Splendid Isolation

*The eruption of the Laacher See volcano and southern
Scandinavian Late Glacial hunter-gatherers*

Splendid Isolation

The eruption of the Laacher See volcano and southern Scandinavian Late Glacial hunter-gatherers

By Felix Riede

Laboratory for Past
Disaster Science

*Volcanic eruptions and
prehistoric culture change*

Aarhus University Press | 🏃

Splendid Isolation
© The author and Aarhus University Press 2017
Cover: Jørgen Sparre
Cover illustration: Adaptation by Kristoffer Akselboe
of the original painting *Moesgård Strand* by Janus la Cour, 1890
Layout and typesetting by Anette Ryevad, www.ryevadgrafisk.dk
This book is typeset in ITC Legacy Serif Std and printed on 130g Luxo satin

Printed by Narayana Press, Denmark
Printed in Denmark 2017

ISBN 978 87 7124 127 3

Aarhus University Press
Finlandsgade 29
DK-8200 Aarhus N
Denmark
www.unipress.dk

INTERNATIONAL DISTRIBUTORS:

Gazelle Book Services Ltd.
White Cross Mills
Hightown, Lancaster, LA1 4XS
United Kingdom
www.gazellebookservices.co.uk

ISD
70 Enterprise Drive, Suite 2
Bristol, CT 06010
USA
www.isdistribution.com

Published with the financial support of the Danish Council for Independent Research | Humanities
(grants number 11-106336 and 6107-00059B)

PEER REVIEWED

/ In accordance with requirements of the Danish Ministry of Higher Education and Science, the certification
means that a PhD level peer has made a written assessment justifying this book's scientific quality.

MIX
Paper from
responsible sources
FSC® C010651

Contents

Preface

This book has been a long time in the making. I can clearly remember the rare day when – sometime in the latter half of my doctoral research – the idea come to me that my data on the size and shape of Late Glacial projectile points, the tephra fallout distribution of the Laacher See eruption and the then still new models for the loss of technological complexity may be related in interesting ways: The 'Laacher See hypothesis' was formulated. My Ph.D. research was about the period and region in question, but it was thematically quite distinct. Yet, connecting these elements turned out to be by far the most productive and controversial discovery generated from that research. Since then, for the last ten years, I have been pursuing, evaluating, testing, rejecting, and ultimately returning to this 'Laacher See hypothesis'. The project to which this book originally was linked has long since ended, but a new and bigger one is gathering pace just now. The Danish Council for Independent Research, to whom I am greatly indebted, has generously provided financing for both projects. In four years time we will know a great deal more about these curious Late Glacial foraging societies, about the Laacher See eruption, and how we might be able to articulate it with contemporary concerns of catastrophe and climate change.

Colleagues and friends too many to name have played a part in shaping this book throughout the years. Nick Conard invited me to present in Tübingen and advised me to frame the notion of impact as a hypothesis. You may not remember it, Nick, but that was a great idea. Erik Brinch Petersen, Mikkel Sørensen and Kristoffer Buck Pedersen have been stimulating interlocutors; always pointing the way towards where I need to turn my attention. Early on, Oli Bazely and Jeff Wheeler willingly collaborated, and volcanologists Claire Horwell, Peter Baxter as well as Clive Oppenheimer generously shared their expertise. Clive also welcomed me at the Department of Geography back in Cambridge when I was on research leave. Ofer Bar-Yosef kindly sponsored my prolonged stay at Harvard's Department of Anthropology, where most of this book was written. My colleagues at Aarhus University have been supportive throughout, and I sincerely cherish the collegiate environment we have built up. At Aarhus University Press, Sanne Lind Hansen has shown the necessary patience to nurse this project to completion.

Throughout researching for and writing this book, I have also been so fortunate to become father to two lovely boys. So a substantive thanks goes, of course, to my wife Christina, to Alexander and to Oskar for going along with my particular interests. Thanks to all.

Højbjerg, March 2017

Front page inset image: When Shelley wrote *Frankenstein*, and Turner painted his famous red sunsets, they were strongly inspired by the unusual natural phenomena generated in the wake of the eruption of Tambora volcano (Indonesia) in 1815. These works of material culture are examples of the complex effects that far-away volcanic eruptions can have on people entirely unaware of such causal connections. The inset is based on a landscape painting by Janus La Cour (1837-1909) depicting Moesgård beach near Moesgård Manor, where the Aarhus University Department of Archaeology and Heritage Studies is housed and where I have my office. The painting is modified towards the red scale as if it was bathed in a volcanic sunset (Zerefos, et al. 2014), and brings the far-field effects of volcanic eruptions right home. This is what a distant volcanic eruption might look from where I live. The inset image was constructed by Kristoffer Akselbo.

Chapter 6

Chapter 7

List of tables

Chapter 1

Splendid isolation

1.1 Introduction

The year is 12,800 BP. Europe is entirely occupied by people of the so-called Upper Magdalenian culture. Well, not entirely...one small region, southern Scandinavia differs markedly from its neighbours. With a nod of appreciation to Uderzo and Goscinny, this rather flippant introductory sentence sets the scene for this book. Based on the better part of ten years of research, and standing on the shoulders of many scholarly giants, this work is about a remarkable hunter-gatherer culture found only in southern Scandinavia during the middle part of the so-called Late Glacial, the *Bromme culture*. But this book is also – indeed, perhaps more so – about what came before the Bromme culture, namely the Federmessergruppen, and the way in which these two archaeological entities are linked together by one of northern Europe's last truly large volcanic events, the eruption of the Laacher See volcano located in present-day western Germany (Fig. 1.1). Volcanoes and their eruptions have long captured the imagination and attention of academics and the public alike (Sigurdsson, 1999). Perhaps it is not surprising given the incredible forces volcanoes at times unleash that the mere mention of archaeology and volcanoes conjures up images of Pompeii, of destruction and death, and almost universally carries with it moral connotations of sin, of punishment, of apocalypse (Pomeroy, 2008; Sigurdsson, 2000b; Sigurdsson and Lopes-Gautier, 2000). This book does include the description of an intense and violent event, and while a consid-erable number of pages will be devoted to discussions of how the eruption may have affected, in very real and negative terms, animals, plants and humans, it is decidedly not an argument for some blunt and simple causality. Rather, this book endeavours to use the volcanic eruption as an analytical mirror to investigate the social structures and actions of individuals and communities both before and after the event. Calamities lend themselves to both affective and effective narrative, but emerging trends in a diverse range of disciplines within risk reduction research (Birkmann et al., 2010; Olshansky et al., 2012), historical and anthropological disaster science (García-Acosta, 2002; Oliver-Smith, 1996), historical sociology (Sewell, 1996a, 1996b), and archaeology (Grattan and Torrence, 2007; Grattan, 2006) suggest that rapid-onset, extreme events such as volcanic eruption may i) be causally related to periods of intense social change, and ii) provide potentially unique analytical opportunities for investigating social structures and processes surrounding such episodes of change (Riede, 2011a, 2013a, 2014g). Social change and the relationships between past human societies and their environment are mainstays of archaeological inquiry. Yet, relating general changes in the environment to cultural changes remains challenging, not least because there usually are critical and different dating uncertainties attached to both domains of information (Baillie, 1991). Yet, extreme events such as earthquakes, tsunamis and, above all, volcanic eruptions offer

Figure 1.1 *The caldera relict of the Laacher See volcano today (from http://www.fdwallpapers.com).*

one form of resolution here: They are often associated with the formation of stratigraphic marker layers whose formation is widespread in space and can be considered instantaneous in archaeological, geological and evolutionary time: isochrons. Archaeologists working in the European Late Glacial have long been aware of the potential chronological utility of such layers (e.g. Behlen, 1905; Schwabedissen, 1954), and, importantly, recent years have seen marked improvements in the detection and analysis of particles of volcanic origin embedded in both environmental and archaeological stratigraphies that are not visible to the naked eye through so-called micro – or cryptotephra analysis (Lane et al., 2014; Lowe, 2011; Lowe and Alloway, 2015; Sarna-Wojcicki, 2000; Swindles et al., 2010; Turney and Lowe, 2001). This powerful methodological extension and the resulting tephra isochrones assembled into so-called tephrochronological lattices now offer the opportunity not only to improve the dating of individual eruption events, to link different volcanic provinces together, but also to link different kinds of sedimentary archives (e.g. terrestrial, lacustrine, marine and ice core records). This, in turn, opens for the opportunity to compare, contrast and thereby clarify the impacts – or otherwise – of past volcanic events on human communities in the near- and far-fields of such eruptions (Riede and Thastrup, 2013).

The term catastrophe derives from the Ancient Greek καταστροφή, and according to the Oxford English Dictionary (www.oed.com) refers to both "an event causing great and usually sudden damage or suffering; a disaster" – its catastrophist meaning – but in a more ancient meaning it also refers to "the denouement of a drama", its turning point. Likewise, the term apocalypse derives from ἀπό and καλύπτω meaning to "uncover, reveal". In the following, I attempt to do justice to the dual meaning of both terms; I will both critically address and contextualise the arguably disastrous impact of the Laacher See eruption on contemporaneous communities, and I will do so by using the event as a narrative juncture and social-analytical caesura. In sum, the argument laid out in the following chapters is about a catastrophe, but it is not catastrophist in nature.

1.2 Setting the scene

Around 20,000 years ago, the Scandinavian ice sheet reached its maximum extent. Arctic desert regions locked in permafrost and devoid of vegetation extended several hundred kilometres to the south of the ice's edge, pushing plant and animal communities into refugia at lower latitudes, especially to the Franco-Iberian region, Italy and the Balkans (Hewitt, 1999) as well as perhaps some cryptic refugia further north (Stewart and Lister, 2001). Despite evidence for sporadic, perhaps exploratory excursions northwards dated close to the Last Glacial Maximum (LGM; see Terberger and Street, 2002), humans, too, had abandoned northern Europe at this time (Burdukiewicz, 2001).

While information on past climate, derived from traditional sources such as pollen, has long shown that the period around the LGM was harsh in terms of both temperature and aridity, the new climatic proxy data derived from the Greenland ice-coring projects clearly demonstrates that the amplitude as well as magnitude of the climatic changes that occurred at the end of the Pleistocene far exceeded any changes experienced by human populations in the Holocene, and that some of these changes occurred on timescales below one or two human generations – well within human experience (Burroughs, 2005).

The period following the LGM is known as the Late Glacial or the Last Glacial Interglacial Transition (LGIT), which, as the latter term suggests, chronologically bridges the period from the height of the Last Ice Age to the beginning of our current Interglacial, the Holocene. The Late Glacial has been subdivided into a series of stadial (colder) and interstadial (warmer) phases, and the period of particular interest here starts approximately 14,000 years, and ends 12,000 years, before the present. It is in this period that human populations expanded into the previously depopulated landscapes of Northern Europe. The western sector of Europe was colonised by forager groups bringing with them a repertoire of tools that are most commonly referred to as Magdalenian, while Eastern Europe saw the expansion of the makers of so-called Epi-Gravettian tool-kits. This re-colonization process was contingent both on the ecological and geomorphological consolidation of previously glaciated landscapes, the successive northward movement of biotic communities of which these hunter-gatherers were members, as well as on a number of key inventions that facilitated the development of a recognisable Arctic adaption more or less akin to that documented in the ethnographic record of northern peoples (Hoffecker, 2005a, 2005b; Riede and Tallavaara, 2014). Living at very low population densities (Bocquet-Appel et al., 2005; Riede, 2009a) these Late Glacial hunter-gatherers faced environmental upheavals that would have posed a series of social, ecological and demographic challenges for those groups moving into the empty and peripheral landscapes of northern Europe (Kelly, 2003; Mandryk, 1993). While this colonisation process can, at a very general and geographically coarse level, be described as a rapid 'filling up' of the northern regions (e.g. Fort et al., 2004), analyses at smaller scales suggest a pronounced staggering of settlement phases contingent on, for instance, specific landscape types as well as the –at times – erratically oscillating climate of the Late Glacial (Conneller, 2007; Riede, 2007b). While regions closer to the ecologically more stable and continuously productive refugia in south-western Europe arguably show cultural sequences of more gradual change, peripheral regions preserve only fragments of such sequences (Pettitt, 2008). This fragmentary picture may at times be aggravated by the less complete preservation of archaeological sites in more northerly areas, but it more importantly and most likely quite accurately reflects the fact that peripheral regions were only occupied ephemerally and episodically, and that these regions at times saw unique cultural changes related to and rooted in their remoteness.

Much previous research has focused on collating regional archaeological sequences (see chapters in Barton et al., 1991; Burdukiewicz and Kobusiewicz, 1987; Larsson, 1996; Soffer and Gamble, 1990; Straus et al., 1996 and references therein), while more recent work has attempted to better understand the mode and tempo of, as well as the motivation for,

Event stratigraphy		ice core approx. years of onset (BP)	Chronozones	Population events	Techno-complexes
	Holocene	11,500			
GS-1			Younger Dryas	Contraction	*Ahrensburgian*
	GI-1a	12,650	Late Allerød	Splendid isolation	*Brommean*
			LAACHER SEE ERUPTION		
	GI-1b	12,900	Gerzensee Oscillation	Decline	*Federmesser-gruppen*
	GI-1c	13,150	Early Allerød	Resettlement	
	GI-1d	13,900	Older Dryas	Abandonment	*Hamburgian*
	GI-1e	14,500	Bølling	First settlement	
GS-2	GS-2a	16,900		First expansions into C Europe	
	GS-2b	19,500			
	GS-2c	21,200			S Scandinavia not settled
		21,800			
GI-2			Last Glacial Maximum	Refugium phase	

Table 1.1 *The general event-stratigraphic chronological and terminological framework used in this book. Adapted from Gamble and colleagues (2005). GI = Greenland Interstadial, GS = Greenland Stadial.*

this colonization endeavour. Beginning with the landmark contribution of Housley et al. (1997), long strides have been made in our understanding of the continental-scale patterns and processes in the human re-colonization of northern Europe. Gamble and colleagues (2004; 2005) have assembled a synthetic scaffold for the discussion of the human re-colonization of northern Europe that incorporates recent insights from both environmental sciences (Lowe et al., 2008) and from population genetics (Forster, 2004). This framework will serve as a general chronological and terminological anchor here (Table 1.1).

As the title of this book and of this chapter alludes to, isolation and splendour are important notions in understanding the making of, in particular, the Bromme culture. The idiom 'splendid isolation' requires comment, however: Initially coined to describe the foreign policy of the British Empire in the late 19th century (Charmley, 1999), this evocative term has since been transferred to discussions of Easter Island art (Kjellgren, 2001) and to South American mammals (Simpson, 1980). Although perhaps best known in its original political meaning, it is really the latter two uses that are most germane here. The great palaeontologist George Gaylord Simpson's

treatise *Splendid isolation. The curious history of South American mammals* charts the changing dynamics of contact and isolation and their respective impacts on the evolution of South American mammal communities. Likewise, Kjellgren's lavishly illustrated volume *Splendid isolation: Art of Easter Island* demonstrates how cultures, too, evolve when isolated. In fact, even ultimately maladaptive practices can evolve under such circumstances, as exemplified by the demographic decline amongst Easter Islanders, which can also be linked to their geographic remove and their life without neighbours (e.g. Diamond, 2010a; Good and Reuveny, 2006; Mieth and Bork, 2010; Rolett and Diamond, 2004). In the same vein, the present book is about similarly changing trajectories of isolation and contact amongst late Ice Age hunter-gatherers in southern Scandinavia, and it will use an evolutionary theoretical framework not unlike the one of Simpson, but one applied – in line with recent developments in evolutionary archaeology (Shennan, 2008, 2011a, 2011b) – to culture change. The isolation experienced by Late Glacial foragers in southern Scandinavia may, at least in parts, have been splendid in the sense that they found themselves in an area extremely rich in one of their key natural resources, flint, as well as perhaps other resources such as preferred

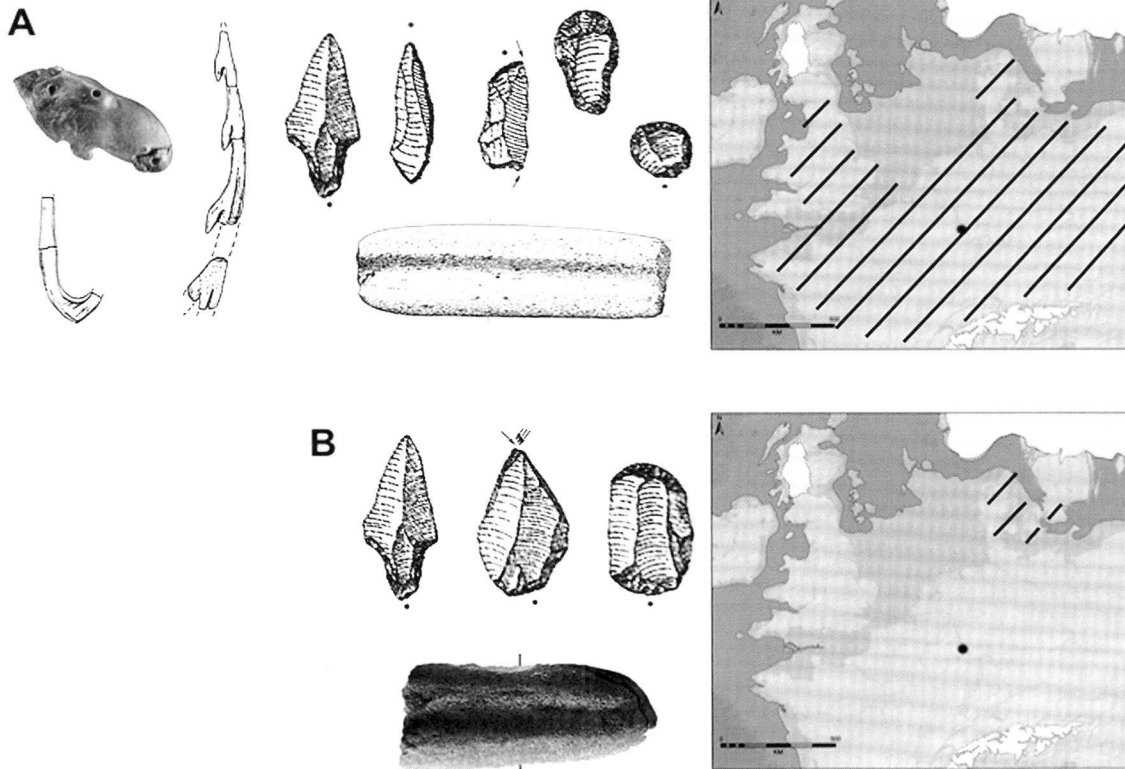

Figure 1.2 *Schematic showing the contrasts between the Federmessergruppen of the early and middle part of the Allerød and the Bromme culture of the late Allerød/early Younger Dryas. Federmessergruppen sites have yielded evidence of art here exemplified by the magnificent amber elk head from the site of Weitsche in northern Germany, organic technologies such as harpoons and fishhooks as well as a range quotidian stone tools such as the characteristic arch-backed points, large tanged points, small and large scrapers and burins. Auxiliary stone tools such sandstone shaft-smoothers are also known, at times even decorated. In contrast, the Bromme culture is only defined by the presence of large tanged points, large scrapers and miscellaneous burins. A single shaft-smoother from a possible Brommean context is also known. See Chapters 4-6 for further discussion and references.*

large game animals, fowl, and fishing grounds. Yet, this small group of foragers also diverged markedly in its cultural make-up from those of contemporaneous communities elsewhere in Europe. In the regions today encompassed by Denmark, the very tip of southern Sweden, and the very northern end of Germany, a unique archaeological phenomenon can be defined: the Bromme culture. Named after the eponymous excavation site where it was first recognised (Mathiassen, 1946), this archaeological culture is characterised by four features (Fig. 1.2):

1. There is a real net increase in sites belonging to this culture in southern Scandinavia.
2. It is geographically circumscribed at a time of otherwise general cultural homogeneity over a large region.

3. It is characterised by a simplified toolkit and tool production techniques at a time of otherwise increasing toolkit diversity.
4. It is characterised by large and rather heavy tools at a time of increasing use of very small stone tool components in the form of backed elements and microliths elsewhere.

These four traits not only distinguish the Bromme culture markedly from the cultures that, in southern Scandinavia, came before (the Federmessergruppen) and after (the Ahrensburgian culture), but they also go strongly against the grain of general contemporaneous cultural developments and thus need explanation. Attempts to correlate the emergence of this culture with general patterns of climate or environmental change, or simply with the abundance of high-quality flint resources in the area, fail to account satisfactorily for the specificity of these characteristics, especially as some of the observed changes imply a loss of ostensibly adaptive technologies such as the bow-and-arrow (Dev and Riede, 2012; Riede, 2009d).

This book then is not really a monograph about the Bromme culture in a traditional sense. Instead, it is problem-oriented and analytical, offering one possible explanation for the emergence and fate of the Bromme phenomenon in southern Scandinavia. The explanatory nexus of this book is the event that arguably gave rise to the isolation of these forager groups, which in turn precipitated the cultural changes alluded to above: Around 13,000 BP – and BP here stands for the conventional 'before AD 1950' – the Laacher See volcano in present-day western Germany erupted cataclysmically. This eruption is very well-investigated from a volcanological perspective (Schmincke, 2006; Schmincke et al., 1999). Indeed, the Pompeii-like preservative covering of its fallout contributed significantly to the archaeology of the near-field area in the Rhineland (Baales, 2002b). Yet, few – Thissen (1995) and Mania (2003) among them – have as yet considered in detail how this eruption may have affected the ecology, economy, and the social as well as religious lives of contemporaneous forager groups not only in the immediate vicinity of the volcano but far away from it. Having noted a potentially remarkable chronological and spatial exclusivity of the Laacher See eruption and its attendant fallout on the one hand, and the Bromme culture in southern Scandinavia on the other, I some time ago proposed the 'Laacher See hypothesis' for the origin of the Bromme culture (Riede, 2007a, 2008b). This hypothesis was specifically geared at addressing the seemingly paradoxical notion that the impact of this eruption should be more pronounced with distance from the eruptive centre. The Laacher See hypothesis has not gone unchallenged, primarily on the ground of archaeological evidence or lack thereof (Sørensen, 2010; Weber et al., 2011). Yet, numerous subsequent interdisciplinary studies have provided insights into the chronology of this interesting time period (Riede and Edinborough, 2012), the extent of the

ash fallout (Riede et al., 2011c) as well as the likely mechanisms of ecological impact (Riede and Wheeler, 2009; Riede and Bazely, 2009; Riede and Kierdorf, in prep.) and subsequent social and technological changes (Dev and Riede, 2012; Riede, 2009d, 2011a, 2014b, 2015). These studies have each tested or further substaniated, different facets of the Laacher See hypothesis. This book follows up on, updates, and extends these efforts by attempting to map and analyse the wider extent of impact and change following the eruption. More broadly, it also attempts to use the event as an analytical mirror onto the societies and their internal dynamics prior to it. Quite critically, this means inverting our perspective from looking primarily at the post-eruptive changes and the Bromme culture to considering, on an even footing, the pre-eruptive Federmessergruppen. In this way, post-eruption changes may be linked to salient patterns of vulnerability amongst these Late Glacial foragers. In addition, this consideration of the Federmessergruppen allows the explicit identification of a source population for the more sustained immigration of foragers into southern Scandinavia following the LSE.

As disaster scientists have pointed out for a long time and repeatedly, an extreme event (volcanic eruption, earthquake, tsunami, etc.) in itself does not make a catastrophe. Catastrophes emerge only in the interaction of such events with particular human societies in particular places and times (Alexander, 2000; O'Keefe et al., 1976; Oliver-Smith, 1996). The historical, political, social and economic constellations of the affected societies vary, thus making them critical parameters in any analysis of causality in relation to impact and to vulnerability.

1.3 Outline of the book

In considering historical disaster research, García-Acosta (2002: 50) has argued that disaster events can be both "triggers" of social change and "revealers" of such changes. This dual function of disasters thus provides an unusual and potentially productive analytical angle on the function of societies both past

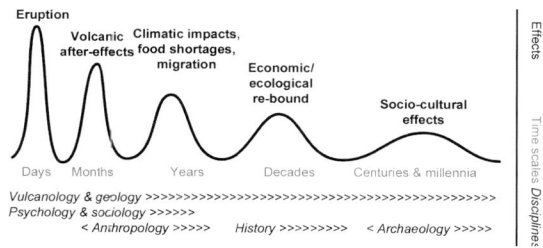

Figure 1.3 *The temporal dimensions of various disciplines studying the impact of extreme events on human societies along the 'vibrating rubber-band' model of volcanic after-effects of de Boer and Sanders (2002).*

and present: If a given disaster acts as a catalyst of change, such changes are rooted in the ongoing and historically constituted social and natural entanglements of the affected societies with the world around them. Moreover, these processes of change and the structures and actions they reflect are thrown into analytical relief precisely because of the perturbation constituted by the disaster event. Finally, because these processes unfold over time, chronology is an important dimension. If the impact and responses at different temporal scales are related to pre-disaster (social and natural) constellations, then disciplines such as sociology and anthropology can study immediate post-disaster responses and their attendant immediate pre-disaster vulnerabilities. Archaeology, in contrast, has the prerequisite data on such relations in the long-term (Fig. 1.3).

But first things first: The remaining bulk of this chapter asks what there is to explain at all. In posing this question, I aim to uncover some of the assumptions that have made addressing the uniqueness of the Bromme culture difficult to the point where it is in fact often simply ignored. Chapter 2 picks up the theme of disaster and catastrophe and unpacks these terms from a perspective that makes them useable in specifically archaeological and historical contexts. The response of individuals, communities, and of cultures to extreme events cannot be understood without reference to key elements such as vulnerability, resilience and adaptation, and without looking in a broad comparative fashion at the parameters that again and again have been considered critical in structuring

human responses to volcanic eruptions. At the same time, Chapter 2 also introduces elements of understanding disasters that will be particularly relevant for linking the Laacher See eruption to Late Glacial societal changes, and for how disaster science may benefit from also drawing on archaeological data. Chapter 3 will then very briefly introduce volcanism in general, and explosive volcanism in particular. Much has been written on volcanic activity from a geological perspective by scholars better placed to provide such comprehensive reviews (e.g. Francis and Oppenheimer, 2004; Robock and Oppenheimer, 2003; Schmincke, 2004). The first half of this chapter serves as a prelude to a consideration of the specific event in question here, the Laacher See eruption. The second part of Chapter 3 summarises the main eruption parameters of this cataclysm and its unfolding in the near-field. Much has been written about the Laacher See eruption, as it has been the object of intense study by volcanologists, especially during the latter half of the 20th century. In particular, the efforts of Hans-Ulrich Schmincke, his students and colleagues have provided remarkably detailed insights into the eruption dynamics and likely climatic impacts of this event. Both popular and technical summaries of these results are widely available (Schmincke, 1988, 2006, 2010). Complementary to these focused volcanological investigations, some recent efforts have also looked closer at the extent and nature of the ash (= tephra) fallout from this eruption in the medium- and far-fields (Riede, 2012b; Riede et al., 2011c). The tephra fallout, its crude thickness, the season of deposition, latitude and the economic systems affected by it all play important roles in shaping the dynamics of impact from proximal to distal (see, for instance, Thorarinsson, 1979).

Chapter 4 focuses on the hunter-gatherer communities in northern Europe prior to the eruption: the Federmessergruppen. I will sketch out what we know about the technology, economy and social structure of these groups, highlighting in particular those aspects that I consider important for then understanding how an event such as the Laacher See eruption could have affected them in the way it did. Chapter 5 draws on the previous chapters in charting the "progression of vulnerability" (Wisner et al., 2004: 87) – an approach developed by disaster scientists to interrogate causality in calamities – of Late Glacial societies in different regions across Europe in relation to the effects of the Laacher See eruption. Importantly, these effects varied from region to region, as did the ecological and social configurations with which they interacted. Inspired by the notion of 'natural experiments of history' (Diamond and Robinson, 2010), I here take a geographically broad *synchronic comparative* perspective that illustrates how the responses of these small groups of highly mobile hunter-gatherers changed depending on both the specific hazards to which they were exposed, but also their position within wider networks of alliance, trade and contact. Chapter 6 finally turns more specifically to the Bromme culture and looks at what happened, or may have happened, in southern Scandinavia following the Laacher See eruption. This chapter considers in some detail both the particular properties of the Bromme culture and places it in a *diachronically comparative* manner within a wider context of how hunter-gatherer societies elsewhere and at other times have responded to hazards such as volcanic eruptions. By the end of this chapter it should be evident that although detailed considerations of vulnerability, impact and change in response to volcanic eruptions as far back in time as the Late Glacial are fraught with issues of data resolution, linking the emergence of the Bromme culture to the Laacher See eruption is consistent with the available information and provides a genuinely novel way of looking at this instance of prehistoric culture change. The combined synchronic and diachronic views of Chapters 4 and 6, articulated by the theoretical and comparative apparatus concentrated in Chapter 5, together provide a hopefully stimulating view on Late Glacial societies in northern Europe, not least because much conceptual, empirical and analytical work remains to be done for further evaluating the predictions and hypotheses it generates.

The concluding Chapter 7 sketches out a roadmap for how the study of past extreme events and their impacts or otherwise on traditional societies may be of some use in understanding the effects of such events in the present. On the whole, disaster science remains dominated by natural and engineering science approaches. Whilst detailed natural scientific knowledge of a given event is critical in understanding its impacts, an equally thorough understanding of the affected communities, their economies, ecologies, religious structures, and how all of these have developed over time can be said to be just as important – especially if the aim is not only to retrospectively relate post-event impacts to pre-event patterns of vulnerability but to use such analyses to reflect on (a) the societal impacts of extreme events, and on (b) how efficiently and effectively to prepare for future calamities. Arguably, history matters when investigating the relationship between human communities, present-day vulnerability and extreme events (Bankoff, 2004; Boonstra and de Boer, 2014). Following García-Acosta (2002: 65) "emphasis should be placed on understanding the surrounding and prior sociocultural context and vulnerability to the effects of a certain hazard. Examining one of the key theoretical issues in any disaster research – the multidimensionality of disasters as expressed in the concept of socially constructed vulnerability – deepens our knowledge of hazards themselves; to determine the cause of calamitous incidence, recurrence, and probability; to differentiate scale, intensity, and duration; to understand how to face disasters or avoid them".

The aim of this book is not, of course, to argue that archaeological data can directly reduce vulnerability, although they occasionally can make very practical suggestions (Sheets, 2012). Instead, this book first and foremost aims to explain one particular instance of dramatic cultural change – the emergence of the Bromme culture – in the wake of a rare but intense event. A corollary of this study is that other episodes of marked culture change in deep time but also in more recent periods may profitably be seen through the lens of vulnerability and in relation to extreme events (e.g. Dumond, 2004; Jacoby et al., 1999; Maschner and Jordan, 2008; McCormick, 2008; Mc-

Cormick et al., 2007; VanderHoek and Nelson, 2007), although it is equally important to remember that extreme events can lead to positive as well as negative changes (Grattan and Torrence, 2007; Grattan, 2006; Torrence, 2016). Such a perspective articulates quite seamlessly with current thinking in risk reduction research. Disasters always have winners and losers (Scanlon, 1988), and they may offer windows of opportunity for instigating social change at a variety of scales (Birkmann et al., 2010). As Birkmann and colleagues have noted, it is important to distinguish between impact – the destructive direct or indirect consequences of an extreme event – and change in the wake of such an event. Making such a distinction in archaeological practice can be difficult due to methodological challenges or issues of data-resolution, but is ultimately helped by the temporal distance and the long-term perspective. Yet, this seemingly trivial but hitherto clearly underappreciated differentiation goes some way towards relegating the insidious effects of catastrophist thinking.

A final, related and not merely epiphenomenal aim is to suggest that the archaeological record may be seen as the material precipitate of the kind of "social memory...based on diachronic long-term observations" (Lorenz, 2013: 14) that feeds resilience. The effects but also the mechanisms of culture change identified in archaeological and historical case studies of past extreme events such as the one presented in this book can serve as vital input – a kind of "usable past" (Stump, 2013: 269) – for historically informed, evidence-based recommendations for how to cope with and handle such events in the present day and in the future (Riede, 2011a, 2013a, 2014c).

1.4 A very short history of the Bromme culture and the Federmessergruppen in southern Scandinavia

It can be said that research into the Bromme culture now goes back more than 100 years, with the discovery, in 1913, of a large tanged

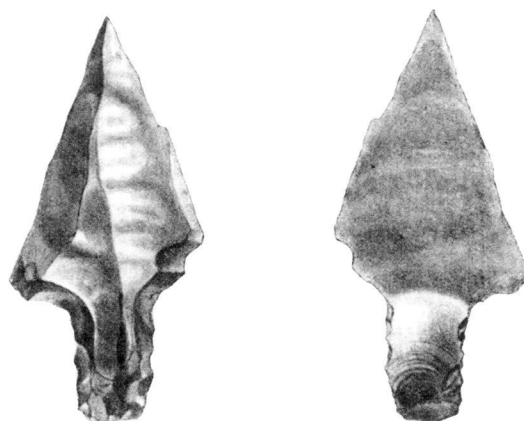

Figure 1.4 *The large tanged point found at Nørre Lyngby, modified from Jessen and Nordmann (1915). See also Fischer et al. (2013b) for further detailed analysis of this object as well as the antler implement found nearby.*

point (Fig. 1.4) in ancient freshwater deposits uncovered by coastal erosion at Nørre Lyngby in the very north of Denmark (Jessen and Nordmann, 1915). Previously, a club- or axe-like implement of reindeer antler was also discovered in the area, further supporting the view that both objects date to a period prior to the end of the Last Ice Age. The Nørre Lyngby locality has been the subject of repeated palaeo-ecological and archaeological investigations over the years, and we do have a fairly clear picture now of the nature of the highly dynamic local environment during the middle part of the Late Glacial – it is characterised by a mix of species that today prefer rather different (boreal, steppe and tundra) environs (Aaris-Sørensen, 1995; Fischer et al., 2013b; Iversen, 1942). In contrast, additional archaeological finds from the area remain scarce, and dating of the antler implement (as well as other similar objects elsewhere – see Sommer et al., 2011) question the strict contemporaneity of these artefacts (Fischer et al., 2013; Stensager, 2004).

Nonetheless, the then-perceived association between these evidently man-made objects with animals and plants that had long since disappeared from the region have prompted archaeologists to define a new culture, the 'Lyngby culture' (Schwantes, 1923a, 1923b). Prehistorians in Europe at the time – especially outside France – still struggled with making sense of the very basic geographic and chronological components of their regional records. Adding to the almost universally rising national and indeed nationalist sentiments, defining regional archaeological cultures was rather fashionable. It allowed countries to effectively stake a claim to the Palaeolithic, and to establish a kind of pedigree in relation to a particular area (Rowley-Conwy, 2006; Sommer, 2000, 2008; Tomášková, 2003; Trigger, 1989). The term 'Lyngby culture' was swiftly adopted by other archaeologists working in northern Europe and several single finds of both reindeer antler 'axes' and large tanged points were added to its roster (e.g. Berthelsen, 1944). This new entity was readily accepted by the archaeological community and reified by the rapid appearance of the term 'Lyngby culture' in contemporary archaeological textbooks: Ekholm's (1926) eponymous entry in the *Reallexikon der Vorgeschichte* and Clark's (1936) discussion of it in his ground-breaking synthesis of Late Palaeolithic and Mesolithic archaeology in northern Europe did their part for putting the 'Lyngby culture' firmly on the archaeological map.

It was not before 1944, however, that the first excavation of a true site – rather than the more or less random discovery of surface finds – from this culture became reality. Discovered by the very active amateur archaeologist Erik Westerby and subsequently excavated under the auspices of the National Museum of Denmark by Therkel Mathiassen (1946), a small site near the hamlet of Bromme on Zealand in eastern Denmark was investigated. This site yielded numerous lithics – large tanged points, flake and blade scrapers and burins – as well as faunal remains and pollen. Relative palynological (Iversen, 1946) and subsequent absolute radiometric dating (Heinemeier and Rud, 2001) place this site in the later part of the Allerød chronozone. As the site did not yield reindeer axes, it was initially used to define yet another culture, the Bromme culture, which was thought to be axe-less and older than the Lyngby culture, which in turn was seen as the link to the later and now defunct 'Inland Mesolithic' (see Andersen and Sterum, 1971). Competing and complementary culture-historical schemata for the region became increasingly convoluted (e.g. Clark, 1950; Rust, 1951), often

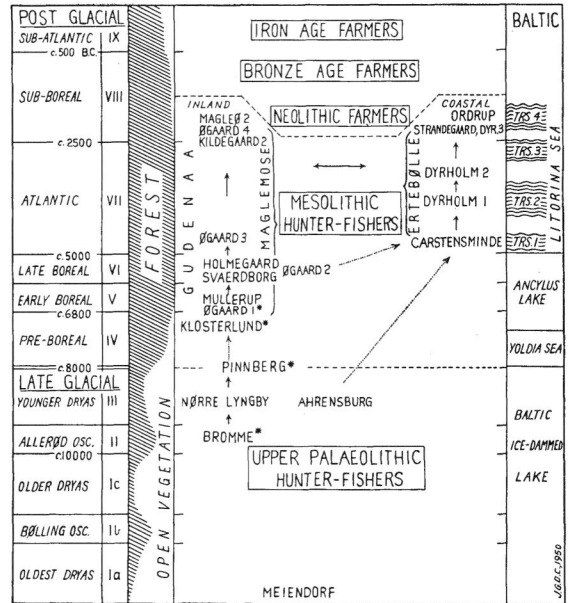

Figure 1.5 *Cultural scheme for the Late Palaeolithic and Mesolithic of northern Europe by Clark (1950).*

boldly invoking – somewhat paradoxically but in full agreement with the general explanatory Zeitgeist of the day – migrations from far-away places as well as subsequent strongly regionalised autochthonous developments (e.g. De Molyn, 1954; Fig. 1.5).

Mathiassen's fieldwork, followed by subsequent excavations of similar but generally less productive sites in southern Sweden (Larsson, 1991; Larsson, 1993; Salomonsson, 1964) and other parts of Denmark (e.g. Andersen, 1970; Andersen, 1972; Madsen, 1983; Mathiassen, 1959), provided additional 'palaeoethnological' evidence for this Late Palaeolithic 'tribe'. Large tanged points became enshrined as the artefact 'type fossil' (cf. O'Brien and Lyman, 1999) of this culture, and many subsequent studies invested the Bromme culture with a kind of territorial reality that is reflected in rather sharply drawn boundaries (Fig. 1.6). The eventual rejection of the term 'Lyngby point' in favour of 'Bromme point' and the amalgamation of the two entities into one (Becker, 1971; Brinch Petersen, 1970) cleared away some of the terminological confusion but, at the same time, also further asserted the exclusive claim of a direct and culture-historically diagnostic relationship between this projectile point

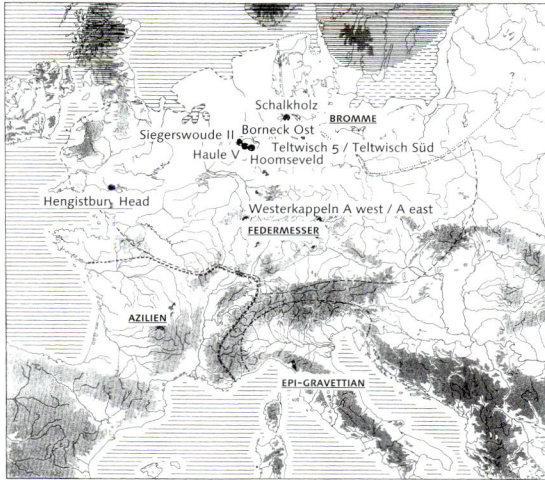

Figure 1.6 *An example map showing the presumed 'territory' of the Bromme culture, from the study of Newell and Constandse-Westermann (1996).*

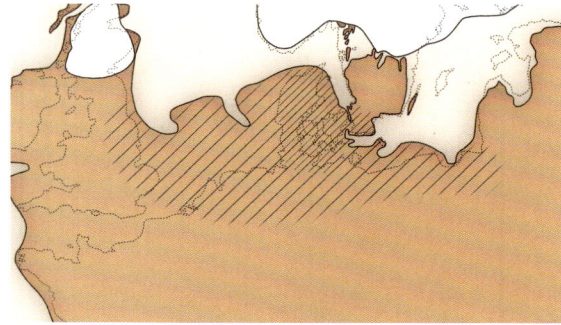

Figure 1.7 *Another example map of the presumed ranging grounds or 'territory' of the Bromme culture. This map distinguished (single/double diagonals) between the 'core territory' of southern Scandinavia and the 'extended territory' where Bromme-like artefacts occur. Originally from Andersson et al. (2004), re-used by Sørensen (2010).*

type and the eponymous Bromme culture. Yet, not too long after the excavation of the Bromme locale, large tanged points began to appear also far afield in sites broadly dating to the Late Glacial. In particular, sites otherwise thought to belong to the regional variant of the overarching European Upper Magdalenian – the so-called Federmessergruppen of northern Germany and the Netherlands – repeatedly and consistently yielded large tanged points that on morphological grounds could not be readily distinguished from 'Lyngby points' (Schwabedissen, 1954). They also became known from France (de Sonneville-Bordes, 1969, 1988), the British Isles (Jacobi, 1980; Mace, 1959), and eastern Europe (Bagniewski, 1999; Ginter, 1974; Gramsch, 1987; Sinitsyna, 2002; Zaliznyak, 1999).

At the same time as these discoveries were made, archaeology moved towards an explanatory approach less interested in migrations, and grounded more in local adaptation and the relationship between economic activities and material culture (Trigger, 1989). Such research questions have long been important in Scandinavian and especially Danish Stone Age archaeology (see Kristiansen, 2002 for perceptive comments on this), and were further boosted by the economic/ecological approaches promoted so strongly by influential scholars

such as Stig Welinder (1983), Erik Higgs (1972) and Grahame Clark (1989; see also Gräslund 2010 for an assessment of Clark's Scandinavian legacy). As a result, the emerging typological overlap between the Bromme culture and the broadly contemporary Federmessergruppen was suggested to reflect, for instance, the seasonally differentiated tool-kit of the same groups of people whose annual round brought them from Central Europe (where they used the arch-backed points characteristic of the Federmessergruppen) to southern Scandinavia (where they instead used the considerably more massive tanged 'Lyngby points'; see Bokelmann et al., 1983; Houtsma et al., 1996). Eventually, a general consensus emerged at this time, which viewed the whole Late Glacial cultural sequence in southern Scandinavia "as a continuous and largely endogenous cultural development" (Eriksen, 1999: 169), although dissenting voices continued to countenance migration scenarios (Brinch Petersen, 2009; Madsen, 1996). In this understanding, the occasional presence of large tanged points, i.e. of supposedly diagnostic 'Lyngby points' on, for instance, the British Isles (Barton and Roberts, 2001); in Poland (Bagniewski, 1997, 1999; Ginter, 1974; Schild, 1975); in the Baltic states including western Russia (Rimantiene, 1971; Šatavičius, 2004; Sinitsyna, 2002; Zaliznyak, 1999); or south-west of the River Elbe (Breest and Gerken, 2008), is commonly interpreted as an ephemeral and episodic presence of Brommean hunters far outside their regular territories brought there by long-range hunting expeditions or in search of specific resources such as haematite. As a result, some now consider the 'territory' of the Bromme culture to have expanded vastly to also include parts of the British Isles, of north-eastern Europe, and north-central Germany (Andersson et al., 2004; Sørensen, 2010; Fig. 1.7). In sum, a variety of different hypotheses for the origin and nature of the Bromme culture have been put forward over the years (Table 1.2). Some of these can

	Hypothesis	Ancestral culture	Selected key sites	Mechanism(s)	Chronology	References
1.	Eastern migration	Aurignacian/Eastern Gravettian	Bromme (DK)	Migration from eastern Europe & diffusion	Bromme thought to span the entire Allerød	De Molyn (1954); Ekholm (1925, 1926)
2.	Contemporaneity	Not specified	Rissen, Wustrow, Grande 1, Sprenge, Calbe-Kremkau (GER)	Boundary formation & diffusion	Contemporaneity; but geographic separation due to ethnic differentiation & adaptation	Schwabedissen (1951, 1954)
3.	Western migration & contemporaneity	Southwestern Magdalenian	Grotte Bâtie (FR); Segebro (SWE)	Boundary formation & diffusion	Contemporaneity; geographic separation due to ethnic differentiation & adaptation	Taute (1968)
4.	Seasonal and/or functional facies	FMG	Schalkholz (GER)	Seasonal mobility & adaptation	Contemporaneity, Bromme as a functional/seasonal facies of FMG	Bokelmann (1978); Houtsma et al. (1996)
5.	Continuity from the Hamburgian	Hamburgian	Løvenholm (DK); Mölleröd (SWE)	*In situ* adaptation	Continuity from Hamburgian to Bromme in southern Scandinavia; role of FMG not considered	Larsson (1993); Madsen (1983)
6.	Continuity from the FMG	FMG	Trollesgave (DK); Klein Nordende (GER)	*In situ* adaptation	'The Bromme complex is interpreted as an offshoot of the Federmesser which developed during the early or middle part of the Allerød'	Fischer (1991: 111); Eriksen (2000)
7.	Repeated immigration	Not specified	Stoksbjerg Vest, Rundebakke, Hasselø Tværvej (GER)	Regional extinction & re-colonisation	Possible hiatus caused by the 250-year long IACP; 'The appearance of the Brommian could...mark a third pioneering event'.	Madsen (1996); Brinch Petersen (2009: 103)
8.	Laacher See-forcing	FMG	Sassenholz, Westertimke, Rissen, Borneck (GER); Jaglisko 3 (POL); Hasselø Tværvej (DK)	Regional demographic bottlenecking	The Bromme culture as derived from peripheral FMG using 'proto-Bromme' large-tanged points as armatures for spear-throwers as supplementary hunting weapon	Thissen (1995); Riede (2007, 2008)

Table 1.2 *Various hypotheses for the origins of the Bromme culture, roughly arranged in the chronological order in which they have been put forward.*

today only be considered as no more than research historical curiosities, their explanations clearly limited by the complete absence of absolute age control and the much more limited number of finds at the time of formulation. Other theories emphasize and prioritise different facets of this culture – chronological, typological, or economic – which are not necessarily mutually exclusive. Importantly, however, many can in principle at least be evaluated empirically (Riede and Edinborough, 2012).

1.5 The 'Bromme problem', or 'Typological Top Trumps'

In a classic review of Late Glacial finds from southern Scandinavia, the Danish archaeologists C.J. Becker (1971: 136) stated laconically that "we cannot solve the problem of the Bromme's origin". More recent reviewers likewise bemoaned that more conclusive interpretations of the Late Glacial record are hampered by "an inaccurate cultural taxonomy" (Eriksen, 1999: 167), and that "the proposed linear development of successive human cultures or technocomplexes has led to a stalemate with no room for alternative views" (Brinch Petersen, 2009: 89). The status of the 'Lyngby point' as diagnostic artefact type has eroded to such a degree that some (usually scholars from outside Scandinavia) outright reject its analytical utility and thereby cast doubt on the existence of the Bromme culture *per se* (Kobusiewicz, 2009a, 2009b). Yet, others (usually Scandinavian scholars) see the Bromme culture as a very real phenomenon, indeed as a "complete adaptation" (Fischer, 2013: 8) to "the improved environmental conditions during the Allerød" (Sørensen, 2010: 277).

These taxonomic uncertainties – boiling down to the question of what elements of material culture can be seen as indicative of the Bromme culture – are reflected well in the diverging geographic projections for this technocomplex (see Figs. 1.6 and 1.7). Rather flippantly, the issue at hand can be described as a game of 'Typological Top Trumps' (Fig. 1.8). Top Trumps is a cherished card game where each card is associated with a series of values.

Figure 1.8 *Typological 'Top Trumps' of Late Glacial armatures and hence cultures.*

Players take turns at calling out the attributes of the top-most card in their own stack in order to beat and thereby win the other's respective card. In its Late Glacial manifestation, certain typological elements such as 'Lyngby points', Federmesser arch-backed points, or other more or less characteristic artefact elements hold *different diagnostic value in different research traditions*. In the Netherlands or Germany, for instance, a site containing Federmesser and large tanged points will normally be classified as a Federmesser site (Houtsma et al., 1981; Paddayya, 1973; Richter, 2001); in Poland, Ginter (1974), Schild (1975) and most recently Kobusiewicz (2009a; 2009b) would want to see large tanged points as integral elements of both Federmessergruppen as well as Ahrensburgian assemblages, but never as indicating the presence of Brommean folk, although others again would like to see these artefacts reflecting the presence of the Bromme culture or some Bromme-like 'eastern equivalent' (Šatavičius, 2004; Sinitsyna, 2002; Szymczak, 1987). In contrast, Danish archaeologists go to great lengths to place such co-occurring elements into several occupation episodes (Johansson, 2003; Petersen, 2006), and demote them to "single finds in other Late Palaeolithic context" (Eriksen, 1999: 165), or simply ignore the presence of the Federmesser component when it comes to assigning a given locality to its right culture-historical berth (e.g. Fugl Petersen, 1994; Knudsen, 1990; Kramer, 1995; Madsen, 1986; Rindel, 1993, 1994a). It seems that the Bromme culture serves as the default Late Glacial technocomplex in southern Scandinavia as soon as large tanged points are in evidence.

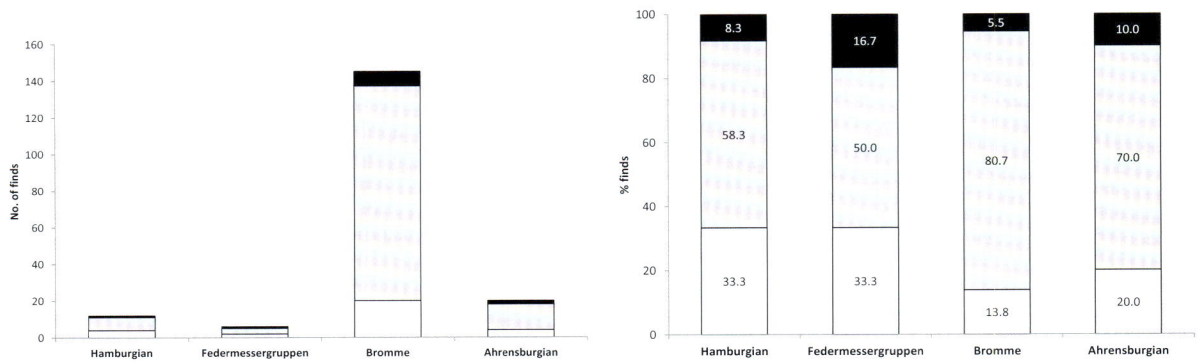

Figure 1.9 The (A) number and (B) percentage distribution of Late Glacial sites assigned to the four different candidate techno-complexes, divided into sites (white), surface finds (grey) and others (black). Note the very strong predominance of inherently problematic surface finds in the Bromme culture.

Besides having created a rather incongruous picture of the Bromme culture, this widespread and regionally specific typological automatism – coupled with the fact that the Bromme culture was already defined so early on – has contributed to i) a reification of the assumed status of the Bromme culture as a southern Scandinavian phenomenon, and ii) a marked over-identification of Bromme localities in that area. Figure 1.9 summarises the assessments of all currently known and registered Late Glacial sites in Denmark. The dominance of Bromme sites is as striking as it is problematic: The actual number of undisputable and sizable Danish Bromme sites (Bro, Bromme, Stoksbjerg Bro, Fensmark, Trollesgave, and Højgård) is low, and all but one of these are located on the eastern island of Zealand. The remainder of possible settlement sites (N= 15), listed recently by Brinch Petersen (2009), are either not excavated, only inadequately documented, or indeed contain Federmesser elements that cast doubt on their taxonomic status. The same difficulty arises more painfully still when it comes to the actual bulk of localities assigned to the Bromme culture: the vast majority are single finds of large tanged points, which are significantly easier to spot in the field and to identify than the more anonymous and smaller arch-backed points that characterise the Federmessergruppen. Here, the well known 'size effect' (Baker, 1978; Dunnell and Simek, 1995; Odell and Cowan, 1987) creates a dual bias in that bulkier materials are easier to find as such (i.e. favouring Brommean assemblages) and in

that the odds are stacked against finding arch-backed points in surface-collected assemblages even if they originally were present (Ammerman and Feldman, 1974). The implication of this is that we are simply unable to confidently assign small unexcavated assemblages of Final Palaeolithic material to either the Federmessergruppen or the Bromme culture.

In addition, and as sketched out above, large tanged points can no longer be seen as indexing the Bromme culture alone. Instead, many of these large tanged points very likely belong to Federmessergruppen contexts (Riede et al., 2011a). To make matters even worse, large tanged points also occur in the later so-called Pitted Ware Culture (Becker, 1950; Iversen, 2010), and some of its point variants cannot readily be distinguished from Late Glacial points when found out of context (Fischer, 1985; Petersen, 2008).

An almost equally large number of sites contain no diagnostic flint elements, but are due to the coarse nature of the flint-working and the large size of knapping products assigned to the Bromme culture. Yet, even dedicated experts in Late Glacial flint-working admit that "some sites and inventories may, with almost equal plausibility be attributed to a local variant of the Bromme or the Federmesser complexes" (Eriksen, 2000: 157), or indeed to later and much more numerous prehistoric activities such as the casual flint-knapping of the late Neolithic and early Bronze Age (see Eriksen, 2010). Many of the flint assemblages

S (large flint nodules)	N (large flint nodules)	S>N
True	True	True
True	**False**	**False**
False	True	True
False	False	True

Table 1.3 *The formal logic of necessity and sufficiency in relation to raw material determinism in the Late Glacial. A true necessary condition in a conditional statement makes the statement true. In formal terms, a consequent N is a necessary condition for an antecedent S, in the conditional statement, 'N if S', 'N is implied by S', or N<S. In other words, 'N is weaker than S' or 'S cannot occur without N'. In the Late Glacial example, it is necessary to have access to large flint nodules in order to make large tools. A true sufficient condition in a conditional statement ties the statement's truth to its consequent. In formal terms, an antecedent S is a sufficient condition for a consequent N, in the conditional statement, 'if S, then N', 'S implies N', or S>N. In other words, 'S is stronger than N' or 'S guarantees N'. For instance, access to large flint nodules guarantees that large tanged points are made. It is the conditional statement highlighted in bold that applies to Late Glacial flint-knapping.*

registered as Brommean have never been assessed by a specialist, some are kept in private possession, and others were catalogued only minimally many years ago. While none of these caveats are meant to imply a necessarily imprecise categorisation of the material in question, in combination they throw additional doubt on the quantity of recorded Bromme sites.

Denmark is blessed with an abundance of high-quality flint nodules that commonly occur also in considerable size (Högberg and Olausson, 2007; Madsen, 1993), and Sørensen

(2010: 273) argues that these raw material preconditions provide "a logical reason for the technological simplification" and general trend towards large-format tools in the Bromme culture. This logic is, however, formally flawed (Table 1.3). Flint-knapping is a strictly reductive procedure, so starting raw material size *constrains* final tool size only when nodules are small, as, for instance, in the Mesolithic of Bornholm (Casati and Sørensen, 2006) or the Federmessergruppen settlements in the flint-poor areas of Hesse in Germany (Loew, 2003).

Biases	Effects on the numerical representation of Allerød-period locales	
	FMG	Brommean
Size effect on discovery probability		+
Size effect on surface representation	-	+
Pitted Ware culture points misclassified as Brommean		+
Arch-backed points classified as lancet microliths or not recognized	-	
Federmessergruppen large tanged points misclassified as Brommean	-	+
Later prehistoric flint-knapping debris misclassified as Brommean		+
Federmessergruppen flint-knapping debris misclassified as Brommean	-	+
Locales with large tanged points and arch-backed elements registered as <u>only</u> Brommean	-	+
Locales with large tanged points and arch-backed elements registered as Brommean <u>and</u> Federmessergruppen sites		+

Table 1.4 *Source critical factors affecting the finding and recording of Bromme and Federmessergruppen material.*

In such cases raw material conditions do provide both a *necessary* and *sufficient* argument for final tool size (Blumberg, 1976; Caumann, 1998). The reverse case is different as the availability of large starting nodules is necessary for the production of large-format tools, yet not sufficient as an explanation for the remarkable size difference between the large tanged points and the slender arch-backed points. Large starting nodules will quite rightly result in larger primary flaking waste and perhaps even engender the kind of more "straightforward" (Madsen, 1992: 128) and "wasteful" (Fischer, 1991: 116) knapping behaviour so characteristic of the Bromme culture, but its influence on the final tool size – especially that of projectile points whose proper function is strongly constrained by ballistic requirements – is, however, limited and demonstrably not determining. The striking difference in the knapping *end products* of the Federmessergruppen and the Bromme culture remains, and accordingly, the literature is riddled with a considerable range of opinions on the function of large tanged points – were they arrowheads, javelin-tips, or lance-heads? Chapter 4 will provide one possible answer.

Albeit difficult to quantify precisely, these source critical issues all combine to not only mimic an overwhelming presence of Bromme material in Denmark, they have also led to a simultaneous underrepresentation of the Federmessergruppen (Table 1.4). Nonetheless, even cutting the Bromme culture down in size in this manner – the net numerical difference in registered sites between the Federmessergruppen and the Bromme culture thus lies around a factor of two rather than a factor of twenty –

does not remove the evident trend towards an increase in the number of both on- and off-site material, which, all things being equal, should indicate an increase in human presence and activity in the landscape.

1.6 Chapter summary and outlook

Have the last 40 years brought us closer to solving Becker's 'Bromme problem'? The argument that the Bromme culture somehow constitutes a perfect adaptation to the landscapes of Allerød-period Scandinavia is difficult to sustain, given that there is little unique about the environment at this time that should lead to the emergence of a technocomplex that is so different from its contemporary counterparts. It has long been known that regional research traditions create and emphasise regional archaeological phenomena (e.g. Sommer, 2000, 2009), especially in the Palaeolithic of Europe where the roots of such regional cultures are often to be found in the 'Race to the Palaeolithic' of the earlier part of the 20th century (McNabb, 2012; Otte and Keeley, 1990). This regionalism – Newell and Constanze-Westermann's "paradigmatic straightjacket of provincialism" (1996: 385) – has, for instance, resulted in a plethora of alternative taxonomic labels for the technocomplexes of the Late Glacial in northern Europe (Table 1.5). In Denmark, too, archaeology is deeply intertwined with romantic and nationalist notions (Damm and Thorndahl, 1987; Høgh, 2008; Klindt-Jensen, 1975), not least in relation to hunter-gatherer studies (Høiris, 1999). The geographic identity of the Bromme culture with the border of the Danish nation state – both the southern Swed-

	Federmessergruppen	Bromme culture
General terms	Arch-backed Point Complex, Rückenspitzen Kreis; Pen-knife groups; Azilian	Tanged-Point Complex; Pedunculated-Point Complex; Stielspitzen-Gruppen
Regional variants	Pre-Masovian; Volkushian; Rissener/Wehlener/ Tjonger Gruppe; Ostromer Gruppe; Atzenhofer Gruppe; Fürsteiner Gruppe	Brommean; Brommian; Lyngby Culture; Perstunian; Old Tanged Point Complex; Lyngby Kreis; Segebro-Bromme Gruppe; Vistulian; North Ukrainian/Baltic Magdalenian; Grenskala/ Vyshagorskaia/Podolskaia groups

Table 1.5 *Examples of taxonomic labels applied to North European Late Glacial technocomplexes.*

ish region of Scania and the northern German region of Schleswig-Holstein once were part of Denmark – reflects the complex linkage between academic knowledge creation and its use as cultural heritage in the service of a national narrative in Denmark (Høgh, 2008; Pentz, 2009), as elsewhere (e.g. Kohl and Fawcett, 1995; O'Connor, 2007; Tomášková, 2003). That said, the Bromme culture really *is* unique in its geographic circumscription, its short duration, and its curious technology. It is, by the standards of the Palaeolithic, a very special phenomenon. In the remainder of this book, I will argue not only that the Bromme culture requires an equally special explanation, but that it offers at the same time an unparalleled analytical opportunity to investigate the causal relations that drive material culture change in the past.

Chapter 2

Vulnerability, events and cultural evolution

2.1 Introduction

The previous chapter sketched out the overall framework and problem that this book is trying to address. It introduced the major characters – the Federmessergruppen and the Bromme culture – of this Late Glacial drama, and suggested that these two technocomplexes are linked though an ancestor-descendant relationship whose defining caesura was the eruption of the Laacher See volcano in present-day western Germany. Before looking in more detail at volcanic activity in general, at the Laacher See eruption in particular and at how it affected landscapes, fauna, flora, and foragers in Europe, a key concept needs elaboration: vulnerability. In this chapter, vulnerability is defined and placed in a relationship with ad-

aptation and adaptability. Finally, first steps are taken towards a science of past disasters that builds bridges between the natural scientific view of hazards – especially volcanic eruptions – the archaeological and environmental records, and a broader understanding of how history unfolds that is grounded in equal parts in historical sociology and evolution theory.

2.2 Eyjafjallajökull

In AD 2010, from April to October, the Icelandic volcano Eyjafjallajökull erupted (Fig. 2.1). This eruption was small and "ordinary" (Davies et al., 2010: 608) by the standards of glob-

Figure 2.1 *One of thousands of captivating images of the 2010 eruption of Eyjafjallajökull. Shown here is volcanic lightning during the top-crater eruption. Arctic Images/Alamy Stock Photo.*

al volcanic activity. Yet, it was *perceived* and *experienced* as catastrophic by many. Although local farms were affected and although the landscape remains barren in the volcano's immediate vicinity (Fig. 2.2), its awesome display of geological force also attracted badly-needed tourists at a time of economic troubles (Benediktsson et al., 2011). As Iceland regularly experiences eruptions, communities and authorities are reasonably well-equipped to swiftly assess the risk and to respond to it (e.g. Gislason et al., 2011). As a result, the local effects of this eruption were minor. However, the ash it generated was transported to Europe with paralyzing, economically disastrous consequences (Pedersen, 2010). Flights were grounded due to the threat of volcanic ash particles to aviation (Langmann et al., 2012), sparking a virtual mobility-related panic that affected millions of people in Europe and beyond (Guiver and Jain, 2011; O'Regan, 2011). Budd et al. (2011) proffer some of the staggering numbers: 108,000 flights were cancelled, 10.5 million passengers affected – and this does not count all those (like myself) who decided not to travel just in case they were going to be affected – and the

aviation industry suffered losses in excess of 1.5 billion Euros. How can such an insignificant geological event cause so much trouble, such high costs? The answer to this question rests not in 'nature', not in the volcanological properties of the eruption. These do, of course, also have a role to play, but causal in a more salient and significant way are the economic, social, and cognitive structures and systems that it interacted with. European airspace is the premier hub of today's global 'aeromobility' that is so defining of our times (Fig. 2.3; Urry, 2007, 2009). The remarkable effects of the Eyjafjallajökull eruption can therefore not be sought in its inherent, geophysical properties, but rather in the complex ways in which it interacted with the affected societies and their ways of socially, cognitively, legally and technologically handling this event (Alexander, 2013; Donovan and Oppenheimer, 2011, 2012, 2013; Lund and Benediktsson, 2011).

In line with the eruptions of Mount St. Helens of 1980 (see, for instance, Carson, 2000 – but there are innumerable works on this eruption and its myriad effects), the Parícutin eruption

Figure 2.2 *The area around Eyjafjallajökull some seven months after the eruption. Photo: the author.*

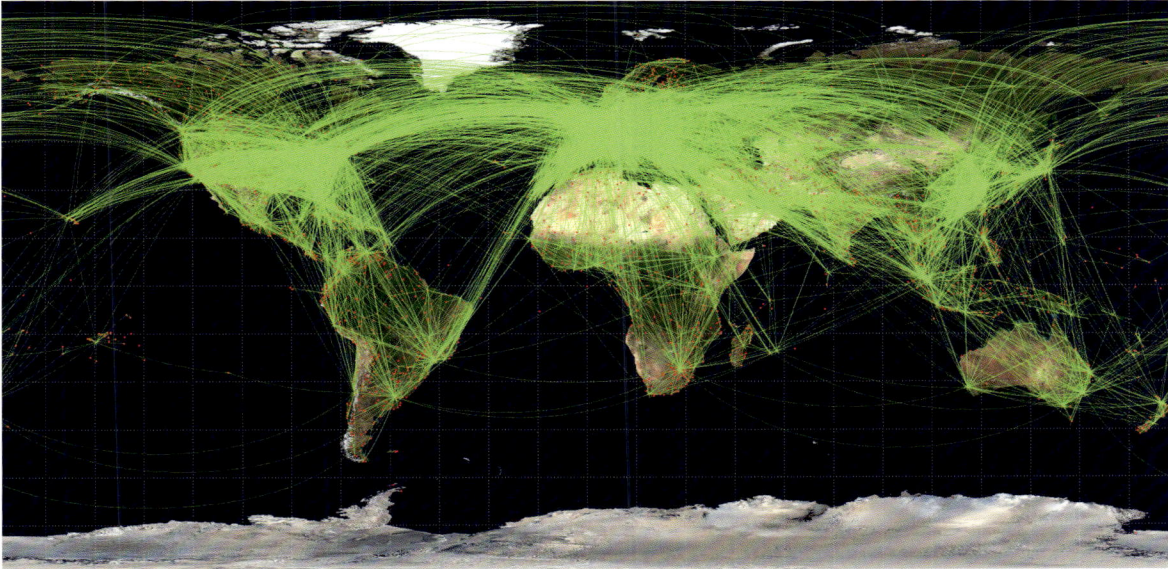

Figure 2.3 *The global 'aeromobile' network of the present day, from http://openflights.org. Note the extreme node density in Europe.*

of 1943 (Luhr and Simkin, 1993) and a handful others, the Eyjafjallajökull eruption is one of a few such events that has been comprehensively studied from both a natural and social scientific perspective. It thus serves to underline the notion that this kind of extreme geophysical event is not to be considered causal of any kind of impact or human cultural responses in isolation, but rather that it poses a complex of risks or hazards; a disaster then emerges at 'the interface between an extreme physical event and a vulnerable human population' (Susman et al., 1983: 264). In addition – and this observation is at the same time more mundane but also perhaps more critical – the Eyjafjallajökull eruption offers, owing to its remote island location, a drastically simplified distinction between proximal and distal impacts. Its effects underline that the nature and magnitude of hazard and impact of a given eruption change, potentially dramatically, from proximal (= the area immediately around the erupting volcano) to distal (= the area far away from the volcano) along the transect (or transects) of its fallout.

At first glance, it may seem paradoxical that impact increases with distance, but this is what November (2008: 1523) calls the "spatiality of risk", where impact is not alone determined by proximity to a hazard, but by pre-event vul-

nerability. Human populations in particular are bound together in complex social, demographic, and economic networks that – in addition to underlying differences in local ecology conditioned by, for instance, latitudinal gradients – reflect this spatial variation. It is arguably the fragility or otherwise of these social networks that determine the extent of impact, and the specific structures that steer cascading effects such as those observed in the wake of the Eyjafjallajökull event (Helbing, 2013; Helbing et al., 2006).

The anatomy of this eruption also exposes another important dimension of human impact: time. Over time, the eruption evolved from harmless or even beneficial spectacle to severe threat, and back to a resource to be exploited. Time plays an important role in the relevance and perception of this hazard, but this 'temporality of risk' plays a yet greater role once we consider that its impact was dependent on the *specific* point in time at which the eruption occurred. Had this eruption occurred in AD 1010 the effects would have been rather different (cf. Dugmore et al., 2007): Local farmers (without tractors, plastic seals for fodder, stored clean water, etc.) would likely have been less able to cope with its impact right there and then, but people in the eruption's far-field possessed means of transport somewhat less

Figure 2.4 *A material culture assortment assisting in coping with the proximal impact of the Eyjafjallajökull eruption: (A) eye and mouth protection, rapid personal transport vehicles (from http://www.16lovers.com/syningar/nigeriusvindlid/ islandssvindlid/bref-1-volcanic-eruption/); (B) heavy machinery, plastic seals for fodder, spacious and fairly tight buildings (from http://blogs.sacbee.com/photos/2010/04/iceland-volcano-part-two.html); (C) running water, safety equipment, electricity (from http://saigonocean.com/trangAlbertDong/ Info/InfoSceneVoca.html).*

susceptible to volcanic ash. The effects would have been different again if it had occurred in 11,010 BCE, when Iceland was unoccupied and such a minor eruption would most likely not have been noticed by anybody anywhere. This thought experiment underlines the distinction between a natural event free of human dimensions, and a catastrophe that by definition is the result of the interaction between such an event and human individuals, communities, or societies.

Finally, it is worth drawing attention to the materiality of the eruption. Contemporary Icelanders use a wide variety of rugged, heavy-handed engineering and containment measures designed to limit the damage of volcanic eruptions to the immediate environment, and to preserve, for example, crucial infrastructure elements such as bridges. There is sophisticated monitoring equipment as well as specific tools and machines associated with these volcanic landscapes, which although seemingly wild are heavily modified by human intervention. In addition, both state and local communities offer warning and relief measures in the case of volcanic eruptions that provide a safety net

for local farmers who themselves employ modern farming and transport technology to, for instance, move livestock out of harm's way swiftly, and to protect themselves, their animals and their supplies against the ash (Fig. 2.4; Bird and Gísladóttir, 2012; Bird et al., 2011). Yet, most catastrophes result in both winners and losers (Scanlon, 1988), and shortly after the end of the eruption the local farming family put into place a purpose-built visitors centre and gift shop selling not only their own produce, bottled ash from the eruption, but also Eyjafjallajökull-branded clothes, mugs, and other paraphernalia (http://www. icelanderupts.is/en). Thus, the eruption has engendered its own material culture, both generic and specific.

The volcanic vignette used to open this chapter has served to highlight how these key facets of volcanic activity and its human impact can provide avenues into analysing such events – not as sensationalist spectacles but as crucial threads in the fabric of human prehistory and history. The Eyjafjallajökull eruption and its effects make clear that it is *not* the geological properties of a given eruption alone that make it a catastrophe. But what then, are the factors that do? Disaster scientists use two related terms as conceptual foci for discussion of the susceptibility of human individuals, and especially of human communities, to extreme events such as volcanic eruptions: vulnerability and resilience. The United Nations Office for Disaster Risk Reduction defines vulnerability as "[t]he characteristics and circumstances of a community, system or asset that make it susceptible to the damaging effects of a hazard" (http://www.unisdr. org), in other words "the potential for loss" (Cutter, 1996: 529). A hazard, in turn, can be understood as any threat to the livelihood and lives of people. Today, such threats come more and more in the guise of technological or social calamities such as oil spills, famine, and warfare, but natural events beyond the making and influence of people still do occur. In addition – and I will return to this point later – 'social' calamities such as famine and warfare are often intimately and part-causally related to natural events. Volcanic eruptions are but one hazard in a broad portfolio of geological calamities that befall human societies (e.g. Kusky, 2003). In fact, an estimated 9% of the world population, that is upwards of 455 million people, live within zones of high volcanic risk, especially in poorer and more urbanized countries (Chester et al., 2001; Small and Naumann, 2001). At the time of writing, these estimates are already more than ten years old. Small and Naumann (2001) employed a total global population figure of merely 5.2 billion. This has since risen to well over 7 billion (see http://www.census.gov/population/popclockworld.html), and given the dramatic and on-going rise in global and especially low-latitude population densities (Roberts, 2011), the actual number of communities and individuals at risk from volcanic hazards today must be considered much greater (Huppert and Sparks, 2006).

2.3 Vulnerability and resilience

An important complement to the notion of vulnerability is resilience. Resilience captures how well communities and individuals are able to cope with and withstand catastrophes. Together these two terms frame the ability of communities or individuals to accommodate perturbations that go beyond – often way beyond – what is regularly experienced. The terms are often connected to 'adaptation' and 'adaptive capacities' (cf. Hufschmidt, 2011), but this linkage is problematic. Adaptation strictly speaking is the result of a diachronic, historical or evolutionary process that matches a given organism or population to its environment or, occasionally, a process in which organisms modify environments to better suit their selective requirements (Lewontin, 1978; Odling-Smee et al., 2003). Also in terms of material culture, which is the particular focus of this book, the term adaptation should likewise

Evolutionary classifications of traits/behaviours	Description	Related disaster risk reduction terms
Adaptive behaviour/ adaptability	Adaptive behaviour is functional behaviour that increments reproductive fitness	Adaptive capacity
Adaptation	An adaptation is a character favoured by natural selection for its effectiveness in a particular role	Pre-industrial coping mechanisms/ traditional ecological knowledge; evolved resilience
Current adaptation	A current adaptation is an adaptation that has remained adaptive because of continuity in the selective environment	Evolved resilience
Past adaptation	A past adaptation is an adaptation that is no longer adaptive because of a change in the selective environment	Pre-industrial coping mechanisms/ traditional ecological knowledge
Exaptation	An exaptation is a character that now enhances fitness but was not built by natural selection for its current role	Designed resilience
Dysfunctional by-product	A dysfunctional by-product is a character that neither enhances fitness nor was built by natural selection	Some spurious pre-industrial coping mechanisms

Table 2.1 *A classification for different behaviours or features of organisms or population with regard to their match to their environment. Only evolved matches can be termed adaptation, but adaptation is not the same as resilience, from (Laland and Brown, 2002).*

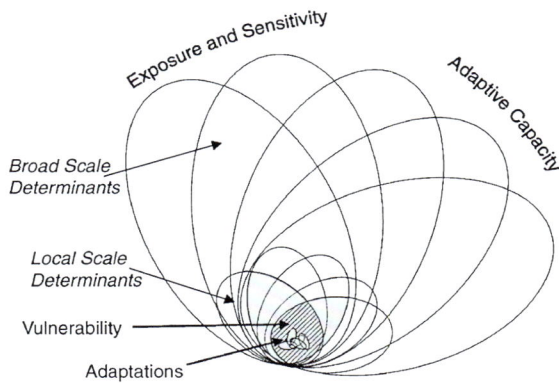

Figure 2.5 *The relationship between adaptation, adaptability and vulnerability, where true adaptations are a sub-set of community/population adaptive capacity in intersection with vulnerability and exposure. From Smit and Wandel (2006).*

be reserved to changes in a particular trait that demonstrably take place over time and due to selection (O'Brien and Holland, 1990, 1992). Not discriminating sharply between resilience and adaptation is analytically problematic as resilience references flexibility, adaptability and future events, whilst adaptation is the end-result of a process and thus references the past. In fact, there are several other distinct classifications for a given feature or behaviour (Laland and Brown, 2002), but all require information about the trait's history (Table 2.1). Failure to distinguish between true adaptation and its alternatives makes for incomplete and untestable historical narratives.

Vulnerability and resilience therefore relate first and foremost not to adaptation but to *exaptation* or *adaptability*, in other words, to the inherent flexibility of an individual or community to accommodate extreme variations in their environment. In contrast, adaptation is the result of selection and can be said to emerge out of vulnerability, but only if exposure to a given hazard is repeated at sufficiently short intervals for directional change or learning to occur (Fig. 2.5; Smit and Wandel, 2006). In the absence of such *evolved resilience*, it is this flexibility (*adaptability* or *adaptive capacity* – Brooks et al., 2005) and potential previous exposure and latent response mechanisms (*exaptations*) that determine vulnerability/resilience. In combination, this terminology serves to underline that it is not the extent, magnitude and

nature of a given geological hazard *alone* that determine its attendant human impact, but that such effects must be sought in the combination of geological, social and cultural processes (Leroy, 2006; Quarantelli, 1991). Vulnerability's sister-term 'resilience' is derived from its application in ecology (Holling, 1973) and disaster scientists have thought hard about it (Hufschmidt, 2011; Lorenz, 2013; Wolf et al., 2013). With few exceptions (McLaughlin, 2011, 2012), however, the term and its application remains disconnected from recent significant developments in ecology that articulate its hallmark synchronic perspective with the diachronic view of evolutionary theory under the umbrella notion of niche construction or triple-inheritance theory (Laland et al., 1999; Odling-Smee et al., 2013). The latter is readily integrated with archaeological understandings of technology, landscapes and culture change (Laland and O'Brien, 2010; Riede, 2012c; Rockman, 2009; Shennan, 2006) and here furnishes the point of contact between contemporary disaster science and the archaeological record.

Over time, communities can indeed genuinely *adapt* to volcanic hazards. If repeated experiences of volcanic events lead to the accumulation of knowledge on how to handle these, and if this knowledge is consistently transmitted across generations – in most traditional societies through oral media and as stories, myths and legends – some form of adaptation can be achieved (Blong, 1982). These oral encodings are generally known as geo-myths (Vitaliano, 1968, 2007), and many such legends the world over have been argued to reflect real volcanic events (Barber and Barber, 2006). We will return to the issue of how traditional societies handle such awesome events later in this book. For now it suffices to note that only repeated exposure to volcanic events, most often then in the form of high-frequency/low-magnitude eruptions, can lead to adaptation. The opposite scenario, eruptions of low-frequency/high-magnitude type leave societies doubly vulnerable because of the high magnitude of the event itself and because of the lack of previous experience with similar occurrences and their consequences.

2.4 'Dominant' and 'radical' disaster science

Those that study disasters come from very different disciplinary backgrounds: geology, physical and human geography, volcanology, anthropology, sociology, engineering, economics and the political and management sciences. For various reasons, the natural scientific approach, which foregrounds the physical and quantifiable aspects of natural disasters has a tendency to view individuals and society as responding passively to such events, and has long dominated disaster science. This technocratic approach certainly still dominates amongst governments in dealing with climate change and its attendant disasters (e.g. Bjurström and Polk, 2011; Nielsen and Sejersen, 2012), despite the fact that numerous studies have pointed towards the often awkward and occasionally downright counterproductive incompatibility of this way of thinking with local, traditional practices and world-views (e.g. Cashman and Cronin, 2008; Donovan et al., 2011; Lavigne et al., 2008). In a fairly blunt but perhaps not entirely unjust stroke of academic rhetoric, this technocratic and environmental determinist attitude has been labelled the 'dominant' approach, contrasted with its 'radical' critique, which emerged in the early 1980s and maintains that "the 'natural' and the 'human' are... so inextricably bound together in almost all disaster situations, especially when viewed in an enlarged time and space framework, that disasters cannot be understood to be 'natural' in any straightforward way" (Wisner et al., 2004: 9). The vulnerability of individuals, of sub-sections of society, and of society as a whole is given centre stage and this is seen as a product of historical, economic/ecological, and political circumstances at the time of the catastrophe. Beginning with O'Keefe et al.'s (1976) powerful call to arms and the subsequent landmark publication of Hewitt's (1983) edited volume, radical disaster scientists with backgrounds in anthropology, geography, and sociology have challenged the 'tacit assumption of an unexamined normality' (Hewitt, 1995: 322) said to prevail prior to a disaster and have issued 'an explicit call for the study of human agency in disaster research' (Oliver-Smith, 1986: 24).

Interestingly, these sentiments should resonate with a familiar note for archaeologists. In archaeology, the 1980s saw a general reaction against the behaviourist or systemic approaches, which here were given the tag 'processual'. Archaeology's very own but no less 'radical' critique became known simply as 'post-processualism' and although many often rather disparate approaches have developed since (see Hodder, 2001), the call for increased attention to agency – ultimately going back to the influential writings of Giddens (1984) and Bourdieu (1977) – in the past and the multivocality of the record has been one of the loudest, most persistent, and successful (e.g. Dobres and Robb, 2000; Dornan, 2002; Joyce and Lopiparo, 2005). Detecting and analysing agency – the actions and their consequences perpetrated by particular individuals of different gender, class, age and so on – in the deep past is no easy undertaking, but archaeologists have at the very least developed the conceptual apparatus to take on this challenge. In that sense, one of post-processualism's greatest achievements can perhaps be said to be the constant admonition that we need to think of past individuals with desires, ambitions, and conflicts; of communities, even those in the very deep past, as complex, as internally heterogeneous and thus capable of generating and driving social change independently of (supposedly) external environments. Such changes do not simply emerge passively but according to particular, often conflicting and just as often unconscious agendas. Importantly, this heterogeneity also contributes to community resilience by allowing people to draw on informational and social capital in the form of, for example, differential knowledge and know-how or access to resources; at the same time, this heterogeneity may also be the source of vulnerability, especially for those with *limited* access to resources, by preventing effective collective action, or by opening up for social change promoted by particular groups, for instance religious splinter groups (Chester, 2005a). Finally, it is worth noting that variation is also necessary for selection and thus ultimately for adaptation (Lewontin, 1978) bringing us full-circle in linking vulnerability, knowledge, and selection. Much like systemic terms such as resilience, the greater focus on agency is not at all incompatible with a broader evolutionary approach (Riede, 2005a, 2008a; Shennan, 1989, 2004a).

A further grievance 'radical' disaster scientists have levelled against the traditional 'dominant' approach is its 'lack of historical perspective' (Alexander, 2000: 105) with the obvious implication that a more comprehensive inclusion of 'radical' perspectives in *archaeological* studies of *past* natural disasters may be fruitful. However, it is also noteworthy that although 'radical' geographers strive to incorporate notions of agency, history and reflexivity in their studies of disaster reactions, and although they reject viewing societies as functional(ist) wholes at equilibrium, they nonetheless remain firmly grounded in an ecological approach: 'The field of natural hazards is peculiarly adapted to a human ecological approach, for the simple reason that environmental extremes are powerful enough to exert a strong and consistent influence upon social and cultural systems, if not also on physiological ones' (Alexander, 2000: 55). Political ecology thus offers a suitable general framework for disaster scientists interested in vulnerability and deeply concerned with contemporary politics and the engagement with society (Oliver-Smith, 2004). In this, they differ from their post-processual archaeology counterparts, where the adoption of agentive or interpretive approaches usually also entails the outright rejection of the relevance of human evolutionary or behavioural ecology (e.g. Shanks and Tilley, 1993). This anti-scientific stance seems rooted in the philosophical sources that inspired much of this writing. Although post-processualists have made many a valid point, and although these then-novel ways of approaching the archaeological record opened up many new domains of inquiry, the rejection of ecology and evolution as relevant to the study of the past is arguably based on a fundamental misunderstanding of these concepts (Riede, 2005a; Riede et al., 2012).

Archaeology (especially the Palaeolithic variant) fares best – that is it can utilise its specific data more fully – when human individuals and societies are seen as part of larger ecological constructs (Butzer, 1982, 1990; Mithen, 1990; Welinder, 1978). Such a view does not deny individual agency, but recognises that the kind of structures created by the material world – natural and built – and the inertia of cultural systems constrain potential actions to a significant degree and that ecological factors also impact political decision making (Shennan, 2004b). In particular, there are two pertinent extensions to the basic paradigm of human ecology (cf. Hardesty, 1972; Hardesty, 1975):

1. Much of the human niche is constructed by humans themselves, often in previous generations. This entails that a large number of selectively relevant behaviours reference not a kind of virgin natural environment, but rather that they must be seen in the context of 'inherited ecologies' or 'inherited niches' (Odling-Smee, 2007). The niche construction or triple-inheritance model of cultural evolution accounts for such processes (Odling-Smee et al., 2003). This overarching body of theory and its attendant methods are eminently applicable to human ecology of the present (Laland et al., 1999; Odling-Smee et al., 2013) and can equally well be exported to past ecological/archaeological contexts (Laland and O'Brien, 2010; Riede, 2012c).

2. In small-scale societies, the transmission of knowledge about the world – today often termed local or traditional ecological knowledge (TEK) – is critical for succeeding in that world. Scholars working with contemporary societies dealing with climate change or rapid-onset hazards stress as much (Lorenz, 2013; Wisner, 2010). Likewise, archaeologists increasingly view knowledge of, for instance, landscapes, technologies, resource distributions and social connections as factors that shaped past human social and economic behaviour – and their resilience – in important ways (e.g. Redman, 2005; Smith, Bruce D., 2009). It is the social transmission of culturally specific information – descent with

modification – that (by and large) shapes human adaptation (O'Brien and Holland, 1992; Shennan, 2011a) and this is true as much of artefact production and use as it is of ecological knowledge (Rockman, 2009; Strickland, 2006). The focus on cultural and ecological knowledge transmissions imbues the otherwise primarily synchronic perspective of ecology with a dynamic sense of diachronic change, of evolution, over time. At the same time, it opens up for a greater sensitivity to cultural inertia. Many systems of cultural transmission in traditional societies are rather conservative (Tehrani and Riede, 2008), and such inherent conservatism may lead to behaviours being drastically mismatched vis-à-vis newly-occupied landscapes (Alexander, 2000) or recently changed environmental regimes (Laland and Brown, 2006; Willerslev, 2009).

This dual focus on human ecology and knowledge – the transmission of which provides an evolutionary diachronic dimension to the basic ecological outlook – allows for a salient articulation of (some elements of) contemporary disaster science and (some elements) of contemporary archaeology by way of a knowledge-centred/evolutionary political ecology of past disasters (cf. McLaughlin, 2011, 2012; McLaughlin and Dietz, 2008).

2.5 Towards a science of past disasters

Space, time, and the material correlates of past peoples are the trinity that together make archaeological data and that are the building blocks of historical narrative and explanation. The same holds true for the study of impacts, changes, and vulnerability in relation to natural hazards present and past (Table 2.2). The strong emphasis in contemporary social science approaches on the political and social root causes of disaster can be seen as the natural consequence of human niche construction processes that over time have increasingly tipped the balance of human

existence – ecologically speaking – towards constructed environments and technological contexts. In the past, natural environments and their economic affordances likely played a greater role, but then as now such forces and structures will always have underdetermined the specific ways in which individuals and communities reacted.

Since the 'radical' critique of the 1980s, rallying calls for routinely including historical dimensions in the study of vulnerability have been sounded repeatedly and from different disciplinary corners (history/sociology: Bankoff, 2004; environmental science: Leroy, 2006; archaeology: Sheets and Grayson, 1979), yet they have only sporadically been answered (see chapters in Cooper and Sheets, 2012; Mauch and Pfister, 2009; Schenk, 2009a), in part at least because the methods of historical and archaeological research each require specialised knowledge and skills that at times leave little time or energy for such broader interdisciplinary engagements, and because their disciplinary discourses are difficult to unite with the no less arcane fields of Risk Reduction Research and disaster science (Dix, 2008; Dix and Röhrs, 2007). The continuing emphasis on technocratic risk reduction solutions finds one of its perhaps most stark reflections in the allocation of research funds: Despite there being a fair share of social science disciplines amongst the ~30 stakeholder disciplines in the field of Disaster Risk Reduction (Alexander, 1997),

Variable domain	Impact variable	Variable effect	
Geological	Magnitude	Low	High
	Speed of onset	Slow	Rapid
	Duration	Short	Long
	Recurrence	Frequent	Rare
	Area coverage	Limited	Extensive
Societal	Population density	Low	High
	Type of society	Flexible	Rigid

Table 2.2 *Basic natural hazard and some societal characteristics that structure the severity of impact, expanded from Leroy (2006).*

approximately 95% of the available funding goes towards natural science and engineering projects (Alexander, 1995). Arguably, the measures advocated by the latter disciplines have not, however, resulted in the hoped-for disaster panacea (Oliver-Smith, 2004), and cost-effective and lasting vulnerability reduction and disaster mitigation – especially in contexts where technological relief measures are prohibitively expensive to implement or where the nature of the calamity makes such implementations difficult or impossible – can be greatly improved via a more balanced approach that integrates both natural and social sciences.

Economic development and its attendant parameters such as wealth inequality, centralised market distribution structures, population increase, as well as urbanisation are often put forward as key variables creating and amplifying vulnerability (e.g. Birkmann et al., 2013; Cutter et al., 2003). Interestingly, archaeological and historical analyses of disaster impacts diverge in their general conclusions with regard to the way in which development intersects with vulnerability and resilience: whilst historians tend to argue that development ultimately increases resilience and indeed that disasters spur on development (Helbling, 2006; Pfister, 2009), archaeologists see the emergence of centralised political systems and market economies as a key factor that leads to increased vulnerability (Fitzhugh, 2012; Sheets, 2001, 2008, 2012). Although seemingly in opposition, these diverging observations can to some degree be reconciled with reference to Gilbert White (1974) who already noted a long time ago that effective post-industrial or comprehensive responses to disaster incorporate elements of pre-industrial as well as industrial social configurations (Table 2.3). Yet, the many known cases where, in particular, colonial interventions have led to increased vulnerability amongst indigenous populations suggest, however, that not all forms of development benefit resilience, whereas – vice versa – not all forms of indigenous or pre-industrial response can be seen as effective or useful (Chester et al., 2012; Kuhlicke, 2010). In addition, White's tripartite distinction of social responses into pre-industrial, industrial, and post-industrial does not easily

Response types and characteristics		
	Pre-industrial	*Industrial*
Adjustment range	Wide	Restricted
Actors	Individuals, households, small groups	Authorities, authority-coordinated groups
Relation to nature	Harmonisation with	Technological control over
Capital investment	Low	High
Spatial variability in responses	High	Low
Response flexibility	High	Low
Loss perception	Perceived as inevitable	Losses may/should be reduced by government action, technology, science & development
Time-depth	Deep, where there is previous hazard knowledge, traditional responses are evolved	Shallow, industrial responses first emerge from mid-19th century onwards and often suppress or replace (especially in marginal and colonised areas) traditional responses

Table 2.3 *Pre-industrial and industrial responses to natural hazards. After White (1974) and Chester et al. (2012). Post-industrial or comprehensive response approaches combine the most effective elements of both, although, arguably, such mitigation measures have not been implemented anywhere in the world yet.*

facilitate a more detailed assessment of vulnerabilities and resilience strategies amongst traditional societies, which clearly differ along many more salient dimensions than merely economic organisation. Given the considerable recent interest in the potential of traditional knowledge informing more inclusive community-level participatory approaches to risk reduction and coping in general (Adger, 2006; Agrawal, 1995; Berkes, 2007; Hastrup, 2009; Lorenz, 2013; van Aalst et al., 2008; Wisner, 2010) and also with specific reference to volcanic hazards (Cashman and Cronin, 2008; Cronin et al., 2004b; Cronin and Cashman, 2007; De Bélizal et al., 2012; Donovan et al., 2011), deciding which pre-industrial and industrial elements are best incorporated into a comprehensive disaster response approach remains a pressing empirical question.

A science of past disasters does not so much challenge but complement other approaches to the investigation of natural hazards (Riede, 2014f). It does, however, add an important further dimension to our knowledge base – the long-term perspective (see Fig. 1.3). This long-term view requires bridging numerous disciplines as it articulates with geology and its allied fields on the one hand (the natural science of deep-time) and anthropology and sociology on the other (the social science of the present day). Navigating such diverse disciplinary waters can be difficult, but it is doubly relevant in that it not only informs us about the vital magnitude/frequency relationship of the hazard in question, but it also allows us to trace post-event cultural change back to pre-event vulnerabilities, and to perhaps uncover causality. The depth of this time perspective and the focus on materiality and the landscape scale are, in combination, unique to archaeology and circumvent the bias – inherent in the vast bulk of historical documents – towards the filtered experiences of the establishment, the male, the learned, and the privileged (e.g. Schenk, 2009b). Such documents certainly can and do yield important information (Dix and Röhrs, 2007), but unless alternative data sources are incorporated they also set clear limits to what can be known about past calamities.

In archaeological terms, stratigraphy provides the material instantiation of time, segmented into more or less clearly discernable units. Importantly, many extreme events (e.g. earthquakes, tsunamis/storm surges, volcanic eruptions) leave methodologically convenient stratigraphic traces in the geological and archaeological records that facilitate the precise and accurate correlation between sites and regions. Volcanic eruptions and their often very widespread ash blankets are particularly germane here as this fallout – whilst certainly dangerous in its own right (Thorarinsson, 1979), it is also much less of a destructive or erosive agent than earthquakes and tsunamis – forms visible or at times invisible but microscopically detectable layers. The formation of such layers can be considered instantaneous from an archaeological perspective, forming so-called isochrons that provide artificial time markers, t_0, in relation to which pre-event (t_{-1}, t_{-2}, t_{-n}) and post-event (t_{+1}, t_{+2}, t_{+n}) patterns and processes can be investigated. This temporal control allows near- and far-field effects to be investigated comparatively, and climatic and environmental records to be directly linked to sequences of culture change (Riede, 2014g).

2.6 Tephrochronology

Environmental scientists have been busy identifying, tracing and dating such volcanic fallout layers in different kinds of terrestrial, marine, and lacustrine archives as well as in the Arctic and Antarctic ice-cores for some time. Archaeologists are now following suit (Lane et al., 2014; Riede and Thastrup, 2013). Volcanic ash is also known as tephra, a term derived from Greek τεφρα meaning 'ashes', although this is in many ways an unfortunate misnomer. Volcanic ash is decidedly not the product of organic combustion, but rather it is rock powder generated in an extremely high-powered environment where both native (surface) rocks as well as the magma connected to the eruption itself are torn asunder. Truly distal tephra particles are usually glassy and can retain their characteristic bubble-infused and sharp-edged form, although the shape, size, degree

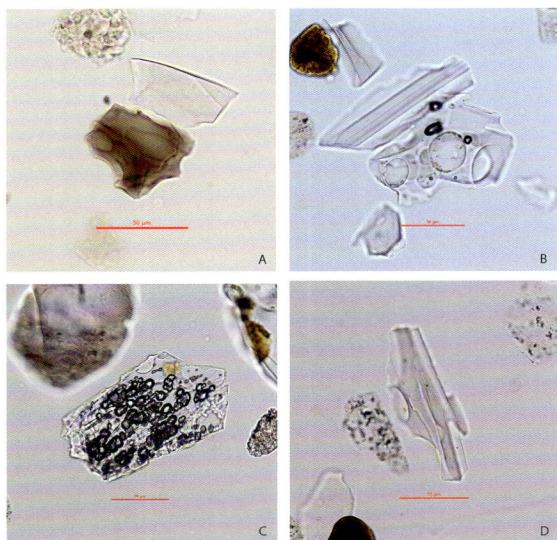

Figure 2.6 *Examples of tephra shards from a locale in northern Denmark. The morphologies seen here are by no means exhaustive. From Riede and Thastrup (2013).*

of vesicularity, and colour of tephra particles can vary substantially (Figure 2.6). Tephra is commonly further divided by size classes into ash (<2mm), lapilli (2-64mm), and bombs or blocks (>64mm), the latter of which can reach considerable sizes.

The frequency of eruptions that likely resulted in widespread fallout deposits throughout the Quaternary is substantial (Bryson et al., 2006; Crosweller et al., 2012; Siebert et al., 2010), with periods of rapid melting of inland ice masses such as the Late Glacial being marked by particularly high rates of volcanic activity in Europe at least (Nowell et al., 2006; Pagli and Sigmundsson, 2008; Sigmundsson et al., 2010). Pioneering near-field work was carried out on Iceland in the first half of the 20th century by Thorarinsson (1944), and by the early 1980s the prospect of a superregional, far-field tephrochronology was first aired (Thorarinsson, 1981). Indeed, thanks to the many Icelandic eruptions through the millennia (Lacasse and Garbe-Schonberg, 2001; Larsen and Eiríksson, 2008; Thordarson and Larsen, 2007) and the considerable methodological advances in recent years (Blockley et al., 2005; Swindles et al., 2010) that have facilitated the discovery and secure identification of so-called crypto- or microtephra otherwise invisible to

the naked eye, there now exists an ever more robust tephrochronological lattice – largely made up of Icelandic eruptions and their products – for the Late Pleistocene and Holocene of the north-western Atlantic seaboard (Haflidason et al., 2000; Hall and Pilcher, 2002; Pyne-O'Donnell et al., 2008) as well as parts of Scandinavia (Wastegård, 1998, 2005) and northern Germany (van den Bogaard and Schmincke, 2002; van den Bogaard et al., 1994).

In central Europe, the palaeobotanist Franz Firbas (1949) suggested already in 1949 that tephra layers originating from the Late Glacial Laacher See eruption could be used as a chronostratigraphic marker for the Allerød chronozone in Europe north of the Alps. This enthusiasm was mirrored by the archaeologist Schwabedissen's (1954) remark on how this tephra layer could be used in a similar way in archaeological investigations both close to and at some distance from the eruptive centre. Yet, it was first in the 1980s that more extensive distribution maps for the Laacher See tephra were presented (van den Bogaard and Schmincke, 1985) and its potential as a powerful chronostratigraphic marker highlighted (van den Bogaard and Schmincke, 1988). It took some additional years until archaeologists haltingly suggested a possible relationship between this eruption and contemporaneous cultural changes (Thissen, 1995) and some decades until a more coherent hypothesis for this impact, its impact mechanisms and consequences was formulated (Riede, 2007a, 2008b).

In brief, tephrochronology achieves its greatest utility if and when discrete visible or invisible layers of volcanic particles (a) originate from known-age and short-lived explosive volcanic events that (b) left a widespread deposit of particles, which (c) can be securely identified via petrological and/or geochemical methods. Knowledge of the source of the tephra is not strictly required and several important isochron markers (e.g. the so-called Borrobol Tephra) are only known from distal occurrences. In this way, the study of far-field tephra occurrences also feeds back into the study of the eruption frequency/magnitude behaviours of volcanic systems, which in turn has important implications for risk assessments in relation to future eruption events (Lawson et al., 2012; Swindles et al., 2011). Tephrochronology is most commonly used as part of Quaternary scientific studies of environmental change, and offers a unique and powerful way of dating and linking different sites and archive types (ice-cores, terrestrial, marine, lacustrine). The volcanological background to tephrochronology as a method, attendant techniques, and regional applications have been reviewed a number of times (Alloway et al., 2007; Dugmore and Newton, 2009; Sarna-Wojcicki, 2000; Turney and Lowe, 2001), most recently and extensively by Lowe (2011). Adding archaeological stratigraphies to this list of archives (e.g. Balascio et al., 2011; Housley et al., 2014; Housley et al., 2012; Lane et al., 2014; Lowe et al., 2012) then turns tephrochronology into a cornerstone method for a science of past disasters that focuses on volcanic activity (Riede, 2013a, 2014g; Riede and Thastrup, 2013).

2.7 Event horizons

The increasing use and resolution of tephrochronology has resulted in what can probably rightly be described as a revolution of our understanding of Late Glacial climate and environmental change: the creation of an event stratigraphy. The usefulness of the older framework based on the palynologically-derived chronozones of Mangerud et al. (1974) has been increasingly eroded by the inherent time-transgressiveness of changes in local and regional plant communities. Whilst such regionality to a very large degree quite accurately reflects actual past environmental differences between different areas, it has led to a terminological confusion and great difficulties in correlating such successions between regions (de Klerk, 2004; Litt et al., 2003).

Tephrochronologists have suggested one solution to this issue. The high-resolution climate proxy data from the Greenland ice-coring projects is put forward as a northern hemisphere reference, a so-called stratotype. In the ice cores several major climatic transitions can be identified, which relate quite

directly to major reconfigurations in ocean circulation and their down-stream changes in wind patterns, sea-ice accumulation and drift, and temperature regimes (e.g. Andersen et al., 2004; Johnsen et al., 2001; Rasmussen et al., 2006; Sigl et al., 2013; Steffensen et al., 2008). In addition to the numerous chemical climate proxies that can be retrieved from the ancient ice layers, volcanic ash or aerosols can also be recovered (Abbott and Davies, 2012; Fiedel et al., 1995; Zielinski et al., 1996; Zielinski et al., 1994). Of course, the climate change recorded in the ice cores is, as such, only valid for Greenland. Yet, tephra layers found there can also be found in other archives outside Greenland. Once found and identified, key layers can be used to both precisely and accurately investigate the similarities, differences and potential lead-lag-effects that characterise different environmental systems and regions located at different latitudes and at varying distances from Greenland without prioritising one archive type over another *a priori* (Davies et al., 2012; Lowe et al., 2008; Turney et al., 2006). This event stratigraphy recognises that even during the Late Glacial – a period of general climatic instability to begin with – several episodes of severe, sudden, and prolonged change can be isolated (see Table 1.1).

This renewed focus on rapid environmental change – on events – has prompted a widespread interest amongst archaeologists in the question of whether cultural changes may have been equally rapid. In relation to individual cases this is ultimately an empirical question. The notion of major changes in human societies coming about in an event-like fashion receives support from a perhaps unlikely corner: historical sociology. In an effort to extend the earlier discussions on structure and agency by Giddens (1984) and Bourdieu (1977), the historical sociologist Sewell (1996a, 1996b, 2005) suggested that major social change, seen historically, is eventful and full of "radical contingency" (Sewell, 1996b: 263). According to Sewell (1996a: 861-879), such event horizons are characterised by ten particular features:

1. *Historical events are cultural transformations...events are, literally, significant: they*

signify something new and surprising. They introduce new conceptions of what really exists...of what is good...and of what is possible... This implies that symbolic interpretation is part and parcel of the historical event.

2. *Historical events are shaped by particular conditions...the small but locally determining conditions whose interaction in a particular time and place may seal the fates of whole societies.*

3. *Historical events are characterized by heightened emotion...Most social scientists avoid emotion like the plague. They seem to fear that if they take emotion seriously as an object of study, they will be tainted by the irrationality, volatility, subjectivity, and ineffability that we associate with the term – that their own lucidity and scientific objectivity will be brought into question. But if, as I would maintain, high-pitched emotional excitement is a constitutive ingredient of many transformative actions, then we cannot afford to maintain this protective scientific distance.*

4. *Historical events are acts of collective creativity...Dislocation of structures...produces in actors a deep sense of insecurity, a real uncertainty about how to get on with life... In times of structural dislocation, ordinary routines of social life are open to doubt, the sanctions of existing power relations are uncertain or suspended, and new possibilities are thinkable. In ordinary times, cultural schemas, arrays of resources, and modes of power are bound into self-reproducing streams of structured social action.*

5. *Historical events are punctuated by ritual... Students of ritual disagree about precisely how ritual should be defined; among the characteristics that have been proposed to mark off ritual from other types of social action are the formalization and repetition of gesture, the theatrical character of the action, the invocation of supernatural forces, the demarcation through gesture of sacred from profane persons, places, and activities,*

and the delineation of particular stages in 'the ritual process'.

6. *It is the creation of this sense of communitas that gives rituals their psychological and social power. In episodes [of eventful change], the usual process is reversed: rather than the ritual inducing the emotional excitement and the sense of communion, the emotional excitement and sense of communion – what Durkheim would call the collective effervescence – induce those present to express and concretize their feelings in ritual.*

7. *Historical events produce more events... Events are sequences of ruptures that effect transformations of structure. If structures are multiple and overlapping, it follows that any transformation of structure has the potential of touching off dislocations and re-articulations of overlapping or contiguous structures.*

8. *To become definitive, re-articulations of structures must gain authoritative sanction... Authoritative re-articulations, however, are likely to take place at power nodes that command an adequate geographic and institutional scope.*

9. *Historical events are spatial as well as temporal processes... We usually think of the event as a temporal category. But it is impossible to analyze an event without encountering spatial processes...historical events can be defined at least in part by a prodigious expansion in spatial reach of what are initially local phenomena.*

10. *Defining the boundaries of a historical event requires an act of judgment...the complexity of events is not limited to their fractal character. Events are also overlapping and interpenetrating. If it is true that structures form a loosely articulated network, and if we define events as sequences of occurrences that transform structures, then...each of these transformations will have a different spatial and temporal range. Once again, deciding*

how to bound an event is necessarily a matter of judgment. One may state as a rule of thumb that how an analyst should delimit an event will depend on the structural transformation to be explained.

Sewell's characterisation of historical events is necessarily grounded in part in his own work on the French Revolution. Yet, his insistence on contingency and unpredictability, but also on the role of psychology and of ritual and religion match the descriptions of causal relationships in hazard responses offered by 'radical' disaster scientists (Hoffman and Oliver-Smith, 1999, 2002; Wisner et al., 2004). Archaeological applications of Sewell's approach are emerging (Beck et al., 2007; Bolender, 2010) and natural hazards can arguably serve as "triggers" (García-Acosta, 2002: 57) and "social catalysts" (Kreps, 1998: 32) that change, arrest or accelerate trajectories of culture change. It is interesting to note in this context that numerous scholars do in fact see a connection between volcanic activity – the infamous Laki fissure eruption of 1783 – and the unfolding of the French Revolution, Sewell's prime case for 'eventful' historical change (Grattan et al., 2003; Grattan et al., 2007; Grattan and Charman, 1994; Witze and Kanipe, 2014).

No doubt, recasting human deep history in eventful terms – especially with regard to the impact of disasters on past human communities – should be done with great care (Grattan, 2010): The actual causal relationship between a given hazard and some observed culture change, no matter how large the hazard, cannot be assumed a priori, but neither should potential connections – likely non-linear and cascading – be ignored. As suggested by Sewell (1996b) in a footnote, there are highly salient similarities between his view of historical change and the punctuated equilibrium paradigm in palaeontology (Eldredge and Gould, 1972; Gould and Eldredge, 1993). Perhaps the duality of periods of stability and periods of change is a general emergent feature of historical processes that unfold in complex and at times unstable relations to other (environmental, ecological/economic or social) components?

One of the most important conceptual contributions of the punctuated equilibrium approach is its insistence on the simple fact that not all biological traits seen in nature can be explained as adaptions. In a powerful critique of overly adaptationist explanations of, in Gould and Eldredge's case, biological features, they argue instead that quite often the historical signal of either past but no longer relevant selection processes, selectively neutral and purely random stochastic evolutionary processes, or indeed decidedly maladaptive traits and/or behaviours is just as strong in the fossil record (Gould and Lewontin, 1979; Lewontin, 1978). Archaeologists have made similar suggestions for prehistoric culture change that happened at temporal scales somewhere between Gould's and Sewell's (e.g. Bentley et al., 2004; Koerper and Stickel, 1980; Maschner and Jordan, 2008; O'Brien and Lyman, 2000; Prentiss and Chatters, 2003; Rosenberg, 1994), and the previous chapter has already cast doubt on whether the Bromme culture can satisfactorily be explained within an adaptationist framework as applied to culture change.

Environments change, at times rapidly, and extreme events do happen. While humans are able to entertain a wide range of future possibilities based on previous experience and the transmission of these experiences in the form of traditional ecological and technical knowledge (Vale et al., 2012), they are not able to clairvoyantly see into the future (Mesoudi, 2008). Rapidly changing environments and rapid-onset natural hazards thus lead, more often than not, to temporary adaptive mismatches between environment and communities. It is at these critical junctures that maladaptations can be identified. In fact, Oliver-Smith and Hoffman (2002: 8) have argued programmatically that 'the degree to which [given hazards] bring about a disaster in a society is an index of adaptation or maladaptation to the environment'. In sum, an integration of archaeology with disaster science at a theoretical level through a focus on eventful changes and the social transmission of cultural knowledge, and at a practical level through the powerful correlation methods of tephrochronology paves the way towards a more integrated study of past natural hazards. Disasters are "revealers" (García-Acosta, 2002: 57) of social tensions and trends, and they can – if stratigraphically represented – serve as effective analytical tools for juxtaposing pre-event and post-event patterns of past environments, material culture, and, by extension, social structures. Vulnerability as a spatially and temporally heterogeneous socio-ecological property serves as a key heuristic for understanding the relationship between a given hazard event and cultural changes – cultural evolution – observed in their wake.

Chapter 3

Explosive volcanism and the Laacher See eruption

3.1 Introduction

The previous chapter has focused on articulating disaster research more broadly with an evolutionary archaeological and deep historical perspective on culture change. In doing so it has highlighted issues of, on the one hand, vulnerability, resilience and the ability of individuals and communities to command knowledge and resources in the face of unexpected calamities, and adaptation on the other. Adaptation can be seen as a form of *evolved resilience*, where specific behavioural patterns, tools, or social strategies have developed in repeated interaction with and exposure to a given hazard type. This chapter now turns to one kind of calamity, volcanic eruptions, their many faces, and their ways of affecting human communities. This chapter is divided into two parts. Part one provides a necessarily abridged introduction to volcanism in general and to explosive volcanism more specifically. Part two then reviews what we know of the Laacher See eruption from a natural scientific perspective. No claims are staked to either comprehensiveness or originality, but an attempt is made to provide an essential backdrop for then considering, in the chapters to follow, how this cataclysmic eruption interacted with contemporaneous Late Glacial human communities.

3.2 The origins of volcanic activity

Volcanic activity ensues when extremely hot, molten, and more or less viscous rock – magma – is extruded onto the surface of the Earth; lava, pyroclastic materials, and/or volcanic gases erupt through one or several openings in the crustal surface termed vents. The openings can be approximately round (craters) or elongated (fissures). When, during or after eruption, craters collapse into the emptied magma chamber underneath, so-called calderas are formed. The bulk of volcanic activity is ultimately the result of plate tectonic activity (Fig. 3.1), where movement and friction between tectonic plates lead to openings through which magma can escape. Consequently, the vast majority of volcanoes on land (sub-aerial) and under water (submarine) are located along plate boundaries, for instance along the so-called 'Ring of Fire' that frames the Pacific Ocean and links the volcanic chains of Japan, Kamchatka, southern Alaska, the Aleutians, the Cascade Range of the United States of America and Canada, Cen-

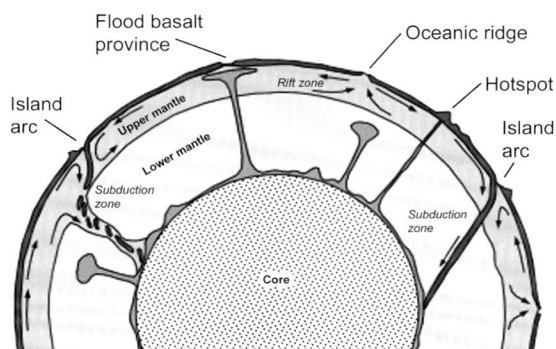

Figure 3.1 *Schematic of the Earth's core-to-mantle layering and the different types of volcanic systems.*

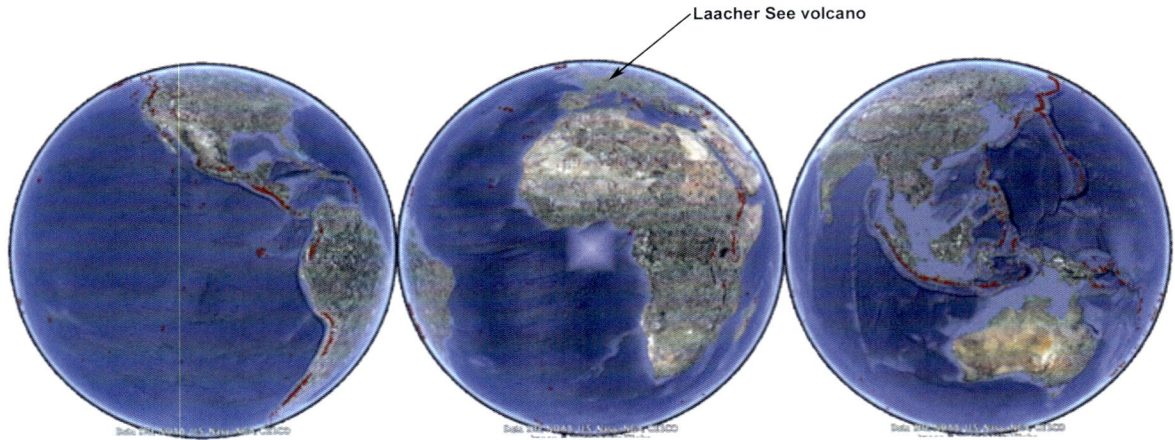

Figure 3.2 *The global distribution of volcanoes. Note the Pacific Ring of Fire and the isolated position of the intra-plate Laacher See volcano. Maps ©Google Earth.*

tral America and the Andes, emerging again in Oceania including Tonga, Vanuatu, New Zealand, Papua-New Guinea, Indonesia, the Philippines, and the Mariana, Izu and Bonin Islands (Fig. 3.2). Here, continental plates either converge (subduction zones) or spread (rift zones) from each other, and both processes can lead to volcanic activity (see, for instance, Scarth, 1994, for an overview).

Volcanoes can also be fed by so-called mantle plumes, which are accumulations of

magma at unusually shallow depths in the Earth's mantle. These features, sometimes in interaction with plate boundaries or rifts, create volcanic 'hot spots' (e.g. Iceland, Hawaii), which often persist over very long times and can rapidly build up critical masses of magma (Druitt et al., 2012). These subterranean blowtorches burn through the mantle, and are the culprits responsible for some of the deep past's largest volcanic events (e.g. the Deccan and Siberian Traps flood basalt provinces – see

Volcano type	Lava characteristics	Opening type	Pyroclastic debris	Location type	
Flood basalt	Very liquid lava	Fissures	None	Sub-aerial	On land
Shield volcano	Liquid lava	Central vent	None	Sub-glacial	On land, under ice
Cinder cone	Explosive liquid lava	Central vent	Very little	Sub-marine	Under water
Composite or stratovolcano	Moderately viscous lava	Central vent	Some		
Volcanic dome	Very viscous lava; sometimes explosive	Occurs adjacent to central vents	Some		
Caldera	Moderately viscous lava; usually linked to large eruptions of composite volcanoes	Central vent	Much		

Table 3.1 *Types of eruptions and their basic characteristics as well as locational variants.*

Hooper, 2000) and have fed many well-known prehistoric and historic eruptions (Huff and Owen, 2013; Robock and Oppenheimer, 2003; Schmincke, 2004).

Volcanic activity has a plethora of faces, ranging from the gentle and barely noticeable extrusion of gas bubbles in water-filled craters, to sluggish so-called effusive eruptions, to explosive and violent super-eruptions that affect climate on a global scale. Volcanoes erupt deep under water, near the surface, on land, and under glaciers (Table 3.1). Despite this evident diversity, volcanoes themselves can be classified into some broad categories, whose genesis and morphology varies along a suite of parameters. One of the smallest categories of volcanoes is the so-called cinder, scoria or splatter cone, an often steep-sided hill formed by largely lava-free eruptions. Bigger eruptions that also extrude lava form so-called stratovolcanoes that are built-up of lava and other ejecta over successive eruptions and can take the steep-sided cone appearance of popular imagination, but can also take considerably more irregular forms with rugged flanks and multiple edifices (volcanic peaks). Finally, shield volcanoes often appear less dramatic, but can be very large indeed. They, too, are the result of eruptions, either in geologically rapid succession, or over long periods of low intensity effusive activity.

Another standard way of classifying volcanic eruptions, or rather the material erupted, is by considering the relationships between its combined alkali content in relation to its silica content, which is commonly presented in a so-called TAS (total alkali versus silica) diagram (Fig. 3.3; Le Maitre, 2002). The increasing availability of accurately measured chemical compositions for volcanic products now allows for a kind of geochemical fingerprinting – encountered already in the discussion of tephrochronology in Chapter 2 – that cannot only link far-field deposits with great confidence to specific eruptive centres, often through the use of multiple bi- or tri-plots that akin to the TAS plot juxtapose different elements, but that also at times allows different eruption phases and with it varying eruption dynamics to be tracked in proximal as well as distal deposits (Pollard et al., 2006). We will

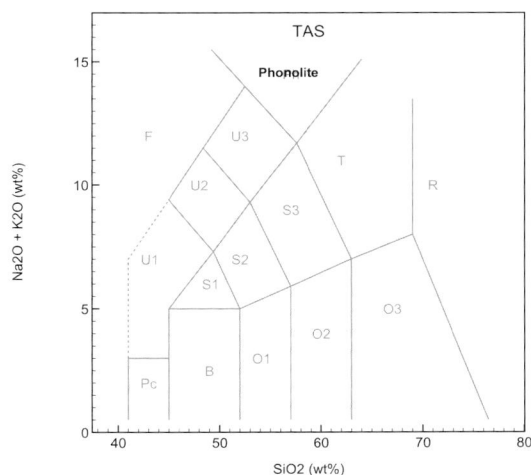

Figure 3.3 *The total alkali versus silica diagram or TAS plot and the divisions into different geochemical eruption products. The Laacher See eruption was phonolitic.*

return to matters of geochemistry later in this chapter.

The products of volcanic activity – for instance, the light and bubble-rich pumice and the durable basalt – have been used in many periods of prehistory and history to fashion tools, and as building material (e.g. Dehn and McNutt, 2000; Newton, 1999, 2001, 2003). Likewise, volcanic soils can be very fertile, although the oft-cited default fertility of volcanic soils is an obstinate myth of remarkable persistence. Volcanic soils become fertile only under the right climatic conditions (mostly in the tropics and sub-tropics) and when the ejecta is adequately mixed with the parent soil (James et al., 2000; Ping, 2000; Ugolini and Zasoski, 1979). Most recently, the geothermal energy stored in and released by volcanic systems is also extensively used (Arnórsson, 2000).

3.3 Rating volcanic eruptions

Volcanic eruptions are commonly assessed using the Volcanic Explosivity Index of Newhall and Self (1982). This scale is roughly similar to the better-known Richter scale for earthquake magnitude in that it is logarithmic, i.e. each step up on the VEI signals a ten-fold increase in magnitude. The VEI is, however, semi-quantitative and amalgamates several eruption parameters

VEI	0	1	2	3	4	5	6	7	8
Description	non-explosive	small	moderate	mod-large	large	--- very large ---			
Ejected volume (m^3)	$<10^4$	10^4–10^6	10^6–10^7	10^7–10^8	10^8–10^9	10^9–10^{10}	10^{10}–10^{11}	10^{11}–10^{12}	$>10^{12}$
Column height (km)	<0.1	0.1-1	1-5	3-15	10-25	>25 ---			
Qualitative description	--- gentle, effusive ---			--- explosive ---		--- cataclysmic, paroxysmal, colossal ---			
Classification	--- Strombolian ---					--- Plinian ---			
	--- Hawaiian ---			--- Vulcanian ---		--- Ultraplinian ---			
Duration of continuous blast (h)		<1 ---				>12 ---			
				--- 1-6 ---					
					--- 6-12 ---				
Tropospheric injection	negligible	minor	moderate		--- substantial ---				
Stratospheric injection	none	none	none	possible	definite	--- significant ---			

Table 3.2 *A schematic tabulation of key parameters making up the Volcanic Explosivity Index, from Newhall and Self (1982).*

such as volume ejected, plume height, eruption duration, and impact on weather systems and climate (Fig. 3.4 and Table 3.2). Whilst largely descriptive, this aggregate classification scheme works reasonably well both for very large (Self, 2006) as well as, in a modified form, for very small (Houghton et al., 2013) volcanic events. As a consequence, it remains widely used. Alternative schemes of classification employ more rigorously quantitative measures of eruption magnitude and intensity to make eruptions comparable and to analytically separate some of the factors that the VEI lumps together (Mason et al., 2004; Pyle, 2000). Eruption magnitude, M, for instance, is derived in this manner:

$$M = \log_{10} \text{(erupted magma mass, kg)}-7 \qquad (3.1)$$

In practical terms, the quantitative magnitude ratings of volcanic eruptions coincide largely with the less rigorous, but more inclusive VEI assessments. Complimentary to M, the rate or intensity of eruption can also be measured. Here, mass eruption rate or its estimates serve as input, and is transformed into a volcanic Intensity, I, measure by this formula:

$$I = \log_{10} \text{(mass eruption rate, kg/s)}+3 \qquad (3.2)$$

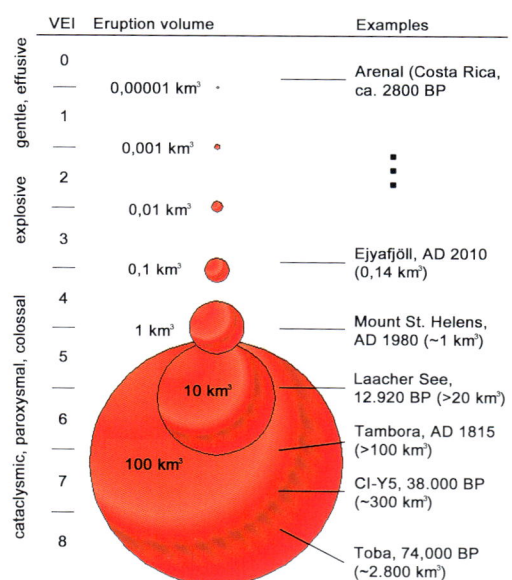

Figure 3.4 *The Volcanic Explosivity Index (VEI), and some example eruptions.*

Eruption year and volcano	Column height (km)	Magnitude (M)	Intensity (I)	Sulphur yield (Mt)	Northern Hemisphere summer surface temperature anomaly (°C)	Recorded near-vent fatalities (N)
AD 1815 Tambora	43	7.3	11.4	28	-0.5	>71,000
AD 1883 Krakatau	25	6.5	10.7	15	-0.3	36,600
AD 1902 Santa Maria	34	6.3	11.2	11	-	7000-13,000
AD 1912 Katmai Novarupta	25	6.5	11.0	10	-0.4	2
AD 1980 Mount St. Helens	19	4.8	10.3	0.5	-	57
AD 1991 Pinatubo	35	6.0	11.6	10	-0.5	1202
13k BP Laacher See	**40**	**6.2**	**11.7**	**150**	**-4.0**	**0**

Table 3.3 *Selected explosive eruptions, their VEI, magnitude and intensity, meteorological consequences and recorded fatalities, compiled from Pyle (2000) and Francis and Oppenheimer (2004). Values for column height, sulphur yield, Magnitude and Intensity are peak/maximum values. For more information and references for the Laacher See values see Table 3.11.*

Generally speaking, there is a positive correlation between *M* and *I* – the greater the eruption magnitude, the greater its intensity (Table 3.3). Intensity relates directly to measures of plume height and usually varies strongly throughout an eruption process, which in turn is reflected in the properties of the resulting stratigraphic columns such as grain size and sorting (Fig. 3.5). Finally, Pyle (2000: 268-269) proposes a measure of destructiveness for a given eruption as the 'area within which human structures would be expected to be completely destroyed as a result of the eruption',

which corresponds to the area affected by lava, pyroclastic flows or surges, lahars, as well as dry and non-compacted tephra fall 10-20cm deep (>100kg/m²). This measure is (as Pyle himself admits) rather arbitrary, especially from a non-geological point of view given that human habitation structures and people's ways of coping with volcanic fallout vary dramatically today, let alone over time. Nonetheless, such a Destructiveness index (*D*) is defined as:

$$D = \log_{10} \text{(total area in km}^2 \text{ affected by ejecta } >100\text{kg/m}^2) \qquad (3.3)$$

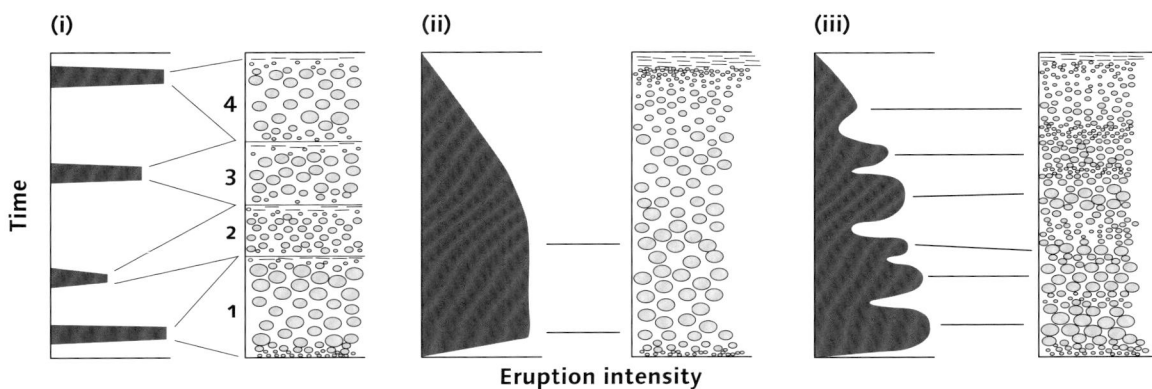

Figure 3.5 *Idealised relation between stratigraphic bedding features, maximum size of eruption products, and eruption intensity. Compare with Figure 3.13 and Table 3.13.*

Eruption year and volcano	Area (km²) covered by			Total area (km²)	Destructiveness (D)
	Tephra fall (>100 kg/m²)	Pyroclastic surges/flows	Lahars		
AD 1912 Katmai Novarupta	30,000	150	–	30,150	4.5
AD 1980 Mount St. Helens	10	600	100	710	2.9
AD 1991 Pinatubo	1700	400	>400	>2500	3.4
13k BP Laacher See	?	**1400**	?	**>1400**	**>3.1**

Table 3.4 *Some historical eruptions and their destructiveness (D), from Pyle (2000). Note that the area covered by a dry, un-compacted tephra with a thickness of 10-20cm (corresponding to 100kg/m²) has not been included in the calculation of D for the Laacher See eruption. Given that compacted primary air-fall thickness values from this event are found at distances of ~250km from the vent, this value may very well be considerable. In addition, the syn-eruptive lahar-like river flood surge along the River Rhine is not considered here.*

and does allow for a rough comparison of the gross destructive potential of eruptions in relation to infrastructure elements (Table 3.4). Devastating events with a *D* value >4 are considered very rare.

3.4 The frequency of volcanic activity

At the time of writing, some 140 volcanoes are active globally, where such activity ranges from mere 'unrest' to 'major eruption' (http://www.volcanodiscovery.com/erupting_volcanoes.html). The majority of the active sub-aerial vents are located along the Pacific 'Ring of Fire' and are unlikely to develop into large-scale events. Small volcanic eruptions are, in fact, a rather common occurrence, at least seen globally. There is a strong relationship between eruption magnitude and frequency, so that low magnitude eruptions occur most frequently (Fig. 3.6). Larger eruptions are increasingly rare events, although Self (2006) does suggest that there is 100% probability that at least one event of M= 6 will occur in the 21st century. Events of greater magnitude still are decreasingly likely (Table 3.5).

Seen over very long times scales, peaks of volcanic activity appear to cluster in certain periods (Sigurdsson, 2000a). One way in which such global increases in volcanic activity can be explained is via differential loading on tectonic

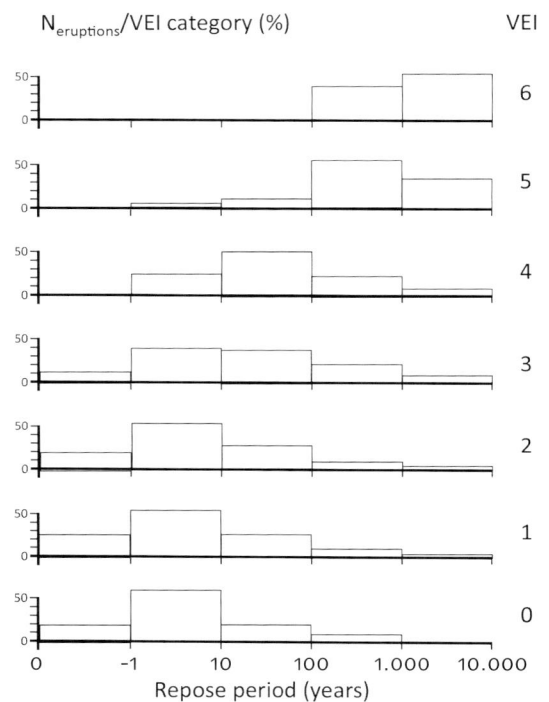

Figure 3.6 *Explosivity and repose between eruption for events of increasing VEI, redrawn from Schmincke (2004).*

plates, in turn related to the changing relationship between sea and ice masses with global climate. Studies in Iceland indeed seem to confirm this hypothesis (Pagli and Sigmundsson, 2008; Sigmundsson et al., 2010) and suggestive time series data for Mediterranean and transalpine European continental volcanism likewise indicate a relationship between global or hemisphere-wide warming and increases in

VEI	Magnitude (M)		Eruption mass (kg)	Erupted magma (km³)	Erupted pyroclastic deposits (km³)	Examples	Frequency (average/100 years)	P_{21C} (%)
5	5		1×10^{12}	0.4	1.0	AD 1980 Mount St. Helens	~10	100
6	6		1×10^{13}	4	10	AD 1883 Krakatau	2	100
7	7	Low	1×10^{14}	40	100	>AD 1815 Tambora	0.1-0.5	10-50
7	7	Moderate	2.5×10^{14}	100	250	7000k BP Kikai-Akahoya	~0.01-0.06	1-6
7	7	High	8×10^{14}	300	750	38k BP CI-Y5	0.001-0.01	0.1-1
8	8	Low	1×10^{15}	450	1000	26k BP Taupa	<0.001	<0.1
8	8	Moderate	2.5×10^{15}	1000	2500	2 ma BP Cerro Galan	0.0003	Negligible
8	8	High	8×10^{15}	>3000	>5000	>74k BP Toba	<0.0002	~0

Table 3.5 *Examples of major (M≥5) eruptions and the probability of similar-sized eruptions occurring in the near future. P_{21c} (%) denotes the estimated probability of an explosive eruption of that size occurring in the 21st century.*

Range of damaging effects (km)			Eruption type	Lava	Tephra	Gases	Pyro-clastic flows	Base surges	Lahar/ mud-flows	Secondary lahar/ flooding	Earthquakes	Tsuna-mis
<50	Proximal		Effusive	XXXX	XXX	XXXX				XXXX	XXXX	
			Mixed	XXXX	XX	XXX		XXXXX	XXXX	XX	XXX	XX
			Explosive		XX	XXX	XXXX	XXXXX	XXXX	XX	XXX	XX
50-500	Medial		Effusive	XX	XX	XX				XX	XX	
			Mixed			XXX			XX	XXXX	XX	XXX
			Explosive		XXXX	XXX	XX		XX	XXXX	XX	XXX
500-1000	Distal		Effusive			X						
			Mixed		XX	X						
			Explosive		XX	X				X		XX
>1000	Ultra-distal		Effusive			X						
			Mixed									
			Explosive		X							

Damaging agent

Table 3.6 *Volcanic hazard phenomena and their likelihood of occurrence proximally, medially, distally, and ultra-distally/ globally. The hazards of specifically explosive eruptions such as the Laacher See event are highlighted.*

volcanic activity in this region throughout the Quaternary (McGuire et al., 1997; Nowell et al., 2006; Watt et al., 2013). Nearly 10,000 volcanic eruptions are known from the Holocene alone (Siebert et al., 2010) and more than 2000 such events are known *and* dated from the late Quaternary (Bryson et al., 2006), a considerable number of which were large (M/VEI≥ 4;

see Crosweller et al., 2012). Taking account of taphonomic and research historical biases, most volcanologists consider these numbers to be severe underestimates of the actual number of eruptions that have taken place.

3.5 Volcanic hazards

The diversity of volcanic eruption styles results not surprisingly in an equally diverse range of output or ejecta types, and each of these types of ejecta in turn constitutes a hazard to people living nearby (near-field/proximally: <50km), in the middle distance (mid-field/medially: 50-500km), far removed (far-field/distally; 500-1000km), as well as potentially ultra-distally/globally (Table 3.6; Blong, 1984; Bolt et al., 1975; Simkin et al., 2001; Tanguy et al., 1998).

Volcanic eruptions are often preceded and accompanied by tremors or earthquakes, and by ground deformation. This is caused by magma moving upwards in the mantle. Once an eruption has begun in earnest, the most immediate hazards are lava flows, bombs, pyroclastic flows, and surges. Lava production is strongly associated with effusive eruption of relatively gas-poor and therefore less pressurised magma. The higher the silica content of the lava, the more fluid and faster-flowing it will be. Lava comes in different chemical compositions and in interaction with the environment (water or wet sediment) will take different forms; it can create major landforms, and is highly destructive in relation to fixed facilities, buildings, and other infrastructural features. It is not, however, very dangerous. In contrast, pyroclastic surges or flows can be very lethal indeed. Pyroclastic flows vary in their genesis, either being the product of a collapsing lava dome, or a collapsing eruption column. Lava dome collapse surges are generally known as *nuée ardentes* (glowing clouds), and when finally coming to rest as black-and-ash deposits. The dynamics of eruption columns are complex, but invariably they will experience collapse, often multiple times (Woods, 1995). The resulting deposits contain mainly pumice and can fill and blanket the existing topography around the eruptive centre. Ignimbrites often contain ejecta in a range of sizes, and when emplaced hot can become strongly welded. These pyroclastic surges are laterally expanding rings consisting of a turbulent mixture of gas and particulate fragments travelling outward from the base of the eruption column.

Explosive eruption can generate tremendous pressure waves and produce sounds that rank amongst the loudest ever recorded. Such eruptions have been heard over distances in excess of several 1000km (Table 3.7), and in the near-field these sounds – estimated for the 1883 eruption of Krakatau (Indonesia) to have reached c. 180 decibels – would have been well above the human pain threshold (c. 134 decibels; see Winchester, 2003). In addition, explosive eruptions cast about with different kinds of pyroclastic material either in the form of debris flows or avalanches, or as projectiles. The gargantuan forces released during Plinian eruptions are often multiples of the most powerful nuclear bombs ever detonated. They effectively turn, as the very term 'pyroclastic' already suggests, most ejected material into quite fine rock powder: tephra with grain sizes <2mm, larger chunks of both magma (2-64mm= lapilli; >64mm= bombs) as well as fragments of the shattered mantle (= xenoliths) are extruded. Volcanic bombs can reach rather large sizes, and, occasionally, directed explosions from lateral vents can also occur casting both fine- as well as coarse-grained material specifically in one direction.

A further class of syn- and post-eruptive hazard phenomena emerges in the interaction of the eruption with water or ice. Sub-glacial eruptions, for instance, can lead to rapid melting of the surrounding ice, which eventually is discharged as a so-called 'jökulhlaup', the Icelandic term that has become the international standard for a sub-glacial outburst flood. Likewise, crater lakes or other bodies of water near an eruption can breach their shores or banks, leading to fast-moving mud or debris flows, so-called 'lahars'. The voluminous input of small particles into the atmosphere during eruptions often leads to increased rainfall, which can further aggravate this risk. Comparable in

Eruption	Sound heard at	Distance from source (km)
Tarawera, 1886	North Cape	500
Taal, 1911	-	240
Sakura-jima, 1914	-	500
Asama, 1911	-	400
Asama, 1958	Sandai	150
Asama, 1958	Gifu	400
Bandai, 1888	Takai-Kori	164
Katmai, 1912	Juneau	1200
Katmai, 1912	Ketchikan	1400
Santa Maria, Cosiguina, 1835	Bogota	1740
Santa Maria, Cosiguina, 1835	Guatemala City	430
Mt. Pelée, 1902 (May 2nd)	-	1280
Mt. Pelée, 1902 (August 30th)	St. Kitts	430
Krakatau, 1883	Rodriguez	4700
Krakatau, 1883	Diego Garcia	3580
	MEAN	1141
	MIN	150
	MAX	4700
	MODE	500

Table 3.7 *Recorded distances at which explosive volcanic eruptions have been heard. Data from Blong (1984).*

consistency to wet concrete and loaded with ejecta small and large, lahars tend to follow riverbeds, and are both extremely destructive as well as extremely lethal. Such dirty mudflows can occur as a primary phenomenon linked to crater-lake outbursts as well as a secondary phenomenon linked to flank landslides, or to the mobilization or erosion of fresh, unconsolidated pyroclastic material. When eruptions occur near larger bodies of water, co-eruptive seismic activity or the high-energy explosions can also generate tsunamis, which constitute a great collateral danger associated with volcanic eruptions.

Finally, the ejection of fine-grained and often voluminous tephra also harbours numerous attendant hazards. In sufficient depth tephra fall can lead to building collapse and can cause serious mechanical and corrosive damage to modern machinery. In recent years,

tephra clouds have become notorious for disrupting flight routes over vast areas (Miller and Casadevall, 2000). Beyond its impacts on modern technology, however, tephra fall carries with it a series of further impacts and hazards. Rather than automatically acting as a fertiliser, tephra blankets disturb the soil balance and can lead to a series of changes, which end in the de facto sterilisation of the land surface (e.g. Gómez-Romero et al., 2006 and Table 3.8), although revegetation can also proceed reasonably rapidly (Dale et al., 2005).

By the same token, such thick covers can affect animals in numerous ways, especially by impeding feeding or by contaminating forage. As it is made up of rock and glass fragments, tephra particles are both hard and usually sharp-edged. It is known from numerous eruptions that chewing on vegetation laden with even quite thin coatings of tephra can

Thin burial (< 5mm tephra)

- No plant burial or breakage
- Ash is mechanically incorporated into the soil within one year
- Vegetation canopies recover within weeks

Moderate burial (5-25mm tephra)

- Buried microphytes (soil algae) may survive and recover
- Larger grasses are damaged but not killed
- Tephra layer remains somewhat intact on the soil surface after one year
- Soil underneath remains viable and is not so deprived of oxygen or water that it ceases to act as a topsoil
- Vegetation canopies recover within next growing season

Thick burial (25-150mm tephra)

- Completely buries and eliminates the soil algae
- Small mosses and annual plants will only be present again in the local ecosystem after re-colonization
- Generalized breakage and burial of grasses and other non-woody plants
- Some macrophytes (aquatic plants) do not recover from trauma
- Large proportion of plant cover eliminated for more than one year
- Buried soil is revitalized when plants extend roots and decaying organic matter from the surface of the tephra layer down to the top of the buried topsoil and affect an integration of the tephra and buried A horizon. Generally accomplished in four to five years
- Vegetation canopy recovery takes several decades

Very thick burial (>150mm tephra)

- All non-woody plants are buried
- Burial will sterilize soil profile by isolation from oxygen
- Soil burial is complete and there is no communication from the buried soil to the new tephra surface
- Soil formation must begin from this new 'time zero'
- Several hundred (to a few thousand years) may pass before new equilibrium soil is established

Table 3.8 *Tephra cover thickness and effects on soil. From www.maf.govt.nz/mafnet/rural-nz/emergency-management/volcanoes/volcano-erruption-impact.*

lead to steep increases in tooth wear amongst, in particular, browsers and grazers. Of the 1931 eruption of the Aniakchak Crater volcano in Alaska (USA), Trowbridge (1976: 73) reports:

> ...that particular time of the year was reindeer fawning time, and on the tundra where the deer are born, the ashes fell so thick as to cover all moss. The adult deer moved on in search of food

> and left the fawns to die. The moss which these deer finally did find was so coated with ashes and grit as to grind their teeth to the gums.

This passage vividly describes how tephra fallout both stimulated animal migrations as well as how it can lead to increased levels of mortality amongst both the old and the young. Likewise, for the eruption of the Parícutin volcano in Mexico, Bolt et al. (1975: 79) recount how:

...herds of cattle had to be moved to other areas, but even so several thousand animals died, partly of starvation due to destruction of grazing areas, but partly because their digestive systems became clogged as a result of eating ashladen vegetation. Another serious effect is the grinding away of tooth surfaces by chewing on ash-covered feed, the teeth eventually becoming so worn down that the animal can no longer eat.

Birds, too, seem to be strongly affected by tephra, and many eruptions are also associated with high fatalities within this group of animals. Returning to Alaska (USA), Martin (1913: 180) reports the following from the eruption of the Katmai volcano in 1912:

At Kodiak, during the tephra fall (300mm), small birds fell out of the air apparently gassed while large birds flew around in panic until they hit something. Afterwards, dead gulls, snipe, ptarmigan and ducks were found everywhere – at sea, buried in the ash and tangled in trees...even at Cold Bay where only 6mm of tephra fell, and at Iliamna Lake where the fall was 25-100mm, many of the small birds died.

Below this level of immediate lethality, volcanic eruptions with their associated landscape change and ash clouds can severely impact the migratory, breeding, and feeding habits of birds (Blong, 1984). Aquatic and wetland environments are also affected, albeit quite variably, by tephra deposition through pollution with particulate matter and a range of chemicals, as well as through acidification (Frogner Kockum et al., 2006; Hotes et al., 2006; Hotes et al., 2004). While the deposition of volcanic material can thus both fertilise as well as poison aquatic environments, microorganisms (e.g. diatoms) in particular can suffer from the changed chemical balance (Flaathen and Gislason, 2007; Jones and Gislason, 2008).

In addition to releasing potentially toxic chemicals in watery environs, tephra also brings these into atmospheric circulation (Pyle and Mather, 2009). Against the backdrop of historic Icelandic eruptions, Thorarinsson (1979) has suggested that the chemical loading of tephra deserves special attention in relation to assessing its hazard potential. Numerous noxious gases are associated with volcanic activity: carbon dioxide (CO_2), sulphur dioxide (SO_2), hydrogen chloride (HCl), hydrogen fluoride (HF), hydrogen sulphide (H_2S), carbon monoxide (CO), radon, various heavy metals as well as highly reactive and potentially dangerous free radicals (Hansell and Oppenheimer, 2004; Horwell et al., 2007; Horwell et al., 2003a; Horwell et al., 2003b). Fluorine (F) and its derivatives in particular can quite easily reach levels toxic for both animals and humans (D'Alessandro, 2006). Importantly, the quantity of chemicals attached to the surface of tephra particles increases with distance from the vent (Fig. 3.7). This is because smaller particles travel farther and as the relationship between particle volume and surface area changes in favour of the latter as particles become smaller (Kittleman, 1979; Óskarsson, 1980). Whilst only sparse data exist on how tephra-deposited F eventual becomes bio-available (Cronin et al., 2000), numerous cases are known where tephra deposition demonstrably has led to fluorosis and subsequent massive increases in life-stock and wild animal mortality (e.g. Araya et al., 1990; Cronin et al., 2003; Flueck and Smith-Flueck, 2013; Georgsson and Petursson, 1972). Likewise, numerous historical cases of more chronic fluorosis in both humans and animals living in volcanically active regions are also known (Garrott et al., 2002; Petrone et al., 2011; Weinstein, 2005). A point worth noting is that one of the symptoms of fluorosis – which swiftly kills in its most acute form, but otherwise attacks the teeth, antler and bone tissue – is the softening of dental enamel (Fejerskov et al., 1988; Thylstrup, 1978; Thylstrup and Fejerskov, 1978), a consequence that is particularly well-described in deer today living in industrially polluted regions (Kierdorf and Kierdorf, 1997; Kierdorf et al., 1996; Kierdorf et al., 1993; Richter et al., 2010; Zemek et al., 2006). In an important recent study, Flueck and Smith-Flueck (2013) were able to document the development of severe fluorosis as well as mechanical tooth-wear in Patagonian red deer following the eruption of the Puyehue-Cordon Caulle volcano (Argentina) in 2011. One and a half years after the eruption juvenile animals in particular had grossly elevated levels of bone fluoride, and displayed all tell-tale symptoms of severe dental fluorosis. None of these animals had been able to conceive, and the authors stressed the far-reaching ecological effects of the eruption on an important species such as red deer. Furthermore, it is known from other Argentinian eruptions (e.g. Hudson volcano, 1991) that effects mediated by windborne tephra continue to plague humans and animals due to the remobilisation of particles by wind over periods of >20 years (Wilson et al., 2011). Reverberating through ecological networks and up and down trophic chains, increased morbidity and mortality coupled with decreased fertility in a key stone species such as the red deer has major effects on other species – especially their predators (cf. Garrott et al., 2002).

In addition to fluoride, tephra-borne sulphide, too, may be implicated in animal pathologies such as the lethal ruminant-specific neuropathologic condition of polioencephalomalacia, where sulphide ingestion leads to metabolic imbalance and brain tissue damage (Gould, 1998). In addition to its toxicity, sulphide is argued to be particularly damaging for mosses and lichen, the dominant forage of reindeer (see VanderHoek, 2009).

A further hazard dimension linked to the changing grain size composition of tephra fallout is its impact on respiratory health. The more explosive an eruption, the finer the resulting rock powder (Rose and Durant, 2009) – and the finer the rock powder, the greater the health hazard (Horwell, 2007). Particulate matter (PM) smaller than 63μm can penetrate the upper respiratory system and enter deep into the lungs, where such mechanical obstruction but also the chemicals that are attached to these miniscule particles can cause irritation and damage (Fig. 3.8; Baxter, 2005; Durand and Grattan, 2001; Horwell, 2007; Horwell and Baxter, 2006). Particles become hazardous at sizes <15μm in aerodynamic diameter, and can penetrate further into the pulmonary system as size decreases. Particles <10μm (the 'thoracic fraction') may cause asthma and severe breathing difficulties, and those <4μm (the 'respirable fraction') will settle in the alveoli bringing with them the greatest health hazard.

Acute manifestations of tephra-related health effects, which have been observed during or following the eruptions of Mount St. Helens (USA), Cerro Negro (Nicaragua), Mount Ruapehu (New Zealand), Guagua Pichincha (Ecuador) and Irazu (Costa Rica), include asthma attacks, bronchitis, breathlessness, chest tightness and wheezing. These are

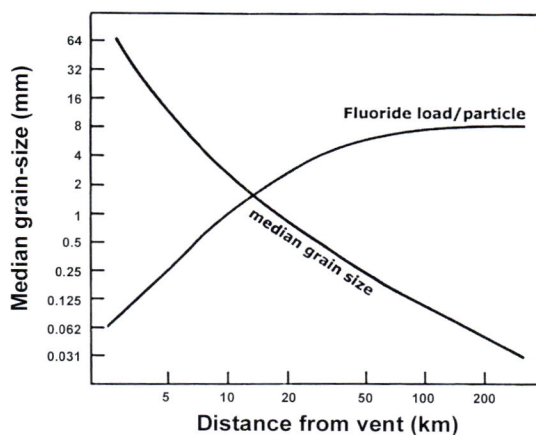

Figure 3.7 *Idealised relationship between distance from vent and median grain size composition of tephra fallout. As grain-size decreases and surface area increases in relation to particle volume, chemical load increases. Modified from Kittleman (1979).*

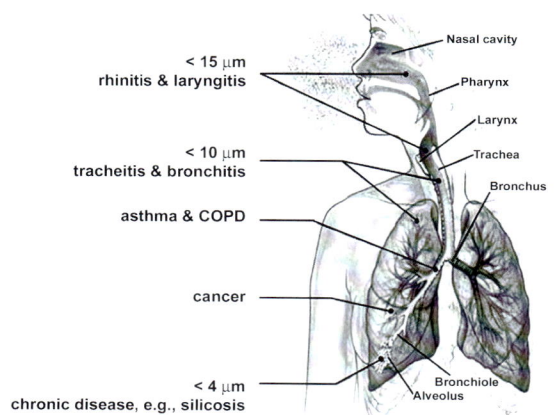

Figure 3.8 *The human pulmonary system and the reach of particulate matter of different sizes. From Horwell and Baxter (2006).*

brought on by fine-grained tephra particles entering and lining the airways. To previously undiagnosed people, especially children, the onset of asthma attacks can be frightening. In the elderly, they can be fatal. The effects on prior sufferers' afflictions can be exacerbated (Baxter et al., 1983). On the whole, mortality related to this impact mechanism is low, but people's day-to-day performance and wellbeing can be severely reduced, while morbidity is raised.

In addition to acute effects, long-term (years to decades) exposure to respirable tephra, analogous to the occupational exposure to fine dust, potentially leads to the development of chronic conditions such as silicosis or chronic obstructive pulmonary disease (COPD). Both are brought on by respirable particles penetrating deeply into the lungs, leading to scarring in the case of silicosis and the irreversible narrowing of the airways and chronic mucous hypersecretion in COPD. Cases of chronic respiratory health effects following volcanic eruptions have not yet been observed, but the database is minimal and the risk remains difficult to quantify. It is worth noting in this regard that unconsolidated tephra remaining exposed on the land surface following an eruption can easily be remobilized by strong winds (Scasso et al., 1994). Such ash storms lead to repeated exposure to hazards similar to the original ash-fall, lead to ash dune formation,

and may contribute to the development of more chronic versions of respiratory as well as chemically induced ailments. With these effects lasting for >20 years following an initial eruption, ash storms are implicated in "starvation, severe tooth abrasion, gastrointestinal problems, corneal abrasion and blindness, and exhaustion" (Wilson et al., 2011: 223). Finally, this hazard does not discriminate between animals and humans, although, with their snouts close to the ground much of the time, animals may be affected more strongly by this hazard agent than humans.

3.6 Volcanic eruptions and climate change

Famously, the eruption of the Tambora volcano (Indonesia; see Sigurdsson and Carey, 1989) in 1815 led to 1816 being called the 'year without summer' in the north-eastern USA, the maritime provinces of Canada, as well as southern and central Europe (Oppenheimer, 2003; Stommel and Stommel, 1983). Harvests failed in many regions (although not in Scandinavia, Finland or European Russia; see Neumann, 1990), leading to severe fluctuations in grain prices, which in turn impacted economic and political balances in the affected areas and their neighbours (Auchmann et al., 2012; Krämer, 2009; Stothers, 1984). Some-

Weather/climate effects	Mechanism	Onset	Temporal extent
Reduction of diurnal cycle	Blockage of shortwave and emission of longwave radiation	Immediately	1-4 days
Reduced tropical precipitation	Blockage of shortwave radiation, reduced evaporation	1-3 months	3-6 months
Summer cooling (Northern Hemisphere, tropics, subtropics)	Blockage of shortwave radiation		1-2 years
Stratospheric warming	Stratospheric absorption of shortwave and longwave radiation		
Winter warming (Northern Hemisphere)		6 months	Following winter(s)
Global cooling	Blockage of shortwave radiation	Immediately	1-100 years
Ozone depletion, enhanced UV radiation	Dilution, chemical reactions on aerosols	1 day	1-2 years

Table 3.9 *Common effects on climate and weather following large explosive eruptions, following Robock (2000).*

what more apocryphally, the unusual weather phenomena – blood-red sunsets, discoloured moons, increased precipitation – inspired romantic poets of the day such as Lord Byron to dystopically forecast the end of the world, although Byron himself was not aware of the causal link between his apocalyptic weather experiences and the far-away eruption. Byron (1839) wrote (in 1816), in his poem *Darkness*:

> *I had a dream, which was not all a dream.*
> *The bright sun was extinguish'd, and the stars*
> *Did wander darkling in the eternal space,*
> *Rayless, and pathless, and the icy earth*
> *Swung blind and blackening in the moonless air;*
> *Morn came and went – and came, and brought no day...*

A range of typical effects on climate following volcanic eruptions are now known (Table 3.9). The reduced temperatures recorded in areas far away from the volcano have been suggested to primarily be the result of changes in radiation budgeting due to voluminous sulphur dioxide (SO_2) and sulphuric acid (H_2SO_4) aerosol input (Fig. 3.9). Complex and heterogeneous chemical reactions at different altitudes often lead to a range of climate and weather anomalies (Cole-Dai, 2010; Mather et al., 2003; Robock, 2000), although these can vary strongly from region to region even for very large eruptions (Timmreck et al., 2010). There may be important differences between high- and low-latitude eruptions in this regard, as they respectively dump aerosols into hemispherically more closed or more open circulation systems. Generally, tropical eruptions appear to have a greater potential for impacting global climate. Nonetheless, models of high-latitude eruptions suggest that they, too, can significantly affect climate and weather at great distances (e.g. Oman et al., 2005). Some of these effects, such as untimely darkness, increased precipitation, the formation of the unusual mammatus cloud type (Fig. 3.10; Durant et al., 2009) and lightning strikes (Fig. 3.11), are linked to the ash itself, as they are related to the ejected particulate matter and generated in what is often referred to as 'dirty thunderstorms' (An-

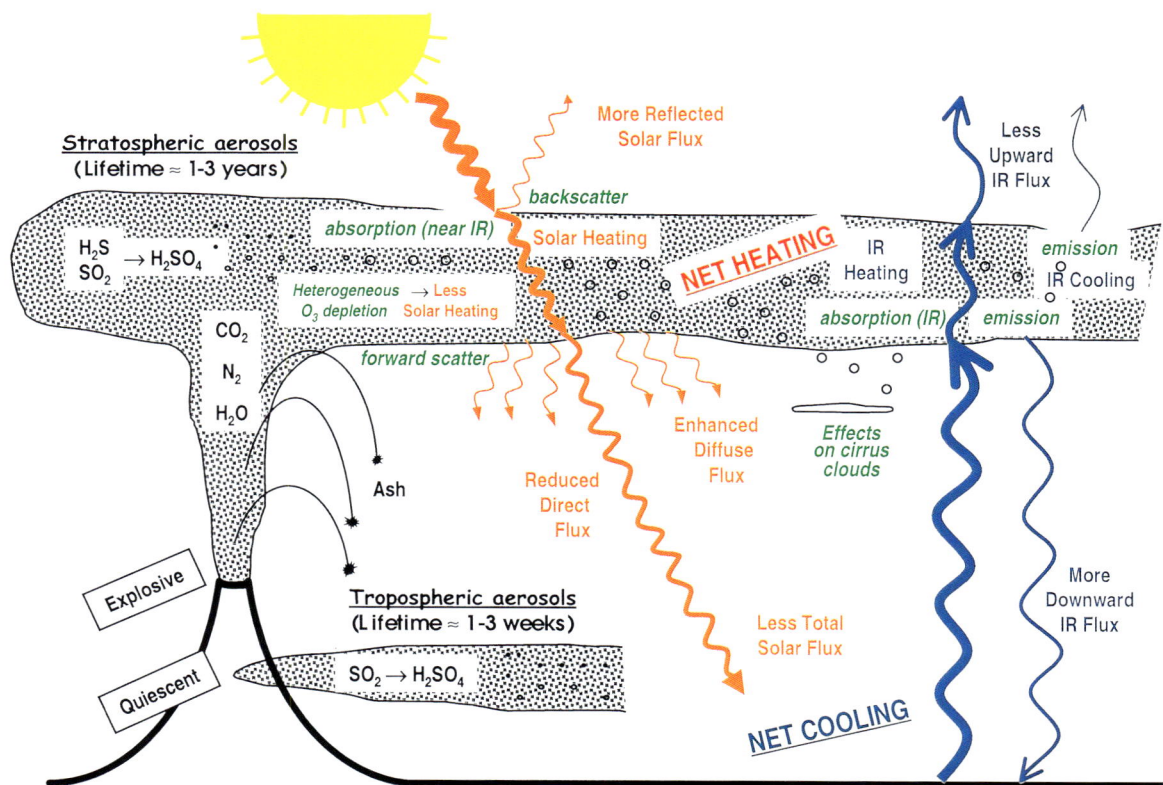

Figure 3.9 *Model relationship between volcanic particulate matter/aerosol input and climate impact.*

Figure 3.10 *Example of so-called mammatus clouds often seen in conjunction with volcanic eruptions (NOAA Photo Library).*

Figure 3.11 *Volcanic lightning during the 2008 Chaiten eruption (Chile, May 3rd, 2008, © C. Gutierrez/UPI.*

derson et al., 1965; Thomas et al., 2007). In contrast, more general effects on temperature and climate can be spatially and temporally disarticulated from the actual eruption and fallout cloud.

3.7 Changing hazard dynamics

With some hazard agents extending further from the eruptive centre than others, the abridged tabulation and discussion provided here already hints at the changing hazard potential and dynamic of a given eruption. Interestingly, the likelihood of a hazard occurring does not in a straightforward way correspond to the likelihood of these leading to fatalities. The rapidly moving and extremely destructive pyroclastic flows have claimed most lives, followed by what Simkin et al. (2001: 255) term 'indirect causes' such as famine, conflict and the like resulting – presumably – from the economically and politically destabilising conditions of an event such as a volcanic eruption. In addition, it is also interesting to note that tephra fall is linked to a great range of potentially interacting hazards that although not as bluntly lethal as those occurring in the near field, are nonetheless associated with the highest incidence of fatal events in recent times. Against this background, Simkin et al. (2001: 255) suggest that "increased attention should be paid to tephra". This sentiment is echoed by Charman et al. (1995: 807) who argue from a prehistoric perspective that "the absolute quantity of tephra is not necessarily directly proportional to the environmental impact". This varying impact may in part be related to

the time of year during which tephra is deposited because, as Thorarinsson (1979: 180) has noted:

> [t]he damage to vegetation caused by tephra layers as such not only depends on the thickness of the layer but is also greatly influenced by the time of year when the tephra fall takes place and the weather conditions during or following the eruption. A thin layer of tephra deposited during the growth season may do much more harm than a thicker layer deposited in other seasons.

In sum, tephra-specific hazards are less visual and less spectacular but therefore also more opaque in their causality. This, in turn, makes them hard to understand and to mitigate. Increases in reported post-traumatic stress symptoms in the wake of volcanic eruptions may be related to these variable and difficult-to-explain effects (Adams and Adams, 1984). They are multidimensional and, in combination, can lead to both severe reductions in viability of landscapes as well as to fatalities.

Seen in the context of other geological, hydrological and biological disasters, volcanic eruptions are by no means the biggest killer. However, what volcanic eruptions almost inevitably and on a large spatial scale do lead to are homelessness and displacement (Table 3.11; see also Annen and Wagner, 2003; Witham, 2005). As later chapters will argue, it is these less dramatic and less mechanistic effects of volcanic hazards that likely played a critical role in what transpired in southern Scandinavia following the Laacher See eruption.

3.8 Anatomy of an explosive eruption – the Laacher See event

The Laacher See volcano is part of the East Eifel volcanic field, Rhenish Shield (Germany), which itself is part of the Central European alkaline Cenozoic intraplate province. The caldera that resulted from crater collapse at the time of eruption now presents itself as a picturesque lake, approximately 2.5km × 1.8km (3.31 km^2) in size and with

Impact/ response type	N$_{events\ recorded}$	N$_{people\ affected}$
Killed	~250	~90000
Injured	~150	~16000
Homeless	~100	~300000
Migrating	~250	~5000000

Table 3.10 *The changing effect dynamics of volcanism in relation to human communities. After Witham (2005).*

Characteristic	Description	Reference
Best estimated dates based on various approaches	12,916 cal BP 12,900±560 (Ar^{40}/Ar^{39}) 12,880 varve years BP 12,980-12,890 (μ= 12,940±25) cal BP 13,034 cal BP	Baales et al. (2002) van den Bogaard (1995) Brauer et al. (1999) Bronk Ramsey et al. (2015b) van Raden et al. (2013)
Correlated geophysical, cosmogenic, and climatic events	"acid rain, increased rain fall, reduction of solar radiation and drop of temperature"	Schmincke (2006: 152); see also Graf and Timmreck (2001)
Fallout directions	NE>SSW	van den Bogaard and Schmincke (1984)
Maximum height of Plinian column	< 40km	van den Bogaard and Schmincke (1985)
Minimum height of Plinian column	> 20km	Schmincke et al. (1999)
Volume of extruded magma	≥20km^3 or 6.3km^3 (dense rock equivalent, DRE)	Schmincke et al. (1999)
Estimated discharge rate	3-5 x 10^{8}kg/s	Schmincke (2006)
Eruptive temperature	250 °C (pyroclastic flows); 8800 °C (magma)	Schmincke (2006)
Sulphur injected into the atmosphere	1.9-15 x 10^{12}g	Schmincke et al. (1999)
Sulphate signal in Greenland ice core NGRIP	Not yet detected	cf. Abbott and Davies (2012)
Area covered by pyroclastic currents	> 1400km^2	van den Bogaard and Schmincke (1984)
Area affected by ash fallout	> 315,000km^2	Fisher and Schmincke (1984); Riede et al. (2011c)
Cooling induced	1-2°K	Graf and Timmreck (2001)
High-latitude (>60° N) amplifying factor for cooling	+4 (late winter)/-4 (late summer) °K	Graf and Timmreck (2001)
Regional abandonment	Affected part of the North European Plain	Riede (2007a, 2008b, 2012b, 2016)
VEI	6	Newhall and Self (1982)
Magnitude (M)	6.2	after Mason et al. (2004)
Intensity (I)	11.5-11.7	after Pyle (2000)
Destructiveness (D)	≥3.1	after Pyle (2000)

Table 3.11 *Summary of key characteristics of the Laacher See eruption.*

a maximum depth of 52m. Prior to historic and recent lowering of the lake level, the water table reached some 15m higher than it does at present and the crater remnant in total measures c. 3.8km × 3.0km (Goepel et al., 2014). On its south-eastern shore thrones the once powerful monastery of Maria Laach (Kremer, 1995). Today, the location of the Laacher See volcano places it in the densely settled Neuwied Basin between the cities of Bonn and Koblenz at approximately 50° 25' N, 7° 16' E (Schmincke, 2006; Schmincke et al., 1999). Scientific interest in the Laacher See and the forces that have created it go back to the days of nascent scientific enquiry in the 18th century (Schmincke, 1988, 2010). Table

3.11 provides a schematic overview of the key characteristics of this eruption.

With a minimum calculated eruption magnitude, $M = 6.2$ and a peak eruption intensity, $I = 11.7$, the Laacher See eruption (LSE) ranks globally as a very intense volcanic event of fairly large proportion (cf. Table 3.3). In the words of Newhall and Self (1982: 1232) it was "cataclysmic, paroxysmal, colossal", and it certainly was one of the largest Northern Hemisphere eruptions of the Late Pleistocene. The Laacher See volcano is fed by an intraplate mantle plume (Ritter et al., 2001) that has recently been made clearly visible using tomographic methods (Zhu et al., 2012). This mantle plume continues to be active, currently reflected in carbon dioxide rising to the surface at various locations around the caldera lake (Aeschbach-Hertig et al., 1996; Gal et al., 2011).

During eruption, the rising magma's interaction with groundwater resulted in a highly explosive phreatomagmatic eruption that was at its most intense over a period of a few days or weeks, but probably lasted several months in all (Litt et al., 2008). Van den Bogaard and colleagues (1990) have calculated that near- and far-field fallout deposits constitute 88% of the erupted tephra volume, pyroclastic flow deposits 10%, and base surge deposits 2%. Up to 64% of all material was ejected during the initial and likely most intense phase of the eruption (c. 10h).

Stratigraphic correlations of LSE deposits in terraces of the River Rhine had long suggested a late Ice Age date for the Laacher See event (e.g. Ahrens, 1927), and Firbas (1953) arranged for the LSE to be ^{14}C-dated already shortly after the invention of the technique by Arnold and Libby (1949). It has since been dated quite accurately and precisely by a variety of techniques – varve counting (Brauer et al., 1999), single crystal laser fusion ^{40}Argon/^{39}Argon dating (van den Bogaard, 1995; van den Bogaard et al., 1987), AMS radiocarbon dating (Hajdas et al., 1995), dendrochronological approximation (Baales et al., 1999; Baales et al., 2002) and most recently Bayesian chronological modelling (Bronk Ramsey et al., 2015a) – to just under 13,000 calendar years BP, which places it very close to the beginning of GS-1

in Greenland and around 200 years prior to the onset of the Younger Dryas. Different authors do use slightly different dates (see Table 3.11 above), but all cluster around 13,000 years BP and virtually all dating methods overlap at 1σ or certainly at 2σ (see van Raden et al., 2013). Future work concerned with identifying actual traces of the Laacher See eruption in the Greenland ice-cores may eventually resolve this remaining uncertainty, although issues of correlating the LST with local and regional environmental sequences, which may very well show some lag in response time to the climatic shifts recorded in the Greenlandic ice-cores, remain as pressing and difficult as ever.

In advance of the LSE, the East Eifel province had undergone several phases of volcanic activity from approximately 700 ka BP (Schmincke, 1999). These pulses of volcanic activity resulted, for instance, in the explosive formation of the phonolitic Rieden and Wehr calderas from 430,000-380,000 and 215,000-115,000 years ago, respectively (van den Bogaard et al., 1987, 1989; Wörner et al., 1988). In addition to these relatively large events, there is evidence for up to 300 smaller basaltic eruptions between approximately 700,000 and 10,800 years ago that have created the numerous scoria cones and maar features so characteristic of the region (see Frechen, 1995; Litt et al., 2008; Schmincke and Mertes, 1979; Zolitschka et al., 1995). Interestingly, the resulting landforms are also closely linked to, in particular, Middle Palaeolithic archaeology in the region (Baales, 2002b; Conard, 1992).

Despite repeated suggestions of multiple Late Glacial eruptions (Frechen, 1952; Housley et al., 2013; Schirmer, 1995), it is currently believed that the entirety of Laacher See tephra is derived from the most recent phonolitic, i.e. sil-

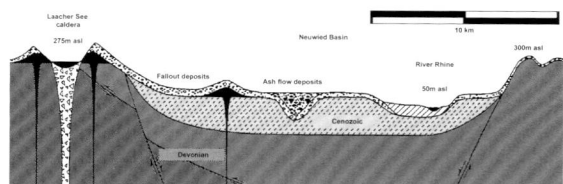

Figure 3.12 *Schematic of the topography around the Laacher See caldera; modified from van den Bogaard et al. (1990).*

Phase	Eruption type	Height of column	Primary air-fall trajectory
ULST	Phreatomagmatic	Low	SW
MLST-C3	Plinian	High	NE
MLST-C2	Phreatomagmatic	Low	S
MLST-C1	Plinian	High	NE
MLST-B	Plinian	High	NE
MLST-A	Phreatomagmatic	Low	S
LLST	Plinian	High	NE

Table 3.12 *Laacher See eruption type, column height and air-fall trajectory by eruption phase. Based on van den Bogaard and Schmincke (1985) and Schmincke (2004).*

ica-undersaturated, and volatile-rich eruption of the Laacher See volcano focused on here, and that the modern basin morphology can be attributed to this event in combination with post-eruptive sedimentary processes (Fig. 3.12). The LSE tapped into a strongly zoned phonolitic magma chamber (van den Bogaard and Schmincke, 1984, 1985; van den Bogaard et al., 1990; Wörner and Schmincke, 1984). The upper part of the magma reservoir was characterised by highly pressurised phonolite magma. Repeated interaction with groundwater resulted in an initial highly explosive phreatomagmatic and Plinian stage as well as intermittant explosivity. The material deposited during the first phase is known as the Lower Laacher See Tephra (LLST). Subsequent phreatomagmatic (MLST-A) and Plinian phases tapped crystal-poor, moderately evolved magma (MLST-B), and crystal-poor, mafic phonolite magma (MLST-C), producing pyroclastic fall and flow deposits together known as the Middle Laacher See Tephra (MLST). The final phreatomagmatic phase tapped a crystal-rich, mafic phonolitic magma, and deposited the Upper Laacher See Tephra (ULST). The height of the eruption column varied with the intensity of the eruption (Table 3.12). Different stratigraphic sections in the proximal area of the eruptive centre reflect these changing eruption dynamics. The LLST/MLST/ULST near-field master tephrostratigraphy for this event has been derived from such a composite of proximal ejecta sequences and has drawn on an extensive suite of petrographic and chemical properties available at such lo-cales (see Ginibre et al., 2004a; Ginibre et al., 2004b; Harms et al., 2004; Schmincke et al., 1999 for more detailed information).

3.9 Near-field deposition

An estimated area of >1400km^2 was completely covered in pyroclastic flow, surge and fallout deposits ranging from 50 to 1m thickness (see

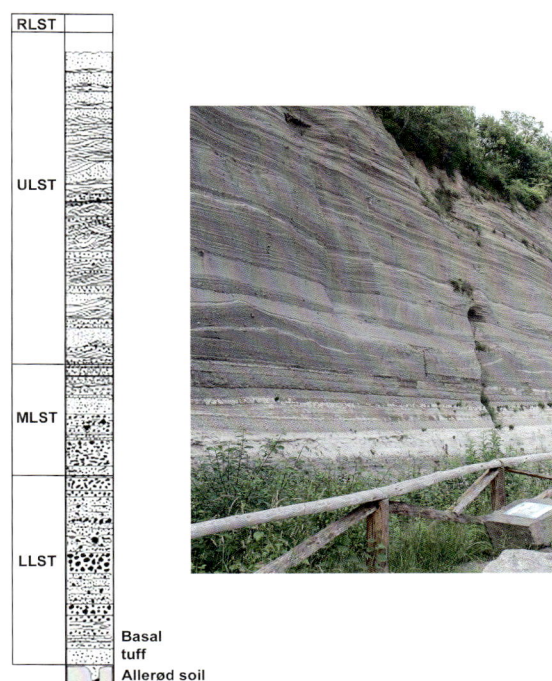

Figure 3.13 *The near-vent deposits at the famous Wingertsbergwand, and its idealised stratigraphic sequence (left, the so-called Mendig sequence or facies; modified from Harms and Schmincke, 2000). Photo by the author.*

Figure 3.14 *Example of a burned tree trunk preserved in Laacher See deposits. Photo by the author.*

Fig. 3.13), and including blocks, bombs, xe-nolithic mantle fragments as well as welded and unconsolidated tephra deposits (Fisher et al., 1983; Freundt and Schmincke, 1985; Schumacher and Schmincke, 1991; van den Bogaard et al., 1990). Interestingly, recent finds of rather stupendous amounts of pyroclastic material deposited in a cave system approximately 75km to the north-east of the Laacher See underscores the power of the eruption (Dorsten and Harries, 2007; Dorsten et al., 2007). Further to the north-east, in regions such as the valley of the River Lahn and the Taunus Mountains – some 100km from the eruptive centre, tephra cover was probably still thick and continuous with clast sizes in the lapilli range. Here, several eruption phases are well represented judging by the diversity (in colour, density, porosity) of ejecta encountered (cf. Lang, 1954; Röhr, 1987; Weyl, 1961).

Much like at Pompeii, this thick pyroclastic blanket covered, sealed and thereby preserved a prehistoric landscape nearly 13,000 years old. Subsequent industrial activity has allowed for detailed reconstructions of Allerød-age

topographies (Ikinger, 1996), and has led to the discovery of animal tracks (Baales and von Berg, 1997) as well as macrobotanical remains ranging from leaves to charred tree trunks (Fig. 3.14) to entire burned woodlands (Street, 1986) that have been instrumental in the accurate and precise dating of the event both in terms of placing it on a calendric timescale and in terms of the season of eruption, which has been narrowed down to late spring/early summer (Baales et al., 1999). In addition, a plethora of archaeological sites have been discovered, including miniscule locales made up of no more than a casual fireplace and a handful of lithics (von Berg, 1994a) as well as some of the richest archaeological locales of this period (see Baales, 2006; Baales and Street, 1996, 1998, 1999; Street and Baales, 1997) to which the next chapter will return.

At the nearby River Rhine, these deposits built up to form a dam, which in turn led to the formation of a substantial lake and widespread upstream flooding and attendant downstream channel drying. Nearest to the eruptive centre the River Rhine today has an average discharge rate of c. 2000m³/s (Kwadijk, 1991). Assuming a roughly similar discharge rate for the period around the end of the last Ice Age, the respective drying and flooding caused by the LSE dam would have had dramatic and highly visible consequences in regions both up- and perhaps especially downstream of the Eifel. Lake formation and rising water levels would have affected major tributaries in the Middle Rhine (Lahn, Mosel and Main) as well as the very northern part of the Upper Rhine (Park and Schmincke, 2009).

Water-rafted pumice and other overbank features suggest that this dam broke already during or shortly after the eruption – perhaps owing to strong earthquake activity – causing one or several gargantuan lahar-like flood waves of 'dirty' water highly saturated with small and large particulate matter from the eruption and erosive action around the temporarily expanded lake (Park and Schmincke, 1997, 2009). Numerous locations in still active as well as abandoned channels along the Lower Rhine downstream from the Laacher See volcano preserve river-rafted pumice (e.g. Choi et al., 2007; Crommelin, 1963; Kasse et al., 2005; Lauer et al., 2011; Paas, 1961) that has now been traced all the way to the English Channel (Hijma et al., 2012). In fact, Verbraeck (1990) and Cohen (2003) report a 30cm-thick pumice layer that can be followed the entire 200km-

long distance from the German-Dutch border at Emmerich (itself located c. 170km downstream of the eruptive centre) to the Hook of Holland. Recent research suggests that these lahar-like river tsunamis may, on their own or in interaction with subsequent hydrological changes during the Younger Dryas, have led to a major reconfiguration of the Rhine delta (Erkens et al., 2011; Janssens et al., 2012).

3.10 Far-field deposition

During the LSE, a significant amount of pyroclastic material was injected into the upper atmosphere, and was dispersed via atmospheric vectors (i.e. wind). The distal distribution pattern of these airborne ejecta was defined by the changing eruption column height, the regional weather patterns and altitudinally varying winds at the time of eruption (van den Bogaard and Schmincke, 1985). As a result of this process, distal tephra deposits may only represent fragments of the idealised proximal tephrostratigraphy. The distal deposits are also composed of the smallest and lightest particles capable of being held aloft for an extended period of time, i.e. glass shards. The distal deposits, therefore, may not represent the full range of physical characteristics displayed by proximal tephra sequences. Thus, whilst it is

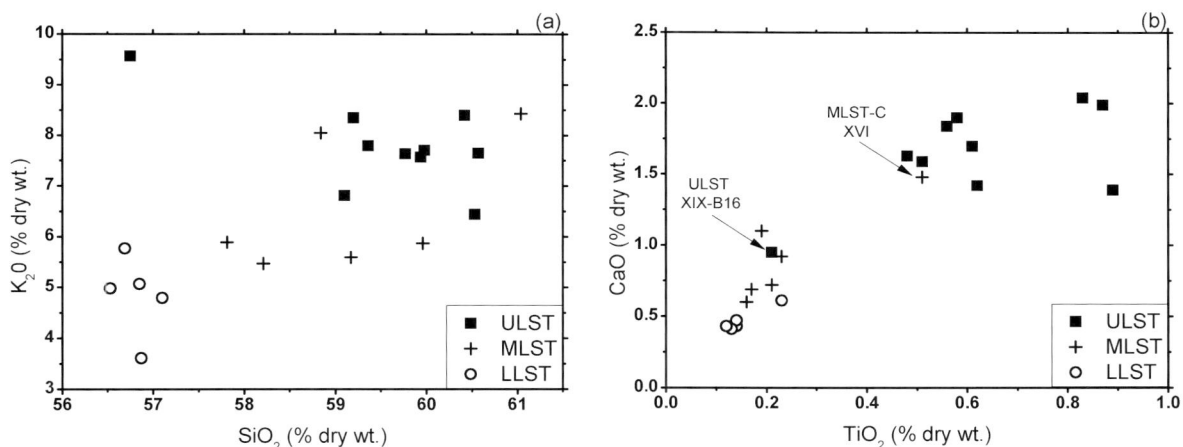

Figure 3.15 a/b *Scatter plots showing (a) potassium oxide (K_2O) versus silicon dioxide (SiO_2), and (b) calcium oxide (CaO) versus titanium dioxide (TiO_2), using published proximal pumice matrix glass data from Harms and Schmincke (2000). Whilst these scatter plots demonstrate clearly the systematic variation in the LST chemistry, they also show how the chemical compositions of samples from the MLST and ULST units overlap. Data and sample names from Harms and Schmincke (2000).*

possible to use tephra shard morphology and lithology as well heavy mineral content to discriminate proximal LST deposits (van den Bogaard, 1983; van den Bogaard and Schmincke, 1985), comparable glass geochemical analysis is required to securely link distal fallout deposits to their proximal counterparts. As virtually all major and trace element concentrations vary systematically throughout the LST sequence, it is in principle possible to distinguish and identify LLST, MLST, and ULST deposits on the basis of whole-rock compositions (proximal) and glass shard compositions (proximal and distal).

However, attributing shards from distal sites to individual eruptive phases is often problematic, because proximal reference data sets are often only partly available or published. For the LSE, van den Bogaard and Schmincke (1985) have provided full end-member compositions (LLST-I, MLST-B-XIII, MLST-C-XIV, and ULST-XX), and a statistical evaluation of the Na_2O-K_2O-CaO ratios based on electron microprobe analyses of an impressive sample of around 500 glass shards from the entire near-vent LST reference section. In addition, Harms and Schmincke (2000) provide average matrix glass compositions of a further 21 samples from part of that near-vent LST reference section. Yet, the presence of scatter and overlaps in glass composition, as evident in existing analyses of this proximal tephra sequence, makes it difficult to unanimously divide samples into truly discrete eruption phases on the basis of geochemistry. This is illustrated here in Figure 3.15 a and b, borrowed from Riede et al. (2011c). Note that here sample MLST-C-XVI in particular is assigned to the MLST unit of the so-called Mendig sequence (see Fig. 3.13 above) close to the caldera (Harms and Schmincke, 2000), but the abundance of some elements appears to link it to the ULST unit. This sample comes from a layer close to the MLST-ULST-boundary, making it possible that there is some sediment mixing at this point, or that the unit boundary is not clearly defined chemically. Additionally, one of two pumice samples from ULST XIX-B16 in the Mendig facies (Harms and Schmincke, 2000) from the middle of the ULST unit shows

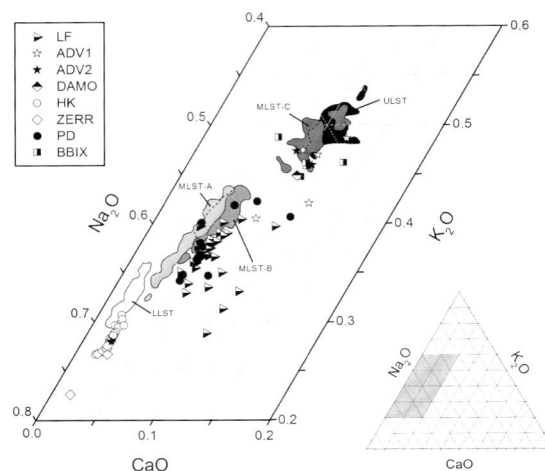

Figure 3.16 *A tri-plot of Na_2O:K_2O:CaO ratios of glass shards from several mid-field locales on the main northeastern fallout lobe, plotted against the reference fields of van den Bogaard and Schmincke (1985). Some of the scatter in the results obtained by Riede et al. (2011c) can be explained by methodological differences, but it should be noted that the most likely phase-attribution of some of these samples does not correspond to the previous phase-specific mapping of the north-eastern LST fall-out.*

a glass composition closely related to that of the MLST unit. This anomaly could either accurately represent magma chemistry or mixing (e.g. Wörner and Wright, 1984), or may be the result of depositional processes, or of sample selection. At present these issues cannot be satisfactorily resolved, but it is worth underlining that in all cases LST deposits can easily be distinguished geochemically from products derived from other volcanic provinces in Europe (i.e. Iceland, Jan Mayen, the Mediterranean, and the Chaîne des Puys).

Nonetheless, LLST glass shard compositions can securely be distinguished from MLST-B on the basis of, for instance, ternary diagrams (Fig. 3.16). Similarly, MLST-B compositions are distinct from MLST-C and ULST glass shards. Significant overlap exists between the glass shard and matrix glass compositions of MLST-A versus MLST-B, and the glass shard and matrix glass compositions of MLST-C versus ULST, the differences and similarities of glass compositions reflecting primary zones of stratification and mixing of phonolite melt in the Laacher See magma chamber prior to and during the eruption. Additional discrepancies of the now traditional zonation of the

$N_{countries}$	Country	N_{LST}
1	Germany	440
2	France	100
3	Switzerland	34
4	Luxembourg	13
5	Belgium	12
6	Netherlands	6
7	Poland	4
8	Denmark	3
9	Italy	2
10	Austria	2
11	Sweden	2
12	Lithuania	1
13	Russia	1
	Σ	620

Table 3.13 *Present-day countries where Laacher See ejecta have been fcund, as per mid-2016.*

Laacher See eruption and its cartographic projection come from well-investigated distal sections. Working with material from Vallensgård Mose on Bornholm (Denmark), Turney et al. (2006) demonstrate that either the zonation or rather its spatial projection into the eruption's far-field needs revision. Likewise, Riede et al. (2011c) could not find a definite match between their geochemical data for seven distal locations in the north-eastern fallout lobe and their hypothesized eruption phase. More strikingly still, Housley et al. (2013) have not only provided clear evidence for the dispersal of LST into western Poland, but have also fingerprinted tephra there to the ULST phase that has hitherto been linked exclusively to the southern dispersal lobe. Most recently, Bronk Ramsey et al. (2015c) also report a large sample of LST geochemistry that presents a relatively poor fit to previously published data. In sum, the LST fallout maps produced in the 1980s represented a major leap forward in the appreciation of the Laacher See eruption, its impact

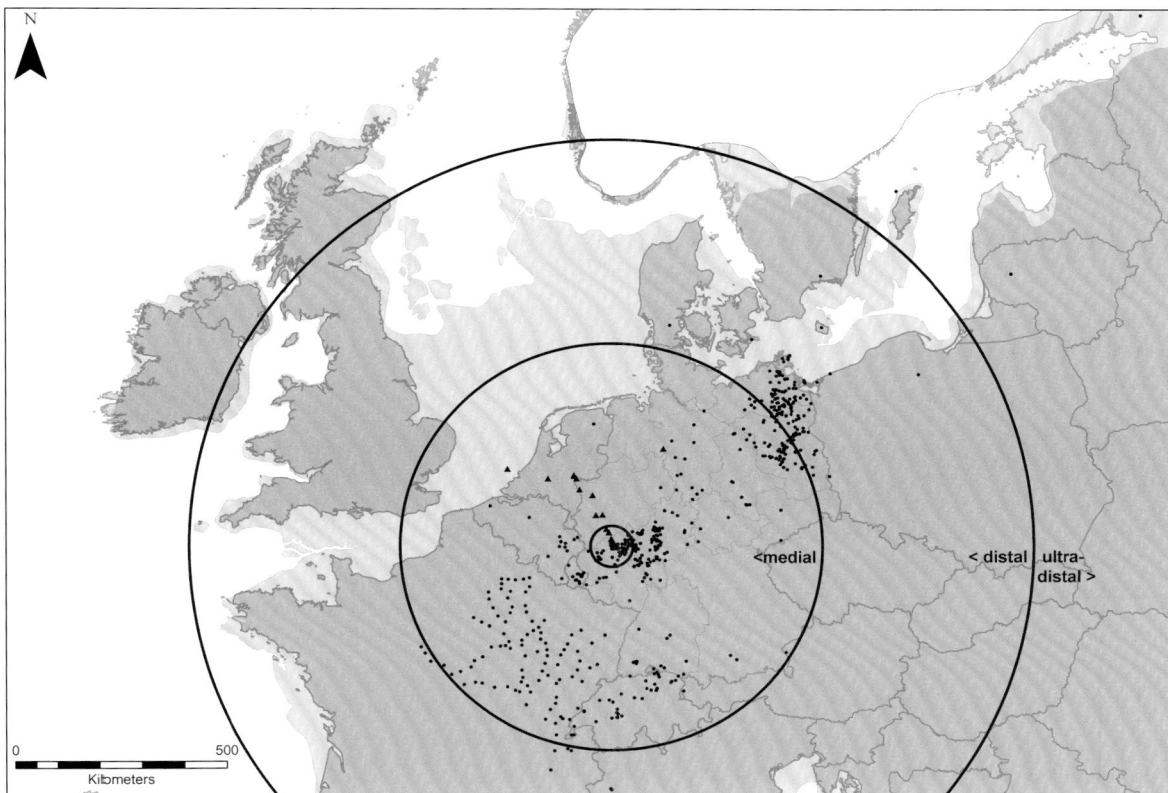

Figure 3.17 *The spatial distribution of occurrences of Laacher See tephra across Europe. The concentric circles mark the proximal (≤50km), medial (50-500km), distal (500-1000km), and ultra-distal (>1000km) fallout zones. Circles mark airfall tephra, triangles mark fluvial deposits.*

Site name	Country	State/Region	Latitude	Longitude	Profile name	Thickness (cm)
Trou Jadot	B	Liege	50.5	5.6	CCSA/CCSB	
Trou Walou	B	Liege	50.6	5.5		
Grotte du Coléoptère	B	Province de Luxembourg	50.4	5.5	in E5	
Vallensgård Mose	DK	Bornholm	55.2	14.9		0.1
Slotseng	DK	Sydjylland	55.3	9.3	SSB	
Sacrower See	GER	Brandenburg	52.4	13.1	SAC05/15	3.0
Hennigsdorf	GER	Brandenburg	52.6	13.2	Schönwalde P Schö 2	3.0
Rüsselsheim 122	GER	Hessen	49.8	8.4		
Mühlheim-Dietesheim	GER	Hessen	50.1	8.9		Traces only
Mardorf-Schweinsberg	GER	Hessen	50.4	8.7		2.0
Rothenkirchen	GER	Hessen	50.7	9.7	Profile 20/5-20	Traces only
Weimar-Niederweimar	GER	Hessen	50.8	8.8		
In der Seckbach	GER	Hessen	50.8	8.9	Se-1-12	50-100
Wartbergsiedlung	GER	Hessen	50.8	8.9	Wb-1/-1a/-2	50-100
Wittelsberg	GER	Hessen	50.8	8.9	La-1-3	20-50
Marienbach	GER	Hessen	50.8	8.9	Ma-1-4	>10
Kleinseelheim	GER	Hessen	50.8	8.8	Ei-1/2	50-100
Amöneburger Becken	GER	Hessen	50.8	8.9	Md-1 & -2; (Se-12a/ Rau-5a/Rau10)	60-90
Dorla	GER	Hessen	51.2	9.3	Road-cut	
Prelitzsee	GER	Mecklenburg-Vorpommern	53.4	12.8	Profile 4, 5 & 8	
Löddigsee	GER	Mecklenburg-Vorpommern	53.4	11.9		
Zillmannsee	GER	Mecklenburg-Vorpommern	53.4	12.9		
Wollgrasmoor	GER	Mecklenburg-Vorpommern	53.5	14.3		
Bartmannshagen	GER	Mecklenburg-Vorpommern	54.1	13.1	Profile 4	1-2

Distance from vent (km)	Fan direction	Archaeology	Deposit condition	Deposit	Reference
	SSW	FMG	Secondary	Fall	Toussaint and Becker (1992)
	SSW	FMG	Secondary	Fall	Pirson and Juvigné (2011); Pirson et al. (2004); Pirson et al. (2006); see also Lacroix (1993) and Renson et al. (2002)
	SSW	Magdalenian, Ahrensburgian	Primary	Fall	Juvigné (1977); see also Dewez (1975)
730	NE	Mesolithic (see Casati and Sørensen, 2006)	Primary	Fall	Usinger (1977); Turney et al. (2006)
	NE	Hamburgian, FMG	Primary	Fall	Larsen and Noe-Nygaard (2014)
460	NE	Later prehistoric / historical	Primary	Fall	Enters et al. (2010)
480	NE	FMG	Primary & secondary	Fall	Kloss and Wechler (1987); de Klerk (2006)
	NE	FMG	Primary & secondary	Fall/ Fluvial	Loew (2005)
	NE	FMG	Primary	Fall	Fruth (1979, 1994)
100	NE	Mesolithic	Secondary	Fall	Bos (2001); Litt et al. (2003); Andres et al. (2001)
	NE	FMG	Secondary	Fall	Fiedler (1976); Hofbauer (1985, 1992); Riede (2012)
	NE	Mesolithic	Primary	Fall	Schirmer (1998, 1999); Bos and Urz (2003)
120	NE	Medieval	Primary & secondary	Fall	Rittweger (1997)
120	NE	Medieval	Primary & secondary	Fall	
120	NE	Medieval	Primary & secondary	Fall	
120	NE	Later prehistoric/ historical	Primary & secondary	Fall	
120	NE	Later prehistoric/ historical	Primary & secondary	Fall	
120	NE	Mesolithic and later prehistoric	Primary & secondary	Fall	Andres et al. (2001); Rittweger (1997)
	NE	Fragment of human skull, possibly Late Palaeolithic	Secondary	Fall	Fiedler (1994)
	NE	Ahrensburgian (see Terberger, 1996); Mesolithic (see Schoknecht, 1959)	Primary	Fall	Kaiser (1998)
	NE	Neolithic	Primary	Fall	Jahns (2007); Becker and Benecke (2002)
	NE	Ahrensburgian (see Terberger, 1996);	Primary	Fall	Kaiser (1996, 1998)
	NE	Mesolithic (see Schoknecht, 1959)	Primary	Fall	Kaiser (1998)
570	NE	Later prehistoric/ historical	Primary & secondary	Fall	Kaiser and Janke (1998)

Table 3.14 *Continues* ⟶

Site name	Country	State/Region	Latitude	Longitude	Profile name	Thickness (cm)
Endinger Bruch	GER	Mecklenburg-Vorpommern	54.2	12.9	Hoher Birkengraben (de Klerk 2002)	
Bettenroder Berg IX	GER	Niedersachsen	51.5	10.0	Westprofile, layer 16	20-40
Bettenroder Berg I	GER	Niedersachsen	51.5	10.0	S- and N-Profile, layer VI	20-30
Reinhausen 36/Abri Bettenroder Berg XI	GER	Niedersachsen	51.5	10.0	W-Profile, Layer 5	20-25
Reiffenhausen 23/Abri Schierenberg I	GER	Niedersachsen	51.5	10.0	O-Profile, Layer 12	41202.0
Reinhausen 39/Abri Immengrund I	GER	Niedersachsen	51.5	10.0	NO-Profile, Layer 9	41202.0
Reinhausen 38/Abri Bettenroder Berg XIV	GER	Niedersachsen	51.5	10.0	SW-Profile, Layer 5	10.0
Reinhausen 37/Abri Bettenroder Berg XIII	GER	Niedersachsen	51.5	10.0	SW-Profile, Layer 5	10.0
Seck-Bruch	GER	Niedersachsen	52.4	9.4	SB 1, 3 & 5	0.5
Arendsee	GER	Niedersachsen	52.9	11.5	ARS 1	
Thür	GER	Rheinland-Pfalz	50.4	7.3		300
Bassenheim	GER	Rheinland-Pfalz	50.4	7.5		
Wannenköpfe	GER	Rheinland-Pfalz	50.4	7.4	Profile B/D	30-90
Tönchesberg	GER	Rheinland-Pfalz	50.4	7.4	Tö1/Tö2	200.0
Rübenach	GER	Rheinland-Pfalz	50.4	7.5		
Urbar	GER	Rheinland-Pfalz	50.4	7.6		
Rauschermühle bei Plaidt	GER	Rheinland-Pfalz	50.4	7.4		
Kettig	GER	Rheinland-Pfalz	50.4	7.5	W-O Profile	150-450
Miesenheim II/III/IV	GER	Rheinland-Pfalz	50.4	7.4	Multiple cores	300-400
Andernach-Martinsberg	GER	Rheinland-Pfalz	50.4	7.4	Profile Schaffhausen	400

Distance from vent (km)	Fan direction	Archaeology	Deposit condition	Deposit	Reference
	NE	FMG (see Kaiser et al., 1999; Street, 1996; Terberger et al., 1996)	Primary & secondary	Fall	Lane et al. (2012)
230	NE	FMG	Primary & secondary	Fall	Grote (1988, 1994, 1999)
230	NE	FMG	Primary & secondary	Fall	Grote (1988. 1990. 1994. 1999); Ahl and Meyer (1994)
230	NE	Mesolithic and later	Primary	Fall	
230	NE	Mesolithic and later	Primary	Fall	
230	NE	Metal Ages	Primary	Fall	
230	NE	Metal Ages	Primary	Fall	
230	NE	Metal Ages	Primary	Fall	
280	NE	Ahrensburgian	Primary	Fall	Dietz et al. (1958)
	NE	Later prehistoric/historical	Primary	Fall	Christiansen (2008)
10	PX	Woodland with traces of human occupation	Primary	Fall	Bolus (1992)
	PX	Isolated fireplace & artefacts	Primary	Fall	
10	PX	Middle Palaeolithic	Primary & secondary	Fall	Frechen (1995)
10	PX	Middle Palaeolithic	Primary & secondary	Fall	Conard (1992)
	PX	Isolated fireplace & artefacts	Primary	Fall	Bolus (1992)
	PX	FMG	Primary	Fall	
	PX	Find of human remains	Primary	Fall	Frechen (1953); Bolus (1992)
10	PX	FMG	Primary	Fall	Baales (2002)
10	PX	Various locales around Miesenheim have yielded isolated fireplaces (III) and remains of woodland with traces of human occupation	Primary	Fall	Bolus (1992); Scharf et al. (2005)
10	PX	FMG	Primary	Fall	Numerous, but see e.g. Bosinski and Hahn (1973); Veil (1982); Kegler (2002)

Table 3.14 Continues ⟶

Site name	Country	State/Region	Latitude	Longitude	Profile name	Thickness (cm)
Gönnersdorf	GER	Rheinland-Pfalz	50.4	7.4	Profile A	345
Niederbieber	GER	Rheinland-Pfalz	50.5	7.5		100-200
Bad Breisig	GER	Rheinland-Pfalz	50.5	7.3		
Geiseltal	GER	Sachsen-Anhalt	51.3	11.8	near Krumpa	5.0
Gaterslebener See (=Ascherslebener See)	GER	Sachsen-Anhalt	51.8	11.4	A1/A6 (Grube Georg)/Profile A (Grube Konigsaue)	0.8-13
Weinberg bei Schadeleben	GER	Sachsen-Anhalt	51.8	11.4		4-13
Schadeleben	GER	Sachsen-Anhalt	51.8	11.4	A3/A4 Tagebaurest Nachterstedt, Feld Schadeleben	3-10
Torbiere di Trana	I	Piemonte	45.0	7.4		
Wegliny	PL	Lubuskie	51.8	14.7		
Burgäschi	CH	Basel	47.2	7.7		
Lac Loclat	CH	Neuchatel	47.0	7.0	L-P1A	0.5
Weiher	CH	Schaffhausen	47.7	8.9	694 775/288 050	
Egelsee Frauenfeld	CH	Thurgau	47.6	8.9	707 200/268 475	0.5

Table 3.14 *Sites with traces of Laacher See tephra and archaeological remains nearby or in association. FMG= Federmessergruppen; PX= proximal. Sites with stratigraphically or otherwise associated material from Federmessergruppen contexts are listed in bold.*

and the chronostratigraphic usefullness of its tephra. Yet, given their age and recent methodological developments in the tephrochronology of the Late Glacial, it is not surprising that these maps are due a modification both in terms of the suggested isopach positions and values as well as in terms of the phase representations.

Reconstructed degassing dynamics of the LSE (Textor et al., 2003) and climate models suggest that the atmospheric input of aerosols from this eruption resulted in altered Northern Hemisphere weather patterns for some years (Graf and Timmreck, 2001), which is duly reflected in terrestrial and lacustrine records across Europe (Birks and Lotter, 1994; de Klerk et al., 2008a; Merkt and Müller, 1999). Depending on the height of the eruption column and prevailing winds, tephra from this

eruption was transported over large parts of Europe, from Italy in the south to the margins of the inland ice near present-day Gotland in the north, and from the Ardennes in the west to Poland in the east (Fig. 3.17). Occurrences of Laacher See-tephra (LST) at some distance from the eruptive centre have been known and discussed since the late 19th century (Brauns, 1886, 1892; Sandberger, 1882a, 1882b; von Dechen, 1881). As already noted, the potential of the LST to provide a major temporal marker for the Allerød chronozone of the Late Glacial was suggested already by the environmental historian Firbas in 1949, although at that time it was widely thought that the Laacher See caldera was the result of numerous eruption events (e.g. Frechen, 1952; Frechen, 1953) – in fact, some still argue for multiple eruption (Schirmer, 1995). Subse-

Distance from vent (km)	Fan direction	Archaeology	Deposit condition	Deposit	Reference
11	PX	Magdalenian	Primary	Fall	Bosinski (1979, 2007)
20	PX	FMG	Primary	Fall	Bolus (1992)
	PX	FMG	Secondary	Fluvial	Grimm (2004)
340	NE	Mesolithic and later	Primary	Fall	Böttger et al. (1998); Mania and Toepfer (1971)
330	NE	Magdalenian (see Mania, 1967)	Primary	Fall	Frechen (1952); Müller (1953); Strahl (2005)
330	NE	FMG	Primary	Fall	Mania (1967, 2003); Toepfer (1965)
330	NE	FMG	Primary	Fall	Knuth and Thomae (2003)
	SSW	Later prehistoric/ historical	Primary	Fall	Schneider (1977); Eicher (1987)
	NE	FMG, Ahrensburgian, Mesolithic (see Masojć et al., 2007)	Primary	Fall	Housley et al. (2013)
	SSW	Magdalenian	Primary	Fall	Martini (1971)
380	SSW	Magdalenian, Neolithic	Primary	Fall	Rolli et al. (1994)
	SSW	Magdalenian	Primary	Fall	Hofmann (1963)
340	SSW	Neolithic	Primary	Fall	

quent studies argued for a revision of this view and for a single major eruption responsible for all Allerød tephra deposits that can be linked to Eifel volcanism (Fisher et al., 1983; van den Bogaard, 1983; van den Bogaard and Schmincke, 1984). These research efforts also yielded a considerable number of distal occurrences and presented them, for the first time, in a systematic cartographic fashion (van den Bogaard and Schmincke, 1985, 1988). These maps were based on approximately 40 securely identified and some additional but less certain data points from six countries (see van den Bogaard and Schmincke, 1985: Supplementary Table B). Renewed efforts to collate LST data points from the literature and from regional databases have increased the number of occurrences more than ten-fold (Riede and Thastrup, 2013; Riede et al., 2011c). At the time of writing, 622 LST data points are known – not all equally well-published or certain, it has to be said – coming from 13 countries (Table 3.13). Collecting these data required a major literature search effort well beyond standard databases as these occurrences are mentioned across a range of different disciplines – volcanology, geology, soil science, palynology, geography, and archaeology, as well as unpublished grey literature sources (i.e. regional natural resource management agencies, conservation agencies, etc.) – and in many languages (German, English, Dutch, Italian, French, Danish, Polish). Notably, the most recent additions to the north-eastern lobe from, for instance, northern central Poland (Wulf et al., 2013), south-eastern Denmark (Larsen and Noe-Nygaard, 2014) as well as north-western Russia (Andronikov et al., 2012), but also ultra-distal locales such as Gasserplatz (van Mourik et al., 2013) and Höllerer See (Klee et al., 1993) in Austria as well as a series of locales in northern Italy (Eicher, 1987; Finsinger et al., 2008) have extended the known distribution of the LST substantially. In part, these new discoveries are driven by better and more precise methods as well as field investigations at ever increasing resolution. It is highly likely that many more LST find localities will be discovered in the future.

Remarkably, too, an increasing number of archaeological sites preserving either LST cryptotephra layers or layers easily seen by the naked eye have emerged in the process of assembling this database. In fact, some of the best-preserved and most massive far-field LST strata come from archaeological sites (e.g. Grote, 1994; Mania, 2003) – and these are sig-

nificantly thicker than suggested by the fallout maps generated in the 1980s. Whilst not all archaeology associated with LST layers is also directly related to the eruption event, upwards of 20 LST localities do preserve traces of Late Glacial habitation (Table 3.14). The general pattern here is that LST caps occupation at these sites, which if at all are first re-occupied many centuries or even millennia later. The following chapter will look in greater detail at these sites, and at the nature and timing of pre-eruption Federmessergruppen occupation, land-use and economy. Thereafter, the ways in which the LSE impacted these communities will be put into focus, charting the progression of vulnerability in relation to the numerous hazards generated by the LSE outlined in this chapter.

Chapter 4

Before the eruption – the Federmessergruppen

4.1 Introduction

The previous chapter briefly reviewed volcanic activity with the specific aim of highlighting the ways in which explosive volcanism in particular may impact landscapes, plants, animals, and people. This generic discussion of explosive volcanism was followed by a specific introduction to the Laacher See eruption, its dating, timing, and unfolding. Numerous potentially hazardous effects of this eruption have been alluded to – the locally massive fallout deposits even far removed from the eruptive centre, the fine-grained nature of the very hard and abrasive ash carrying with it harmful chemicals, the increased and untimely precipitation and lightning strikes, as well as regionally varying climate and weather impacts. Yet, in order to understand how these potential hazards became actual hazards, we need to consider in greater depth the communities they affected. This chapter therefore focuses on the so-called Federmessergruppen, a regional archaeological phenomenon that was widespread on the North European Plain at the time of the Laacher See eruption. Chronology, typology and technology, as well as economy will be touched upon, but much like the last chapter, this section is not meant to be an exhaustive treatment of the Federmessergruppen. Instead, this chapter should be understood as a review of those features of this culture – of these small hunter-gatherer groups operating at the northern periphery of the human world at that time – that are particularly germane to understanding how they interacted with the Laacher See eruption and its aftermath.

4.2 Origin of the Federmessergruppen

The term 'Federmesser' was first used by R. R. Schmidt (1908: 76) to describe arch-backed points belonging to archaeological inventories that bridge the link between the Palaeolithic cultures of the Ice Age and, as was argued then, the Neolithic cultures of the following warm period. This somewhat quaint label – using one now obsolete technological element (the penknife) to describe another even more obsolete one (the flint-tipped arrow) – was subsequently adopted by Schwabedissen (1944) who provided extensive initial discussions of the variability found within this group (Fig. 4.1) and offered a first synthesis of the knowledge available at the time (Schwabedissen, 1951, 1954). He described the Federmessergruppen as both a cultural, spatial and chronological phenomenon clearly linked to the Late Upper or Final Magdalenian, a late stage in *l'age du renne* of western Europe, which, then as now, remains the best-known period of the European Palaeolithic (see, for instance, de Sonneville-Bordes, 1963; Lartet and Christy, 1875; Paniagua, 1926; Straus et al., 2012).

The people carrying with them the technology summarily referred to as Federmessergruppen were not the first to enter the far northern

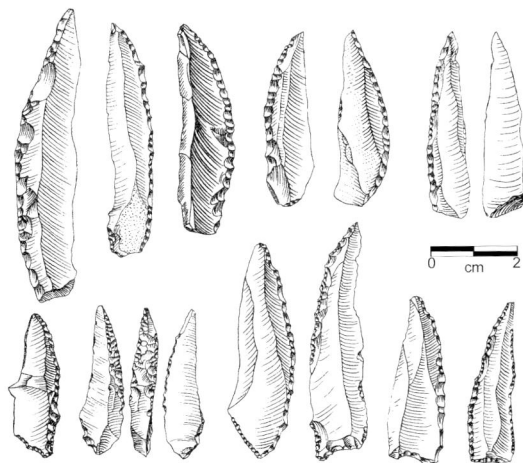

Figure 4.1 *Form diversity within the category 'Feder-messer' as perceived by Schwabedissen (1954).*

reaches of the Great North European Plain. Before them came the Hamburgian culture, dated to the earlier and very first warming period of the Late Glacial (GI-1e/Bølling; see Grimm and Weber, 2008; Weber and Grimm, 2009). This initial colonization was most likely unsuccessful and the Hamburgian culture disappeared prior to the arrival of the folk of the Federmessergruppen. Although ultimately deriving from the same ancestral Magdalenian cultural background, the material culture differences between the reindeer-hunting Hamburgian and the economically less specialised Federmessergruppen are so marked that these two groups probably represent two subsequent colonisation pulses (Brinch Petersen, 2009; Riede, 2014e). It has been argued elsewhere (Riede, 2007b, 2009b) that the Hamburgian occupation may have failed due to the increasing strain of maintaining viable bio-social groups in the face of ever-increasing mobility, but the exact processes of such a cultural collapse remain to be clarified (Riede, 2014d). At any rate, the Federmessergruppen – in southern Scandinavia – appear to conform more closely to the suggested strategy of a pioneering hunter-gatherer society rather than a residential one, although different locales may represent a changing trend, as discussed in more detail below (Table 4.1).

4.3 Federmessergruppen chronology

Much like in all other prehistoric periods on the North European Plain, the vast bulk of Fe-

Domain	Pioneer	Post-pioneer
Landscape knowledge	Limited	Extensive; landscape marking through art
Resource focus	Animal focus, periodic shortages dealt with by range relocation, smaller assemblages	Broad spectrum, intensive; larger faunal assemblages; periodic shortages dealt with by diversification, storage and exchange
Mobility strategy	High residential and logistic mobility, high range mobility	Differentiated settlement systems; site specialization
Regional variation	Low	High
Locational strategy	Short-term redundant use of known places	Territorial with specialized activity locations; multi-season; more evenly distributed
Technology	Portable, high-quality raw material; long use-life OR simple with few tool types; small-medium assemblages	Task-specific and/or expedient tools; large and small assemblages; local raw materials
Storage	None	Possible
Stratigraphic position	Underlying/pre-dating a developed phase; duration 500-600 years	Underlying or post-dating a pioneer phase

Table 4.1 *Trait list across eight archaeological signature domains for distinguishing Palaeolithic pioneering and post-pioneering groups. Trait descriptions from Kelly and Todd (1988), Davies (2001), Housley et al. (1997), and Hazelwood and Steele (2003).*

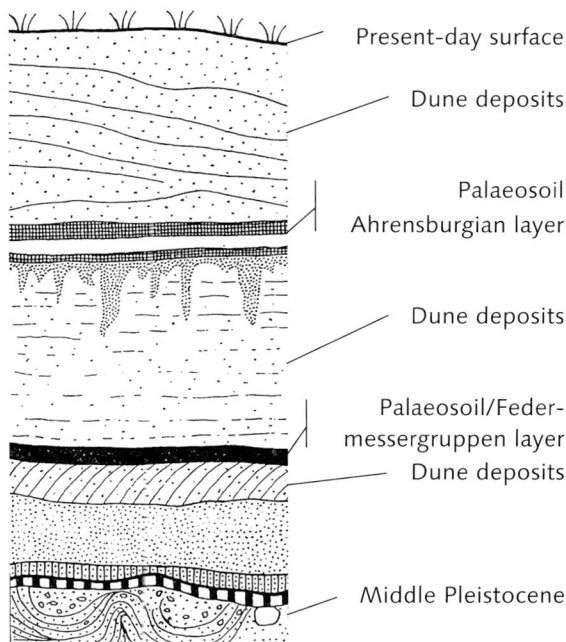

Figure 4.2 *The important stratigraphic sequence found by Schwabedissen at Rissen, north of Hamburg.*

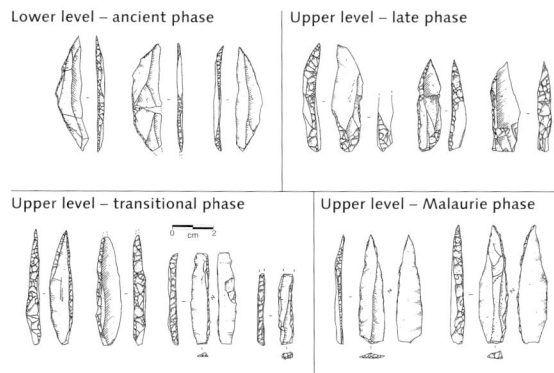

Figure 4.3 *Lithic developmental scheme for the Late Glacial in northern France, as seen at the important site of Le Closeau. Modified from Bodu and Valentin (1997).*

dermesser locales are either surface collections or lack any kind of informative stratigraphy, rendering the definitive dating of individual localities very challenging indeed. Yet, by excavating the important stratified dune site of Rissen north of Hamburg (Schwabedissen, 1949), by swiftly grasping the opportunity to have these important finds both pollen-analysed and radiocarbon-dated, and by placing the locality in a wider geographic context, Schwabedissen (1958) was able to provide a best-estimate date for the Federmessergruppen to the Allerød chronozone (Fig. 4.2). As Federmesser locales are also found beneath the tephra of the Laacher See eruption in the Rhineland, this event proved critical for anchoring this technocomplex in time already at that point.

Subsequent fieldwork in, for example, the Paris Basin and adjacent regions (Bodu, 1998; Bodu and Valentin, 1997; Fagnart and Coudret, 1997), in the Benelux region (Dewez, 1975), on the British Isles (see Pettitt and White, 2012 for an up-to-date summary), and in southern (Taute, 1972) and central (Küssner, 2007, 2010) Germany has provided further stratigraphic evidence of the general succession of Late Magdalenian – Federmesser – and,

where present, Ahrensburgian or else early Mesolithic. Likewise, Federmesser occupation in the Netherlands tends to be associated with the so-called Usselo horizon, a consistent soil-formation layer found across large parts of the North European Plain that is dated to the Allerød (Kaiser et al., 2009). It is in southeastern and northern France where a gradual and uninterrupted evolution from the Late Magdalenian into the Federmessergruppen and further into the so-called Laborian with its characteristic basally retouched 'Malaurie points' can be observed, although even the latter area may have been abandoned during parts of the very cold Younger Dryas (Fig. 4.3; Fagnart et al., 2000; Thévenin, 1997). Following the suggestion of Thévenin (1997), the emergence of the Federmessergruppen – already then characterised by both arch-backed and large tanged points – can be traced back to the so-called Valogurian of south-eastern France, where stratified cave and rock-shelter sequences date the appearance of Federmesser-like elements and large tanged 'pointes de Teyjat' into the times just prior to the Allerød. These groups, he argues, then moved up the Saône, Rhône and Rhine corridors to the Upper and Middle Rhineland, a notion supported by the movement of lithic raw materials (Floss, 2000) and decorative objects made from far-travelled raw materials (Álvarez-Fernández, 2001) along these river valleys. Similar raw material provenance studies then demonstrate that these forager groups from there moved further up onto the North European Plain, both along the Lower Rhine and Meuse valleys (Baales, 2001; Floss, 1994) and along the somewhat smaller valleys of the central German Rivers Main, Fulda, Lahn, Schwalm, Eder, and Leine (Riede, 2012b).

The stratigraphic anchoring provided by these key cave and deep open-air sites can be supplemented with a, by now, reasonably substantial database of radiocarbon and other absolute dates. This suite of dates is not without problems, however, as the dating of, for instance, charcoal from open-air sites is riddled with methodological difficulty (e.g. Crombé et al., 2013; Vermeersch, 1977). The stratigraphic integrity of sequences can be poor, allowing for contamination from younger strata. In addition, forest fires were abundant during the Allerød leaving charcoal traces that may have nothing to do with human presence (Crombé et al., 2013; Lanting and Van der Plicht, 1996). As a consequence, ^{14}C-dates are often obtained on material that may not relate to the archaeology in question. The reverse is also evident: Many objects of clear human manufacture – antler axes, harpoons, etc. – are also dated, but these are usually not found in secure contextual association with lithic material and are thus no great help in differentiating the various technocomplexes (e.g. Clausen, 2003). Similarly, cut-marked or otherwise humanly modified faunal elements constitute another category of dated material. Yet, again, links between these and nearby lithic material can be rather weak.

In an effort to meet these methodological challenges head on, all available dates for the very northern extension of the Federmessergruppen have been subjected to a standardised evaluation procedure that examines each date's technical quality as well as culture-historical relevance (Pettitt et al., 2003). This approach has already been applied with some success to investigate the transition from the Federmessergruppen to the Bromme culture in southern Scandinavia (Riede and Edinborough, 2012), and new dates have since been obtained or become available (Fischer, 2013; Fischer et al., 2013a; Galiński, 2007; Tolksdorf et al., 2013; Turner et al., 2013; Veil et al., 2012). All these dates are listed in Appendix I, the auditing criteria used for evaluating their quality and relevance in Appendix II. Even a cursory glance at this table shows that all the recently obtained dates on material that is reasonably clearly linked to diagnostic lithic material place the Federmessergruppen in the earlier part of the Allerød. Indeed, sites along the southern margin of the North European Plain such as Weitsche and Grabow, but also Federmessergruppen sites slightly further afield, such as Reichwalde in very eastern Germany (Friedrich et al., 2001; Vollbrecht, 2005), date to very early in the Allerød if not even slightly before it. In northern Germany, too, the site of Borneck (Rust, 1958) has yielded an early Allerød date, although the link of the dated bone, which is unmodified, to the settlement site is not certain (Riede et al., 2010). Similarly, the oft-cited early dates for the Federmessergruppen occupation at the complex locale of Klein Nordende (Bokelmann et al., 1983) must be seen with caution. These dates, reported only incompletely in a footnote to the site report, were obtained on unmodified twigs of hawthorn (*Hippophaë*) from a layer that was thought to be identical to a find-bearing stratum elsewhere at Klein Nordende. However, the stratigraphy at the site is complex and the lithic material could easily have moved into this layer post-depositionally. Given these observations and the possible importance of this site, a fairly extensive re-dating programme was initiated some years ago (Riede et al., 2010). Dating of a cut-marked femur of elk (*Alces alces*) from the site has produced a fairly late Allerød date (KIA33951: 11,035±50, ∂^{13}C= -20.45±0.14‰), whilst re-dating of what remained of Bokelmann and colleagues' original samples moves the *Hippophaë*-layer even further back in time (*Betula* sp., KIA47282 [from KI-2124]: 12,040±110, ∂^{13}C= -29.25±0.26‰ and *Salix* sp., KIA47283 [KI-2152]: 12,230 ± 50, ∂^{13}C= -29.92±0.22‰). Finally, dating of a cut- and impact-marked reindeer antler attests to a still earlier presence of people at the site, presumably of the Hamburgian culture (KIA47280: 12,290±50 BP, δ^{13}C= -19.41±0.18‰, and KIA47281: 12,120±40, ∂^{13}C= -19.36±0.25‰). Sadly, none of these dates conclusively resolve the chronological position of the Allerød-age human pres-

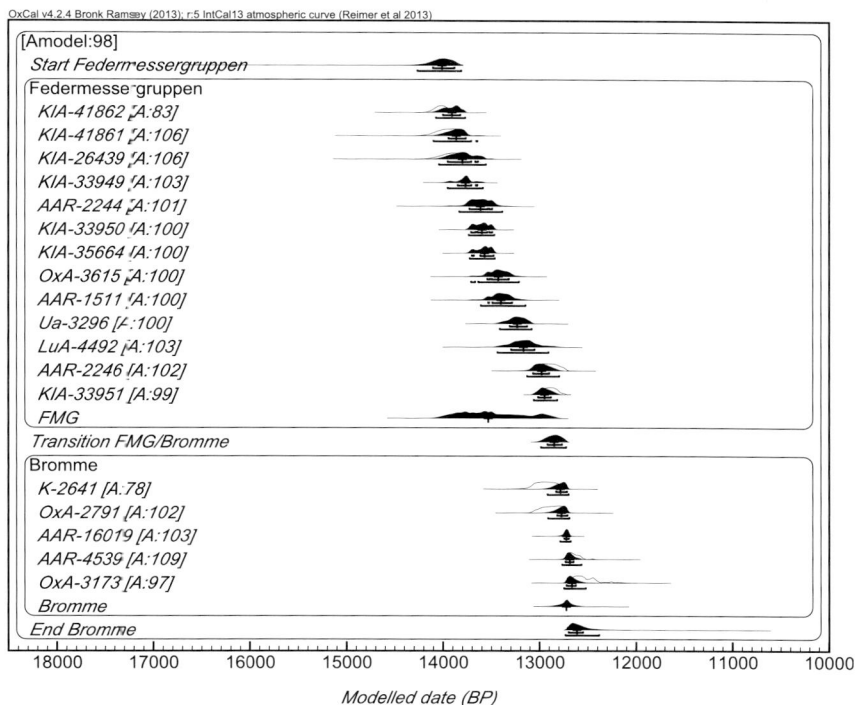

Figure 4.4 *A simple two-phase Bayesian model for the Federmessergruppen and the Bromme culture. The data used are listed in Appendix I. All dates with a quality score ≥27 are used in the final model. For a more detailed treatment of this dating approach see Riede and Edinborough (2012).*

ence at this locality, as the young date on the elk bone evidently relates to later occupation episodes that are also stratigraphically clearly separated from the lower find-bearing layer. If anything, the re-dating of Bokelmann's plant samples from the *Hippophaë*-layer make it less likely that the formation of this layer is contemporaneous with the deposition of the Federmessergruppen settlement remains. In fact, it may rather relate to the presence of Hamburgian hunters at the locale, an association that would gel better with the botanical and ecological interpretation of that layer, i.e. it being a manifestation of early Late Glacial warming in northern Germany associated with GI-1e (the 'Meiendorf' phase; see de Klerk, 2004). Riede et al. (2010) have discussed the site's dating problems in some detail.

Looking at the younger end of the radiocarbon dates for the Federmessergruppen also shows an interesting pattern. Here, high-quality dates linked securely to diagnostic flint artefacts do not occur after 11,000 uncalibrated BP. In combination, even these preliminary observations on the radiocarbon dates for the Federmessergruppen on the Great North European Plain suggest a chronological range for this technocomplex from 12,000 to 11,000

uncalibrated BP. Placing the suite of dates into a Bayesian calibration model using the OxCal software (Bronk Ramsey, 2009) and following Pettitt et al. (2003) in only including dates of a certain technical and contextual quality sets the transition from Federmessergruppen to Bromme culture to the period just after 13,000 calibrated BP (Fig. 4.4).

4.4 Federmessergruppen ecology and economy

If the Late Glacial on the whole can be described as a period of pronounced and rapid climatic and environmental change, then the Allerød chronozone can be said to have offered some respite. Regional temperature reconstructions based on ecologically sensitive beetle (*Coleoptera*) assemblages indicates quite strong regional differences that underline basal latitudinal gradients as well as the differences between wetter and milder maritime and dryer and colder continental climatic regimes (Fig. 4.5; Coope and Lemdahl, 1995; Coope et al., 1998). After the brief cold of the Older Dryas/GI-1d, both climate and environments began to stabilise, even eventually in southern

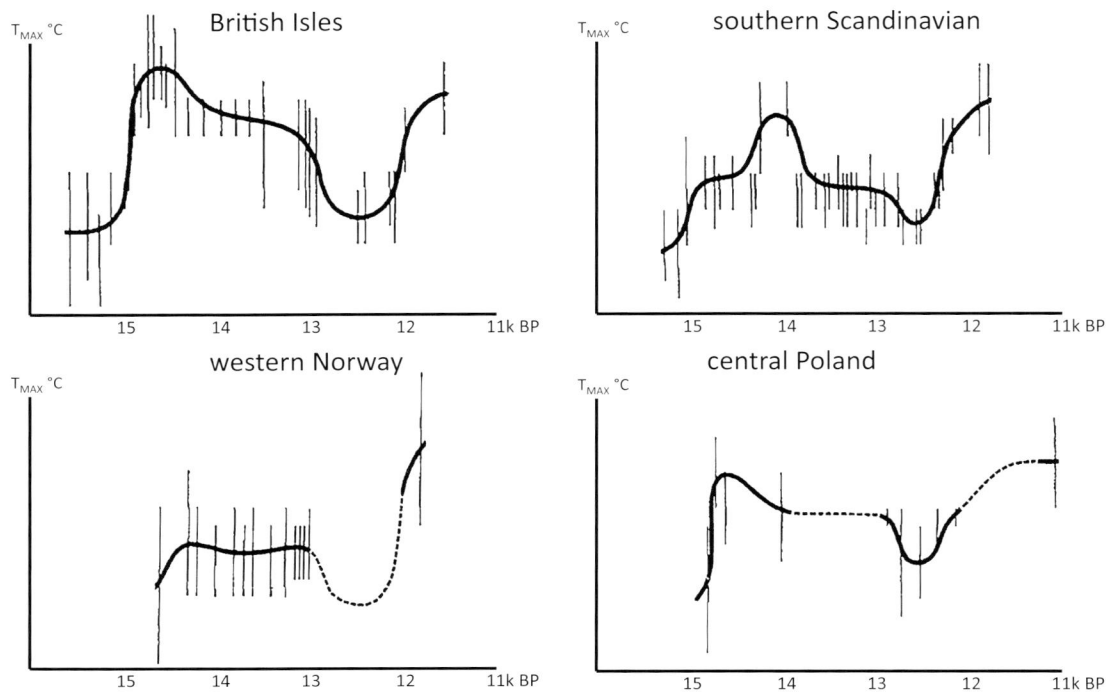

Figure 4.5 *Comparison of reconstructed mean July temperatures (T_{MAX}) for four regions in northern Europe throughout the Late Glacial, based on temperature-sensitive insect assemblages. Note the large number of samples for southern Scandinavia and its significantly later warming when compared to the British Isles and Poland. Redrawn from Coope and Lemdahl (1995).*

Scandinavia (Bennike et al., 2004; Coope and Bocher, 2000; Lemdahl et al., 2014; Mortensen et al., 2014b; Mortensen et al., 2011). As noted above, Aeolian deposition abated and soil development commenced many places. With this, plants and animals began to migrate northwards in greater number and diversity (e.g. Aaris-Sørensen, 2009; Noe-Nygaard et al., 2006). In the Rhineland as well as the British Isles, numerous faunal assemblages are known and attest to quite diverse open woodland faunal communities (Baales et al., 2002; Currant and Jacobi, 2001; Street and Baales, 1999). Northern communities were similar in composition, albeit less diverse (Table 4.2).

Of those species present in Allerød landscapes, many were hunted. Federmessergruppen economy, whilst no doubt decidedly oriented towards large mammals, contained a broad spectrum of other species (Baales and Street, 1996). Smaller mammals such as beaver and hare were hunted, and fish remains become more common at this time (Álvarez-Fernández, 2011; Le Gall, 1992, 2003) as do the implements, fishing hooks and gorges

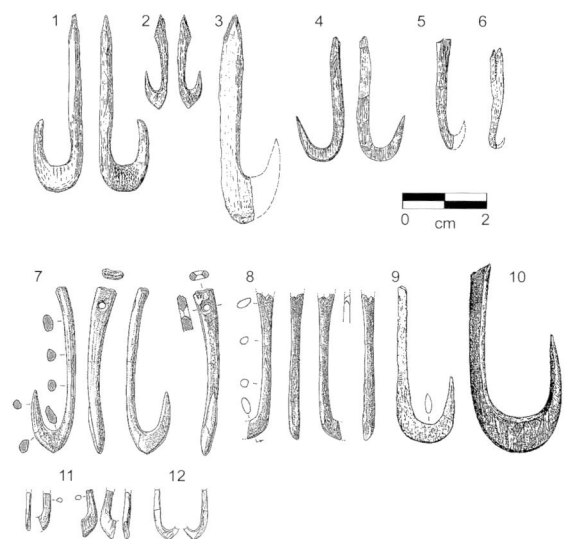

Figure 4.6 *Fishing hooks from Federmesser contexts. 1-6: Wustermark 22 (north-eastern Germany), made of ungulate bone, except 4 which is made of fossil mammoth ivory; 7: Bois-Ragot (France); 8: Pont-d'Ambon (France); 9: Gratkorn (Austria), 10: Braunsbedra (eastern Germany); 11: Klein Lieskow (eastern Germany). Modified from Gramsch et al. (2013).*

(Fig. 4.6), used to catch them (Cziesla, 2001; Pasda, 2001).

Figure 4.7 *First Nation Americans hunting elk whilst swimming. Note that the weapon tip in question here is made of stone. From http://americanart.si.edu/collections/search/artwork/?id=3008.*

Barbed points are another technology that may reflect an increasing use of water-bodies as hunting-grounds. These occur in a variety of forms, equipped with both finer and larger barbs (Cziesla and Pettitt, 2003). Although rarely associated with fauna, when such associations do exist – at Poulton-le-Fylde (Lancashire) on the British Isles, for instance (Hallam et al., 1973) or at the site of Kettig in the Rhineland (Baales, 2002a) both dated to the earlier part of the Allerød – they are associated with large terrestrial rather than marine animals. Ethnographic accounts of similar strategies (Fig. 4.7) have led to the suggestion that these points, as parts of harpoon-like weapons, were used to hunt swimming land mammals (Petersen, 2009; Pettitt and White, 2012), a supposition broadly supported by the occurrence of these implements far inland, and generally in close demonstrable association with water-bodies.

It is unclear whether these harpoons were delivered unaided, or with the help of a spear-thrower (Fig. 4.8). Spear-throwers, also

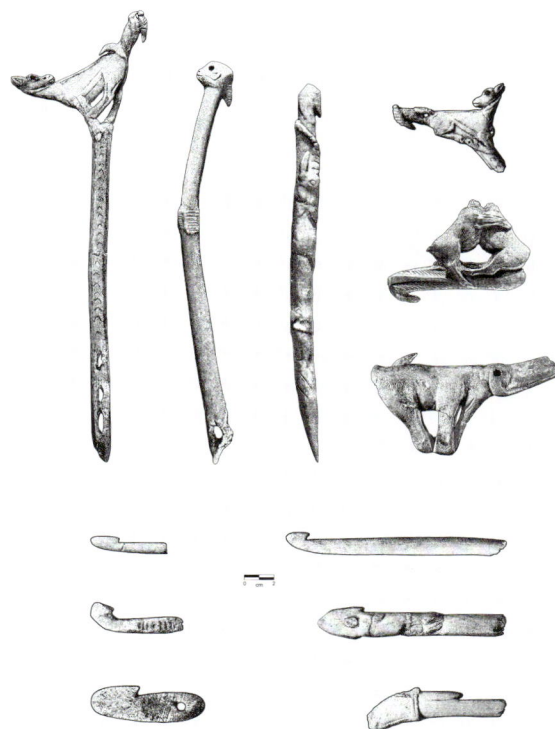

Figure 4.8 *Decorated and plain spear-thrower fragments from the Late Magdalenian/Federmessergruppen contexts. From Stodiek and Paulsen (1996).*

Animal	Taxonomic identification to genus/sp.	species	Regions of Federmessergruppen occupation SC	W	E	N
Elk		*Alces alces*		1		1
Giant deer		*Megaloceros giganteus*				1
Arctic fox		*Alopex lagopus*	1	1		1
Auochs		*Bos primigenius*	1	1		1
Bovids	Bovidae		1			
Bison	*Bos/Bison*		1	1		1
Steppe bison		*Bos primigenius*		1		
Wolf		*Canis lupus*	1	1		
Dog		*Canis lupus familiaris*	1	1		
carnivore	Carnivora		1	1		
Red deer		*Cervus elaphus*	1	1		1
deer	Cervidae		1	1		1
Roe deer		*Capreolus capreolus*	1	1		1
Ibex		*Capra ibex*	1	1	1	
Beaver		*Castor fiber*	1	1		1
Horse	*Equus* sp.		1	1	1	1
Wolverine		*Gulo gulo*	1			1
Musk ox		*Ovibos moschatus*	1			
Reindeer		*Rangifer tarandus*	1	1		1
Chamois		*Rupicapra rupicapra*	1	1		
Wild boar		*Sus scrofa*	1	1		1
Brown bear		*Ursus arctos*	1	1	1	1
Polar bear		*Ursus maritimus*				1
Red fox		*Vulpes vulpes*	1	1		
Mammoth		*Mammuthus primigenius*	1			
Sheep		*Ovis aries*	1			
Mouse	*Apodemus sp.*		1	1		
Yellow-necked mouse		*Apodemus flavicollis*	1	1		
Wood mouse		*Apodemus sylvaticus*		1		
Vole/lemming	Arvicolinae					1
Water vole		*Arvicola terrestris*	1	1		1
Barbastelle		*Barbastella barbastellus*	1			
Russion desman		*Desmana moschata*				1
bats	Chiroptera		1	1		
Hamster	*Cricetus* sp.			1		
Common hamster		*Cricetus cricetus*	1	1	1	
Dzungarian hamster		*Phodopus sungorus*		1		
Bank vole		*Myodes glareolus*	1	1	1	
Northern red-backed vole		*Myodes rutilus*		1		
Collared lemming	*Dicrostonyx sp.*		1	1		
Lagomorphs	Lagomorpha			1		
Hare		*Lepus sp.*	1	1		1
Mountain hare		*Lepus timidus*	1	1		1

Common name	Genus/Family	Species				
Norway lemming		*Lemmus lemmus*	1	1		1
Badger		*Meles meles*	1	1		
Vole	*Microtus* sp.		1	1		1
Field vole		*Microtus agrestis*	1	1	*1*	
Common vole		*Microtus arvalis*			*1*	
Field/common vole		*Microtus arvalis/agrestis*	1	1		
Singing vole		*Microtus gregalis*	1	1		1
Snow vole		*Chionomys nivalis*	1	1	*1*	
Tundra vole		*Microtus oeconomus*	1	1	*1*	1
Alpine marmot		*Marmota marmota*	1	1		
Weasel	*Mustela* sp.		1			
Stoat		*Mustela erminea*	1	1		
Common weasel		*Mustela nivalis*	1	1		
Steppe pika		*Ochotona pusilla*	1	1		1
Rodents	Rodentia		1			
Red-toothed shrews	*Sorex* sp.		1	1		
Common shrew		*Sorex araneus*	1	1		1
Pygmy shrew		*Sorex minutus*	1	1		1
European vole		*Talpa europaea*	1	1		
Mouse-eared bat	*Myotis* sp.		1			
Common long-eared bat		*Plecotus auritus*	1	1		
Horseshoe bat	*Rhinolophus* sp.		1			
Common/Hazel dormouse		*Muscardinus avellanarius*	1			
Mouse/rat	Muridae					1
Black rat		*Rattus rattus*	*1*			
Pine vole		*Microtus subterraneus*	1		*1*	
Red squirrel		*Sciurus vulgaris*	1			
Moles	Talpidae		1			
Ground squirrel	*Spermophilus* sp.		1			1
Shrews	Soricidae		1			
Northern birch mouse		*Sicista betulina*	1	1		1
European water shrew		*Neomys fodiens*	1	1		
Noctule	*Nyctalus* sp.			1		
Steppe polecat		*Mustela eversmanni*	1			
Common vole		*Microtus arvalis*	1			
Marten	*Martes* sp.		1			
Pine marten		*Martes martes*	1			
Edible dormouse		*Glis glis*	1			
Wildcat		*Felis silvestris*	1			
White-toothed shrew		*Crocidura leucodon/ russula*	1			
Vole/lemming	Arvicolinae		1			
Long-tailed field mouse		*Apodemus sylvaticus*	1			
SUM			71	53	10	30

Table 4.2 *Animal species known from different regions of Federmessergruppen settlement. Data and regional divisions from Fahlke (2009) who also further discusses the ecological implications of these patterns. Taxa noted in italics are only uncertainly represented in the respective regions.*

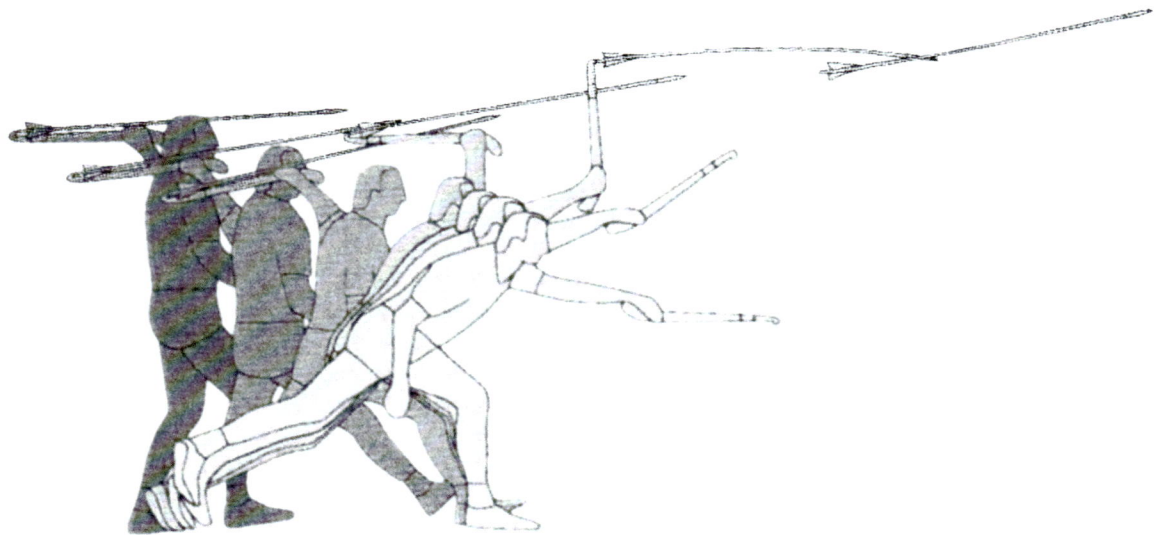

Figure 4.9 *The launching sequence of a dart using a spear-thrower, modified from Stodiek and Paulsen (1996).*

known as atlatls, are extensions of the arm that significantly amplify the – compared to other primates (see Roach et al., 2013) – already powerful natural throwing ability of *Homo sapiens* (Fig. 4.9). The projectiles thus delivered are generally termed darts in order to distinguish them terminologically from hand-thrown spears or javelins and thrusting lances. Fragments of atlatls, occasionally elaborately decorated, are known from this period (Cattelain, 2004, 2005; Garrod, 1955; Grünberg, 2006; Stodiek, 1993; Szmidt et al., 2009), although most date to the millennia just preceding the Allerød and none are from

southern Scandinavia (see Riede, 2010a). While it is widely assumed that bow and arrow technology was introduced in northern Europe during Magdalenian times at the latest (Rozoy, 1989; Shea, 2006), there is in fact good circumstantial evidence from the stone tool aspect of contemporaneous tool-kits for the use of both the spear-thrower as well as the bow in the Federmessergruppen. The lithic component of past weapon delivery systems was only minor compared to the various and varied organic components – in fact, the importance of each component is, as Stodiek and Paulsen (1996) have wryly noted, inversely correlated with its

Material	N weapon elements	% of whole weapon	Chance of preservation
Stone	4	10	Very high
Antler	2	10	High to medium
Bone	2		
Wood	10		
Cordage	11		
Hide/leather	3	80	Medium to poor
Feathers	3		
Mastic	6		

Table 4.3 *Stone Age weapon components and the chances of survival of the different components, from Stodiek and Paulsen (1996).*

likelihood for surviving the vagaries of time (Table 4.3).

Fortunately, the functional requirements of projectile weapons reference invariant laws of physics and, in order to function adequately, points, hafting, shafts, and weapons must conform to specific shape and weight parameters (Beckhoff, 1966; Christensen, 1986; Cotterell and Kamminga, 1990; Hickman, 1937; Kooi and Bergman, 1997). By taking such a (baseline) engineering/ballistics approach, it is possible to say quite a lot about past weapon systems on the basis of their tips alone. Interestingly, Federmesser assemblages from England (Barton, 1992; Jacobi, 1980; Mace, 1959), France (Alaux, 1972; Champagne and Espitalié, 1970; de Sonneville-Bordes, 1969) and the Netherlands (Houtsma et al., 1981; Paddayya, 1973) in the west, to Poland (Bagniewski, 1999; Siemaszko, 1999a, 1999b) and Lithuania (Sinitsyna, 2002) in the east, with evident concentrations of occurrence in the 'heartland' of Federmessergruppen settlement in northern Germany (Breest and Gerken, 2008; Taute, 1968), consistently contain large tanged points, albeit in usually low numbers. In Denmark, too, the association of arch-backed Federmesser and large tanged points is relatively common (Riede et al., 2011a). Table 4.4 provides a preliminary catalogue over those sites where large tanged points co-occur with Magdalenian, Federmesser or Azilian elements.

The morphology of these implements is highly variable, but the systematic difference in size between these Teyjat, Lyngby or Bromme points and the much more slender arch-backed points with which they co-occur side by side is suggestive of differential use contexts. Equipping any projectile with a stone tip significantly increases the weapon's power (Waguespack et al., 2009). The ballistics of such stone tips have been investigated in detail, where the work of Hughes (1998) has provided a robust framework for investigating differences, similarities and trends in prehistoric weaponry. According to Hughes, tip cross-sectional area (TCSA) and tip cross-sectional perimeter (TCSP) values in particular are useful for distinguishing different weapon types. These values are obtained on the basis of quite simple measurements that can often be retrieved even on broken specimens (Fig. 4.10). Tip cross-sectional area is calculated thus:

$$TCSA = 5.0 \bullet \mathit{width} \bullet \mathit{thickness} \qquad (4.1)$$

whereas the tip cross-sectional perimeter, modified by Sisk and Shea (2009) to suit unifacially worked blade- or flake-based armatures, is calculated as follows:

$$TCSP_{unifacial} = \mathit{width} + 2 \bullet \sqrt{((0.5 \bullet \mathit{width})^2 + \mathit{thickness}^2)} \quad (4.2)$$

It has since been suggested that point thickness may vary with the intended length of use-life (curation) of points (Cheshier and Kelly, 2006), leaving width as the single most important variable for discriminating between past weapon types. Other researchers have found tip weight to be a better predictor of weapon type (Bretzke et al., 2006), although as both the cross-sectional values and weight are directly related to overall point size they ultimately measure the same thing, namely that, all else being equal, arrowheads are smaller than dart-points, which are smaller again than spearheads. Plotting maximum width for arch-backed and large tanged points from Federmesser contexts shows that virtually all arch-backed points fall into a very narrow interval between 7 and 14mm, whilst the long tail of mostly higher values is made up of large tanged points only (Fig. 4.11). This suggests that the typological division between large tanged points on the one hand and arch-backed points on the other reflects a functional differentiation between armatures designed for darts and for arrows respectively. Calculating TCSA and TCSP supports this conclusion (see Riede, 2009d). Likewise with regards to weight, large tanged points fall outside the range generally thought to reflect arrowheads: Korfmann (1972) along with numerous other workers (e.g. Beckhoff, 1966; Fenenga, 1953) argues that 5g constitutes an upper weight limit for prehistoric arrowheads, and that early bows were unlikely to have been able to effectively fire heavier missiles. Caspar and De Bie (1996) report an average weight of

Locale	Country	Region
Alt Duvenstedt LA 89		Ldkr. Rendsburg-Eckernförde
Andernach (Martinsberg)		Ldkr. Mayen-Koblenz
Bärenkeller		Ldkr. Saalfeld-Rudolstadt
Berlin-Tegel A /B		Stadt Berlin
Bienenbüttel (FStNr. 15)		Ldkr. Uelzen
Borneck-Mitte		Kr. Stormarn
Brümmerhof (FStNr. 16)		Ldkr. Rotenburg (Wümme)
Brunsmark		Kr. Herzogtum-Lauenburg
Dietesheim		Stadt Mühlheim
Dohnsen-Bratzloh (FStNr. 2)		Ldkr. Celle
Dohnsen-Lührsberg (FStNr. 29)		Ldkr. Celle
Fienerode "Holzbreite"		Stadt Genthin
Flintbek LA 35/LA 118		Ldkr. Rendsburg-Eckernförde
Grande 1		Kr. Stormarn
Groß Lieskow		Stadt Cottbus
Häcklingen (FStNr. 19)	Germany	Ldkr. Lüneburg
Hamfelde		Kr. Herzogtum-Lauenburg
Handeloh (FStNr. 15)		Ldkr. Harburg
Kalbe-Kremkau		Kr. Salzwedel
Kampen (FStNr. 42)		Ldkr. Harburg
Klein Vollbüttel		Ldkr. Gifhorn
Leiferde-Viehmoor I		Ldkr. Gifhorn
Lurschau 5, 7, 18		Ldkr. Schleswig-Flensburg
Martinshöhle		Kr. Iserlohn
Oldendorf (FStNr. 42 und 52)		Ldkr. Rotenburg (Wümme)
Pinnberg		Kr. Stormarn
Querenstede, Fundstelle II		Ldkr. Ammerland
Rietberg		Kr. Gütersloh
Rissen 14, 15/15a, Timmermanns Moorloch		Hansestadt Hamburg
Saaleck		Kr. Naumburg
Sassenholz (FStNr. 78 und 82)		Ldkr. Rotenburg (Wümme)

Reference(s)	Lat	Long	Dating
Clausen and Hartz (1988); Kaiser and Clausen (2005)	54.36	9.59	
Schwabedissen (1954)	50.43	7.40	Underneath LST
Feustel et al. (1971)	50.65	11.07	B 980: 11190±180
Taute (1968); Mey (1962)	52.57	13.28	
Richter (2001)	53.14	10.49	
Rust (1958); Riede et al. (2010)	53.49	10.36	KIA-33950: 11770±55
Gerken (2001a, 2001b)	53.26	9.25	
Trölsch (1976); Ikinger (1998)	53.61	10.74	
Fruth (1979, 1994)	50.12	8.88	Contemporaneous with/older than LST
Breest et al. (1999)	52.82	10.03	
Taute (1968)	52.82	10.02	
Taute (1968)	52.38	12.32	
Zich (1999)	54.23	10.06	
Schwabedissen (1944, 1954); Taute (1968)	53.58	10.38	
Pasda (2002)	51.80	14.45	
Richter (2002)	53.21	10.39	
Schwabedissen (1944); Tromnau (1977)	53.60	10.45	
Breest and Graff (2007)	53.24	9.84	
Schwabedissen (1944, 1954); Taute (1968)	52.65	11.38	
Breest (2004)	53.24	9.77	
Taute (1968)	52.42	10.49	
Ikinger (1998)	52.44	10.44	
Loewe (1998)	54.54	9.47	
Günther (1988)	51.35	7.64	
Gerken (2001a, 2001b)	53.27	9.26	
Rust (1958)	53.66	10.23	
Zoller (1981)	53.15	7.97	OxA-2562: 11840±110; KN-53: 11070±320
Günther (1988)	54.36	9.59	
Schwabedissen (1954)	53.60	9.77	H-75/68: 11450±180
Ikinger (1998)	51.12	11.70	OxA-11890: 12780±60; OxA-11891: 12945±60
Breest and Gerken (2003, 2008)	53.35	9.30	

Table 4.4 *Continues*   ⟶

Locale	Country	Region
Schalkholz		**Kr. Dithmarschen**
Sprenge 4		Kr. Stormarn
Tagebau Cottbus-Nord		Stadt Cottbus
Teltwisch 5		**Kr. Stormarn**
Todtshorn (FStNr. 62)		Ldkr. Harburg
Tolk (A)	Germany	Ldkr. Schleswig-Flensburg
Weitsche		**Ldkr. Lüchow-Dannenberg**
Westertimke (FStNr. 69)		Ldkr. Rotenburg (Wümme)
Wörpeldorf		Ldkr. Osterholz-Scharmbeck
Wulften		Ldkr. Osnabrück
Wustrow		Ldkr. Nordvorpommern
Rotnowo 18		**Gryfice**
Woźnawieś		Grajewo
Jaglisko 3/3a		**Choszczno**
Lurbza		**Prudnik**
Kargowa 'e'	Poland	Zielonogórski
Całowanie		**Otwock**
Siedlnica 17 I/73 & 17 II/78		**Wschowa**
Witow		**Łęczyca**
Hollendskær		**Northern Jutland**
Enslev (Mosely I)		Southern Jutland
Attemose II		Southern Jutland
Gamst Søenge		Southern Jutland
Estrup (HBV 288)		Southern Jutland
Sølystgård (MKH 411/MKH 1111)	Denmark	Southern Jutland
Over Jels (SB 149 [J2] & SB 154 [J9])		Southern Jutland
Stoksbjerg Vest		**Zealand**
Hjarup Mose		Southern Jutland
Sølbjerg (surface finds)		Lolland
Rundebakke		Zealand
Hasselø Tværvej (NM 1 7725/94)		**Falster**
Cat Hole*	British Isles	**West Glamorgan**
Hengistbury Head		**Dorset**

Reference(s)	Lat	Long	Dating
Bokelmann (1978)	**54.24**	**9.27**	
Schwabedissen (1954)	53.69	10.37	
Fries (2005)	51.80	14.41	
Tromnau (1975)	**53.64**	**10.20**	
Breest (2004)	53.23	9.78	
Taute (1968)	54.58	9.61	
Breest and Gerken (2008)	**53.02**	**11.13**	KIA-26439: 11980±120; KIA-35664: 11755±50
Gerken (2001c)	53.24	9.13	
Breest and Gerken (2008)	53.22	8.94	
Ikinger (1998)	52.30	8.22	
Taute (1968)	54.35	12.40	
Galiński (2007)	**53.90**	**15.29**	Poz.-8308: 11100±70; Poz.-8310: 11090±80
Kobusiewicz (2009a, 2009b)	53.67	22.77	
Bagniewski (1999); Masojć (2006)	**53.02**	**15.70**	
Kabacinski and Sobkowiak-Tabaka (2010)	**52.31**	**15.44**	
Kobusiewicz (2009a, 2009b)	52.07	15.87	
Schild (1996); Schild et al. (1999)	**52.00**	**21.33**	Various dates – see Pazdur et al. (2004)
Taute (1963, 1968)	**51.76**	**16.34**	
Chmielewska (1962)	**51.74**	**19.85**	Gro-828: 10815±160[§]
Nilsson (1989)	**57.52**	**9.99**	
Madsen (1986)	56.61	10.12	
Kramer (1995)	55.89	12.25	
Knudsen (1990)	55.49	9.18	
Rindel (1994)	55.49	9.04	
Fischer (1991); Riede et al. (2011)	55.48	9.27	
Holm and Rieck (1987); Holm (1992)	55.38	9.24	
Johansson (2003)	**55.29**	**11.82**	
Andersen (1977)	55.18	9.34	
Petersen and Johansen (1991)	54.76	11.09	
Fugl Petersen (1994, 2001)	55.05	11.78	
Johansen (2000); Petersen (2006)	**54.73**	**11.89**	
Campbell (1977); Jacobi (1980)	**51.61**	**-4.13**	
Mace (1959); Barton (1992)	**50.71**	**-1.75**	TL-dated to early Allerød

Table 4.4 *Continues* ⟶

Locale	Country	Region
Een-Schipsloot	Nether-lands	Drenthe
Norgevaart*		Drenthe
Bois-Ragot (level 5b)		Vienne
Abri de Cabônes		Jura
Grotte de la Grand'Baille		Jura
Grotte de la Bonne-Femme		Ain
La Mairie (Teyjat)		Dordogne
Rochereil		Dordogne
Blassac II		Haute-Loire
Longueroche		Dordogne)
Laugerie-Basse	France	Dordogne
Pis-de-la-Vache		Lot-et-Garonne
Font-Brunel		Dordogne
Tufs		Dordogne
Font-Brunel		Dordogne
Grotte-Bâtie		Lot-et-Garonne
Roc des Abeilles		Dordogne
Morin		Dordogne
Le Martinet		Lot-et-Garonne
l'abri de Fontalès		Midi-Pyrénées
l'abri Dufaure		Landes

Table 4.4 *A preliminary catalogue of Magdalenian/Federmessergruppen sites with large tanged points. The points marked with * most likely represent an earlier Gravettian Font-Robert point. ** may be a forgery (Stapert, 1986). Locales listed in bold are excavated. § These dates are on material potentially unrelated to the human occupation. Note also the close correspondence of Federmessergruppen finds and surface-found large tanged points in eastern Germany (Gramsch, 1987). Within each country, the sites are arranged by latitude from north to south and longitude from west to east.*

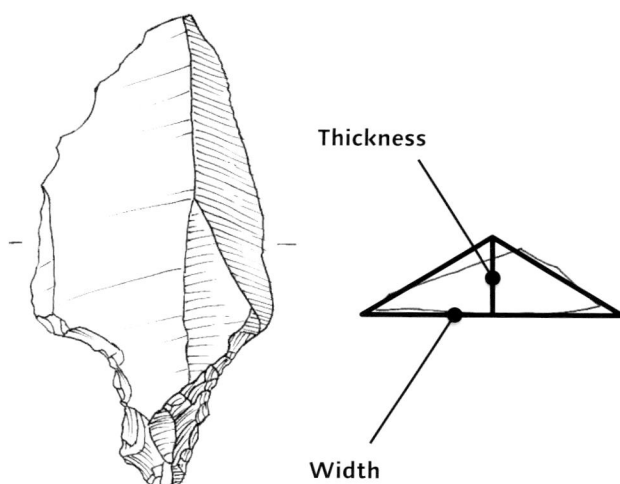

Figure 4.10 *Landmarks for deriving ballistically relevant dimensional values from lithic projectile points.*

Reference(s)	Lat	Long	Dating
Houtsma et al. (1981)	53.08	6.38	GrN-6341: 10495±60 BP[§]
Paddayya (1973)	53.00	6.49	
Célérier et al. (1997); Chollet et al. (1999)	47.20	1.86	
David (1984)	47.17	5.79	Late Magdalenian layer
Desbrosse (1980)	46.09	5.41	Ly-2296: 12620±250
Combier and Desbrosse (1964); Desbrosse (1980)	45.62	5.63	
de Sonneville-Bordes (1969)	45.59	0.58	
de Sonneville-Bordes (1969)	45.30	0.54	
Alaux (1972)	45.17	3.40	
de Sonneville-Bordes (1959)	45.00	1.05	
de Sonneville-Bordes (1969)	44.95	1.00	
de Sonneville-Bordes (1969)	44.93	1.45	
de Sonneville-Bordes (1969)	44.88	0.89	
de Sonneville-Bordes (1969)	44.88	0.89	
Daniel (1970)	44.88	0.89	
de Sonneville-Bordes (1969)	44.88	1.56	
Champagne and Espitalié (1970)	44.86	1.33	
de Sonneville-Bordes (1969)	44.82	0.07	
de Sonneville-Bordes (1959)	44.59	1.01	
Darasse and Guffroy (1960)	44.01	1.29	
Thévenin (1997)	43.53	-1.05	

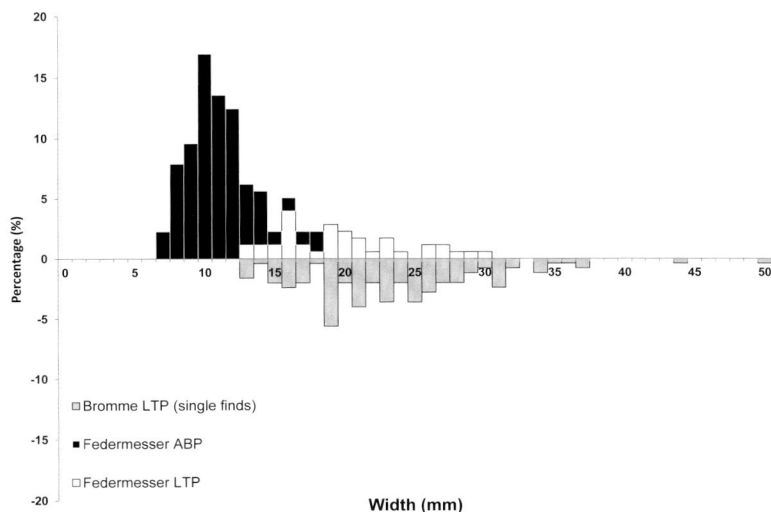

Figure 4.11 *Maximum width measurements for a sample of northern European arch-back and large tanged points from Federmessergruppen (all excavated) and Brommean (excavated and single-found) contexts. ABP= arch-backed point, LTP= large tanged point. Federmessergruppen sample: N_{ABP}= 137, N_{LTP}= 40. Bromme sample: N_{LTP}= 249.*

Draw strength (lb.)	Tip weight (g)
16.50	1.3
25.00	1.7
33.25	2.1
41.50	2.5
49.75	2.9
58.00	3.3
66.25	3.7
74.50	4.2
82.75	4.6-6.6
>82.75	6.6-8.3

Table 4.5 *The relationship between projectile tip weight and bow draw strength in traditional archery. The projectile tip makes up c. 1/7 of the total projectile weight. The generally accepted draw strength range for Mesolithic bows lies between 40 and 70 lb. (see Junkmanns, 2001). Note also that wood suitable for bow-making was very scarce during the Late Glacial in southern Scandinavia. After Korfmann (1972).*

1.5±0.7g for arch-backed points from the Belgian site of Rekem, whereas Holm (1972) reports weights of 5-20g for a substantial sample of complete and near-complete large tanged points from the presumed hunting stand of Ommelshoved on the island of Ærø in south-central Denmark. While arch-backed points thus fall squarely into the weight (<5g) and size (≤14mm) range of lightweight arrowheads, the large tanged points are off that scale for past hunting weaponry (Table 4.5). In conclusion, these considerations suggest that two hunting weapons were in use during the Upper Magdalenian and the Federmesser – the bow and the atlatl – and each was tipped with their own – traditionally typological/culture-historical but actually functional – category of point.

It is reasonably well-attested through observations of recent hunter-gatherers that different weapon systems can be and were used in parallel (Cattelain, 1997), and another way of approaching past weaponry begins with the ethnographic record. In an elegant study that aimed to distinguish arrowheads from dart-points metrically, Thomas (1978) measured the tips of ethnographic stone arrow-

and dart-tip specimens, where the respective weapon type of each projectile was known with certainty. More recently, Shott (1997) extended the sample size and derived discriminant functions for each weaponry type from these data. Much like Hughes (1998), Shott found that, in particular, maximum width (= shoulder width) and maximum thickness performed well as predictor variables. Indeed, iterative testing of function performance against the ethnographic training dataset showed formulae using width only were best at distinguishing between the two weapon types. These formulae are:

$$\text{Arrow} = 0.89 \bullet \textit{width} - 7 \qquad (4.3)$$

$$\text{Dart} = 1.4 \bullet \textit{width} - 16.85 \qquad (4.4)$$

where any specimen of unknown weapon type is classified according to which formula results in the highest value. Shott was thus able to correctly classify the points in his sample of known weapon types at a rate of 89.4% for arrowheads and 84.6% for dart-tips. The uncritical use of discriminant function analysis in archaeology has been warned against recently (Kovarovic et al., 2011), but both statistical arguments as well as archaeological lines of evidence can be harnessed to undergirth Shott's approach. One potential issue with Shott's data is the differential size of the two classes in his training data; there are far fewer darts (N= 39) than there are arrows (N= 132). Yet, applying – as recommended by Kovarovic and colleagues – Sanchez' (1974) proportional chance criterion to Shott's dataset would result in a significantly lower baseline chance-alone weapon type identification of 77.2% for arrowheads, and of only 22.8% for dart-points. The significantly better above-random performance of Shott's formulae for, in particular, dart-points lends confidence to their general utility as one way of deciding which weapon type a given prehistoric projectile specimen was likely part of. Previous replications of this approach using a substantial dataset of Late Glacial projectile points from all the major technocomplexes from northern Europe has yielded encouraging results (Riede, 2009d,

Locale	Region (country)	Lat	Long	Groove size (cm)		Total size (cm)		Cross-section	Reference(s)
				Width	Depth	Width	Height		
Niederbieber*	Stadt Neuwied, Northrhine-Westphalia (GER)	50.46	7.47	1.0	0.2	3.4	2.2	Semi-circle	Loftus (1982), Plate 32, 1
Andernach	Ldkr. Mayen-Koblenz, Northrhine-Westphalia (GER)	50.44	7.40	1.8	0.2	4.4	3.1	Semi-circle	Bolus (2012), Fig. 1, 4
Andernach	Ldkr. Mayen-Koblenz, Northrhine-Westphalia (GER)	50.44	7.40	1.6	0.2	3.1	1.8	Irregular-angular	Bolus (2012), Fig. 1, 5
Rekem 6	Limburg (B)	50.92	5.69	1.1	0.3	3.4	2.1	Semi-circle	De Bie and Caspar (2000), Plate 6, 1
Golßen	Kr. Luckau, Brandenburg (GER)	51.97	13.64	1.8	0.3	2.9	4.4	Unknown	Gramsch (1969); Rozoy and Escalon de Fonton (1978), p. 972, 1
Rekem 6*	Limburg (B)	50.92	5.69	1.1	0.5	4.3	2.6	Irregular-angular	De Bie and Caspar (2000), Plate 6, 2
Finsterwalde 72	Ldkr. Elbe-Elster, Brandenburg (GER)	51.51	13.75	1.4	0.5	5.0	2.4	Semi-circle	Wechler (1988), Fig. 6, 1
Finsterwalde 72	Ldkr. Elbe-Elster, Brandenburg (GER)	51.51	13.75	1.8	0.3	4.8	2.2	Irregular-angular	Wechler (1988), Fig. 6, 2
Lommel	Limburg (B)	51.23	5.31	1.3	-	4.5	-	Unknown	Verheyleweghen (1956), Fig. 21, 1
Rekem 12	Limburg (B)	50.92	5.69	1.1	-	4.5	2.7	Unknown	De Bie and Caspar (2000), Plate 2, 5

Table 4.6 *Shaft-smoothers and their dimensions from Federmessergruppen sites. Objects marked with * are decorated.*

2010a), and strongly support the view that arch-backed points indeed were arrowheads while large tanged points served as tips for atlatl-propelled darts.

From an archaeological point of view it is also very likely that arch-backed points served as armatures for arrows. Use-wear studies on all point forms at the Belgian site of Rekem, dated by AMS radiocarbon date on hafting residue to 11,350±150 (OxA-942, no $\partial^{13}C$ given) has revealed hafting as well as micro- and macro-wear indicating projectile function (Caspar and De Bie, 1996). Intriguingly, none of the larger (>12mm) pointed backed forms – there are no large tanged points in the Rekem assemblage – showed traces of projectile use, and may better be seen as preforms or handheld knives. Elsewhere in Federmesser contexts, sandstone shaft-smoothers are occasionally preserved (Bolus, 2012; Rozoy and Escalon de Fonton,

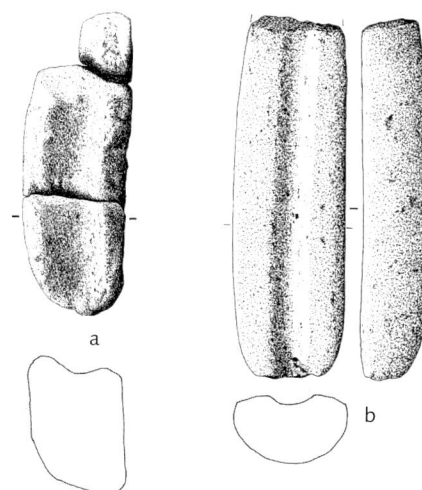

Figure 4.12 *Examples of (a, Golßen) wide- and (b, Rekem) narrow-grooved shaft-smoothers from Federmessergruppen contexts. After Bolus (2012).*

1978), at times even decorated (Loftus, 1982). This often overlooked object type served as an auxiliary tool in the manufacture of arrow- and dart-shafts. The working end of these tools, the groove, thus reflects the outline of the intended shafts size. Although sample size is small (Table 4.6), the dimensions of these grooves among Federmessergruppen shaft-smoothers are again suggestive of two shaft types, one narrower for arrows, one wider for harpoons tipped with organic barbed points and/or darts tipped with large tanged points (Fig. 4.12).

Given the occurrence of large tanged points in Upper Magdalenian contexts in France (de Sonneville-Bordes, 1969), they likely emerged there as supplementary weapon used alongside the bow-and-arrow. With regard to the French sites, de Sonneville-Bordes (1969) noted that reindeer dominated the fauna whenever large tanged points were found. However, 'Teyjat points' usually constitute a minority of armatures at these sites, so linking them mechanistically to dominant or even just common game animals seems unwarranted. Instead, it is possible that arch-backed points were part of the arsenal specifically directed at reindeer (cf. Thévenin, 1997), although the later dominance of arch-backed points in the Rhineland and northern France alongside diverse faunal communities where *Rangifer* at best constituted a minority component again belies such direct linkages. For southern Scandinavia, Bokelmann (1978) suggested that the occurrence of large tanged points correlates with a shift away from the hunting of herd animals such as reindeer towards the hunting of solitary prey such as the elk (*Alces alces*) and giant deer (*Megaloceros giganteus*). Indeed, these larger and heavier projectiles may have been particularly well-suited to the hunting of these large cervids (Tomka, 2013). Finally, Thissen (1995) has suggested that large tanged points may have been part of lances or darts used primarily against marine mammals. Ethnographically, there is some support for the idea that darts were the weapon of choice for kayak-based hunting (cf. Maschner and Mason, 2013) and some indeed want to see the later Bromme culture with its dominance of large tanged points as an eminently marine

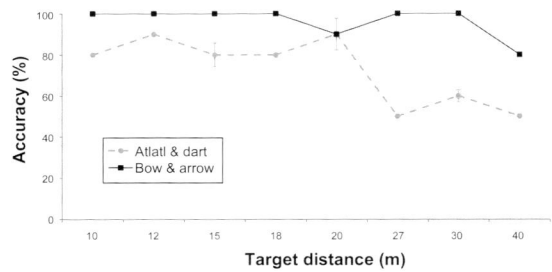

Figure 4.13 *A comparison of the averaged shooting accuracy for bows and spear-throwers delivered by practiced participants during four competitions held in Ramioul (Belgium) and Neuwied (Germany) in the 1990s (Stodiek, 1993).*

adapted phenomenon (Fischer, 2012; Fischer et al., 2013b). Many if not all coastal sites from the Late Glacial are now lost to marine erosion or are deeply buried under sediment following post-glacial sea level rise. Yet, given the early appearance of large tanged points at sites far inland and the absence of any evidence pointing towards complex watercraft (Glørstad, 2013) makes it unlikely that these armatures were designed, from the outset at least, as parts of marine hunting implements.

It is certainly possible that there were regional or chronological differences in hunting strategies and thus in the use of different weapons. It is also possible, however, that the increasing number of Federmessergruppen sites with large tanged points towards the north relates to the different raw material requirements of bows versus atlatls. As shown by, for instance, the classic comparative analysis of Oswalt (1972, 1976), the latter are demonstrably simpler in terms of the components and raw materials required to build a fully efficient tool: the spear-thrower/dart ensemble consists of an average of 5.3 (N= 3) components or techno-units, while the bow/arrow ensemble of an average of 10.8 (N= 25) components. Darts are also simpler with regard to the know-how required to build them, a point to which we will return in the following chapters. The increasingly sparse and low-growing vegetation of the northern regions alone may have led to an increasing reliance on the spear-thrower. By the same token, it should be noted that the bow-and-arrow is generally

Performance characteristic	Stabbing spear	Thrown spear	Atlatl & dart	Bow & arrow
Distance	0	1	1	1
Use in forested environment	1	1	1	1
Variety of positions	0	0	0	1
Motion- and noiselessness	1	0	0	1
Rapid fire	1	0	0	1
Ease of transport	0	0	1	1
SUM_{advantages}	3	2	3	6
Use distances (m)	0	7.8±2.2	39.6±5.5	25.8±2.4

Table 4.7 *Comparison of the relative performance characteristics of different weapon systems, after Hughes (1998), and their respective use distances as known from the ethnographic record (Churchill, 1993).*

considered a superior weapon independently of what game is hunted and in what kind of environment (Table 4.7). Whilst more exacting to make, shooting fast and accurate with the bow-and-arrow is easier to learn as well as easier to execute repeatedly (see Bingham et al., 2013). Experimental evidence in fact suggests that there is a critical difference in efficiency between the bow-and-arrow and the atlatl-and-dart with regard to the kind of distances for which they, according to ethnographic sources, are used most frequently (Fig. 4.13). Although seemingly small, a difference in success margins of only 5-10% would over even short periods make significant differences to the overall hunting success, i.e. the number of calories acquired, and would so have significant adaptive implications (Riede et al., 2011b).

4.5 Federmessergruppen population dynamics

Shennan (2000: 821) has long argued that "the single most important factor in understanding culture change is population dynamics". These demographic dynamics take such a central role because they correlate with changing patterns of group size, density, and interaction, which in turn furnishes the social context for the production and transmission of cultural knowledge. Amongst hunter-gatherers, group size various according to fundamental ecological parameters such as primary net productiv-

ity (Binford, 2001; Kelly, 1995). Other proxies also predict forager population densities quite well. Morin (2008), for instance, has shown that there is a strong relationship between faunal diversity and high-latitude hunter-gatherer population density ethnographically, and has then used these data to model diachronic trends in population density in the Upper Palaeolithic.

Building on this approach, the faunal record for different regions of Europe during the Allerød can then similarly be used to provide point estimates of human population density in these areas. In order to extrapolate Late Glacial population densities, Figure 4.14 plots the relationship between ecosystem diversity measured as the number of large terrestrial mammal species (i.e. excluding micro-mammals such as mice, voles, rats, etc.) present and population density amongst 27 forager populations in North America. Open diamonds denote those groups living in cold and open landscapes, closed circles denote those at home in forested northern/temperate groups. The latter are probably a better analogue for the Late Glacial hunter-gatherers of the Allerød chronozone, although it is also worth noting that contemporaneous faunal communities at least do not have straightforward modern analogues (Aaris-Sørensen, 1995, 2009; see also Stewart and Lister, 2001). There is a strong correlation between mammalian species diversity and forager population density in this data set (r_s=0.62, p<0.002 for the whole data

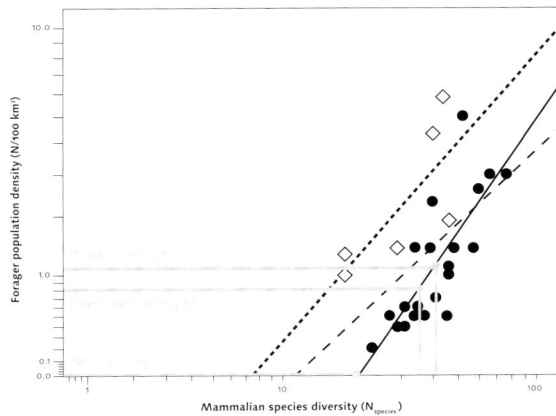

Figure 4.14 *Point estimates of population densities in relation to mammalian biodiversity for 27 recent foragers and selected areas of Late Glacial Europe, from Fahlke (2009).*

set; $r_s=0.82$, $p<0.001$ for cold/open country groups; $r_s=0.81$, $p<0.07$ for temperate grassland groups), which suggests that mammal diversity can be used to estimate forager population densities. Linear fit lines have been added for the whole dataset (wide stippled), the cold/open (narrow stippled) and temperate/ northern forested (solid line) groups, and past population density is found by intersecting the latter line with regional Late Glacial faunal diversity data. Ebbe H. Nielsen (2013) has recently presented such data for Switzerland, Baales et al. (2002) for the Middle Rhineland, and Aaris-Sørensen (2009) for southern Scandinavia. Fahlke (2009) provides a macro-regional overview. Such an extrapolation shows regional differences that almost certainly reflect latitudinal gradients coupled with the proximity to the retreating Alpine and Fennoscandian glaciers. It is worth stressing that the population density suggested for southern Scandinavia by this approach is effectively 0 underlining that forager population density in the Late Glacial of northernmost Europe may have been very low indeed.

Such low population densities are also reflected at the level of individual sites. Bokelmann et al. (1983) highlights the small size of Federmessergruppen sites on the North European Plain, and in comparing features of these settlement sites with a large comparative ethnographic material, Newell and Constandse-Westermann (1996) could not detect *any* definite aggregation camps (see also Hout-

sma et al., 1996). According to their analysis, virtually all Federmessergruppen sites on the North European Plain should rather be seen as short-term hunting or transition camps.

When it comes to site size and structure, there appear to have been definite regional differences. Central German sites, for instance, at least occasionally preserve intra-site spatial patterning suggestive of tent-like habitation structures (Gelhausen et al., 2004; Loew, 2006, 2009), and evidence for long-distance mobility and contact is more frequent than in the North. Such movement of both lithic raw materials and finished products, as well as decorative items such as perforated fossil shells, took place along the major river valleys of the Rhine, Rhone, Saone, and Meuse connecting south-eastern France via Switzerland and the Rhine with northern France and the Benelux region (Álvarez-Fernández, 2001; Crombé et al., 2011; Floss, 1987, 1994, 2000; Rensink, 2000).

To a lesser degree, lithic provenancing data can also be used to trace the tracks of Federmessergruppen expeditions onto the North European Plain towards southern Scandinavia (Riede, 2012b). It is interesting to note in this respect that although many sites of the Federmessergruppen are known in the Low Countries, the east Frisian part of northern Germany is curiously devoid of sites (Schwabedissen, 1954; Schwarz, 1995; Zylmann, 1933). This makes it more likely that settlement in the Netherlands was initiated and remained connected via the Rhine and Meuse valleys, whilst settlement along the River Elbe and in southern Scandinavia occurred via the central German Rivers Main, Fulda, Lahn, Schwalm, Eder, and Leine. Small sites along the Lower Rhine with raw material spectra clearly pointing towards Belgium and the Netherlands mark the former route (Heinen et al., 1996), and Federmessergruppen occupation is well-attested to in the complementary 'destinations' of these mobile foragers in the caves and open-air locales of Belgium and the Netherlands (De Bie and Vermeersch, 1998; Stapert, 2000, 2005). In contrast, traces of Late Glacial occupation in the region connecting the North European Plain with the more southerly upland in the

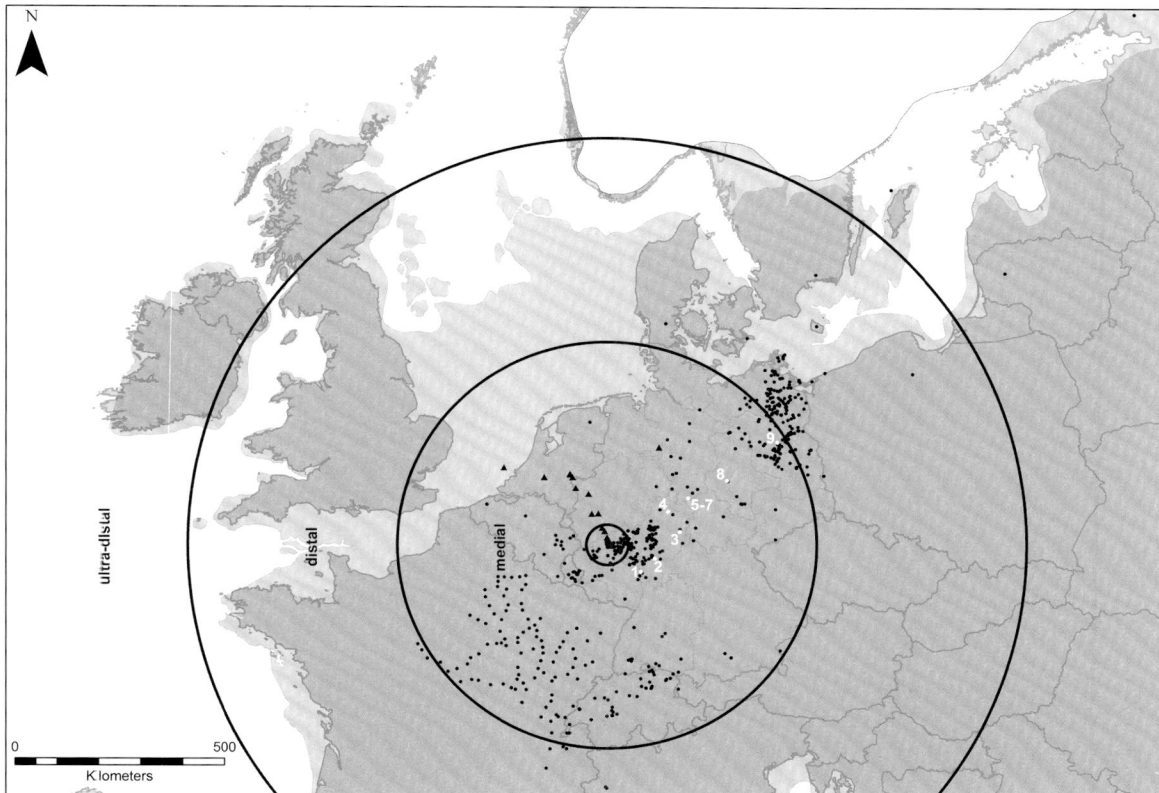

Figure 4.15 *The location of key Federmessergruppen sites connecting the Rhineland with the central part of the North European Plain in relation to the Laacher See tephra fallout and the hazard zonation. 1: Rüsselsheim 122; 2: Mühlheim-Dieteshei.m; 3: Rothenkrichen; 4: Dorla; 5-7: the Leine Bergland rock-shelters; 8: Weinberg Schadeleben; 9: Hennigsdorf. Country borders are shown as are the German Federal State borders. Small black dots= LST air-fall deposits; triangles= LST fluvial deposits marking the areas of downstream river flooding. The concentric circles mark the division into proximal, medial, distal, and ultra-distal sectors.*

southern part of the German Federal State Lower Saxony and, in particular, in Hesse are quite scarce (Fiedler, 1976, 1994; Grote, 1999a). Yet, some of the sites that are excavated there – Rüsselsheim LA122, Rothenkirchen, and a cluster of rock-shelter sites in the valley of the River Leine – can be lined up from the Rhineland to the central part of the North European Plain (Fig. 4.15). These sites provide important clues as to how they served as stepping-stones connecting these regions, and they provide important dating information as each of these sites is associated with Laacher See tephra. Notably, whenever Late Glacial archaeology is found in stratigraphic sequences that also contain LST in Hesse and adjacent regions of the Leine valley and of the Thuringian Basin, human occupation is overlain by Laacher See tephra (Riede, 2016).

All these sites contain different kinds of raw material at varying frequencies. The raw mate-

rials can be related to either specific sources, or to broader regions of origin that nonetheless indicate a direction of movement from whence or to where people were travelling. In addition the varying frequencies of these raw materials (Table 4.8) and the ways in which the different raw materials were used provide indications of the direction of movement. The rationale here is that higher-quality raw materials were used and curated for longer. Thus objects become reduced as groups move away from the source of the material.

The southernmost of these sites, Rüsselsheim LA122 was excavated in 1989 and has been presented extensively by Loew (2003, 2005, 2006, 2009) who interprets it to reflect a short-stay camp of a small group of Federmessergruppen foragers on their way from the north. This inference is supported by a lithic raw material spectrum that is rather diverse for such a small locale with, in all, 17 different raw

Locale	Lat	Long	Stratigraphy	Raw materials present			Comments and references
				Lydite	Baltic flint	Others	
Mecklenburg-W Pomerania							
Endingen	54.25	12.90					Humanly modified horse and giant deer remains ^{14}C-dated to pre-LSE (Kaiser, et al. 1999); LST found nearby (Lane, et al., 2012)
Lower Saxony							
Weitsche*	53.02	11.13			XXX		^{14}C-dated to pre-LSE; amber art objects (Veil, et al., 2012)
Bettenroder Berg IX*	51.46	10.01	FMG|LST| no occupation	X	XX	X	Grote (1994)
Bettenroder Berg I*	51.46	10.01	FMG|LST| no occupation	XX	XX		Grote (1994)
Hesse							
Külte	51.40	9.07		x	x		
Kirchbauna	51.24	9.43		x			Arch-backed point
Dorla	51.17	9.32					Human skull fragment found in (unspecified) association with sediments containing LST
Römersberg	51.03	9.21					
Herbelhausen	51.00	8.98		x			
Gilsa	51.00	9.16					
Reutersruh*	50.93	9.25			x		Luttrop and Bosinski (1971)
Oberrosphe	50.91	8.78		x			
Rauschenberg	50.88	8.92					
Friedensdorf	50.86	8.56		x			
Bürgeln	50.86	8.82					
Neustadt	50.85	9.11					
Anzefahr	50.85	8.86			x		Arch-backed point
Bodes	50.81	9.74		x	x	x	
Mengshausen	50.79	9.62					
Niederjossa	50.78	9.57					
Rhina	50.76	9.68		x			Arch-backed point
Rothenkirchen*	50.73	9.71	FMG|LST| no occupation	XXX	X	X	Hofbauer (1992)
Holzheim	50.49	8.72			x	x	Broken arch-backed point on Baltic flint

Marjoß	50.26	9.51					
Aufenau/ Brückenau	50.25	9.32					
Mittel-Gründau	50.23	9.11					
Breitenborn	50.20	9.10					
Bruchköbel	50.18	8.92					
Mühlheim-Dietesheim*	50.12	8.88	FMG|LST| no occupation	XXX	X	XX	Fruth (1994)
Klein-Welzheim	50.04	9.01		x			
Rüsselsheim 122*	49.99	8.42	FMG|LST| no occupation	XXX	X	XX	Loew (2006a)
Trebur	49.93	8.41				x	Arch-backed point
Wahlen	49.61	8.86		x		x	
Saxony-Anhalt							
Aschersleben*	51.83	11.37	FMG|LST| no occupation		x		Toepfer (1965)
Thuringia							
Abri Fuchskirche*	50.65	11.16		x	x	x	¹⁴C-dated to pre-LSE (Küssner, 2009; Feustel and Musil, 1977)

Table 4.8 *The occurrence of lydite and Baltic flint in mid-field assemblages from Hesse, ordered from N (top) to S (bottom). Relevant locales from Mecklenburg-Western Pomerania, Lower Saxony, Saxony-Anhalt and Thuringia are also shown. Sites marked with * are excavated, all others are surface finds, and are listed (unless specified otherwise) by Fiedler (1994). FMG= Federmessergruppen, LSE= Laacher See eruption; LST= Laacher See tephra; X= present, XX= common, XXX= dominant; x= present, but proportions not known; | indicates stratigraphic separation*

materials represented. Of these, one third is the locally occurring black lydite, which while abundant is only moderately workable and occurs in rather small nodules. Notably, only few projectile points are made from this material, although other tools such as scrapers, burins and less formally modified forms are well represented. A further three raw materials (quartzite, hornstein and diorite) are also local and occur in only small amounts. Some of the raw materials present at the site point towards procurement expeditions reaching a distance of some 30km to the east. Chalcedony and a green Tertiary quartzite derive from these sources – very close to, interestingly, another Federmessergruppen site that dates to before the LSE, Mühlheim-Dietesheim (Fruth, 1979; Fruth, 1994). Of the remaining raw materials, three provide insights into the ranging mobility of this group. There are two types of

vulcanite that occur nearest to the site in the Taunus Mountains to the north, or the Eifel region to the east. In addition, various types of flint also point towards connections to the north and west. While Baltic flint is unspecific in its occurrence north of 51° N, flint from the Meuse gravels directly links this site to the Lower Rhine settlement in Belgium and the Netherlands. Importantly, this raw material spectrum has clear parallels in the larger sites of the Central Rhineland, which in turn also have links to the south and west through the major river valleys (Baales, 2001, 2002a; Baales et al., 1998; Floss, 2000, 2002).

The tools made from the exogenous raw materials were all highly reduced, suggesting that they were part of the initial inventory brought to the site. Furthermore, the topography of the main river courses would have guided foragers not directly northwards from Rüsselsheim, but rather along the River Main and up the River Rhine. Interestingly, too, sites of Federmessergruppen character are absent in the valley of the River Lahn (Terberger, 1993), but not in the other larger river valleys in Hesse, albeit mostly as surface finds (Fiedler, 1994). In combination these features suggest a modest recasting of Loew's original interpretation. It seems most likely that the group resting at Rüsselsheim came from the Eifel region fully equipped with a tool-kit made from the diverse raw materials for which the Eifel sites were major nodes. The site of Mühlheim-Dietesheim perhaps served as an even more temporary camp for the procurement of raw material sources in its vicinity before moving northwards. The site of Rothenkirchen, excavated in 1984 and 1985, in the northern part of Hesse represents the settlement of people returning from the north (Fiedler, 1976; Hofbauer, 1992). Here, the raw material spectrum includes black lydite, hornstein, quartzite, radiolarite, as well as Baltic flint in frequencies that differ significantly from those at Rüsselsheim. Black lydite dominates and is again the raw material that is present locally in greatest abundance. Hornstein, quartzite and radiolarite are also local, although the very minor occurrence of these raw materials and the observation that they occur almost exclusively in the form of finished tools may indicate that these were brought to the site as part of the travelling tool-kit (cf. Richter, 1990). Baltic flint occurs also mainly in the form of tools or as burin spalls. It is a significantly better raw material for flint-working, being both easier to knap and producing finer edges than the local lydite. Its low frequency thus points towards a direct import of this raw material from the north. Although Hofbauer (1992) placed this site into the very late part of the Allerød or the Younger Dryas, this assessment has been shown to be erroneous by a recent tephrochronological re-analysis (Riede, 2012b), which has provided results more consistent with a pre-LSE date for the site.

Definitely dating to before the Laacher See event are the Federmessergruppen sites in the rock-shelters along the River Leine near Göttingen in the very southern part of Lower Saxony. Here, Grote (1988, 1990, 1994, 1999b; 1982) has prospected and excavated several small concentrations of Late Glacial occupation, all of which are capped by layers of primary LST that are up to 40cm thick (Ahl and Meyer, 1994). At two of these sites, the raw material spectrum – consisting of only Baltic flint and black lydite – likewise provides pointers to both the north, in the form of the former, and the south in the form of the latter. The differing frequencies at these two sites may indicate different occupation lengths, although the generally small size and relative lack of diversity in all these Federmessergruppen inventories points, following Richter (1990), strongly to only short and ephemeral occupations by small groups that possibly attempted to cross the raw material-sparse regions of modern-day Hesse and southern Lower Saxony as swiftly as possible.

What may have drawn them northwards? While the general warming and increasing stabilisation of landscapes and vegetation during the Allerød was doubtlessly an enabling factor of such an expansion, I believe that the occasional and on the whole ephemeral occupation of the North European Plain by Federmessergruppen was motivated, at least initially, as much by the search for rare and specific raw materials. Baltic flint may have been one of these resources, but amber would likely have been more valuable, as would the antlers and other parts of large cervids such as elk, reindeer and giant deer that were becoming increasingly rare – extinct even – in Central Europe at this time, but were becoming abundant in the north (Fahlke, 2009; Riede et al., 2010). The early Allerød dates for the Weitsche site that has yielded several art objects made of amber (Veil et al., 2012), and the hunting episodes of giant deer and horse at Endingen (Kaiser et al., 1999; Street, 1996; Terberger et al., 1996) and of giant deer at Lüdersdorf (Bratlund, 1993), likewise dating to the first part of the Allerød chronozone, reflect such targeted exploitation of specific resources in the context of a complex economy where, following the costly-signalling theory of Zahavi and Zahavi (1997), both calories as well as prestige could ultimately be converted into reproductive payoffs (Plourde, 2008).

4.6 Federmessergruppen material culture diversity and settlement in southern Scandinavia

With its roots in the Upper Magdalenian, the Federmessergruppen emerged out of a tradition of complex and diverse material culture (e.g. de Sonneville-Bordes, 1963) in both the lithic and organic parts of the repertoire. At the same time, the Federmessergruppen, together with its southern counterpart the Azilian was also partaking in a general trend – the so-called 'azilianisation' – towards less complex and more straightforward lithic production sequences that resulted in an overall much more generic flint-working technology (Chollet et al., 1999; De Bie, 1999; Loew, 2005; Valentin, 2008; Valentin et al., 2004). In this, the spatially extensive homogeneity of material culture is maintained, and "regional differences are reduced and may to a certain degree be related to raw material constraints" (De Bie and Vermeersch, 1998: 37).

In his classic treatise on the northern European Federmessergruppen material Schwabedissen (1954) identified three regional/chronological sub-divisions, a western Tjonger group, an early Rissener group and a later Wehlener group, where the latter two were also thought to differ slightly in the occurrence and frequency of certain tool types. The Rissener group should, according to Schwabedissen, contain large tanged points, while the Wehlener group should contain the eponymous Wehlener scrapers, which are equipped with invasive tang-forming retouch. Later work, however, has expressed doubts in relation to the validity of these groupings without being able to propose alternative finer-grained classifications (Houtsma et al., 1996; Ikinger, 1998). The variability in the lithic repertoire of the Federmessergruppen thus appears mute in terms of spatially or chronologically subdividing this technocomplex.

With this repertoire (see Fig. 4.16), the Federmessergruppen entered the North European Plain along two routes – a western route into Belgium and the Netherlands – and an eastern route into the Thuringian Basin (Küssner, 2007, 2010) and Lusatia (Pasda, 2002,

2007; Vollbrecht, 2005), and further into Lower Saxony, Schleswig-Holstein, and eventually southern Scandinavia. The Federmessergruppen settlement in the latter region, at the very edge of the Late Glacial human world, is so ephemeral that some older culture-historical schemes ignore it outright. Some small but regular sites (Slotseng B and D – Holm, 1991, 1996), the occasional atelier or workshop site (Egtved – Fischer, 1988) as well as a diffuse spread of single finds (Fischer, 1991; Madsen, 1983) do attest to the presence of these foragers in southern Scandinavia. In fact, an off-site perspective that concentrates not only on sites, but includes also the changing frequencies of single finds in between denser settlement regions and actual sites may be best suited for understanding the Federmessergruppen settlement in the region (Riede et al., 2011a). In his seminal work on off-site archaeology, Foley (1981: 163) suggested that "the archaeological record of mobile peoples should be viewed not as a system of structured sites, but as a pattern of continuous artifact distribution and density...information on land use patterns may in some cases be better obtained through the study of non-discrete artifact distributions in specific zones than from orthodox site distributions". Especially, if the culture-historical 'corrective' of Chapter 1 is accepted, and large tanged points together with the tanged Wehlener scrapers and small thumbnail scrapers are seen as indicative of a Federmessergruppen settlement rather than that of the Bromme culture, the visibility of this pioneering technocomplex becomes somewhat higher. Along the Jutland Ridge running from Schleswig-Holstein to the northern tip of Denmark, for instance, Federmessergruppen material is often hidden in amateur collections or remains in private possession. Much of this material is only known from surface collections, making it very hard to conclusively decide whether it reflects one or several occupation episodes by one or several technocomplexes. Given the now common co-occurrence of these artifact types together in Federmessergruppen assemblages, it is increasingly likely that these surface collections are in fact exemplars of important and "per-

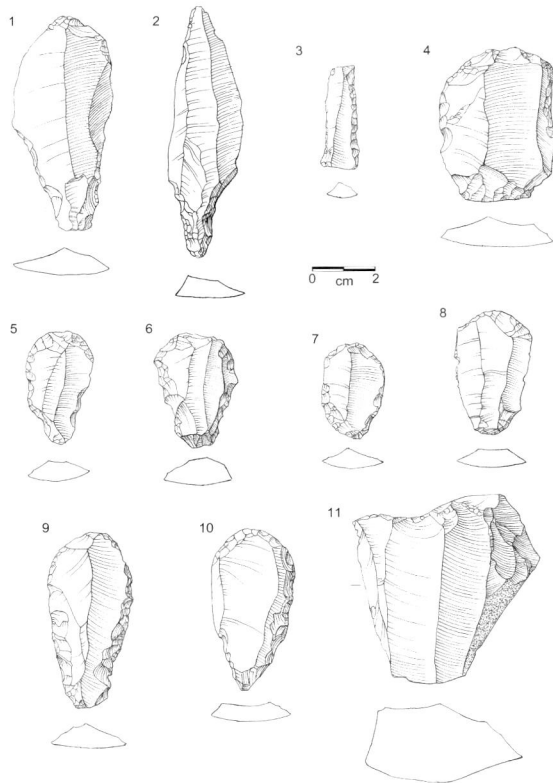

Figure 4.16 *Characteristic artefact assemblage containing arch-backed and large tanged points, Wehlener scrapers, and small scrapers. 1: Damaged large tanged point; 2: Large tanged point; 3: Medial fragment of an arch-backed point; 4: Scraper made on a thick blade-like flake; 5-7: Short flake-scrapers with lateral retouch (Wehlen scrapers); 8: Blade-scraper without lateral retouch; 9-10: Blade-scrapers with lateral retouch (Wehlen scrapers); 11: Unidirectional core with minimal platform preparation. Object 1 is from HBV 185 Gamst Søenge, the remainder from HBV 189 Rolykkevej, both located close to Lake Dollerup in southern Jutland.*

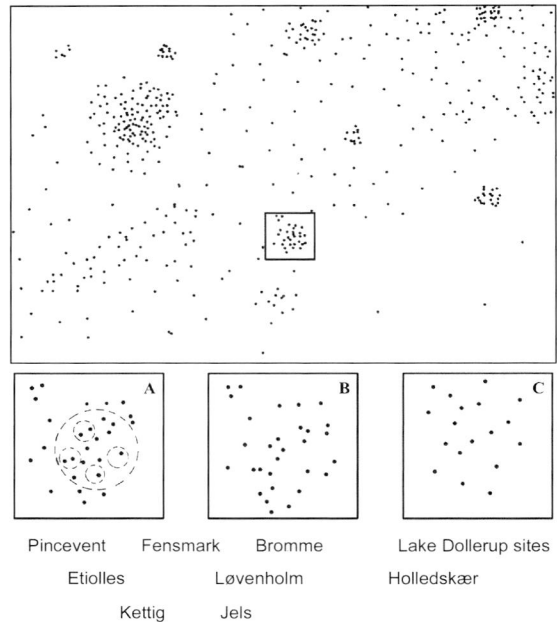

Figure 4.17 *On/off-site schematic – originally presented by Foley (1981) – for the distribution of finds and sites in the landscape and a rough classification of some Allerød-age Late Glacial sites along this continuum. For further discussion of this approach see Riede et al. (2011a).*

sistent places" (Barton et al., 1995: 81) along the site<>single-find continuum (Fig. 4.17). It is even possible that variation in positioning of these sites either on higher ground much like Hamburgian sites (e.g. Slotseng B/D), or close to lake edges in lower elevations much like Bromme or indeed much later Preboreal and Boreal Mesolithic sites (e.g. the locales around Lake Dollerup), hints at differentiated land-use that varied with similarly differentiated economic activities (i.e. reindeer vs. elk/giant deer or beaver hunting and/or fishing). Although not associated with any diagnostic flint material the humanly modified reindeer remains from Nørre Lyngby (cut-marked rib, AAR-1511: 11,570±110, $\partial^{13}C$ (‰)= -17.9) in the

very north of Denmark, and bones and antler from Hasselberga (LuA-4492: 11,300±140, cut-marked antler, Ua-3296: 11,390±90, no $\partial^{13}C$ provided) in southern Sweden may hint at the presence of Federmessergruppen in these remote corners, perhaps specifically for the hunting of these ever more elusive ungulates. The majority of Federmessergruppen sites as well as single finds seem to be tethered to the Jutland Ridge on the Danish mainland and along a north-south transect across Zealand (Eriksen, 1999).

In summary, a picture emerges of Federmessergruppen settlement in southern Scandinavia that is pioneering, most likely seasonal in nature, and ephemeral at best. Actual sites range from small to miniscule, but – in contrast to the preceding Hamburgian – single finds of both arch-backed points as well as the less diagnostic (but much more abundant large tanged points) also speak of human presence in the wider landscape at this time. The Danish Federmessergruppen sites do not contain any evidence of 'exotic' or non-utilitarian items – fossil shells, deer tooth pendants or the like – that could be used to link these sites into the wider networks of trade and mobility of that time, but the presence of amber pieces at the northern German site of Klein Nordende A (Bokelmann et al., 1983) does provide at least some evidence of such connections. Interestingly, Baltic amber only occurs in a few other sites of the Upper Magdalenian/Late Palaeolithic in northern Europe: Gough's and Robin Hood Caves on the British Isles, Weitsche in northern Germany, Champreveyres and Moosbühl in Switzerland, and Les Romains in eastern France (Álvarez-Fernández, 2001; Burdukiewicz, 1999, 2009; Rottländer, 1973; Veil and Breest, 2006; Veil et al., 2012). Federmessergruppen occupation in southern Scandinavia may have been motivated primarily by the exploitation of genuinely valuable resources such as amber, which with its combination of beauty and rarity very likely carried intrinsic cosmological and hence ritual significance. It is ultimately impossible to trace the exact routes of these objects, but they – together with lithic raw material studies – nonetheless attest to the spatially extensive and expansive settlement of the Federmessergruppen in northern Europe (Riede, 2014b). The halting but still progressing landscape development during the Allerød chronozone made it possible for small groups to enter onto the North European Plain. The very early dates for this expansion signal perhaps that competition and social status differentiation may have been pronounced amongst Upper Magdalenian groups (cf. Vanhaeren and d'Errico, 2005), which in part drove the expansion process (Schwendler, 2012).

While we often wonder in awe at the kinds of long-distance networks evidently maintained by Upper Magdalenian hunter-gatherers, it is also worth remembering that the evidence for such exchange activity declined towards the end of the Allerød (Álvarez-Fernández, 2001; Álvarez-Fernández, 2009), and that pioneering societies are more vulnerable to unexpected disturbances – disasters – due to their "pristine vulnerability" (Alexander, 2000: 17). In addition, the Intra-Allerød Cold Period, also known as the Gerzensee Oscillation or Greenland Interstadial 1b (Lehman and Keigwin, 1992; Schaub et al., 2008), began around 13,274 calendar years BP and may have stressed especially more northerly oriented groups considerably. For nearly 300 years average temperatures were lower by 1-2° C, which – if the earlier established relationship between mean annual temperature and forager population densities is accepted – would have resulted in lowered population densities across northern Europe. GI-1b ended around 12,989 calendar years BP and temperatures began to rise again. But right at the end of this cold phase (van Raden et al., 2013) – well documented in climatic and environmental proxies across the North Atlantic (Lowe et al., 2008) – Europe was rocked by an event that was unusual in the extreme and impossible to predict: the Laacher See eruption.

Chapter 5

The progression of vulnerability and the impact of the Laacher See eruption

5.1 Introduction

Chapter 3 ended with a summary of what we know about the Laacher See volcanic eruption, its impact on weather and climate, and the distribution of its fallout. In reviewing the Federmessergruppen settlement of southern Scandinavia and its connections, both social and demographic, to the more densely settled core regions of the Central Rhineland, eastern and northern France as well as Switzerland, Chapter 4 has set the scene for bringing together these disparate insights in an investigation of past vulnerability. The present chapter, then, is a case-study instantiation of some of the ways in which a specific volcanic eruption impacted flora, fauna, and people. In particular, this chapter recapitulates definitions of disaster and hazard and attempts to investigate *causality* in the way the Laacher See eruption affected past communities in the near- and far-field through first examining the specific hazards that followed with the eruption and by then placing these agents of impact in Wisner and colleagues' (2004) Pressure-and-Release and Access Models. Although many alternative models of vulnerability and impact exist (e.g. Birkmann et al., 2013; Cutter, 1996; Fuchs et al., 2012; Hufschmidt, 2011), the advantage of employing the model of Wisner and colleagues is that it is: a) well-established, thus providing an extensive body of case studies for comparison, and that: b) it draws specific attention to both physical geographic, hazard-intrinsic geological, as well as social parameters.

5.2 Disaster defined

Disasters are totalising events (sensu Oliver-Smith, 1998) that often affect and disrupt every part of the social routine, and encompass entire communities – all ages, all social strata and all social groupings – as well as all aspects of the affected environment. There is, however, considerable debate about exactly how to define such events (Oliver-Smith, 1998, 1999; Quarantelli, 1995, 1998), and misunderstandings abound (e.g. Alexander, 2007; Clarke, 2003). Specifically in relation to past disasters, the catastrophist assumption of gloom, doom, death, and of simplistic cause-and-effect patterns continues to hold a powerful sway over historical and archaeological disaster studies (cf. Gräslund and Price, 2012). Arguing against such misguided and misguiding views from a specifically anthropological vantage, Oliver-Smith and Hoffman (2002: 4) offer a definition of disaster as:

> *a process/event combining a potentially destructive agent/force from the natural, modified, or built environment and a population in a socially and economically produced condition of vulnerability, resulting in a perceived disruption of the customary relative satisfactions of individual and social needs for physical survival, social order, and meaning.*

This succinct definition reflects the general consensus that natural disasters are ultimately social phenomena causally related, often in complex ways, to natural hazards. Oliver-

THE PROGRESSION OF VULNERABILITY

ROOT CAUSES

Limited access to
- Power
- Structures
- Resources

Ideologies
- Political systems
- Economic systems

DYNAMIC PRESSURES

Lack of
- Local institutions
- Training
- Appropriate skills
- Local investments
- Local markets
- Press freedom
- Ethical standards in public life

Macro-forces
- Rapid population change
- Rapid urbanisation
- Arms expenditure
- Debt repayment schedules
- Deforestation
- Decline in soil productivity

UNSAFE CONDITIONS

Physical environment
- Dangerous locations
- Unprotected buildings and infrastructure

Local economy
- Livelihoods at risk
- Low income levels

Social relations
- Special groups at risk
- Lack of local institutions

Public actions and institutions
- Lack of disaster preparedness
- Prevalence of endemic disease

DISASTER

This area magnified is the focus of the Access Model (see Fig. 5.2)

RISK=
Hazard x Vulnerability

R=HxV

HAZARDS

Earthquake

Highwinds (cyclone/ hurricane/ typhoon)

Flooding

Volcanic eruption

Landslide

Drought

Virus and pests

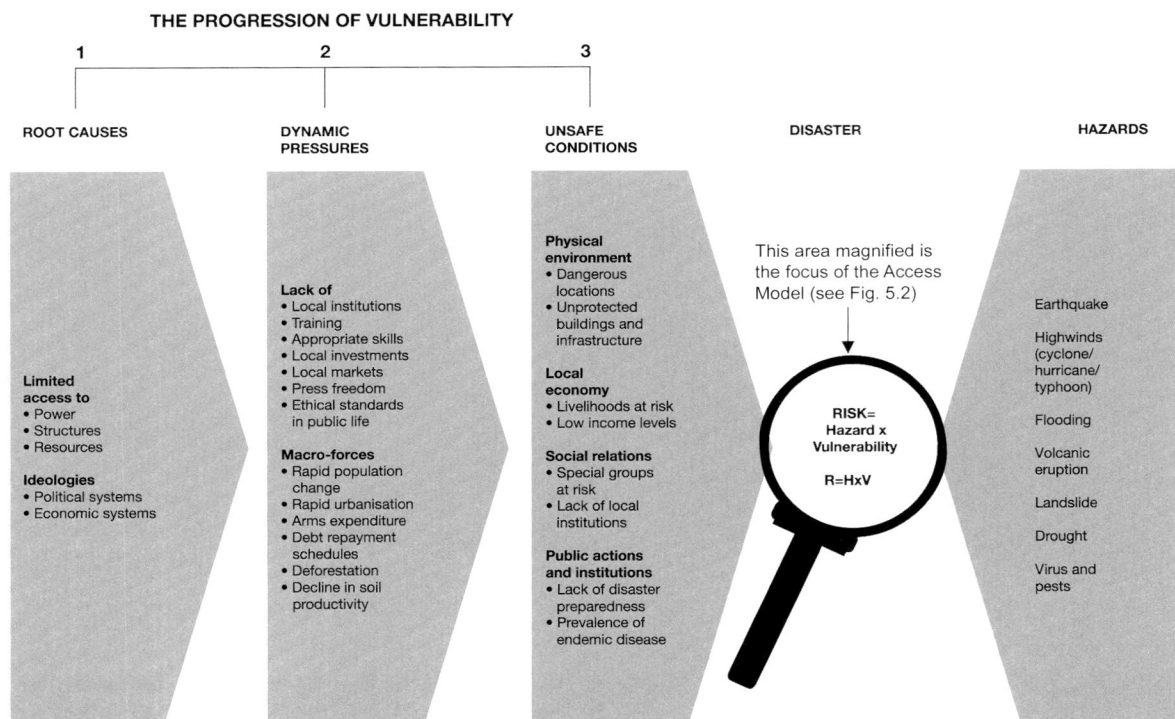

Figure 5.1 *The Pressure-and-Release (PAR) Model of Wisner and colleagues (2004) in its original and generic formulation.*

Smith and Hoffman (2002: 4) also offer a complementary definition of hazard:

the forces, conditions, or technologies that carry a potential for social, infrastructural, or environmental damage... The issue of hazard further incorporates the way a society perceives the danger or dangers, either environmental and/ or technological, that it faces and the ways it allows the danger to enter its calculation of risk.

This chapter focuses on a specific event, the Laacher See eruption some 13,000 years ago and its interaction with on-going climatic and environmental trends, and then proceeds to examine the event's relationship to contemporaneous human communities. The eruption event resulted in a series of hazards of variable spatial scale and temporal duration that acted on communities at different distances of the eruptive centre. Drawing on a broad comparative database of other eruptions and their impacts on ecologies and societies in the recent and deep past, this chapter examines in detail the forces and actions of these hazard agents. In order to facilitate such an

assessment, the fragmentary yet remarkable information available about the Laacher See eruption, its effects, and those communities it affected are here placed within the so-called Pressure-and-Release Model (PAR) of Wisner et al. (2004). This schematic model (Fig. 5.1) consists of four broad components:

1. The hazardous event and its attendant hazard agents.
2. The unsafe conditions intrinsic to local conditions (e.g. economy, ecology, political trends, social tensions, etc.) at the time of the event.
3. The dynamic pressures of on-going processes of social or environmental change.
4. The root causes of deeply entrenched elements of the social fabric amongst the affected communities that make them vulnerable in the first place.

According to Wisner and colleagues (2004: 87) there is a flow or "progression of vulnerability" from the quotidian – but crucial – root causes that are embedded in everyday life to the dynamic pressures that more generally

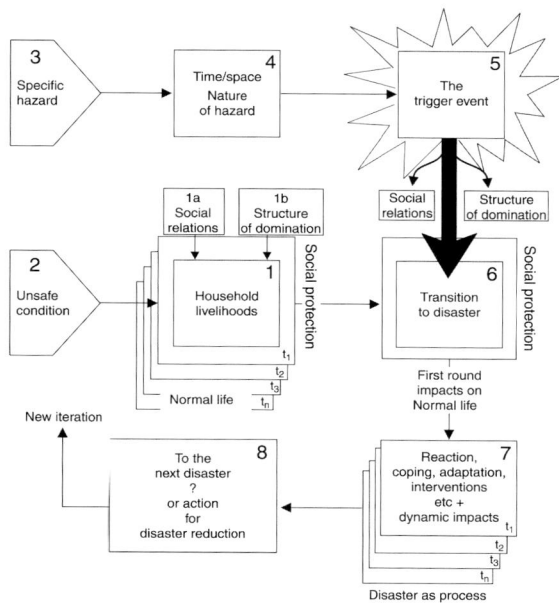

Figure 5.2 *The Access Model that links domestic house-hold-level processes to the impact of disaster. From Wisner et al. (2004).*

affect communities or groups, which in turn generate quite specific unsafe conditions. In the interaction with the hazard event, the vulnerability that has thus progressed crystalizes outwardly and becomes visible as damage, impact, and culture change. The details of this interaction are further analysed using their 'Access Model' (Fig. 5.2) as a guideline, where the specific damages and rearrangements of social ties and entitlements at the household level and at different temporalities are investigated (Table 5.1). The Access Model focuses on the impact of a given hazard on current

and future livelihoods, which is defined as "the command an individual, family or other social group has over...bundles of resources that can be used or exchanged to satisfy its needs. This may involve information, cultural knowledge, social networks and legal rights as well as tools, land or other physical resources" (Wisner et al., 2004: 12).

In combination, the schemata of Wisner and colleagues mirrors similar attempts at providing a vocabulary and taxonomy of hazards and effects by, for instance, Shimoyama (2002). Arguably, the archaeological data at hand may, in their lamentable coarseness, be better suited to more overarching examinations of unsafe conditions, dynamic pressures, and root causes, but the detailed demands of the Access Model remind us to consider individual decision making (i.e. agency) and the production of disaster at the level of families or communities which, if and when successful, yields remarkable archaeological dividends (e.g. Plunket and Uruñuela, 2000, 2008; Sheets, 2002; Sheets, 2011). Likewise, it is here at the individual and household level that salient behavioural and material culture variation and adaptation are generated and transmitted, even though we at times can study only the cumulative and collective outcomes of these myriad actions. Both simpler and more complex models for vulnerability assessment do exist (e.g. Birkmann et al., 2013; Turner et al., 2003), but the PAR Model offers the advantage of being widely used (e.g. Rauken and Kelman, 2010) and of arguably striking a balance between being

Component of the access framework	Typical time period of change after disaster
Class relations	Months-years
Change in political regime	Weeks-years
Household access profile	Immediate/weeks/months
Income opportunities	Immediate-months
Household budget	Immediate-months
Structures of domination	Immediate-years

Table 5.1 *The temporalities of disaster impact in sociological perspective. Note the relatively short chronological horizon of this perspective and its focus on socio-political mechanisms. The archaeological perspective developed here and elsewhere (Riede, 2015) complements this list with a long-term perspective and a greater emphasis on how ecological drivers also affect household access dynamics.*

Figure 5.3 *Near-field Laacher See tephra thicknesses (log cm) in relation to distance from vent (km), based on N= 56 data-points.*

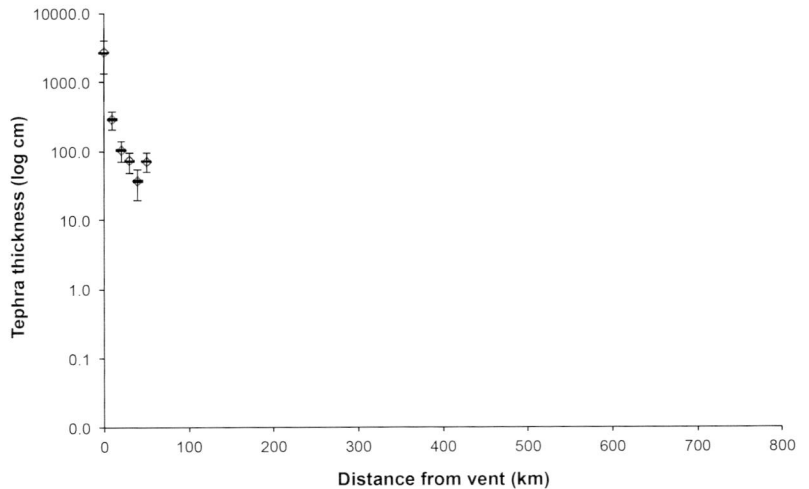

sufficiently detailed for an ambitious and illuminating analysis of a given disaster, yet being neither too detailed nor too data-demanding as to be inapplicable in past disaster science.

5.3 Near-field hazards

As seen in Chapter 3, explosive volcanic activity generates a large number of near-field hazards: tephra fall, poisonous gases, pyroclastic flows and base surges, primary and secondary lahars, mudflows, and flooding, earthquakes, as well as tsunamis. The Laacher See volcano is a good example of all of these hazards if the category 'tsunami' is expanded to include the kind of river flood wave that was the result of the catastrophic dam burst that drained the temporary lake, which formed during the eruption (Litt et al., 2003; Schmincke et al., 1999). Deposits close to the vent reach thicknesses of >50m, which then decrease to c. 10m, 5km from the eruptive centre, and to 4m around the eastern end of the Neuwied Basin. At the somewhat arbitrary cut-off point of 50km distance-from-vent, LST deposits still regularly reached thicknesses of >1m (Fig. 5.3). Tephra compacts easily and given that Thorarinsson (1958), for instance, has calculated that tephra layers 700 years old will have compacted to about 1/3 their original thickness, these recorded tephra blanket thicknesses should (barring secondary accumulation) be seen as minima. In addition,

the dammed lake that formed during the eruption further contributed to altering the near-field landscape in a major way.

The Neuwied Basin around the eruptive centre no doubt was a major settlement hub in northern Europe during the Late Glacial. Its location along the River Rhine and close to the confluence of several major tributaries made the area an important gateway between central and peripheral settlement areas. However, interestingly, recent efforts at refining the chronology of key settlement sites in this region demonstrate that there most likely was a hiatus between the initial and very rich Magdalenian occupation at Andernach-Martinsberg and the later rather more modest remains of the Federmessergruppen (Stevens et al., 2009). [14]C dates for the latter occupation begin before the onset of the Allerød chronozone and span most of its earlier part. They are most probably associated with at least one early and one late occupation episode (Kegler, 2002; Veil, 1982). An early and possibly fairly substantial Allerød human presence in the area is underlined by the otherwise rare burial finds from Bonn-Oberkassel and Irlich, both of which date to around 14,000 cal BP (Bronk Ramsey et al., 2015b; Street et al., 2006).

Although numerous older reports claim to have discovered the remains of human victims killed by the Laacher See eruption and covered by its deposits (Flohr et al., 2004; Schröter, 1998), subsequent research has not been able

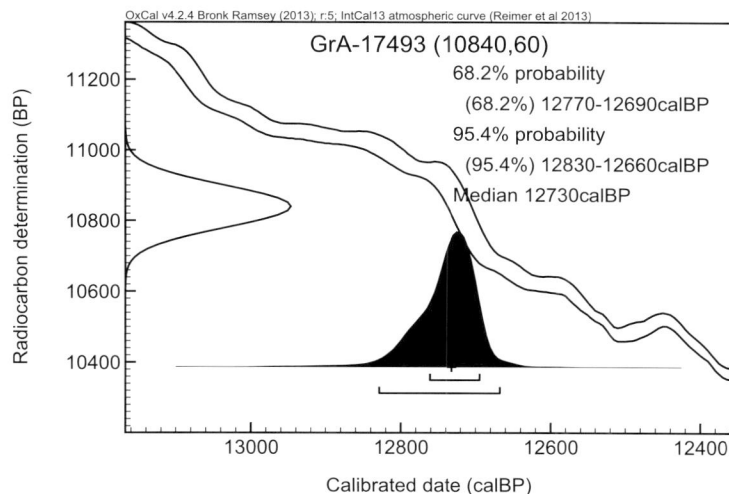

Figure 5.4 *The posterior probability distribution of the most reliable ¹⁴C date from Bad Breisig, calibrated with the OxCal package.*

to verify any of these (Street et al., 2006). Litt and colleagues (2003: 26) thus suggest that "most likely, humans and animals were warned by numerous precursory earthquakes, and left the area", although the presence of at least some animals (capercaillie, brown bear, red deer, and horse) during the eruption is documented by the discovery of their tracks (Baales and von Berg, 1997; von Berg, 1994b). One can also wonder whether people, in the absence of modern seismic measuring equipment and without experience of explosive volcanism in the region, were able to accurately pinpoint the source and cause of such tremors.

In considering the impact of the LSE it is interesting to note that one site, Bad Breisig, close (c. 14km) to the vent on the northern periphery of the affected area and on top of primary and reworked (fluvially transported) Laacher See deposits, is known (Baales and Jöris, 2001, 2002; Grimm, 2004; Waldmann et al., 2001). While this site attests to the presence of Late Glacial foragers in the region some time after the LSE, it may not signal a re-colonisation per se. Ecosystem recovery studies on more recent eruptions indicate that the re-colonisation of volcanic deposits by pioneer species can proceed at a fairly swift pace (Dale et al., 2005; Edwards, 2005), and the relatively high temperatures in the very last part of the Allerød chronozone (GI-1a) may have facilitated such a landscape regeneration. By the same token, however, the near field of

the eruptive centre likely represented a markedly altered landscape that contained many unstable elements, an instability that was further increased by significantly elevated levels of (acid) rainfall in the wake of the eruption (Schmincke, 2006). Flood and overbank deposits containing reworked LSE pumice found at Bad Breisig itself as well as many other places downstream of the Neuwied Basin attest to the on-going syn- and post-eruptive mass wasting by water of the unconsolidated ejecta "that probably lasted for several decades" (Litt et al., 2003: 29). Likewise, remobilisation of the ash by wind also would have continuously altered the landscape and slowed down recovery (cf. Wilson et al., 2011).

It should further be noted that there remains a striking contrast between pre- and post-LSE settlement density in the Rhineland. This may in part be the result of taphonomic factors, i.e. sites sealed by the LST do preserve better, but quite generally single sites really should not be equated with permanent settlement and a widespread human presence (cf. Davey and Innes, 2002). Specifically with reference to the reoccupation of volcanically affected near-field landscapes, Dumond (2004: 113), for instance, reports that the indigenous foragers who lived close to Katmai volcano (Alaska) which erupted in 1912 "were returning to that area in summers for hunting but felt it was still impossible to live there".

Yet, with the site of Bad Breisig at the fore,

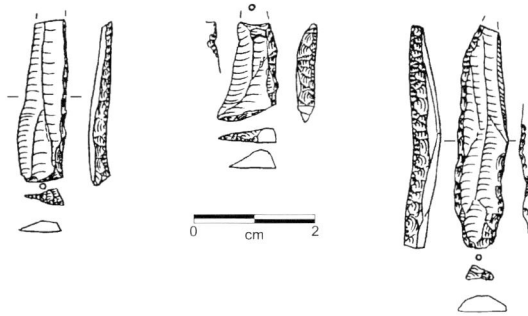

Figure 5.5 *Malaulrie points from Bad Breisig, modified from Baales and Jöris (2002).*

a model positing a rapid "reoccupation of the central Rhineland by Final Palaeolithic hunter-gatherer groups immediately following the Laacher See catastrophe" (Baales et al., 2002: 278) is suggested in many publications (for a recent example, see Fig. 2 in Street et al., 2012). While the faunal assemblage from the site does, with red deer/roe deer and horse, favour a chronological placement into the warmer Allerød rather than the colder Younger Dryas, flint-typologically Bad Breisig exhibits greatest affinity to locales of the Laborian that elsewhere (e.g. the Paris Basin) are quite securely dated to the Younger Dryas. Likewise, the most accurate ^{14}C date (on *Pinus* charcoal) from the site (GrA- 17493: 10,840±60, no ∂^{13}C (‰) given) yields, when calibrated with the IntCal13 curve (Reimer et al., 2013) using the OxCal (v.4.2) calibration package (Bronk Ramsey, 2009), a date range at 2σ of 12,890-12,590 calendar years BP. The posterior probability distribution of this calibrated date (Fig. 5.4) approximates a normal distribution and provides support for an actual date for this site close to the distribution median (12,710 cal BP). Such a date close to, or indeed just after, the beginning of the Younger Dryas in the region would resolve the conflicting chronological indicators and, assuming an eruption date around 12,940 BP, suggest a hiatus of approximately 200 years – with assumed generation times of 30 years (Matsumura and Forster, 2008) seven generations – between the Laacher See event and the relatively ephemeral settlement episode at Bad Breisig.

Finally, the flint typological spectrum pres-

ent at Bad Breisig cannot only be harnessed for chronological information, but arguably also provides evidence for the direction from whence these explorers came. The presence of 'Malaurie points' (Fig. 5.5) characteristic of the Laborian suggest not only a dating into or close to the Younger Dryas, but link the toolmakers and hunters of Bad Breisig to the Paris Basin and other areas to the west. Likewise, the location of the site on the mouth of the east-flowing River Ahr and a raw material spectrum of the tools imported to the locale together point to a movement from the west (Grimm, 2004). Other sites of the Federmessergruppen in the Central Rhineland above the LST or dating to the subsequent Younger Dryas cold phase are not known.

One likely conclusion for the near-field impacts of the LSE on contemporaneous foragers is that the sheer destruction caused by the eruption's ejecta led to a long-term abandonment of the region. The sporadic and perhaps exploratory presence of people in the region after the eruption cannot, in my opinion, be equated with stable and consistent resettlement. Interestingly, other archaeological case studies on how and why traditional societies return to regions heavily affected by volcanic eruption forefront religious rather than economic reasons, as documented separately at various locations in pre-Columbian Mexico by Plunket and Uruñuela (2003) and Sheets (2011) in El Salvador. Although these insights were gained in relation to settled agricultural populations, it is not inconceivable that (albeit unknowable whether) the descendants of those Federmessergruppen folk that had to quickly abandon the hitherto fairly intensely and repeatedly used landscapes of the Central Rhineland felt the desire or obligation to return to the area for reasons other than hunting or the collection of specific raw materials. Assuming those that returned were the descendants of the Central Rhineland's earlier Federmessergruppen occupants, they learned in their western exile new flint-working styles – or, as Ian Hodder (1990: 45) might say, a new "way of doing things" – that is reflected in, for instance, their return with Malaurie points. This may hint at a scenario not very different to that sketched out by Oetelaar and Beaudoin (2005) for the way that forager communities on the Northern Plains of North America coped with the eruption, distal ash-fall and attendant environmental effects of the Mount Mazama/Crater Lake eruption c. 7630 cal BP (see also Beaudoin and Oetelaar, 2003; Beaudoin and Oetelaar, 2006; Oetelaar, 2015; Oetelaar and Beaudoin, 2016; Robertson and Klassen, 2006). With a magnitude (*M*) of 6.8, a VEI of 7 (Bacon and Lanphere, 2006; Zdanowicz et al., 1999), and an extremely wide-spread tephra blanket (Kittleman, 1973; Pyne-O'Donnell et al., 2012), this eruption was somewhat larger than the LSE. In their study, Oetelaar and Beaudoin (2005) focused on far-field communities in southern Alberta at a distance of well over 500km from the eruptive centre. There, too, landscapes became uninhabitable and were abandoned for several hundreds of years. When finally re-occupied, these eruption refugees brought with them a range of new technologies and techniques that they had gleaned from their distant kin in the areas that remained unaffected by Mount Mazama's ash-fall.

In summary, it is likely that the prolonged cooling of the Intra-Allerød Cold Period acted negatively on populations in northern Europe, although faunal and floral resources in the Central Rhineland prior to the eruption appear to have been adequate and varied (Baales et al., 2002). Witham (2005) documented clearly that displacement is the most common effect of volcanic eruption on people. Likewise, it is well known that hunter-gatherers' premier problem-solving strategy involves moving away from it (e.g. Rowley, 1985). The destructive forces of the Laacher See eruption, however, were such that most resources simply became unavailable in its immediate aftermath. The recovery of these resources to a level that warranted resettlement likely took time, and followed a sequence that was difficult to predict. Abandonment thus offered the most sensible and safe solution, although drawing on the reciprocal exchange network of distant kin likely also involved social costs (Minc, 1986; Sobel and Bettles, 2000).

5.4 Mid-field hazards

Moving away from the eruptive centre beyond 50km would mean that the hazard potential of pyroclastic surges and flows diminished. Other hazard agents, however, such as tephra, gases, flooding, earthquakes, and tsunamis come to the fore. Remarkably, a number of archaeological sites in the medial zones are known where human occupation is capped by LST. Under the north-eastern lobe these are Rothenkirchen (Hofbauer, 1992), Rüsselsheim LA122 (Loew, 2005), Mühlheim-Dietesheim (Fruth, 1979, 1994), Weinberg Schadeleben (Mania, 2003) and a series of rock-shelter sites along the River Leine near Göttingen (Grote, 1994). Under the south-western lobe these are Grotte de Coléoptère (Dewez, 1975; Juvigné, 1977), the Trou Jadot (Toussaint and Becker, 1992), and the Trou Walou (Lacroix, 1993; Pirson and Juvigné, 2011; Pirson et al., 2006). The latter sites are located along the outer western extent of the LST at some 120km distance from the vent, the former sites range from 90 to 330km's distance from the Laacher See, where the distal-most locale of Schadeleben still preserves a layer of LST <13cm massive (Fig. 5.6). The large-scale open-case lignite mining in the area in this area has revealed further outcrops of LST which suggest that the landscape was covered continuously – and rather thickly – in fallout ash (Knuth and Thomae, 2003). Likewise, the important but under-appreciated rock-shelters along the River Leine preserve layers of primary air-fall tephra <40cm thick (Ahl and Meyer, 1994); of the nine rock-shelter sites with preserved LST (Abri Lustal II, Abri Stendel XVIII, Bettenroder Berg I, IX, XI, XIII, and XIV, Abri Schierenberg I, Abri Immengrund I), two (Bettenroder Berg I and IX) also preserve occupation layers from the Federmessergruppen (Fig. 5.7).

The overall thickness of LST deposits is declining in the mid-field, following very much the same thinning pattern documented for other eruptions and their fall-out (Bonadonna et al., 1998; Fisher and Schmincke, 1984; Pyle, 1989; Scasso et al., 1994). However, in contrast to previously published and often reproduced maps that suggest thicknesses of around 10cm

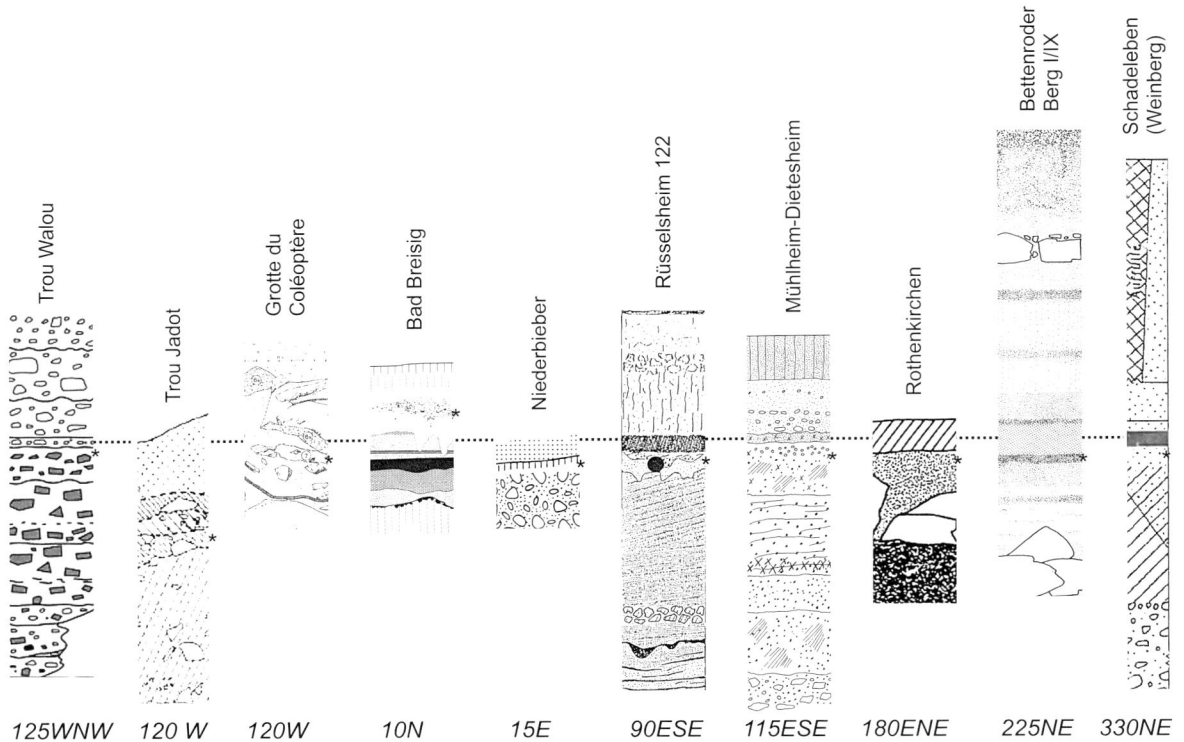

Figure 5.6 *Schematic stratigraphic sequences of Late Glacial archaeological sites with preserved traces of Laacher See tephra. The archaeological layers are marked with *. The distance (in km) and compass orientation to the Laacher See edifice is given. Figure modified from Riede and Thastrup (2013).*

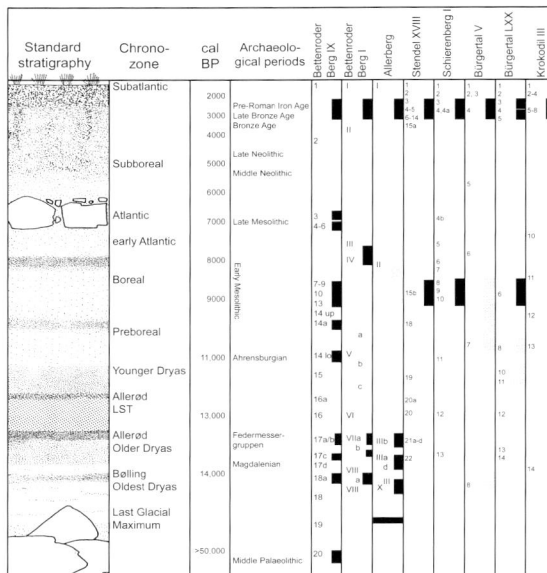

Figure 5.7 *Schematic stratigraphic sequences of selected Leine valley rock-shelters with traces of Laacher See tephra. Note the greater number of sites with traces of pre-Federmesser occupation (i.e. Late Magdalenian), indicating, as in the Rhineland, a decline of overall human activity in this region in the Allerød. Redrawn from Grote (1994).*

for the north-eastern medial fallout zone (e.g. Schmincke et al., 1999), deposits of 100 to 270cm occur at 110km distance-from-vent, thinning to 10 to 30cm at c. 240km's distance, 5-10cm at 340km, and finally to 1-3cm at 500km. Tephra thickness declines considerably faster towards the west and south, although the caveat of compaction needs to be kept in mind in relation to all of these deposits (Fig. 5.8).

The burial of mid-field landscapes by these still rather thick deposits would also have modified these landscapes in a lasting way. In particular in the part of the medial zones closest to the eruptive centre such effects would have been most pronounced. While erosion may have swiftly removed the loose tephra from higher elevations, these were also areas rarely used by contemporaneous foragers. Instead, tephra would have accumulated in river valleys, as is amply documented in, for instance, the Amöneburg Basin of the Lahn valley (Houben, 2003; Rittweger, 2000). Here, the LSE is considered a major agent of land-

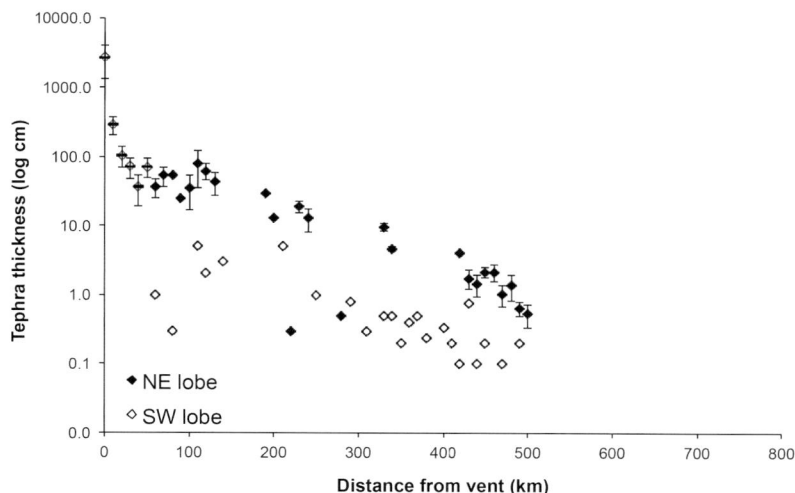

Figure 5.8 *Near- and mid-field Laacher See tephra thicknesses (log cm) in relation to distance from vent (km).*

scape change (Rittweger, 1997), and – importantly – dating of material entrapped in such reworked tephra demonstrates that these landscape alterations continued over 200 years into the Younger Dryas (Andres et al., 2001). Other German rivers also contain traces of LST. Of particular relevance is the River Weser that actually drains into the North Sea far away from the currently known distribution of the LST. Here, rather massive deposits (c. 50cm) of fluvially reworked tephra are recorded in palaeochannels (Caspers, 1993; Lipps and Caspers, 1990). It is impossible to say whether or how long this material has been transported downstream, or whether it is derived from local fallout (<1cm at the nearest locales). Either way, however, it demonstrates the ready availability of large amounts of tephra in river valleys and hints at the potential impact of these eruption products on riverine and lacustrine resources that were becoming more important to hunter-gatherers right at that time.

Further afield the blunt impact of the tephra fallout would have decreased, although the tephra load covering the regions along the River Leine and perhaps even along the Saxony lakeshores near Schadeleben would by contemporary standards still be considered 'thick' or even 'very thick' (see Table 3.8). Such massive tephra fall would likely have arrested soil formation in a major way and the return to productive equilibrium must be measured on decadal or centennial scales. However, in tandem with the decreasing acuteness of the

tephra's sheer destructive action, different and subtler effects would have begun to play ever greater roles. As fallout thickness declined, particle size decreased. With particle size decreasing the respiratory and chemical hazards reviewed in Chapter 3 were aggravated. Detailed data on the grain-size distribution of LST samples spanning the mid-field fallout zone are available, and Table 5.2 compares the grain-size distribution of LST from both the southern and north-eastern fallout fans with the mean and maximum values reported from recent eruptions (Horwell, 2007). With distance from the edifice, the proportion of potentially hazardous particles increases and the values reported for distal locations match or even exceed those documented from other eruptions (Riede and Bazely, 2009). In this, the data from Bettenroder Berg and Schadeleben are especially pertinent, as both deposits directly overlie strata preserving traces of Federmessergruppen habitation.

In Chapter 3 it was noted that historic eruptions have led to starkly increased tooth-wear amongst animals feeding on tephra-laden vegetation. In an effort to quantify this hazard in relation to the LSE, Riede and Wheeler (2009) submitted tooth as well as tephra samples to nanoindentation analysis. Nanoindentation is the method of choice for assessing the hardness and elasticity of a wide range of materials (see Oliver and Pharr, 2010). The tooth samples (lower second molar or its closest functional equivalent) that were analysed came

Sample locales	V E I	Distance from vent (km)	Grain-size (µm) distribution, cumulative % volume						Deposit thickness (cm)
			<1	<2.5	<4	<10	<15	<63	
LSE: NE fan									
Herbstlabyrinth-Adventhöhle caves		75	1-5 mm lapilli. Deposit may be sorted by water action						Blanket cover in cave complex
Gießen (Klein-Linden)		100	c. 15% of sample <150µm, but not further quantifiable; maximum particle size 8mm						25
Raunheim		100	c. 60% of sample >63µm; 35% of sample between 2-63µm, 5% of sample <2µm						18
Marburg$		120	-	-	-	14.3	-	50.5	76
Bettenroder Berg I†		**225**	-	-	-	*14.1*	-	**50.3**	**<40**
Bettenroder Berg IX		**225**	**1.5**	**4.1**	**5.5**	**15.0**	**21.6**	**58.6**	**<40**
Luttersee$		250	-	-	-	28.9	34.8	91.5	1.5
Schadeleben		**330**	-	**11.0**	**20.0**	**42.0**	**52.0**	**92.0**	**<13**
Frankleben	6	340	-	-	-	*31.6*	50.0	97.5	4.2
Großer Bolchow*		450	1%= clay, 85%= silt, 14%= fine sand= 100% <63µm						1-2
LSE: S fan									
Booser Weiher		22	-	11	16	19	24	34	20
Moosbrucher Weiher		29	-	9	11	12	16	22	20
Schalckenmehrener Maar		40	-	14	17	17	20	29	20
Mürmes		40	-	12	16	21	23	31	20
Hitsche		42	-	4	6	8	12	16	20
Hinkelsmaar		50	-	8	10	12	20	32	20
Vance		150	-	20	29	40	50	73	3
MEAN, all recent	3.1	40.7	1.0	3.6	5.6	12.0	16.6	43.4	n/a
MAX, all recent	6	378	4.8	11.6	16.9	32.8	43.4	83.7	n/a

† Values given in% weight by Ahl and Meyer (1994).
$ These are averaged values from multiple samples from the same locality.
* After Mundel (2002).

Table 5.2 *The measured and calculated grain-size distributions of tephra samples from the NE and S fallout lobes. They are compared, at the bottom of the table, with the mean values of previously reported volcanic particle-size measurements from on-going, recent and historic eruptions (Horwell, 2007; Horwell and Baxter, 2006). The figures for the health-pertinent fraction given in italics are calculated following the predictive model of Horwell (2007) and have the following upper/ lower error fits: Marburg: 19.9/10.2; Bettenroder Berg I: 19.8/10.1; Luttersee: 40.5/20.6; Frankleben: 44.2/22.5. For the original Laacher See-tephra data from Gießen see Weyl (1961); for Marburg see Lang (1954); for Bettenroder Berg I see Ahl and Meyer (1994); for Luttersee and Frankleben see Frechen (1952); for Schadeleben see Knuth and Thomae (2003); for Raunheim see Becker (1967); for all southern lobe localities see Jungerius et al. (1968). The grain-size distribution at Bettenroder Berg IX was determined using laser-diffraction, following the method of Horwell (2007). Sites where the Laacher See-tephra overlies archaeological deposits are highlighted in bold.*

from modern examples of many of the Allerød-period animals that were economically important amongst Federmessergruppen hunters (*Alces alces* – elk, *Castor fiber* – beaver, *Cervus elaphus* – red deer, *Equus* sp. – horse, *Oryctolagus cuniculus* – rabbit, and *Rangifer tanrandus* – reindeer), as well as from modern examples of the hunters themselves (i.e. *Homo sapiens*).

Likewise, tephra samples covered the length and breadth of the mid-field north-eastern fallout lobe. The results are clear: Each analysed tephra sample is significantly harder than any part of any of the analysed teeth (Fig. 5.9). In fact, the difference in hardness is greater than 20%, which is the lower limit for scratching (i.e. wear) to occur. In order to further evalu-

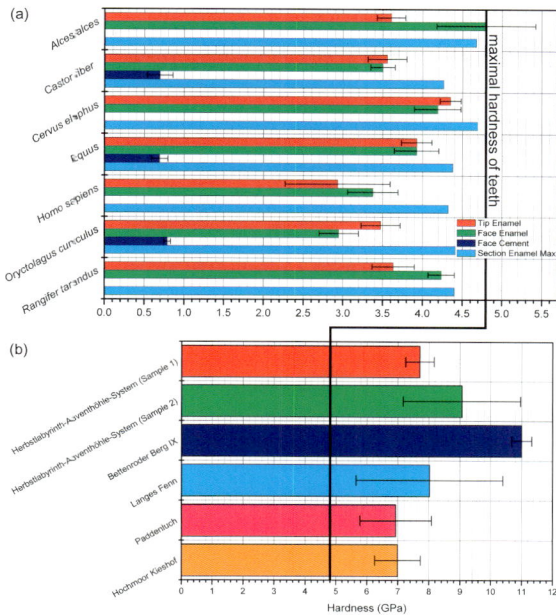

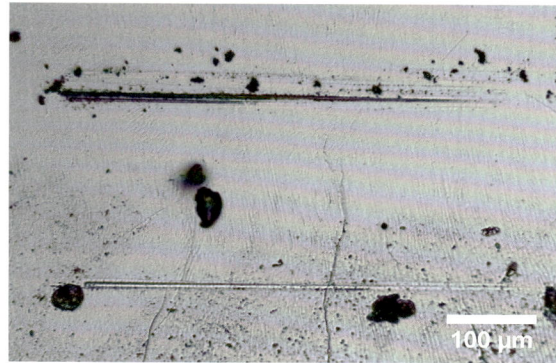

Figure **5.10** *Results of an informal scratch test to simulate the effects of chewing on Laacher See tephra, where a piece of tephra was mounted on the nanoindenter and used to scrape across the tooth surface. Photo: J.M. Wheeler.*

Figure **5.9** *Hardness values (in GPa) for (a) human and animal teeth and (b) Laacher See tephra from a range of mid-field sites.*

ate the degree to which such wear would have occurred, Riede and Wheeler (2009) mounted a particle of tephra from Bettenroder Berg IX – where it is directly associated with an underlying Federmessergruppen settlement horizon – to an indenter tip holder. And then used it to apply a scratch on the chewing (occlusal) surface of an elk molar. Simulating mastication, a load that gradually increased from 1-100 millinewtons (mN, a unit of force), was used over the length of the scratch. This load is at the lower end of the forces generated during chewing (e.g. Rues et al., 2008). The tooth surface was severely affected, without the tephra particle being altered significantly (Fig. 5.10). One can speculate that such an effect would have been particularly dramatic for ruminants that spend a considerable amount of their waking time chewing food.

Once such rather unpalatable forage was swallowed, fluoride and/or sulphide poisoning, too, may have acted on contemporaneous fauna and perhaps foragers. As noted in Chapter 3, gauging the eventual bio-availability of, for instance, fluoride adhering to tephra is difficult. We do know, however, that at least the initial values for both sulphur and fluorine in near-field LST deposits were very high,

with some component particles of especially the early LLST that dispersed preferentially to the north-east being "extremely F-enriched" (Harms and Schmincke, 2000). If humans and animals were affected by fluorosis, the enamel softening often observed as part of this condition, would have further exasperated the already increased mechanical toothwear (Fig. 5.11). The effect of the Laacher See tephra and its chemical adherents must unfortunately, for the time being, remain a working hypothesis. Animal remains from *just* above the LST are extremely rare in Europe, and a preliminary investigation of dental samples from the Azilian site of Rochedane in the French Jura, for instance, did not yield any definite positive identification of fluorosis. At that site, at least one red deer (from layer A4) shows anomalous $\delta^{18}O$ values in its bone phosphate, which has been directly linked to a decrease in temperature caused by the LSE (Drucker et al., 2009). The immediate relevance of this single sample to the question of potential mechanical or chemical tephra impacts is questionable, however. Rochedane is located 350km to the south of the Laacher See edifice, and nearby sites with LST record thicknesses of no more than 0.5cm. In addition, the south-going ULST eruption phase may not have carried as much fluoride as those phases whose ejecta was preferentially transported to the north-east. In order to better evaluate this hypothesis then, future

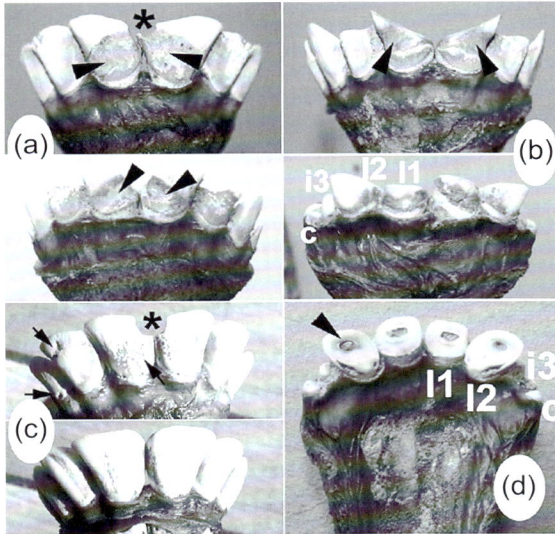

Figure 5.11 *Mechanically worn and fluorosis-affected teeth in Patagonian red deer* (Cervus elaphus) *following the eruption of Puyehue-Cordon Caulle in 2011: (a) Damaged incisor (I1) that has lost its enamel in many places (arrow) and that is broken (asterix); (b) uneven incisor arcades with reduced functionality; note that the deciduous (juvenile) teeth (c/i3) are particularly strongly affected by enamel loss; (c) Full-sized I1 in two sub-adults of recent emergence (upper: female, breakage and pitting), and due to habitat used with abundant leafy forage (bottom: male, only slight pitting); (d) deterioration of the new permanent incisors is so advanced that all of the posterior enamel is worn off and the dental pulp cavity is exposed (arrow). From Flueck and Smith-Flueck (2013).*

work along these lines must focus on finding, dating and analysing pertinent faunal remains, especially under the north-eastern tephra lobe.

Volcanic eruptions – especially violent explosive ones – are universally linked to earthquake occurrences. It has already been suggested that precursor rumblings may have alerted people in the Rhineland that danger was at hand, and there is one site towards the northeast in the mid-field that preserves traces of the power of these tremors. In the Harz Mountains, at a distance of 260km from the Laacher See, an underground cavity formed during the Eemian Interglacial c. 127-115 thousand years ago, collapsed with sedimentation beginning with a turbulent mixture of LSE fallout tephra and local parent rock and clay (Meischner and Grüger, 2008). Notably, sites such as the Bettenroder Berg locales are merely 30km away as the crow flies from this direct piece of evidence for mid-field earthquake activity connected to the LSE.

A final mid-field effect that will be considered here is the Laacher See eruption's impact on climate. Models suggest that the eruption led to short-term temperature fluctuations in Europe whose modularity and severity varied quite strongly from region to region (Graf and Timmreck, 2001), although the critical initial aerosol (sulphur) input parameter must probably be considered a conservative lower limit (Schmincke et al., 1999). Nonetheless, these models suggest winter warming and summer cooling of up to 4° K for the three years following the eruption. Numerous environmental

Figure 5.12 *Depressed tree-ring widths from Late Glacial Switzerland. Narrow rings indicate sub-optimal growing conditions (reduced summer temperatures and/or increased precipitation). The Laacher See eruption is reflected in the tree rings of the pines* (Pinus) *from Dättenau (Switzerland), directly underneath the southern LST fallout lobe at a distance of c. 350km SSE of the edifice. The tree rings display a growth disturbance lasting 5-8 years. This X-ray photograph shows normal growth rings in sector (a), very narrow tree-ring sequence in sector (b), three more rings of smaller width in sector (c), and normal rings in sector (d) following recovery. From Friedrich et al. (1999).*

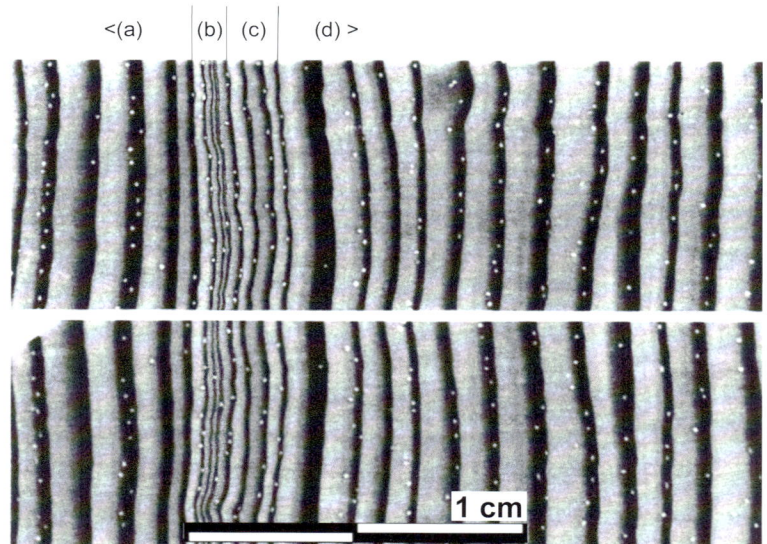

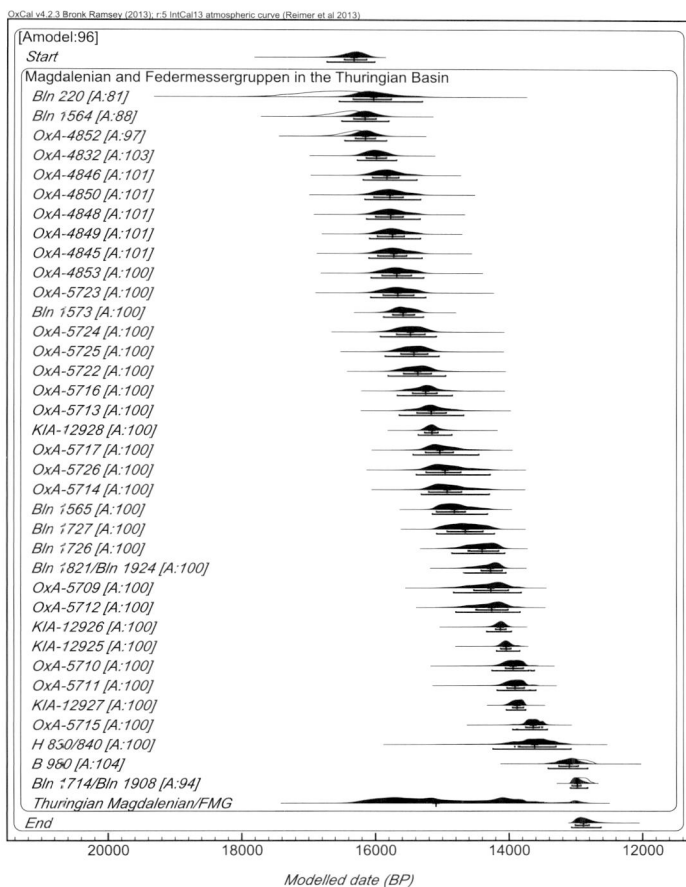

Figure 5.13 *Radiocarbon dates for the Magdalenian and Federmessergruppen occupation in the Thuringian Basin. This date set has been evaluated for reliability by Küssner (2009) and is analysed using OxCal 4.2 (Bronk Ramsey, 2009) and the IntCal13 atmospheric curve (Reimer et al., 2013) as a single-phase model. At 1σ the age range for the end of Federmesser settlement in the region is 13,020-12,800 cal BP (m= 12,890).*

proxies mirror or indeed exceed this marked negative climate forcing of the Laacher See eruption. Tree-rings from contemporaneous Dättenau pines from Switzerland show definite disturbances in the latter part of the Allerød, where tree-rings reflecting about eight years of growth are severely reduced in width (Fig. 5.12), interpreted to reflect reduced summer temperatures and/or increased precipitation (Friedrich et al., 1999). Likewise, Merkt and Müller (1999) have shown that sedimentation regimes in Central Germany – exemplified by the Hämelsee site located at the very edge of the tephra fallout in Lower Saxony – was strongly disturbed for up to 20 years following the deposition of even that very minor fallout layer. Again, this disturbance may have been due to a period of heavy rains. A final twist in the assessment of the climatic impact of the LSE (and volcanic eruptions in general) is that we have apparently been systematically underestimating the climatic forcing effects of even minor volcanic eruptions in baseline assess-

ments derived from recent eruptions (Ridley et al., 2014).

Stratified sites dating to the Allerød in the mid-field of the Laacher See eruption's fallout are scarce. In the south, these are generally deep cave sites, which do not present ideal sediment traps for tephra. Consequently, no such sites are known as yet. To the west and the north-east, however, such sites are known and none preserve traces of human occupation following the LSE. Human remains in these sites are again absent, although a skull was reportedly found underneath Laacher See tephra near Dorla in Hesse (Fiedler, 1994), but efforts to locate and date it have so far been unsuccessful. It is likely that loss of human life in the mid-field as an immediate consequence of the LSE was again limited. However, the negative impacts on resources and livelihoods would, via the varied and variable hazard agents described here, been substantial.

Eriksen (1996) suggested some time ago that the Thuringian Basin experienced a settle-

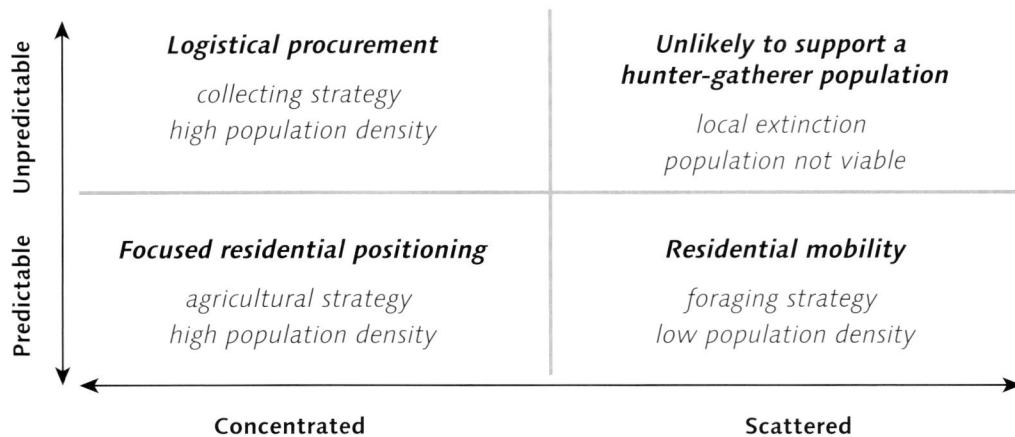

Figure 5.14 *A model for forager mobility in relation to spatial/temporal resource distributions. The effects of the Laacher See eruption may have pushed the balance of resource strategies from the lower right-hand (forager) quadrant towards the upper right-hand one, i.e. towards non-viability. From Whallon (2006).*

ment hiatus towards the end of the Allerød. More recent research in the region (Küssner, 2007, 2009, 2010), including radiocarbon dating and re-dating of key sites and single finds (Grünberg, 2006), hints likewise at a marked reduction in human activity and population density in the latter part of the Allerød. Indeed, the radiocarbon record suggests a settlement hiatus from about 13,000 years BP (Fig. 5.13). Similarly, Riede (2012b, 2016) has argued on the basis of the – admittedly limited – stratigraphic evidence from Late Glacial sites in Hesse and southern Lower Saxony that this region, too, became depopulated. Here, the definite association of find-bearing layers directly underneath the LST strongly suggests that people left the area in response to this event. Further still to the north, stratigraphic associations of Federmessergruppen sites and LST do not exist. The only candidate site, Henningsdorf near Berlin, is controversial. Here, Kloss and Wechler (1987) argued that a lacustrine pollen sequence preserves traces of anthropogenic landscape modification that was then linked to a nearby site of the Federmessergruppen. A critical re-interpretation of the pollen data by de Klerk (2006), however, suggests that a case for human impacts on the landscape – very difficult to detect this far back in time (Bos and Janssen, 1996) – cannot be sustained, thus removing the stratigraphic association between the LST and the settlement waste.

In summary, the blunt landscape impacts coupled with the various changes in plant and animal composition following the LSE in the mid-field under the north-eastern fallout lobe may have made it difficult or, at the very least, not worthwhile for foragers to continue using these landscapes. Whilst the affected regions are dotted with undated locales from the Federmessergruppen, whenever dated, they are placed to before the LSE. The different temporalities of the various hazards and their spatial variation may have made it difficult for contemporaneous foragers to predict the seasonal and locational availability of key resources at crucial points in the seasonal cycle. With resource predictability in space and time as a key variable determining hunter-gatherer mobility strategies, such coupled decreases in predictability would suggest concomitant increases in mobility and/or reciprocal kin-based exchange (Fig. 5.14; Kelly, 1995; Whallon, 2006). Evidence for the latter – at least in the form of the 'currency' of social exchange dominant during the preceding Magdalenian: fossil shells, amber, and animal tooth pendants – is conspiciously absent from post-LSE contexts in northern Europe (Álvarez-Fernández, 2001) and suggests a contraction or temporary collapse of these Palaeolithic safety nets (Riede, 2014b). In the absence of other options, mobility – migration and relocation – may have been the only option.

While directly damaging tephra impacts may have decreased with distance from the vent, access to key physical resources would, correspondingly, have been more critical – at least to the north-east where natural latitudinal gradients resulted in ever shorter growing seasons, less resilient ecosystems, and topographically less varied landscape affordances. Interestingly, the Belgian cave sites that preserve traces of LST also do not show evidence for re-settlement either. Despite the very minor amount of tephra that travelled to the west, these communities may, nonetheless, have retreated further into Central France or towards the Netherlands where the frequency of radiocarbon dates does at least suggest an increase in human activity (Riede, 2008b). The communities under the southern fallout lobe were perhaps only barely affected, although the number of sites securely dated to the Federmessergruppen there is virtually nil and stands in contrast to the rich record of the preceding Magdalenian (Newell and Constandse-Westermann, 1999; Street et al., 2002). One possible effect of the Laacher See eruption's southern fallout may be the regionalisation seen during the very end of the Allerød and in the Younger Dryas. In the Jura Mountain and the western part of Switzerland, the Azilian persists, while further to the east on the Swiss Plateau the so-called Fürsteiner facies emerges (Nielsen, 2009). This geographically and chronologically restricted phenomenon has been described as a "locally degenerate variant of the Magdalenian" (Bandi, 1968: 119) and is said to be associated with an increase in site number (Nielsen, Ebbe H. 2013). While the degenerate nature of the Fürsteiner may be debatable, the observed regionalisation in itself may reflect a reorganisation of seasonal rounds and a more pronounced tethering to particular resources that ultimately resulted in decreased contact between regions followed by the development of more localised identities and styles. Possibly significant here is also the fact that it is the eastern part of Switzerland rather than the western part, which remained connected to the wholly unaffected communities in eastern and central France, where regionalisation occurred. In a similar way, Schönweiß (1992) has argued that the very latest part of the Late Glacial sees the emergence of a regional group

in northern Bavaria, the Atzenhofer Gruppe, characterised by specific combinations of Federmesser styles and the utilisation of diverse but almost, perhaps even entirely, regional raw materials. Whilst poorly constrained chronologically, the geographic distribution of this facies – interestingly – appears framed by the Laacher See tephra fallout to the west and north. Further still to the east, Vencl (1970; 1987) has postulated a Late Glacial facies, the Ostroměr group, entirely without arch-backed points. Whether this area experienced a real decline or disappearance of this armature (and with it possibly also bow-and-arrow technology) during the Late Glacial is unclear, however. The absence of points can be the result of simple stochastic factors, or it could here be due to the potentially strong research historical bias. Indeed, both the Atzenhofer and Ostroměr groups are most probably methodological artefacts in need of critical revision (cf. Sauer, 2017).

5.5 Far-field hazards

As we move into the far-field of tephra deposition, the remaining hazard agents are the tephra itself, gases, flooding, and tsunamis. Laacher See tephra did not travel further to the south or west than about 500km, although the distribution clearly shows the deflecting effect of the Alps. Tephra did travel further along the north-eastern trajectory, in part because this lobe carried substantially more material, was carried by the predominant winds, and was unobstructed by topographic barriers. The northernmost currently known find location of LST offshore from present day Gotland (Påhlsson and Bergh Alm, 1985) is c. 1100km from the eruptive centre and was then just south of the retreating Fennoscandian glaciers. Most likely, the north-eastern plume was carried even further to the north-east – recently underlined by indirect evidence from the Karelian Isthmus (Andronikov et al., 2012; Andronikov et al., 2014) – and deposited ash on the since long-gone ice-sheet. Tephra thicknesses in the far-field vary between 3cm just beyond 500km's distance and 0.1cm at 730km's distance on the island of Bornholm

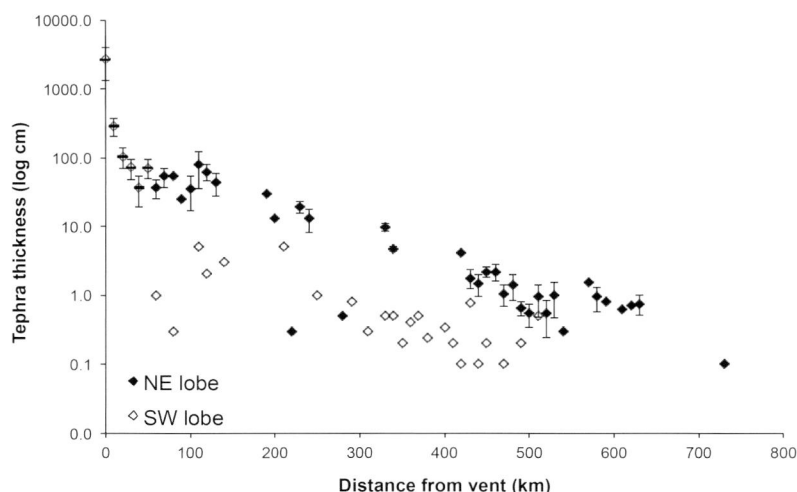

Figure 5.15 *Near-, mid- and far-field Laacher See tephra thicknesses (log cm) in relation to distance from vent (km).*

in the Baltic Sea (Fig. 5.15), where still two eruption phases (LLST and MLST-C2) can be recognised (Turney et al., 2006; Usinger, 1977). Original tephra thicknesses may have been much greater, and the density of find spots in the north-eastern far-field – Theuerkauf (2003) mentions > 120 locales – strongly suggests that the cover was widespread. Detailed micromorphological studies suggest that such layers consist of both primary and reworked in-wash material and that biological activity initially ceased with deposition (de Klerk et al., 2008a). In addition, it is strongly noteworthy that virtually all the LST localities known in north-eastern Germany are macro-tephras, i.e. they are visible to the naked eye despite 13,000 years of taphonomic distortion. Systematic investigations of the distal LST using modern techniques of tephrochronology are only now beginning, and have already yielded at least one tentative data-point far removed from any of the three major tephra dispersal lobes, Kostverloren Veen in the Netherlands (Davies et al., 2005).

The continuous, albeit thin, ash-fall cover across as 150km-wide belt in present-day north-eastern and westernmost Poland makes it likely that the tephra-related hazards described in the section above would have remained active in the far-field. Both mechanical abrasion and the potentially harmful chemical load of the ash particles would have also affected animals and humans. It is difficult to evaluate to what degree the gradual thinning of the layer thickness and the correspondingly decreasing grain size of the deposited particle populations would have balanced each other out in relation to the overall hazard level (cf. Thorarinsson, 1979). At any rate, the direct environmental impact of the tephra deposition would have been fairly minor at this remove, although several potentially important effects have been documented. High-resolution studies of changes in pollen frequencies and the occurrence of lake-dwelling organisms (diatoms) suggests that trees and shrubs were little affected by the ash, although juniper and Artemisia species (mugwood, wormwood and sagebrush) appear to have increased, whereas values of pine pollen decreased to ~0 (de Klerk et al., 2008b). The mechanisms driving these floral changes remain unclear, but appear wide spread in the region. In parallel, plant communities close to mires and lakes were significantly affected with willows, sedges, and grasses increasing significantly after the eruption (Theuerkauf, 2002). This may have been caused by eutrophication of wetlands after the input of sulphuric acid, and/or a temporary rise in lake levels due to the already alluded to increase in precipitation. As lake levels subsided again, the dried-up shores would have provided a suitable habitat for these species to spread (Theuerkauf, 2003). Experimental studies of the effect of tephra deposition on wetlands suggests that while thinner layers are less likely to lead to longer-term changes, smaller grain size does increase the tephra impact (Hotes et al., 2004). Yet, both

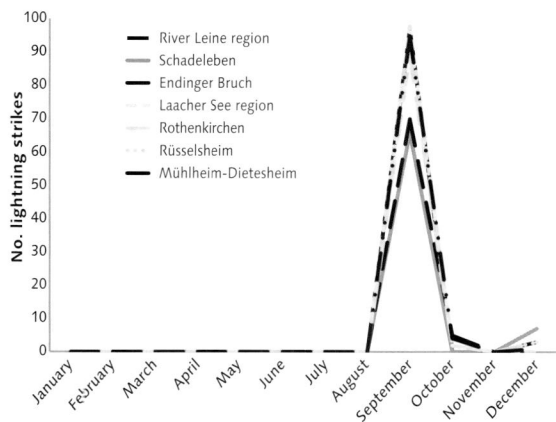

Figure 5.16 *Lightning strike frequency (for the year 2005, arbitrarily selected) in north-eastern Germany, centred on sites with known Federmessergruppen archaeology and Laacher See tephra (20 km radius). Data from http://www. blibis.de/.*

lake level rise and eutrophication could have strongly affected people. Water-bodies were major attractors of human occupation in the Late Glacial (Fischer, 1985, 1991), and sudden lake level rises – secondary flooding – in the already low-lying and wet landscapes of the North European Plain may have made traditional settlement locations somewhat less attractive. More significantly perhaps, eutrophication may have had more severe consequences for the economic attractiveness of these sites. Well-studied in the context of recent industrial and agricultural pollution of water-ways (see, for instance, Dodds and Whiles, 2010; Smith, Val H., 2009), "this nutrient enrichment, or eutrophication, can lead to highly undesirable changes in ecosystem structure and function" (Smith, Joel B. et al., 1999: 179) in the form of an increased biomass of toxic or inedible phytoplankton, blooms of zooplankton and algae, changes in macrophyte species composition and biomass, decreases in water transparency, oxygen depletion and increased incidences of fish kills, as well as significant negative changes in the appearance of these water-bodies, in particular foul smells and strongly altered colours. Algal blooms can be fatal to animals drinking water from such over-enriched lakes (Braun and Pfeiffer, 2002) and given that some of the contemporaneous major game animals such as elk spend considerable amounts of time in the water, impacts on wetlands may

have thus cascaded through the trophic chain. Tephra is known to have such effects in freshwater, i.e. lakes and streams (e.g. Dirksen et al., 2009; Frogner Kockum et al., 2006).

The only far-field site where archaeological remains can with some certainty chronologically be related to LST is at Endingen. Here, humanly modified bones of elk, giant deer and horse have been found, which have been dated to 11,555±100 (UZ-3798, giant deer antler) and 11,830±50 (UZ-5681, horse rib) respectively. Although lithic material is absent from the site, it is thought to relate to the Federmessergruppen occupation in the immediate area and wider region (Kaiser et al., 1999). Subsequent tephra research in the vicinity of the original find locality of the bones has revealed a microscopic but clearly detectable layer of LST (Lane et al., 2012). At present the Endinger Bruch locality marks the north-western most occurrence of LST along this far edge of the north-eastern lobe.

An additional effect observed in the wake of the LSE in the far-field is an increase in violent thunderstorms and forest fires started by lightning (de Klerk et al., 2008a). Such storms as well as forest fires are not unusual in boreal-type environments, but those following the LSE would have been remarkable and likely awesome in several ways. First, volcanic lightning differs in intensity and direction (cloud-to-cloud) from regular cloud-to-ground lightning. In addition, such volcanic discharges generally occur in what is called 'dirty thunderstorms' that travel with, and are generated by, the atmospheric effects of the ash cloud (Anderson et al., 1965; Thomas et al., 2007). Today, lightning occurs in north-eastern Germany in a very seasonally defined pattern. The vast majority of strikes occur between August and October (Fig. 5.16) – not in late spring/ early summer as they would have following the Laacher See event.

In summary, the environmental effects of the LSE in the far-field are clearly visible in multiple proxies at numerous locations. Other likely impacts, such as increased mortality among birds, and potential changes in migration patterns remain entirely invisible for some time. Observations from recent eruptions, as

Species		Migratory?
Duck	*Anatidarum sp.*	X
Goose	*Anser sp.*	X
Gull	*Larus argentatus/ fuscus/marinus*	X
Ptarmigan	*Lagopus lagopus*	
Sandpiper	*Calidris alpina*	
Common crane	*Grus grus*	X
Barnacle Goose	*Branta leucopsis*	X
Spotted Crake	*Porzana porzana*	x
Swan	*Cygnus sp.*	X
Whooper Swan	*Cygnus cygnus*	X
Golden Eagle	*Aquila chrysaetos*	
Ruff	*Philomachus pugnax*	X
Lark	*Alaudidarum sp.*	
Carrion crow	*Corvus corone*	

Table 5.3 *Summary table of known bird species from the southern Scandinavia Late Glacial, including the Bølling, Older and Younger Dryas chronozones. Data from Bratlund (1999), Krause and Kollau (1943), and Aaris-Sørensen (1999). Additional mainly marine bird species are known from northern Scandinavia (see Lie, 1990). X indicates migratory behaviour today, small x indicates possible migratory behaviour.*

outlined in Chapter 3, suggest that birds are strongly affected by volcanic ash (cf. Edwards, 2005), but avian faunal material from the Late Glacial is scarce. Of those species that are known (Table 5.3), several migrate currently across the region in northern Europe affected by tephra fallout, and many did so when the eruption and its tephra output would have been most intense (Berthold, 2001; Elphick, 2007). Those that survived may have altered their migration routes following the eruption in accord with the landscape, climate and environmental changes related to it (cf. Pautasso, 2012; Tøttrup et al., 2008).

Few, perhaps even none of these changes are, however, on a scale that would likely have affected humans in a major way. Yet, as argued before, the simple fact that weather and environments fluctuated unseasonably and un-

predictably at a point just following a nearly 300-year-long period of already deteriorated climatic conditions may have made certain regions – namely those preferentially affected by tephra fallout – significantly less attractive for human settlement. With the varying temporalities of the hazard agents listed here, this reduced attractiveness may, in the first instance, have been grounded in actual and clearly observable effects on weather, climate and environments. Hunter-gatherers can be said to be extremely sensitive to environmental clues, seeing environs not so such much as arrays of economic resources, but as offering certain affordances that are intimately related to, but not determined by, the actual underlying ecology (e.g. Ingold, 1986; Rockman, 2003). While many of the effects – especially if acting in synergy – of the Laacher See eruption on local and regional ecologies in southern and northern Europe suggest some form of mechanistic forcing relationship between the eruption and contemporaneous foragers' responses, these forcing factors clearly do not explain the specificity of the responses already hinted at in Chapter 1, and neither do they explain why impacts appear to have increased with distance from the eruptive centre. There has been considerable debate lately about whether past people responded to changes in weather or in climate, especially in relation to social memory (i.e. traditional ecological knowledge), resilience, and vulnerability (Bell, 2012; Cooper, 2012; Davies, 2012; Gronenborn, 2012; Pillatt, 2012a, 2012b; Wilkinson, 2012). Climate can be defined as "the sum total of the weather experienced at a place in the course of a year and over the years" (Lamb, 1972: 5), and hunter-gatherers in particular are highly responsive to changes in weather and in landscapes, and they arguably employ many more senses in this than merely the visual, which is so heavily prioritised in contemporary Western discourse (Ingold, 2000, 2004, 2005, 2007, 2010). This view of the nature of forager landscape perception and use – what Tim Ingold (2011) terms the 'weather world' – is difficult to implement in an analytically precise way in the deep past, but provides a rich and theoretically expanded backdrop to a consideration of the numerous arguments that have been made about the combined, unusual, unseasonable and unpredictable impact of the LSE on regional *weather*, *climate*, *environment*, and *landscape*. Traditional systems ecological views of past hunter-gatherers would require long-term environmental or climate impacts as causal factors for cultural changes (usually seen as adaptation). In contrast, sensitivity to weather and to the usually animistic worldview of especially northern hunter-gatherers (Plumet, 2006) suggest that it is perhaps as much the varying temporalities of change as well as the ways in which these changes are experienced that are germane to *cultural* responses. The intimate linkage between the physical and the spiritual world in hunter-gatherer societies (e.g. Jordan, 2003) then provides a further stepping stone towards also considering seriously the psycho-social and religious effects of a high-magnitude event such as the Laacher See eruption, given that such responses to extreme events including volcanic eruptions have left clear traces in the historical and oral records of pre-industrial people (Chester and Duncan, 2007; Chester et al., 2012; Dietrich, 2012; Dove, 2008, 2010).

Volcanic eruptions are sensorially violent events, and they are commonly described as such (Holmberg, 2013). In line with arguments for a sensorially more holistic or syn-aesthetic approach to archaeology (Howes, 2006), the following section will therefore attempt to capture and investigate in a quasi-phenomenological manner and in the likely chronological sequence of their occurrence some of the more elusive experiences and effects associated with volcanic eruptions. In contrast to similar studies of either place-based ritual or indeed quotidian sights, sounds, and smells associated with past landscapes (e.g. Goldhahn, 2002; Hamilton et al., 2006; Rennell, 2012), this investigation focuses on how the everyday was – for some time – violently turned on its head.

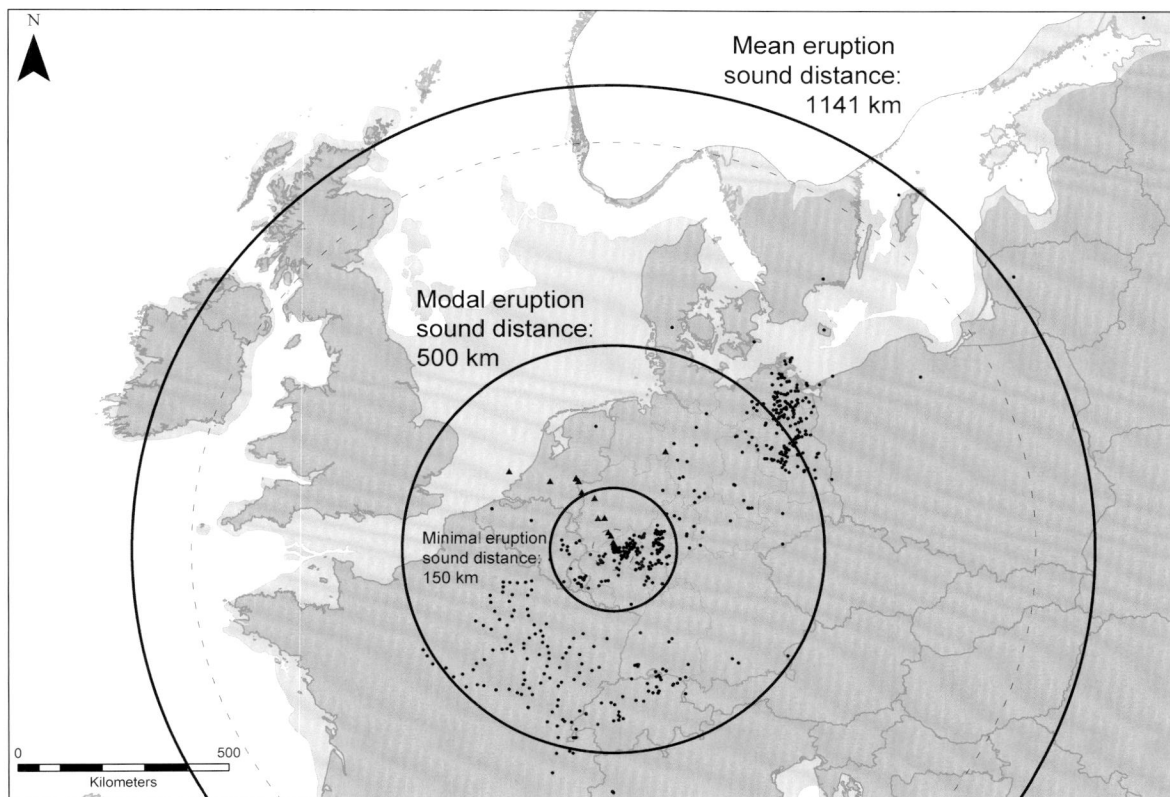

Figure 5.17 *The Laacher See eruption's graded soundscape projected onto a palaeogeographic map of Late Glacial Europe, including extent of the Laacher See tephra fallout. The distance values are calculated using the data of Blong (1984).*

	Relative soundscape composition (%)			
	Natural	Human	Technological	Σ
Traditional societies	69	26	5	100
Medieval, Renaissance & pre-industrial societies	34	52	14	100
Industrial societies	9	25	66	100
Today	6	26	68	100

Table 5.4 *The relative distribution of noise sources and levels in traditional, pre-industrial, industrial, and contemporary society. From Schafer (1973).*

5.6 The time of darkness

In his book *Time of Darkness*, Russell Blong (1982) interrogated the relationship between actual volcanic events and how they become embedded in the traditional corpus of knowledge about hazards, responses, and landscapes. These legends, as well as literary sources going back further still (e.g. Friedrich, 2009) and contemporary eyewitnesses (Bird and Gísladóttir, 2012) report of the overwhelming daytime darkness that attends volcanic fallout. Yet, even before darkness would have descended – to briefly hark back to the flippant reference to Asterix and Obelix that opened this book, when the sky fell on people's heads – they would have *heard* and *felt* the eruption. As was noted in Chapter 3, volcanic eruptions have produced some of the loudest noises ever recorded, and projecting the data available on the spatial extent of these sounds onto a map of Late Glacial northern Europe, it is evident that the near-, mid- and far-fields were affected (Fig. 5.17). In the near-field the initial explosions would likely have been literally deafening; in the far-field people would have struggled to make sense of the noise, especially in the absence of any obvious source. In recent descriptions of volcanic explosions, they are almost universally referred to as heavy gunfire (Blong, 1984). In ancient descriptions of volcanic explosions, the clanging of metal on metal is commonly used (Friedrich, 2009), to the degree that the Classical gods of iron-working (Hephaistos and Vulcan) were thought to reside inside volcanoes. We cannot know what analogy, what cultural idiom Late Glacial hunter-gatherers would have employed, given that they knew neither cannons nor iron. In fact, traditional societies experience overwhelmingly low and predominantly natural noises in their everyday (Table 5.4; Schafer, 1973), and acoustic ecologists and environmental psychologists agree that loud, violent and on-going noise generates considerable stress (Mace et al., 1999; Sundstrom et al., 1996).

One caveat here is that the distances that sounds travels are also dependent on local topography and atmospheric factors, i.e. they rarely radiate out from source in a perfectly circular form. In principle, the propagation of sound can be modelled using GIS (Reed et al., 2012), but attempts to implement these on the massive sub-continental scale required here went beyond the computing power available. Yet, the simple model presented in Figure 5.17 indicates that the explosions of the LSE – perhaps especially those of the so-called *Big Bang Layer* (cf. Schmincke, 2004) at the very end of the LLST phase – may have been heard, ominously, over large parts of Europe.

Simultaneously with the first sound waves, pressure waves would have radiated out from the Laacher See edifice. Above-ground shockwaves generated by volcanic eruptions, too, are known to travel considerable distances, where the general rule is that the more explosive the eruption, the more powerful the shockwaves. Now drawing on the data listed in Table 3.7, plotting these distances on a map of Late Glacial northern Europe again shows how they most probably extended powerfully into the mid-field, and possibly much further (Fig. 5.18).

Following these immediate effects, the eruption column would have become visible.

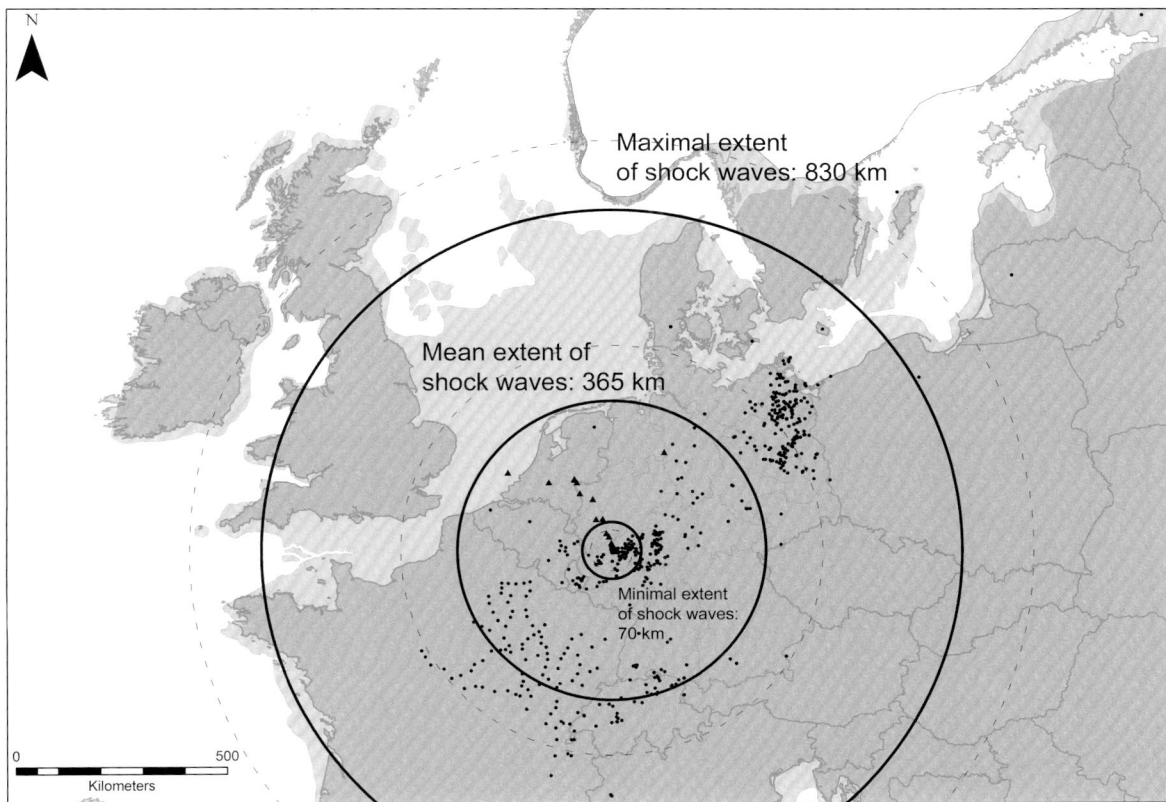

Figure 5.18 *The Laacher See eruption's graded 'shock-scape', i.e. the possible and likely distances travelled by shock waves generated by this eruption projected onto a palaeogeographic map of Late Glacial Europe, including the extent of the Laacher See tephra fallout. The distance values are calculated using the data of Blong (1984).*

Visibility, in turn, depends on atmospheric conditions and the distance of the observer. We cannot know specific variations in day-to-day visibility, but given the likely length of the eruption over several weeks or months, the column and its extension north- and southwards would almost certainly have been visible far and wide some of the time. Indeed, (conservatively) taking the column to be equal to a point source centred on the Laacher See, a simple view-shed analysis again projected onto Late Glacial northern Europe shows that, assuming good visibility, the eruption column would have been visible not only in the southern and western mid-fields or north-eastern far-field, but indeed over large parts of Europe for the entire time the eruption column attained heights >5km (Fig. 5.19). Important to remember here is that the tephra plume would have been displaced along the major wind vectors and that these ash-vanes would likely have appeared as a dark and possibly thunder-and-lightning-filled wonderwall across the land-

scape. If caught in these clouds, people would have experienced the intense darkness alluded to above. Darkness has recently been the subject of ethnographic inquiry, and numerous researchers have pointed out that for many traditional societies darkness is associated with spiritual activity, with altered physiological and psychological states, and with danger (Bille and Sørensen, 2007; Galinier et al., 2010; Williams, 2008). Unusual cloud formations (e.g. mammatus clouds), high, acidic and unseasonable rainfall, strangely-coloured sunsets, and so-called Bishop's Rings around the sun (Bishop, 1886a, 1886b) – all well-known far-field weather effects of volcanic eruptions (e.g. Stommel and Stommel, 1983; Stothers, 1984) – may have further contributed to the awe-inspiring and perhaps ecologically and cosmologically confusing nature of the event.

In addition to sight and sound, further sensorial incongruities between the regular state of the environment and the effects and products of the Laacher See eruption can be listed.

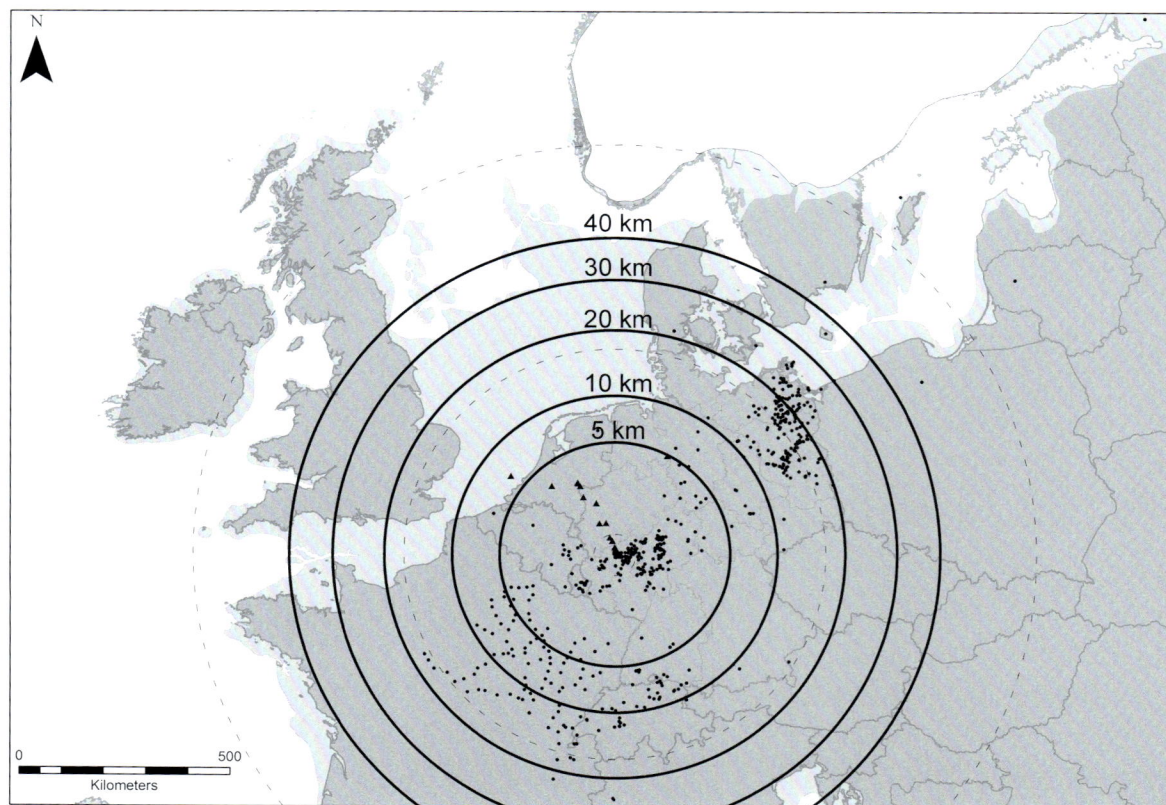

Figure 5.19 *The Laacher See eruption's graded view-scape projected onto a palaeogeographic map of Late Glacial Europe, including the extent of the Laacher See tephra fallout. Distance radii were calculated following http://mintaka.sdsu.edu/GF/explain/atmos_refr/horizon.html.*

Potentially, foul smells of ammonia and sulphur – which were emitted by the LSE in stupendous quantities – may have been carried on the wind – which evidently blew into the direction of the major fallout lobes – away from the eruptive centre. These smells often are associated with supernatural beings, or places, and elicit strong emotional responses (e.g. Grattan et al., 2002). Furthermore, the tephra itself would have precipitated like snow, but unlike snow it occurred in the warm part of the year, and it was neither cold nor wet, nor would it melt away – it felt *very* different. The ethnographer Teit (1930) has related a story from the Nespelem, part of the Salish First Nation of the Western Plateau (Canada), about such 'dry snow' that fell in 1770. The ash-fall, whose cause was not immediately apparent, was conceived of as an ill portent and treated with apprehension. People stayed indoors dancing and

Component of the access framework	Typical time period of change after disaster
Access to biotic and abiotic resources	Immediate-months/years
Negative respiratory health impacts	Immediate-years
Increased dental wear	Immediate-years
F-poisoning	Immediate-years
Change in weather/climate patters	Immediate-decades
Change in social network structure	Years-decades

Table 5.5 *The suggested temporalities of the Laacher See eruption's impact.*

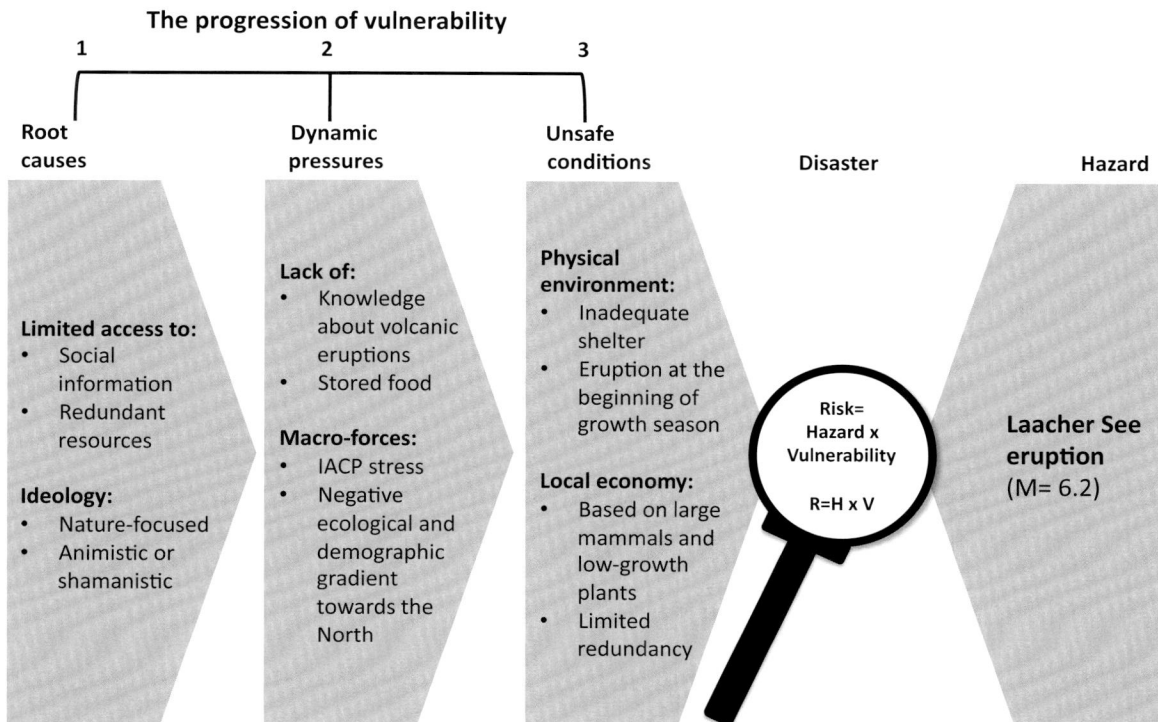

The progression of vulnerability

| 1 | 2 | 3 |

Root causes

Dynamic pressures

Unsafe conditions

Disaster

Hazard

Limited access to:
- Social information
- Redundant resources

Ideology:
- Nature-focused
- Animistic or shamanistic

Lack of:
- Knowledge about volcanic eruptions
- Stored food

Macro-forces:
- IACP stress
- Negative ecological and demographic gradient towards the North

Physical environment:
- Inadequate shelter
- Eruption at the beginning of growth season

Local economy:
- Based on large mammals and low-growth plants
- Limited redundancy

Risk= Hazard x Vulnerability

R=H x V

Laacher See eruption (M= 6.2)

Figure 5.20 *Pressure-and-Release Model for the Laacher See eruption.*

praying in order to arrive at an explanation and to alleviate fear. It is impossible to know, of course, whether any Late Glacial groups engaged in this kind of behaviour. However, it is tempting to suggest that unusual and causally opaque changes in weather and landscape would be seen as significant by people who presumably were supremely in tune with the signs and rhythms of the natural world. A broader comparative perspective on human responses to volcanic disasters underlines the strong propensity of people the world over, and living in different kinds of societies, to infuse volcanic disasters with supernatural agency, and with cosmological and often also with political significance (Cashman and Giordano, 2008; Chester and Duncan, 2007; Hamilton, 2012).

Magdalenian foragers had occasionally experienced small-scale volcanic eruption in the Massif Central (Raynal et al., 1994; Vernet and Raynal, 2000). Particularly noteworthy is the site of Abri Durif at Enval (see Bourdelle, 1979; Bourdelle and Merlet, 1991; Liabeuf et al., 1997), where a merely 2cm-thick ash-fall (the 'Les Roches' tephra dated by an AMS radiocarbon date, Gif TAN 91102: 12,010±150 BP, i.e. to about one thousand years prior to

the LSE), directly covering an Upper Magdalenian settlement layer, led to the permanent abandonment of this site and possibly to long-lasting changes in settlement pattern (Raynal and Dougas, 1984; Vernet and Raynal, 1995). We cannot know whether this event and its effects – perhaps a form of cultural trauma (Sztompka, 2000) – subsequently became part of the oral history of these people, locally, regionally, or in a wider cultural collective. The Eifel was much less volcanically active within the chronological bracket of the Magdalenian, however, and traditional knowledge of the specific volcanic nature of this area and the potential consequences of an eruption was likely minimal. If anything, the Les Roches event may have primed those experiencing the eruption in the near-field to abandon the area. To people roaming northern Europe, i.e. in the very far-field of the eruption, attributing a source and a cause to the effects of the eruption may have been more difficult still, although they could very likely deduce that this source lay to the south. The effects of the eruption, when it eventually subsided after several months of on-off activity, reverberated and trickled through the trophic chain at speeds unique to each effect (Table 5.5); access to numerous essential resources was made difficult for contemporaneous foragers, and the progression of vulnerability in the eruption's far field is presented schematically in Figure 5.20.

In summary, this chapter has argued that the Laacher See eruption's hazard dynamics changed in important ways along the proximal-to-distal transect. Blunt measures of destruction only partly capture the impacts of the eruption on key resources for Late Glacial hunter-gatherers. The unavailability of such resources – and in the absence of other buffering options – these communities arguably chose to move. Southern Scandinavia was already a known area that offered the kinds of biotic (animals and plants) and abiotic (lithic resources and potable water) resources these foragers used. With the source of their troubles to the southwest, moving away from it to the northeast may have been a sensible action to take. This is, at any rate, the argument made here: The landscapes affected by tephra fallout in northern Europe were abandoned or largely abandoned and people moved more decisively into southern Scandinavia. A useful comparison here may come from New Zealand (Lowe et al., 2002; Lowe et al., 2000) and Papua-New-Guinea (Blong, 1982), where volcanically affected landscapes were at times deemed *rahui* – 'prohibited access' – or *tapu* – entirely no-go.

Likewise, Rowley (1985:15) has noted for the Inuit of the Canadian Arctic "another common cause for migration was a belief that the land had become unhealthy" in the wake of, for instance, some catastrophic event, and that people would not move back into a given area for many generations even if it offered abundant game and other resources. These cultural restrictions on land-use may initially have been sparked by volcanic activity and may indeed have served the very real function of delimiting danger zones, but were also heavily invested with supernatural propositions of causality with the consequence that, as Lowe et al. (2002: 152) noted, "any violation of the *tapu* status, or sin (*hara*), was likely to bring upon a calamity". It is impossible to know for sure whether such notions are applicable for the Late Glacial, but they are fully in line with a historicised and cultured approach to landscapes (Gosden and Lock, 1998).

In southern Scandinavia, the latter part of the Allerød not only, arguably at least, experienced an increase in settlement activity, but also saw the emergence of a regionally specific and material-culturally remarkable technocomplex: the Bromme culture. The next chapter will look more closely at this phenomenon and the way in which it may be related to the eruption of the Laacher See eruption.

Chapter 6

After the eruption – the Bromme culture

6.1 Introduction

The previous chapter considered the effects and impacts of the Laacher See eruption following a transecting line of proximal to distal, along the major fallout lobes to the west, south, and the northeast. In thinking about the manifold effects of this eruption on landscapes, plants, animals, and humans emphasis was placed on whether these impacts affected access to resources, and on the temporality of the induced changes. An argument was made that the initially destructive and, to Late Glacial foragers perhaps confusing and worrying, effects of the eruption led to a temporary abandonment of some of the affected landscapes, or at the very least a major change and reduction in the way these were used. It is argued that this abandonment was initially created by "ecological roadblocks" (VanderHoek and Nelson, 2007: 133) that in turn led to a reduction of contact between groups. This relative isolation may then have led to *weak regionalisation* in northern Bavaria in the form of the Atzenhofer Gruppe, in Bohemia in the form of Vencl's armature-less groups, and in Switzerland in the form of the Fürsteiner facies, and *strong regionalisation* in southern Scandinavia in the form of the Bromme culture. Itself to all intents and purposes unaffected by tephra fall, located away from the fallout, and perhaps even benefitting from both the eruption-induced climate variation and the general warming trend during the latter part of the Allerød, southern Scandinavia offered itself as a suitable refugium for those forag-

ers vacating the affected parts of the North European Plain. In addition, the local richness in high-quality flint and the increasing local concentration of sought-after big game (Mortensen et al., 2014a) may have further attracted Late Glacial hunter-gatherers – who had been exploring the area before the Laacher See eruption – to the region.

This chapter will consider the Bromme culture, its origin, technology, economy, ecology, and population dynamics in more detail. In doing so, this chapter will argue that the Bromme culture should really be seen not as a separate culture on a taxonomic par with the Federmessergruppen, but as a rather short-lived variant of it that came to an end already in the first part of the Younger Dryas. The Bromme culture shows all the hallmarks of a bottleneck origin, and it arguably presents a case of "the disappearance of useful arts" (Rivers, 1912: 109) – a reduction in technological capital that may come about due to the social isolation of small populations (Henrich, 2004).

6.2. Origin of the Bromme culture

Chapter 1 already sketched out the various hypotheses that have been put forward for the origin – in time and space – of the Bromme culture over the years (cf. Table 1.2). Many of these can safely be relegated to discussions of research history, while others deserve more serious consideration. It seems that for many years, the general consensus has been that the Bromme culture emerged during the early part of the Allerød, from either a Hamburgian (Holm and Rieck, 1992) or Federmessergruppen (Fischer, 1991) substrate. Either developmental sequence has been seen as a gradual emergence of a regionally specific technocomplex in "a continuous and largely endogenous cultural development" (Eriksen, 1999: 169). Alternative versions have been mooted, however. In these, the Bromme culture (as well as all or most of the other Late Glacial technocomplexes in the region) are seen as migration phenomena (Madsen, 1996), although it has been pointed out that such hypotheses rarely, if ever, provide explicit statements on where people would have come from. In Brinch Petersen's (2009: 103) words "very often the new culture seems to appear as a *deus ex machina*, with no obvious ancestor".

At the time the Bromme culture was first defined, the recognition of a likely ancestor was indeed not straightforward and the question often left unanswered (Becker, 1971; Clark, 1950); publications in the middle part of the 20th century continued to avow the distinctiveness of the Bromme culture (Schwabedissen, 1954), which at this point – i.e. after the excavation of the eponymous settlement near Sorø on Zealand (Mathiassen, 1946) – had become a well-established technocomplex. Yet, despite – or perhaps rather because – of this alleged distinctiveness, finding an appropriate origin for the Bromme culture proved difficult. Indeed, Becker (1971: 136) stated plainly that by the early 1970's "we cannot solve the problem of the Bromme's origin".

To a large degree these conflicting suggestions can be resolved by considering how research history has, by chance and necessity rather than design, conditioned the frame of empirical reference for their proponents. Until about the 1990's very little Federmessergruppen material, for instance, was known from Denmark, all of which in the form of surface finds (Andersen, 1977; Fugl Petersen, 1973). In contrast, early Late Glacial Hamburgian sites have been known for longer (e.g. Holm and Rieck, 1983, 1987), giving rise to suggestions that the Bromme culture derived from this

technocomplex (Holm and Rieck, 1992) – despite the major typological and technological differences that exist between these groups. Seriation techniques were used to investigate this assumed transition (Madsen, 1992), but their results never sufficiently verified; indeed, given that seriation methods presuppose cultural continuity (Dunnell, 1970; O'Brien and Lyman, 1999) they are patently unsuitable to investigating issues of discontinuity. Furthermore, subsequent absolute dating has also revealed a clear difference in time between the Hamburgian and Bromme cultures (Riede and Edinborough, 2012; Riede et al., 2010).

Since the 1990's the number of Federmessergruppen sites and surface finds has steadily increased (Fugl Petersen, 1994; Hirsch and Madsen, 2012; Holm, 1991), and Federmessergruppen components have been recognized at an ever increasing number of locales (e.g. Andersen, 2016; Johansson, 2003; Petersen, 2006). Where dated directly, these fall into the earlier part of the Allerød, i.e. GI-1b or c (Riede and Edinborough, 2012). This in turn has led to the recognition that there is a close affinity, both in typology and technology, between the Federmessergruppen and the Bromme culture (Eriksen, 2000) and that the latter most likely derives from the former (Riede, 2013b; Riede et al., 2011a). It thus seems most likely that the observed culture change from Federmessergruppen to Bromme culture in southern Scandinavia bears traces of continuity as well as discontinuity. There is a certain continuity of tool forms (large tanged points, flake scrapers and miscellaneous burins) and technology (straightforward knapping of local raw materials). The Bromme culture can also be said to economically and ecologically represent a more settled variety (cf. Table 4.1 and see Brinch Petersen, 2009; Riede, 2005b). At the same time, the Bromme culture diverges from the Federmessergruppen – and indeed from the general culture-historical trend observable in Europe at this time – on several counts:

1. It is geographically circumscribed at a time of otherwise general cultural homogeneity over a large region.
2. It is chronologically short-lived at a time

of otherwise general cultural longevity.

3. It is characterised by a simplified toolkit and tool production techniques at a time of otherwise increasing toolkit diversity.

4. It is characterised by large and rather heavy tools at a time of increasing use of very small stone tool components in the form of backed elements and microliths elsewhere.

In sum, a likely ancestor for the Bromme culture has now been identified. What remains controversial, however, are the mechanism, timing and process of this change. Arguably, the 'Laacher See hypothesis' offers a solution to Becker's 'Bromme problem' (see also Riede, 2013b, 2014a, 2017).

6.3 Bromme culture chronology

Already when the original 'Lyngby point' (see Fig. 1.4) was discovered at Nørre Lyngby in the very north of mainland Denmark in 1913, its association with Late Glacial freshwater deposits provided dating evidence (Jessen and Nordmann, 1915). It was suggested that the point is of Younger Dryas age (Iversen, 1942). Yet, given the lack of additional lithic material associated with this object it is – ironically given its iconic status in the Bromme culture's research history – not at all clear whether this projectile point reflects the presence of Federmessergruppen in the area or of the Bromme culture. Indeed, later direct dating of a hu-

manly modified horse rib from Nørre Lyngby (AAR-1511: 11570±110, $\partial^{13}O$= -17.9‰) attests to the presence of people in the area well before the Younger Dryas and well before the Laacher See eruption. To further complicate the matter, the equally iconic 'Lyngby axe' found in the area (although not together with or even at the same time as the lithic point) has since been dated to the early Holocene (AAR-8919: 9110±65; see Stensager, 2004). There is, however, no direct contextual relation between any of the lithic material in northern Jutland and these radiocarbon dates.

The Bromme culture took shape more fully and became more firmly fixed in time with the excavation of its name-giving site (Mathiassen, 1946), the sensational discovery and subsequent investigation of which escalated into an unfortunate dispute over intellectual property rights between the National Museum and the discoverer of the site, Erik Westerby (see Eriksen, 2012; Fischer, 2002; Westerby, 1985). At any rate, palynological and geological analyses placed the settlement into the Allerød and possibly the early Younger Dryas (Iversen, 1946). Subsequent radiocarbon dating further confirmed these relative age estimates (Heinemeier and Rud, 2001). Likewise, geological observations at both Segebro in Scania (Salomonsson, 1962, 1964) and at Bro on Funen (Andersen, 1970, 1972) indicate a chronological position of the Bromme occupation during the late Allerød or early Younger Dryas (Table 6.1). Whilst these two localities themselves have yielded no organic remains and their ages thus

Site	Evidence type	Allerød		YD		Reference(s)
		Early	Late	Early	Late	
Bro	Flint frost shattering			1		Andersen (1972)
Bromme	Pollen, geoarchaeolgy	1	1	1		Iversen (1946)
Nørre Lyngby	Pollen, geoarchaeolgy			1		Iversen (1942)
Segebro	Pollen, geoarchaeolgy	1	1	1		Salomonsson (1964)
Consensus dating		**2**	**2**	**4**	**0**	

Table 6.1 *Non-radiometric dating evidence for the Bromme culture. The consensus of these variable and fairly weak indicator dates points towards the late Allerød and in particular the early Younger Dryas (YD) – when temperature dropped sufficiently to produce strong frosts. See also the discussion in Eriksen (2002).*

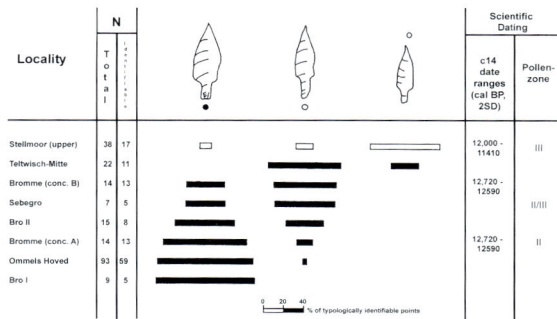

Figure 6.1 An attempt to address the internal development of Bromme formal tool technology using seriation. Sample sizes and external dating evidence is sparse. The significant chronological gap between the latest Brommean assemblage and the Ahrensburgian material from Stellmoor (upper layer) speaks against strict cultural continuity (thus violating one of the foundational assumptions of seriation; see Dunnell, 1970; Lyman and O'Brien, 2006; Madsen, 1988). Redrawn from Fischer (1978).

cannot be cross-checked with radiocarbon dating, two other sites – Fensmark and Trollesgave – have been dated absolutely (Fischer, 2013; Fischer et al., 2013a). In addition, and in accordance with the earlier relative as well as absolute age determinations, all newer ^{14}C dates also fall into the very latest part of the Allerød and the earliest, warmer part of the Younger Dryas, likely before the cold-induced collapse of the Allerød forest ecosystem (cf. Fischer et al., 2013a). Furthermore, two ^{14}C dates on surface-found 'Lyngby axes' from Arreskov on Funen and Mikkelsmosse in Scania have also yielded late Allerød/early Younger Dryas ages. These may be linked to a Bromme presence in the island part of Denmark and southern Sweden.

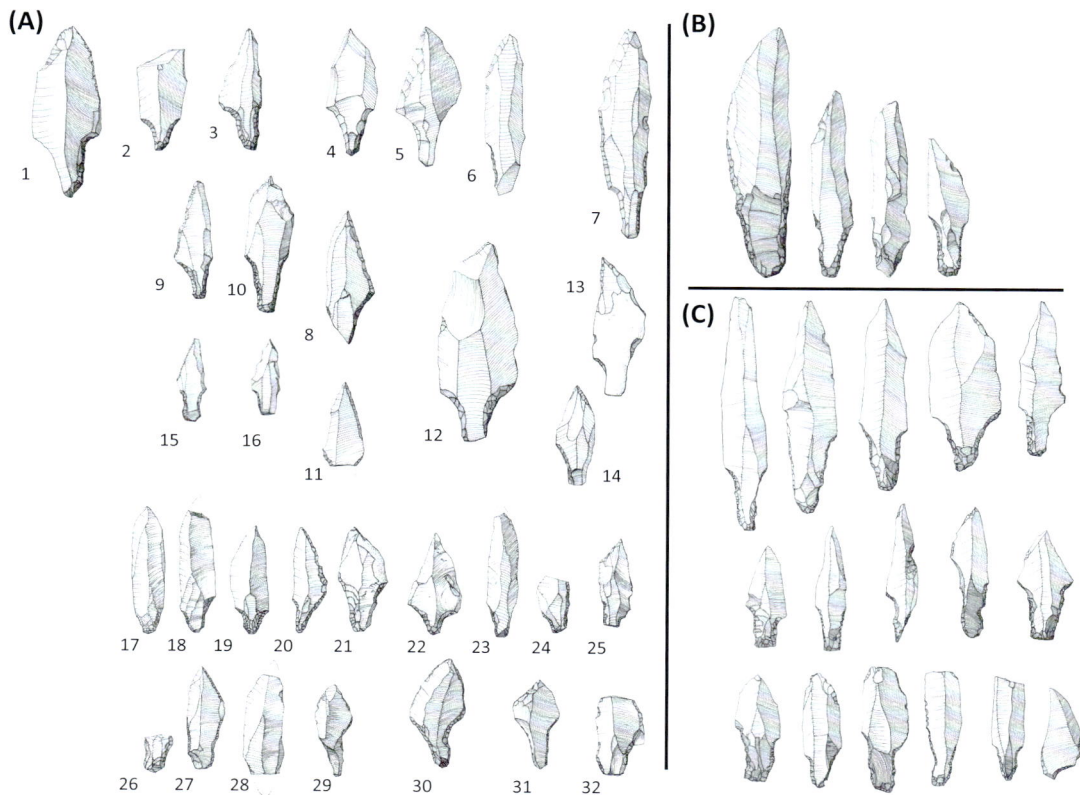

Figure 6.2 The morphological variability within the category 'large tanged point' observed in selected Federmessergruppen sites and a single Brommean locale. (A): France: 1-3: Roc des Abeilles; 4-8: Pis-de-la-Vache; 9: Bois-Ragot level 5b; 10: Grotte de la Bonne-Femme; 11: Grotte du Morin; 12: Laugerie-Basse; 13-14: Abri de Fontalès; British Isles: 15-16: Hengistbury Head; Germany: 17-19: Borneck-Mitte; 20-21: Grande 1; 22: Rissen 14; 23: Häcklingen; 24: Schalkholz; 25: Bärenkeller; 26: Mühlheim-Dietesheim; 27: Alt Duvenstedt LA89; Poland: 28: Jaglisko 3; The Netherlands: 29-31: Norgervaart – but note that these points may be forgeries; 32: Een-Schipsloot; (B) Denmark: Hjarup Mose; (C) locus classicus Bromme. Note: All points are redrawn from the listed publications to approximate scale. References for all Federmessergruppen sites can be found in Table 4.4.

The dating of the Bromme culture into the Allerød and the beginning of the Younger Dryas has stimulated various views on how it is related with technocomplexes both before and after. Seriation methods were employed to investigate the internal development of the Bromme culture and to link it to the Ahrensburgian culture (Fischer, 1978; Fischer and Nielsen, 1986). Based on rather small sample sizes, the use of individual knapping attributes only, and the very limited external dating information available for cross-checking (Fig. 6.1), the results of these studies must be seen as speculative at best. What does remain clear, however, is the striking variability of projectile point forms as well as burins in the Bromme culture (see Buck Pedersen, 2009). Whilst it is possible that some of the points known from Bromme assemblages are unfinished or were never selected for actual usage, the lack of standardisation observed in all Bromme inventories remains large (Fig. 6.2) – and contrasts with the rather more formal tool, blank, and core shapes of the Hamburgian, Federmessergruppen, as well as (albeit perhaps to a lesser degree) the Ahrensburgian. In summary, whilst there may be slight trends of changing lithic technology they remain difficult to substantiate in part because of the short span of the Bromme culture in the order of only 200-330 years (Riede and Edinborough, 2012) and in part because we lack chronological control of individual assemblages.

6.4 Bromme culture ecology and economy

As elsewhere on the North European Plain, Bromme culture sites with organic preservation are rare. This makes it difficult to reconstruct economic and ecological relations with certainty. Yet, as the dating of the Bromme culture suggests, these hunter-gatherers were strongly tied to the sparse forest ecosystem – with stands of birch, rowan, juniper, aspen, willow, pine, grasses and herbs – that developed during the relatively warm and stable Allerød (Kolstrup, 2002). Notably, this was a development with both a temporal and spa-

tial gradient, i.e. less isolated, fragmented and vulnerable stands of trees developed first in more southerly areas and last, if ever, in the northern part of Late Glacial Denmark (Bennike et al., 2004; Bokelmann, 1978; Iversen, 1947; Mortensen, 2007).

These forests were inhabited by an interesting community of mammals that finds no match in contemporary ecosystems, a so-called non-analogue species composition (Stewart and Lister, 2001): Reindeer (*Rangifer tarandus*), elk (*Alces alces*), giant deer (*Megaloceros giganteus*), horse (*Equus caballus*), beaver (*Castor fiber*), brown bear (*Ursus arctos*), as well as carnivores such as the wolf (*Canis lupus*), and the wolverine (*Gulo gulo*) (Aaris-Sørensen, 1995, 1999; Aaris-Sørensen and Liljegren, 2004). The arrival of these species in southern Scandinavia was, much like that of plants, structured in time and space (Aaris-Sørensen, 2009; Riede et al., 2010). During the Allerød, this faunal species composition, whilst non-analogue or disharmonious, maintained a certain degree of stability and greater diversity, at least when compared with the periods before and after, that were characterised by a marked species turn-over and dramatically increased rates

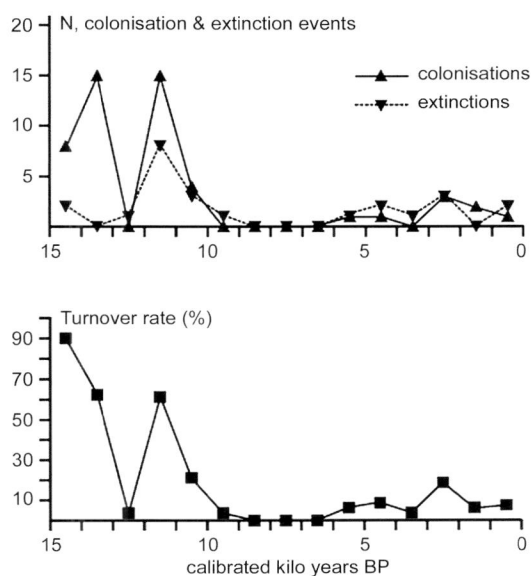

Figure 6.3 *Southern Scandinavian animal communities: (A) Faunal colonisation and extinction dynamics over time; (B) Turnover rate, a measure of change in community composition. Both are counted in 1000-year time slices and are from Aaris-Sørensen (2009).*

of extinction (Fig. 6.3; Aaris-Sørensen, 2009; Sommer et al., 2011).

Those animal species directly associated with sites of the Bromme culture are elk, reindeer and possibly horse (Madsen, 1983; Mathiassen, 1946). However, the stratigraphic and contextual association of the horse bone with the lithic material at the Bromme locale is uncertain, and subsequent radiocarbon dating has been unsuccessful (Heinemeier and Rud, 2001). The presence of reindeer may also have been limited, at least when compared to the colder Bølling and Younger Dryas episodes (Riede et al., 2010; Sommer et al., 2014). Beaver bones , too, were found at Bromme as were the remains of lake fish. Whether *Megaloceros* was hunted during the Bromme culture remains speculation. Taken together – and interpreted liberally – these faunal associations point to a more or less specialised open woodland hunting economy. The limited number of potential prey species may have driven this specialisation.

Seen against the background of southern Scandinavian Allerød ecology, it seems that while the entry of Federmessergruppen in the region may have been motivated in large part by the preferential availability of large mammal species such as elk and giant deer (as well as other resources such as high-quality flint and amber), the economy of the later Bromme culture is focused on these animals by necessity rather than choice. Importantly, the selected prey species of the Bromme culture logically represent only a fraction of those available in more southerly regions, where even the primarily cold-adapted reindeer, weathered the Allerød (Sommer et al., 2014) and remained present in small numbers all the way into the Holocene (Drucker et al., 2011). This restricted economy would have provided markedly less behavioural manoeuvrability – resilience, adaptability – in times of crisis, such as when the Allerød ecosystem came under increasing strain in the early part of GI-1.

What weapons did Brommean hunters use? In Chapter 4, a range of quantitative and ethnographic comparative approaches was used to argue that large tanged points are most parsimoniously interpreted as dart tips. These appeared first in Upper Magdalenian contexts associated with the emergence of the Federmessergruppen, and became a widespread albeit secondary armature along this entire technocomplex' range. Previous experimental studies, in particular the works of Fischer et al. (1984) and Fischer (1989) are in opposition to the interpretation of large tanged points as dart-tips. However, as has been noted many times before, experimental studies at best demonstrate what is possible and never what *was* in prehistory (Thomas, 1978). In this vein, Christensen (1986: 119) has pointed out that students of prehistoric weaponry can generally be divided into two camps: The 'possibilists' who argue on the basis of replication trials for what is feasible, and the 'empiricists' who examine actual patterns in the archaeological record and try to interpret these, usually according to some previously formulated hypothesis. The shooting trials of Fischer and colleagues were conducted in the spirit of 'possibilism', and notably with the original aim of deriving micro- and macroscopic fracture patterns that are diagnostic of particular weapon types. However, not only have such endeavours since been shown to be problematic — fractures can at best be used to tell projectiles from non-projectiles (Hutchings, 2011) and even that only after taphonomic issues are taken into due consideration (Pargeter, 2011; Rots and Plisson, 2014). In fact, these uncertainties are fully reflected in the ambiguous results presented by Fischer et al. (Table 6.2). As I have pointed out elsewhere (Riede, 2009d), the interpretation of these results is made difficult by the variable sample sizes of the two experimental series (bow vs. spear), the variable shooting range, and target type. Furthermore, the bow used was of Mesolithic type and made of elm, a raw material not available in the Late Glacial of southern Scandinavia. The comparison of this weapon set with a hand-delivered spear further complicates the matter. Most significantly, however, the actual results obtained are at least as consistent with an interpretation of the 'Bromme points' as spear-tips rather than arrowheads. After all, relative to sample size nearly twice as many

Experimental parameters			Traces					
			Macro			Micro		
Weapon	Target	Distance (m)	N Examined for macro-wear	N, diagnostic macro-fractures	%, diagnostic macro-fractures	N, examined for micro-wear	N, diagnostic micro-fractures	%, diagnostic micro-fractures
A R R O W	Whole boar	10	23	9	39	23	14	57
	Boar leg	4	5	3	60	5	1	20
	Pig w bones	10	42	19	45	12	8	66
	Fish	1-3	10	1	10	4	3	75
	Reeds	-	4	0	0	4	0	0
	Grass & soil	-	7	1	14	5	1	20
	Bush	3	3	1	33	3	1	33
	Tree	4	5	3	60	2	2	100
S P E A R	Boar	3-4	2	2	100	0	-	-
	Boar head	1-3	6	3	50	0	-	-
	Sheep	2	3	1	33	0	-	-

Table 6.2 *Excerpt from the original results table of Fischer and colleagues' shooting trials using large tanged points. Note the variable experimental parameters and the ambiguous.*

spear-points (61%) as arrowheads (33%) show macroscopic wear traces.

Given the size and weight of the large tanged points from Bromme contexts and given that very strong bows were unlikely to have been manufactured at that time, an interpretation of these tips as dart points seems most parsimonious. As noted in Chapter 4, a shift from the use of the more complex to make but easier to use bow-and-arrow, to the simpler but far less accurate and reliable atlatl, may have had significant demographic implications mediated by reduced hunting success. Reduced hunting success in turn would lead to reduced population density, which then impacted on the costs and benefits of cultural transmission, but also made these groups more vulnerable to stochastic fluctuations in the environment that impacted on life-history decisions (Riede, 2009a).

6.5 Bromme culture population dynamics

It is suggested here that the number of people responsible for making and leaving the material culture now labelled Brommean was very low indeed. The presence of the ancestral Federmessergruppen in southern Scandinavia, but also in the adjacent area of northern central Europe was ephemeral and episodic, probably mostly on a seasonal basis. Those sites that either have significant stratigraphies that preserve LST or are radiocarbon dated all point to slight and likely declining population densities prior to 13,000 BP. The presence of people in the landscapes along the northern periphery of the Late Glacial world may additionally have been stressed by the prolonged cold of the IACP. The eventual abandonment of central northern Europe and the concomitant movement of those groups into southern

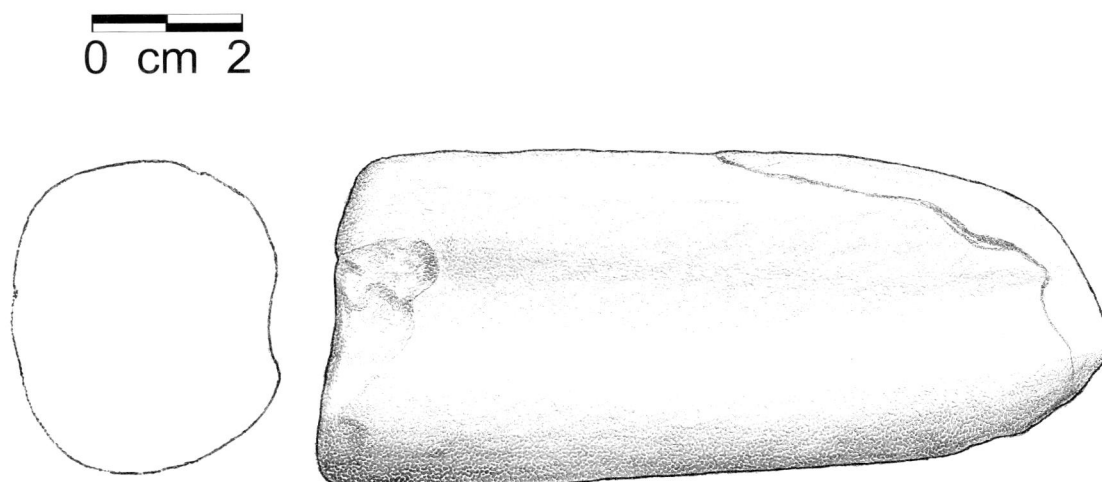

Figure 6.4 *The only known (possibly) Brommean sandstone shaft-smoother from the site of Møllehøje in northern-central Jutland.*

Scandinavia may thus reflect the movement of only few people (Riede, 2012b). The low floral and faunal diversity reviewed above likewise suggests limiting carrying capacity, which translates into small hunter-gatherer groups (see Fig. 4.14). Interesting in this regard is the suggestion that the site of Trollesgave reflects, with a total of ~20,000 lithic pieces, the short-term activity of one family unit (Donahue and Fischer, 2015). By this yardstick, even the largest Brommean sites (see Buck Pedersen, 2009) would not indicate the presence of a substantial population.

Considering the spatial distribution of Bromme locales in southern Scandinavia it is further notable that virtually all large and excavated sites are found in eastern Denmark and Scania (Buck Pedersen, 2009; Mortensen et al., 2014a). Indeed, the occurrence of either tanged Wehlen scrapers, backed elements or both in the typologically classified (but in absolute terms undated) Brommean locales in Jutland (e.g. Enslev, Løvenholm, Hollendskær) suggest that these may belong to the Federmessergruppen rather than the Bromme culture. Nonetheless, independently of whether one considers the locales on Jutland to be Brommean or not, there is little doubt that the great majority of sites, and with them the focus of human activity, was located in eastern Denmark. This perspective – one that rejects claims of Bromme presence in England, Po-

land, Lithuania and other far-away regions as based exclusively on the faulty typological automatism critiqued in Chapter 1 – would make the Bromme a spatially even more restricted phenomenon than previously suggested. Coupling this to the short span of this techno-complex (<300 years) implied by the current radiocarbon record cuts the Bromme culture radically down in size.

Yet, looking again at the correlation between the dating of the Bromme phenomenon and climatic and environmental change, it is equally evident that the Laacher See eruption coincides with the end of the Gerzensee Oscillation (Intra-Allerød Cold Phase, IACP) and the start of a 200-year-long warm phase (GI-1a). This climatic amelioration, together with the abundance of high-quality flint and the presence of (economically and symbolically) valued animal species, such as the elk, not only facilitated the migration of the ancestors of the Bromme culture into southern Scandinavia, but it may have led to the 'splendid isolation' alluded to in Chapter 1. Initially, those groups that migrated away from the darkened skies and the areas covered in LST to the south, lived well. However, the absence of long-distance contacts – there is at the very least no material evidence for such contacts – and the very small population made it difficult to maintain complex technologies. Both demographic parameters as well as raw materials likely played a role: first, small populations have a limited capacity to innovate (Shennan, 2001). Indeed under conditions of low and falling population density, size and/or connectedness, demography can drive the loss of cultural complexity (Collard et al., 2013; Derex et al., 2013; Henrich, 2004; Richerson et al., 2009). The argument here is that the low number of suitable craft role-models or teachers eventually leads to a drop in skill levels, especially in relation to complex technologies – and bow-and-arrow technology is one of those most commonly lost (e.g. Rivers, 1912). The single occurrence of a shaft-smoother from a possible Bromme context in northern-central Jutland from the site of Møllehøje (SMS 329A) would, if its association with the co-occurring Late Glacial lithics is indeed correct, support the notion of spear-thrower use in the Brommean. The working groove of this tool is, even allowing for moderate surface erosion of a size suitable for the production of spear- or dart-, but certainly not of arrow-shafts (Fig. 6.4). In its morphology, this artefact is closer to similar objects found in Federmessergruppen contexts rather than those of the Ahrensburgian, which are evidently used pair-wise and show a more standardised groove size related to the production of arrow-shafts (Riede, 2012a; Riede and Kristensen, 2010).

The simplicity of Bromme technology is not only visible in the shift from arch-backed points plus large tanged points to large tanged points only, but also in the morphology of those points. In an attempt to quantify the functional properties of these Late Glacial projectile points, Dev and Riede (2012) compared both tip angle as well as symmetry of large tanged points from the Federmessergruppen and the Bromme culture with the small tanged points of the Ahrensburgian culture and the tanged armatures of the later Middle Neolithic Pitted Ware Culture. The latter culture's points are notorious for being easily confused with Late Glacial points (Fischer, 1985), and served as a control group in this analysis. It was noted above that the morphological diversity amongst the large tanged points of the Bromme culture is substantial and the results of that study forcefully underline that observation. What is striking is that the highly variable shape of these projectile points can be interpreted to imply a somewhat sub-optimal design of the large tanged points of the Bromme culture (as well as, to a lesser degree, other Final Palaeolithic projectiles). Despite the rather rigorous ballistic requirements of this kind of weaponry (Beckhoff, 1966; Christensen, 1986; Hughes, 1998) they are generally highly asymmetric (Fig. 6.5) and have tip angles that are not considered useful

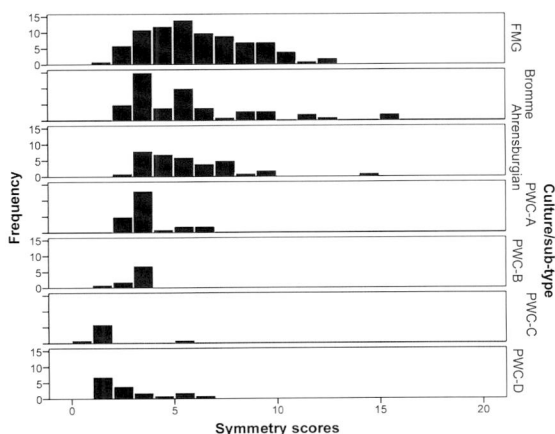

Figure 6.5 Symmetry scores as measured using the approach of Hardaker and Dunn (2005) for a sample of Late Glacial tanged points from the Federmessergruppen (N= 84), Brommean (N= 50) and Ahrensburgian (N= 35) as well as from the Neolithic Pitted Ware Culture (N= 58).

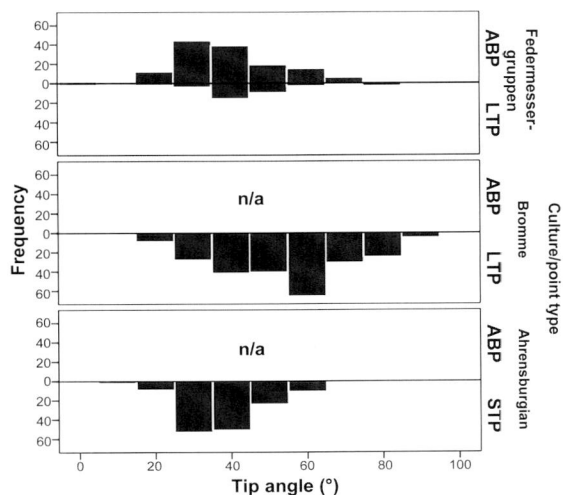

Figure 6.6 Tip angle values amongst selected Late Glacial projectile points. For full details see Dev and Riede (2012).

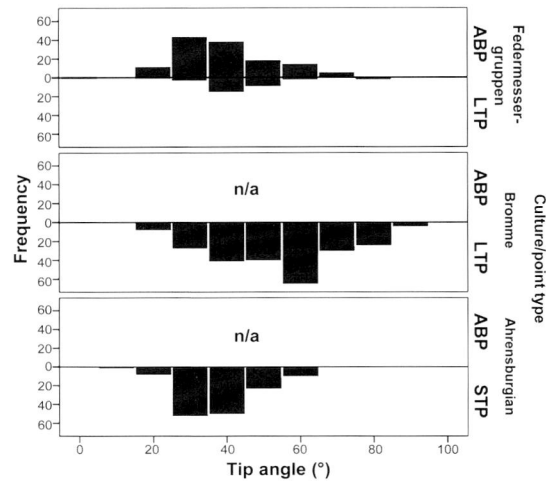

Figure 6.7 *A selection of large tanged points from the hunting-stand/cache at Ommels Hoved; note the generally wide tip angles, the width of the points >20mm and their substantial thickness. Modified from Holm (1972).*

for projectile points (Fig. 6.6). Friis-Hansen (1990: 497, my emphasis) noted that "a wide broadhead with a 30°-40° front angle shows good hide-penetration and cutting qualities *if the two edges are sharp, the blade is thin, and the hide is not too thick*. If maximum hide penetration and bone-splitting capability are needed... the front angle should be no more than 20°". These observations reveal yet another aspect of the Brommean paradox. If the Bromme culture indeed practiced an elk hunting economy, then the optimal design of their hunting armatures should be closer to those alluded to at the end of Friis-Hansen's statement, i.e. broad but also thin and steeply tapering. Elk are the largest extant cervids on par with many African large mammals (see Tomka, 2013) and their hide is thick (Geist, 1999). Yet, Bromme points are – in addition to being rather asymmetric – anything but thin, and their tip angles on average greater than the 50° considered functional by Friis-Hansen. That said, however, using heavier-duty weaponry against large game such as the elk and especially the giant deer may be seen as just the right decision (Tomka, 2013). But: this does *not* explain the disappearance of the slender arch-backed points and neither does it explain the great asymmetry and broad tip-angles observed in the large tanged point projectile-heads (Fig. 6.7).

Connected to technological complexity is the question of suitable raw materials, in particular the all-important organic components. Building a fully functioning bow requires a considerably greater number of components (cf. Oswalt, 1976), especially wood with particular properties. It is possible that, in the Federmessergruppen, these key raw materials were acquired from the more southerly parts of the seasonal round where a greatly expanded range of plant taxa was available (e.g. Baales et al., 2002) and where the growth of trees most likely was less retarded by snow and wind. As travels to the south appear to have been severely curtailed following the LSE, these raw materials could no longer be obtained. Complex technologies such as the bow and arrow are fine-tuned and require all parts to work efficiently. If the capacity to innovate is constrained by population size and one or more critical 'spare parts' become inaccessible, the utility of the entire technological system may collapse (cf. Ugan et al., 2003). In other words, a well-functioning atlatl may be better than a barely functioning bow, and whilst the decision to abandon bow-and-arrow technology may in that sense have been perfectly reasonable, the spear-thrower and dart combination may indeed have been an "adequate technology" (Read, 2006: 164) that serviced all the immediate needs of the newly installed communities in southern Scandinavia. However, the intrinsically lower success rate of dart-hunting (see Stodiek, 1993; Stodiek and Paulsen, 1996) may have posed a demographic challenge to this population. Following this calculation, it can be assumed that bow-and-arrow hunting would have yielded a greater number of calories/unit time spent hunting; this more versatile and reliable technology would thus have made populations less vulnerable to stochastic fluctuations in prey availability.

There has been much discussion about the demography-driven model used here to argue for a loss of cultural complexity following the LSE-induced and perhaps partly self-chosen isolation of southern Scandinavian communities (Collard et al., 2013; Powell et al., 2009; Read, 2006, 2008; Richerson et al., 2009; Vaesen, 2012). In the case of the Bromme culture, it remains clear that the shift from a parallel use of bow-and-arrow and spear-thrower-and-dart technologies to the exclusive use of only the latter, in the absence of significant changes in prey types or overall environs, needs addressing. The most common explanation for the emergence of the Bromme culture found in the literature is curiously deterministic: The abundance of high-quality flint is seen as sufficient to drive this culture change. But why do similar cultures not emerge in other parts of Europe where similarly high-quality stone resources are available? And why is there such a neat fit between the ballistic expectations and ethnographic examples of, on the one hand the slender arch-backed points of the Federmessergruppen and, on the other, the large tanged points that characterise the post-LSE Bromme culture? Why does the entire toolkit of the Bromme culture become so chunky, given that larger is not always better (Kuhn, 1994)? How can we explain the observed regionalisation in the Bromme culture, given that the general trend in this period is one of variable but overall homogenous and expansive technocomplexes? Finally, what does the absence of 'exotic' objects in the Bromme culture signify? Whilst Scandinavian flint may suffice for the making of domestic and quotidian artefacts, hunter-gatherers', lives are not all about the food quest. As suggested by Whallon (2006), by myself elsewhere (Riede, 2014b) and here in Chapter 4, the absence of such 'non-utilitarian' objects – signifiers of social connectedness – in the Bromme culture highlights the social dimensions of the effects of the LSE and of the causal chains leading to the emergence of this technocomplex.

In sum, because the environment does not offer any immediate or logically satisfying explanations, primary causality for the actual shift in technology must be sought in the social or demographic sphere. As has been alluded to on numerous occasions throughout this and the previous chapters, the initial emergence of large tanged points is explained well as the adoption of heavy armatures used primarily against larger prey, such as elk and giant deer, and as a way to fashion functional weapons under constraints of organic raw material availability that became more pressing with northwards expansion. In northern Europe, the organic barbed points in widespread use for the same purpose during the Middle Magdalenian were increasingly phased out and replaced by the much more easily manufactured and more expedient lithic projectile tips (see also Pétillon et al., 2011). Yet, this general pattern does not explain how and why such a supplementary weapon suddenly would replace the otherwise ultimate tool of these hunter-gatherers, the bow-and-arrow – unless we invoke the disruption of networks and population connectivity, and the inability to acquire one or more critical (but unfortunately archaeologically invisible) materials. Together these two factors may explain the abandonment of bow-and-arrow technology at a pace much more rapid than the abandonment of similarly complex technologies in, for instance, Tasmania (Cosgrove, 1995; Diamond, 1978).

6.6 Brommean material culture diversity and settlement in southern Scandinavia

In the foregoing sections it has been argued that the Bromme culture cannot readily be understood as the "first complete adaptation" (Fischer et al., 2013a: 4663) of Late Glacial hunter-gatherers to the particular conditions of southern Scandinavia. Linking these environmental particulars to the specific traits of the Bromme culture – the macrolithic toolkit, the generic production sequence, the exclusive use of large tanged points, and its tight geographic circumscription – is rather environmentally deterministic and adaptationist, yet ignores the fact that what distinguishes the Bromme culture from the preceding and, to the south, contemporaneous Federmessergruppen is the absence of arch-backed points, thumbnail scrapers, as well as the (so far) complete absence of 'exotic' materials that could attest to long-range connections between post-eruption southern Scandinavia and central Europe. Using methods of material culture phylogenetics (cf. O'Brien et al., 2008) and data on the manufacture, morphology

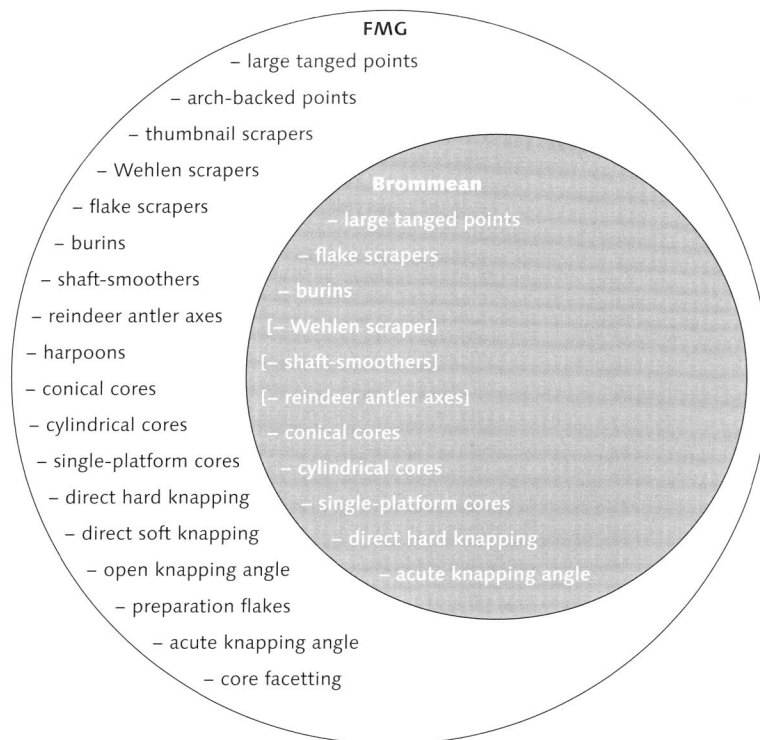

Figure 6.8 *Venn diagram of the logical relation between the Federmessergruppen and the Bromme culture. The typological and technological attributes are selected from the literature: (Hartz, 1987), De Bie (1999), Loew (2005), Madsen (1992, 1996), Richter (2001), and Eriksen (2000). Elements shown in square brackets are only with uncertainty represented. FMG= Federmessergruppen.*

FMG
– large tanged points
– arch-backed points
– thumbnail scrapers
– Wehlen scrapers
– flake scrapers
– burins
– shaft-smoothers
– reindeer antler axes
– harpoons
– conical cores
– cylindrical cores
– single-platform cores
– direct hard knapping
– direct soft knapping
– open knapping angle
– preparation flakes
– acute knapping angle
– core facetting

Brommean
– large tanged points
– flake scrapers
– burins
[– Wehlen scraper]
[– shaft-smoothers]
[– reindeer antler axes]
– conical cores
– cylindrical cores
– single-platform cores
– direct hard knapping
– acute knapping angle

and co-occurrence of projectiles in the Late Glacial of southern Scandinavia, I have previously suggested that the Bromme culture should indeed be seen as a sub-branch of, or clade *within*, the Federmessergruppen (Riede, 2011b). Widening the perspective to other tool classes and stone working aspects, so-called Venn or Euler diagrams (Pakula, 1989; Venn, 1880) can be used to visualise this nested hierarchy. Venn diagrams are simple yet non-trivial graphic representations of the logic relationships between two or more sets (Grünbaum, 1975, 1992a, 1992b). In Palaeolithic archaeology such a formalised approach to investigating the relationships between different technocomplexes has been pioneered by Houtsma et al. (1996), and their approach has also been applied specifically to the Bromme culture by Niekus (1995). Whilst never published, Niekus did find evidence for both a significant overlap between the Bromme culture and Federmessergruppen, as well as a certain degree of uniqueness.

Taking a slightly different approach, the joint presence of typological and technological traits can be transformed into area-proportional Venn diagrams using the VennMaster software (Kestler et al., 2008; Kestler et al., 2005). Given that the Bromme culture is characterised first and foremost by an absence of specific features, it can be readily nested within the Federmessergruppen (Fig. 6.8).

The power of such an analysis should not be overestimated, but it does raise issues of cultural taxonomy and of the most appropriate geographic scale of analysis. As Houtsma et al. (1996: 143) perhaps overly acerbically noted, one needs to "escape the constraints of contemporary national borders and the paradigmatic straight-jackets of provincialism and regional chauvinism" in order to understand material culture changes in the Late Palaeolithic of northern Europe. Yet, the early definition and distinguished research history of the Bromme culture together with the strong regional or even national perspective often adopted in relation to it has arguably led to a biased view of its relation to contemporaneous technocomplexes (more extensively discussed in Riede 2017). Danish archaeology in particular has had and continues to have a strong national, regional and indeed local focus (e.g. Høgh, 2008; Høiris, 2010). Whilst a *regional perspective* is by no means all bad it

Environmental

Cause

- Natural disaster*
- Famine/illness*

Social

Cause

- Anti-social individual
- Fear of revenge
- Feuds
- Fear
- Expansion of territory*
- Search for rich(er) resources*
- Vision
- Desire to die in one's birthplace

Table 6.3 *The causes for migration found in the ethnography and ethnohistory of the Canadian Arctic, after Rowley (1985). Those causes marked with * are likely to have been important in the Late Glacial resettlement of northern Europe. Note that most of the 'social' reasons for migration can be brought on by environmental hardship, whilst subsistence and population failures – even those precipitated by environmental changes or event – also have a social dimension (Mandryk, 1993).*

has, in this instance, led to a certain *regionalism*. This is a well-known problem in studies of the European Palaeolithic in general that has been critically mentioned since the 1990s (Houtsma et al., 1996; Newell and Constandse-Westermann, 1996; Otte and Keeley, 1990). Yet, the early reification of the Bromme culture – *prior* to the more formal definition of the Federmessergruppen by Schwabedissen (1954) – has meant that its existence and reality is rarely if ever questioned.

In discussing the challenges of undue regional focus, Otte and Keeley (1990: 582) at the same time underline that "archaeology...is not an experimental science but must rely on controlled comparisons to evaluate hypotheses and isolate causes. When such comparisons are too local, control of many variables, especially those which transcend or transgress regions, is lost". A comparative approach to understanding the origin and fate of the Bromme culture

has been adopted here, and is also described in more technical detail elsewhere (Riede, 2013a). Such a comparison, whilst by necessity rough and ready, shows that the effects of the Laacher See eruption varied strongly from region to region. Migration appears to have been the major response in some of the most severely affected regions, i.e. the immediate near-field and the central northern parts of the North European Plain (i.e. northern Germany). Such a migratory response is not surprising given that mobility is not only a distinguishing feature of hunter-gatherers in general, but it is their primary crisis management option (Table 6.3; Rowley, 1985). In addition, as we have seen in Chapter 3, the displacement of populations remains by far the most common response to volcanic eruptions, even in historic periods (cf. Witham, 2005).

In sum, the argument presented for the origin, fate and nature of the Bromme culture draws together observations on the uniqueness of this cultural phenomenon, the dating of sites not only in southern Scandinavia but also elsewhere, and the ecological and societal impacts of the Laacher See eruption. The otherwise so potent combination of a culture-historical perspective with contributions from the natural sciences that has characterised Danish archaeology in effect since its very beginning (Kristiansen, 2002) has, for the Late Glacial at least, led to an adaptationist stalemate. Adaptation needs to be demonstrated rather than assumed (Laland and Brown, 2002). The alternative explanation for the remarkable culture changes that happened in southern Scandinavia in the Allerød offered here suggests that adaptation cannot be the driving factor. The approach presented here instead offers a fresh view on the cultural taxonomy of the time (cf. Riede, 2013b, 2014a) and specifies explicit source-sink dynamics: the radiocarbon dates as well as key stratigraphies in northern-central Germany indicate an abandonment of those areas with the LSE. Small Late Glacial hunter-gatherer groups migrated away from these affected areas, carrying with them a legacy of Federmessergruppen technology. Mediated by demographic dynamics, coupled with a more difficult access to the necessary raw materials, bow-and-arrow technology was quickly abandoned in favour of the atlatl. This change is reflected in the lack of slender arch-backed points in Brommean assemblages.

The emphasis here has been on the origin and the internal demographic dynamics of the Bromme culture in relation to the Feder-messergruppen. The very short total duration of the Bromme culture suggested by the radiocarbon dates also raises the question of its end.

Fischer et al. (2013a) suggest that the economy and population of the Bromme culture collapses when the increasing cold of the GS-1 eventually leads to the onset of the Younger Dryas proper, i.e. the shift from the light open woodlands and Boreal-like fauna of the Allerød to the cold steppes and the return of reindeer. Given the length of the Younger Dryas (c. 1100 years) and its division into a very cold first part and a gradually warming second part (Lane et al., 2013), it is possible that southern Scandinavia became initially depopulated only to be re-populated towards the end of this cold phase by groups carrying with them an Ahrensburgian-type tool-kit. The Ahrensburgian could be the result of a meeting between Federmessergruppen groups in the European Uplands and the descendants of the Bromme foragers that were being pushed southwards. Sites with both Federmessergrup-pen and Ahrensburgian technological and typological elements in the Low Countries and in the lower reaches of the River Rhine generally pre-date the northern Ahrensburgian sites and are suggestive of an emergence there (Baales, 1996; Crombé et al., 2014; De Bie, 1999; Vermeersch, 2011, 2013). The miniaturisation of the projectile points in the Ahrensburgian – supported conclusively by the many finds of arrows and some bow fragments at Stellmoor (Rust, 1943) – indicates the reintroduction of bow-and-arrow technology (Riede, 2009d, 2010a), a highly visible technology that, perhaps along with some other archaeologically less tractable elements, was transmitted from the Federmessergruppen to the northern environmental refugees (cf. Carr, 1995). Interestingly, if we accept the importance of projectile points as signifiers of (perhaps primary male) group identity (Sinopoli, 1991; Wiessner,

1983), then the retention of the tanged point morphology could also be interpreted as the long-term retention of important elements of a more or less distinct group identity.

This chapter has focused on Becker's (1971) original 'Bromme problem', that is the question of this technocomplex' origin and fate. It has been suggested that the emergence of the Brommean cannot be adequately understood as a gradual adaptation in perfect synchrony with slowly changing environmental conditions. Instead, this transition was abrupt and relates to the generic stresses that accumulated during the Intra-Allerød Cold Phase, but was 'resolved' – in the term's dramatic sense even 'catastrophically' – by the sudden and wholly unexpected eruption of the Laacher See volcano around 13,000 years ago. The technological and typological poverty of the Bromme culture cannot in a meaningful way be seen as an adaptation, but is the result of a demographic impact on the social transmission of cultural knowledge and know-how, coupled with a potential lack of required organic raw materials and the fact that large high-quality flint nodules were available. This abundance of flint only adequately explains the general increase in the size of knapping debris, not the disappearance of slender arch-backed points, which is interpreted to signal the loss of bow-and-arrow technology. The interplay of these complex factors and the postulated celerity of the transition from Federmessergruppen to Bromme culture leads us back to the consideration of vulnerability and resilience amongst Late Glacial hunter-gatherers in northern Europe and the understanding of this episode as one of 'eventful' change in the sense of Sewell (2005). The next and final chapter will draw these conceptual and empirical strands together, provide an up-to-date sketch of the 'Laacher See hypothesis', and will set this case study in a wider framework of an archaeology concerned with understanding the impacts of climatic change and events on human societies and history.

Chapter 7

Natural hazards and traditional societies past and present

7.1 Introduction

The aim of this book has been to illuminate the remarkable and unusual cultural evolution of Late Glacial hunter-gatherer communities in the middle part of the Late Glacial. During the climatically otherwise relatively mild and stable Allerød Interstadial, northern Europe in general and southern Scandinavia in particular experienced a spurt of culture change that is so special as to require an equally special explanation. The causal root of these changes, it has been argued, lies in the complex interplay between the ecological and societal constellations of the communities in question and the cataclysmic eruption of the Laacher See volcano around 13,000 years ago. An incipient version of this scenario was sketched out some time ago in the form of the 'Laacher See hypothesis' (Riede, 2007a, 2008b).

Combining a detailed empirical treatment of Late Glacial technocomplexes with the conceptual tools of disaster risk reduction research under the theoretical umbrella of 'events' as structuring principles of historical change, this book has significantly expanded upon this earlier working hypothesis. Criticisms in relation to this scenario, voiced both in conversion and in print (Buck Pedersen, 2009; Sørensen, 2010), have contributed to clarifying this position by flagging up key areas of further research. In a suite of publication that followed on from the original formulation of the 'Laacher See hypothesis', a transdisciplinary research programme (sensu Jantsch, 1972) has addressed the likely ecological effects of the eruption

(Riede and Bazely, 2009; Riede and Wheeler, 2009), investigated in quantitative and comparative detail the technological consequences visible in the lithic material of the Bromme culture (Dev and Riede, 2012; Riede, 2009d, 2012a; Riede and Kristensen, 2010; Riede et al., 2011b; Serwatka and Riede, 2016), addressed both the internal chronology and settlement pattern of the Federmessergruppen (Riede, 2012b, 2016) and the Bromme culture (Riede et al., 2011a) as well as the chronological relationship between the Federmessergruppen and the Bromme culture (Riede and Edinborough, 2012), and provided new evidence for the total distribution of the Laacher See tephra (Riede and Thastrup, 2013; Riede et al., 2011c). The latter mapping exercise in turn has become an important research tool for studies that have since added significant new data-points to this fallout distribution – some of which lie far beyond the previously known lobe boundaries (Andronikov et al., 2015; Larsen and Noe-Nygaard, 2014; Wulf et al., 2013). Yet, in investigating the post-eruptive societal effects of the LSE, this research really has highlighted the need to (i) clarify our archaeological systematics for the Late Glacial (Riede, 2013b; Serwatka & Riede, 2016) and to (ii) better understand the pre-eruptive social constellations (Riede et al., 2011a).

There are no such things as natural disasters (Felgentreff and Glade, 2008; O'Keefe et al., 1976; Wisner et al., 2004), and a perspective that roots its understanding of human impact in prior vulnerability and resilience points firmly to pre-event socio-ecological conditions as the explanatory – and by necessity historically constituted – nexus. Archaeologists struggle with the legacy of catastrophism whenever volcanic eruptions or other similarly extreme geological events are invoked as agents, stimulants, or triggers of culture change (Grattan, 2006), a way of thinking history that Pomeroy (2008) caricatured as 'then it was destroyed by the volcano' or that McKibben (2010) brandmarks derisively as 'collapse porn'.

Whilst this book quite deliberately deploys 'catastrophe' and 'apocalypse' as narrative devices, its aim has been to steer clear of clichéd catastrophism. At the same time, in rejection of the adaptationist stance of many other interpretations of culture change in the Late Glacial, this book has endeavoured to avoid environmental determinism. Instead, it has been argued that the Laacher See event can serve as an important analytical mirror onto past societies; a unique and specific event that, in interaction with historically contingent social conditions amongst the affected communities, has produced genuinely historical (i.e. equally unique) outcomes in the sense that these could not be predicted in any meaningful sense by either the pre-existing societal constellations nor the eruption itself. By providing – via the eminently useful tools of tephrochronology (e.g. Lane et al., 2014; Riede and Thastrup, 2013) – a chronological hinge, this event sheds new light on communities both before and after. In this view, extreme events offer a powerful methodological handle on past societal change (Riede, 2013a, 2014g).

But what were these changes? And how can we situate this case study in a wider field of research that is concerned with the impact or otherwise of climate change and extreme events on human societies? This final chapter attempts to draw the main themes and theses of this book together, to summarise the Laacher See scenario, and to make the case for an 'extreme event archaeology' that complements recent efforts to make studies of past environmental impacts relevant within the contemporary discourse on climate change, social resilience and vulnerability (e.g. Djind-

jian, 2011; Hudson et al., 2012; Kirch, 2005; Marchant and Lane, 2014; Mitchell, 2011; Redman, 2005; Sabloff, 2008; Tainter, 2006; Van de Noort, 2011, 2013; van der Leeuw and Redman, 2002).

7.2 The Laacher See hypothesis today

The Laacher See eruption ranks amongst the largest volcanic events that have taken place in the course of human prehistory (Oppenheimer, 2011). Unlike many other similar or even larger events, this eruption happened not on a remote island or at the very margins of human settlement, but it occurred in the middle of the European subcontinent, its fallout covering vast tracts of land that were, at differing degrees of intensity, used by contemporaneous people. While the LSE has long played a role in Late Glacial archaeology, it has primarily been studied from a near-vent perspective (Baales, 2002b). Impacts of this event further afield have rarely been considered (see Thissen, 1995 for an exception), despite the fact that at least medial fallout deposits have been known for some time.

In my view and as argued throughout this book, the impact of the Laacher See eruption on contemporaneous hunter-gatherer groups is best understood as a "convergent catastrophe" (Moseley, 1999: 59) conditioned by a series of "compounding vulnerabilities" (Dugmore et al., 2012: 3658). As the cited references in this spliced-together sentence highlight, other researchers considering, for instance, cultural collapse in the pre-Columbian Andes or the iconic disappearance of the Greenland Norse, have come to very similar conclusions; mono-causal 'catastrophic' explanations are rarely if ever applicable, satisfactory or useful. Dyer (2002: 164) has termed such a model of cumulatively corrosive effects 'punctuated entropy' and defined it as "a permanent decline in the adaptive flexibility of a human cultural system to the environment brought on by the cumulative impact of periodic disaster events. It predicts and explains the nonrecovery of human systems after disaster. The accumulation

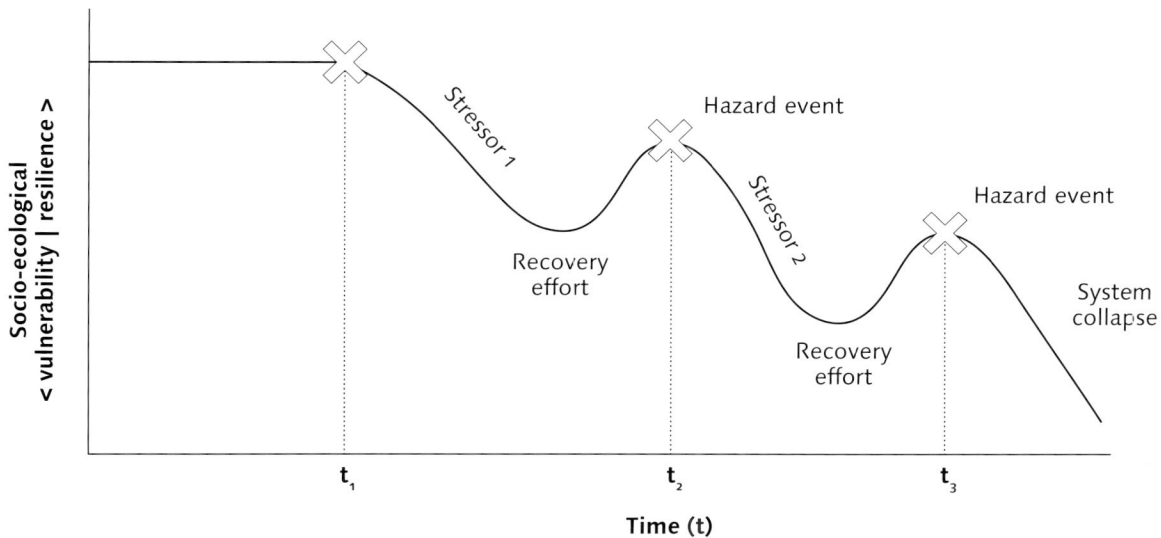

Figure 7.1 *The 'punctuated entropy' model of Dwyer (2002), redrawn. The Intra-Allerød Cold Phase is seen as the initial (longer-term) process stressor, the Laacher See eruption as the hazard event creating a threshold of systemic change.*

of impacts means that the opportunity for recovery is compromised by repeated disruptions to the human system" (Fig. 7.1).

In the Late Glacial, the process in question is the general re-colonisation of northern Europe after the Last Glacial Maximum (Gamble et al., 2005; Riede, 2014e). Humans were part of these expanding but unstable ecological communities that responded individualistically (Lorenzen et al., 2011) to the rapidly changing conditions. Specifically, the pre-event vulnerability amongst northern European hunter-gatherers was conditioned by the prolonged cold of the Intra-Allerød Cold Phase, at the very end of which the Laacher See eruption occurred, combined with the likely lack of traditional knowledge of volcanic eruptions. Whilst small eruptions did impact regional Magdalenian groups in, for instance, the Massif Central (Raynal et al., 1994; Vernet and Raynal, 1995, 2000), these were by all accounts minor compared to the cataclysm of the LSE. The cold of the IACP depressed prey population densities and shortened the growing season for critical plant resources. Via its impact on basic ecological parameters, this cooling likely had impacts on life-history decisions and parameters of Late Glacial hunter-gatherers just as similar episodes have impacted later Mesolithic foragers in Scandinavia (cf. Tallavaara and Seppä, 2012; Talla-

vaara et al., 2010). Yet: it was to these climatic fluctuations that Late Glacial hunter-gatherers probably were supremely adapted. The often rapid climatic changes and their occasionally major amplitude recorded in the Greenland ice-cores represented the more or less daily conditions for these foragers. Their societal normality was highly dynamic, their response flexible and grounded in economic strategies that unfolded around mobility as a means of tracking resources in time and space (Grove, 2009).

Yet, the IACP almost certainly did exert stress upon Late Glacial communities by raising failure risk, especially amongst those operating along the periphery of human settlement. The radiocarbon records for both the North European Plain and the Thuringian Basin show a clear reduction in human activity that – with due caution – can be interpreted as reflecting reduced population densities. These challenges of environmental variability and unpredictability of resources in time and space most commonly led hunter-gatherers to engage in reciprocal exchange relations with groups operating far enough away that synchronic resource depression was unlikely; these relationships show archaeologically as far-travelled 'exotic' and often non-utilitarian items (Whallon, 2006). Interestingly and importantly, these are rare in the pre-LSE

Federmessergruppen when compared to the preceding Magdalenian – implying limited connectedness and thus heightened vulnerability – and totally absent in the Bromme culture – suggesting a major collapse or, at the very least, contraction or reorientation of contemporaneous social networks (Riede, 2014b).

It is these networks that ultimately serve to satisfy those needs of individuals and communities not directly related to the food quest. Likewise, this contracted connectedness feeds into formal models of the demographic conditions necessary for the maintenance of complex technologies such as bow-and-arrow technology. The original formulation of the 'Laacher See hypothesis' also suggested that the so-called Perstunian culture, an "Eastern Equivalent of the Lyngby Culture in the Neman Basin" (Szymczak, 1987: 267) and surrounding drainages of north-eastern Poland, Lithuania, and Belorussia (Bagniewski, 1997, 1999; Rimantiene, 1971; Szymczak, 1999; Zaliznyak, 1999) emerged in the wake of the LSE in a development mirroring the Brommean. However, the reality of the Perstunian culture has to be called into question (e.g. Sulgostowska, 1989). It is more likely that the large tanged points supposedly diagnostic of this technocomplex in fact belong in Federmessergruppen (or Ahrensburgian) contexts in north-eastern Poland as elsewhere (Kobusiewicz, 2009a, 2009b; Riede et al., 2011a; Serwatka and Riede, 2016).

In sum, the chain of causal relations that underwrite the scenario of the societal impact of the Laacher See eruption begins with the small Federmessergruppen communities that explored the North European Plain (including southern Scandinavia) in the early part of the Allerød. This colonisation is fundamentally constrained by local and regional ecologies, in interaction with the available technological solutions (Riede, 2014e; Riede and Tallavaara, 2014). Initially, this colonisation may have been driven by the availability of specific prestige-conferring prey types that had become elusive further to the south (e.g. elk, giant deer), the search for amber as raw material for cultic objects (Veil et al., 2012) or other even

less tractable pull factors of this Palaeolithic way of life (cf. Fuglestvedt, 2012). No doubt, these early Federmessergruppen colonists were "takers of opportunity" (Carlsson et al., 2005: 23), and whilst challenging, the re-colonisation of the recently deglaciated landscapes of the North European Plain came also no doubt with its rewards. Indeed, recent evidence for social and political complexity in Magdalenian communities suggests that the migration of small group northwards may, at least in part, also have been politically driven by offering new horizons away from the manoeuvring and the conflicts that increasingly emerged in the ancestral regions (Schwendler, 2012).

It is important not to conflate etic (external, analyst-chosen) explanations for the re-colonisation and its resulting societal conditions with emic (internal, culturally-specific) explanations for the same process. Yet, notably, ethnographic accounts of the motivations for migrations do underline that both ecological/economic as well as what can be broadly termed political factors motivated people to move (compare Table 6.3). Critical here is that political *as well as* ecological conditions together laid the foundation of what Wisner and colleagues label the locally unsafe conditions and the root causes of vulnerability – also amongst Late Glacial hunter-gatherers. The sequence of colonisation and their distance to core regions of Late Glacial settlement predisposed certain regions to greater or lesser place-based vulnerabilities in that safety networks, economic and demographic margins were critically lowered (Riede, 2013a).

The impacts of the Laacher See eruption on local and regional ecologies at varying temporalities, and the challenges it posed to the world-view of these hunter-gatherer groups, led some groups at least to move their geographic centre of gravity towards southern Scandinavia, possibly with the intention not to return southwards (cf. Henry, 2013). But was this a last resort decision born of desperation and fear? Disasters create winners as well as losers (Scanlon, 1988) and, importantly, they also create opportunities for social change (Birkmann et al., 2010; Olshansky et al., 2012) and for the creation of improved social condi-

Event component	Late Glacial archaeological evidence
Novelty, surprise	Low-frequency/high-magnitude event that was unforeseeable by contemporaneous people
Influence of particular and local conditions	Contingent changes documented in different regions following the LSE
Emotional content	Syn-aesthetic and phenomenological approach
Collective creativity	Changes in tool repertoire that reflect changed every-day routines
Ritual punctuation	Abandonment of exchange ritual practices – a kind of 'ritual failure' at this time (cf. Koutrafouri and Sanders, 2013)
Cascade effects	Migration and changes in settlement patterns that outlast the LSE and its concrete environmental effects
Spatial dimensions of change	Fragmentation of effectively continuous and relatively homogeneous settlement region into several regional clusters (i.e. the Brommean and various 'groups' in southern and central Europe)
Temporal bounding	14C dates and Bayesian models provide increase chronological leverage and place the Brommean into a narrow temporal window between the LSE and the first part of the Younger Dryas

Table 7.1 *Sewell's event criteria and evidence from the Late Glacial.*

tions (Solnit, 2010). The 'splendid isolation' of Late Glacial groups in southern Scandinavia may have been an attractive premise due to 1) the natural richness of the region in flint; 2) the relative abundance of desired prey animals; and 3) the fact that the region was not only unaffected by the LST fallout, but that it may have, as suggested by simulation models of the eruption's aerosol radiative effects (Graf and Timmreck, 2001), experienced additional warming in its aftermath. It is here, the Laacher See hypothesis for the origin of the Bromme culture is in fact reconcilable with alternative theories that stress the favourable, perhaps even outright, "paradisial" conditions of the Allerød (e g. Fischer, 1991: 118).

The view that the LSE opened a window for societal change is also compatible with Sewell's (2005: 227) notion of the historical event: "sequences of occurrences that result in transformations of structures". There is no *a priori* reason that societal transformations in prehistory should follow patterns that are fundamentally different from how historical change unfolds in later periods. Instead, historical changes may serve as detailed instantiations of more general processes that unfold in what has been termed 'deep history' (Shryock

et al., 2011; Smail, 2008). And, while it is difficult to capture the relevant actions of individuals in the temporally more remote reaches of prehistory (e.g. Gravina, 2004), it is not impossible (Gamble and Porr, 2005). Chapter 5 has attempted to show that the impacts of the LSE not only took the form of measurable effects on local ecological networks, but that the sheer unusualness of the event may very well have deeply challenged contemporaneous cosmological and religious conceptions (Ratter, 2013). This challenge in turn would have engendered strong emotional responses as people came to terms with the traumatic aftermath of the eruption – and emotion does play an important role, too, in Sewell's logic of eventful change. Indeed, and as far as they are analytically tractable, the culture-historical caesura created by the Laacher See eruption satisfies the criteria of Sewell's events: a major and rapid episode of culture change that creates novel and lasting new structures and ways of behaving that likely also reflect, to some degree, new ways of thinking (Table 7.1). The emergence of the Bromme culture was characterized by heightened emotion and by collective action that is reflected both spatially and temporally. The Laacher See case study thus offers a perhaps rare but no less powerful example of genuine "palaeo-historical" eventful structural change amongst deep past societies (Audouze and Valentin, 2010).

Still, the Laacher See hypothesis remains just that, a hypothesis. Future studies will be able to further elaborate, to test, and to trowel-truth it by, for instance, investigating contemporaneous locales for cryptotephra where sediment samples or stratigraphies remain. In addition, data repositories such as the Hessian rock-shelter database (Abri-Kataster von Hessen; see Hofbauer, 1991, 1995) could be used to conduct targeted fieldwork at sites in the mid- to far-field. If Federmessergruppen occupation layers and LST are discovered at such potential sites, micromorphology could be deployed in order to establish whether the sites where occupied when the ash fell, or whether they had long since been abandoned. In this vein, a re-analysis of the lithic assemblages from sites where we know occupation layers are covered in or associated with LST (e.g. Bettenroder Berg, Weinberg Schadeleben, Mühlheim-Dietesheim; see Chapter 4) through the lens of 'rapid abandonment' (e.g. Plunket and Uruñuela, 2000, 2003) may provide important clues to on-the-ground decision making processes at the time of eruption, focused by necessity and choice on the material dimensions of disaster response. It would also be paramount to search for well-preserved LST strata in southern Scandinavia, both in environmental as well as in archaeological sequences. The discovery of definite LST in a good environmental context would assist in better understanding the interplay between the pressures of the IACP and the LSE. Finding it in archaeological contexts would allow such sites to be directly linked to the suggested chronological sequence. Finally, more and better radiocarbon dates for this time period, especially for sites outside the LST fallout lobes (e.g. southern Scandinavia) are an archaeological desideratum.

Basic volcanological analyses, too, would likely yield much new information. The number of LST localities is constantly increasing. Besides clarifying recent suggestions of possible precursor eruptions to the major event

at 13,000 BP, this continuous addition of new data-points – some of which reflecting rather massive deposits – arguably warrants a recalculation of ejecta volumes. After all, it has been suggested that 88% of the total material ejected is made up of tephra and adjustments of this volume may have significant impacts on the total estimated volume and hence on the magnitude of the eruption. Such a reconsideration could, given the large number of data-points now available, then be coupled to modelling efforts that could better retro-dict the prehistoric tephra air-fall distribution and its potential regional impact as well as provide fallout scenarios for future eruptions (e.g. Bonadonna, 2006).

The processes leading to the emergence of the Bromme culture and their resulting patterns are compatible, it has been argued, with a general view of a punctuated rhythm of change in history and prehistory. This book has attempted to sketch out a demographically and socially dynamic period, where current national borders and their attendant artificial divisions of the archaeological record of the deep past are meaningless or, worse still, actively distorting our analytical gaze. The dual insistence on the role of demography and on rigorous cultural taxonomy on the one hand, and on the critical importance of the concepts of vulnerability and resilience on the other, links the Laacher See scenario directly to two broader research programmes: evolutionary archaeology (Shennan, 2002, 2008) and climate change archaeology (Van de Noort, 2011, 2013). In the following, I outline how this book contributes to those broader endeavours.

7.3 The contribution to evolutionary archaeology

In evolution in general, demography plays a major role as mediator between the small-scale life-history decisions made by individual organisms in interaction with their local environs and the cumulative and diachronic effects of the sum of these decisions at the population level (Metcalf and Pavard, 2007b); adapting is a demographic process, adaptation its result

(Metcalf and Pavard, 2007a). The Laacher See case study is not hard-line in its evolutionary approach to culture change, but informed by the desire to make this overarching approach more compatible with other ways of thinking historically, ways that place greater – perhaps too great – emphasis on, for instance, agency and the (limited) ability of humans to predict the future and hence to adapt perfectly through entirely cultural means (Mesoudi, 2008; Riede, 2005a, 2006, 2012c; Riede et al., 2012; Shennan, 1989, 2004a, 2004b, 2004c).

I noted in Chapter 2 that there is a remarkable correspondence between the patterns and processes of historical change identified by sociologist Sewell and palaeontologist Gould respectively. This congruence suggests that there may be a process generality as to how history unfolds, a generality that is grounded in Darwinian principles active across scientific domains (Mesoudi, 2007; Mesoudi and O'Brien, 2009; Mesoudi et al., 2004, 2006; Mesoudi et al., 2010; Offer, 2010; Runciman, 2005). It is noteworthy in this context that the use of phylogenetic analytical techniques borrowed from evolutionary biology – but clearly applicable as a general heuristic tool across historical disciplines, too (e.g. Atkinson and Gray, 2005; O'Hara, 1997; Platnick and Cameron, 1977) – paved the way for the development of the Laacher See hypothesis and the eventual cultural taxonomic revision of the Brommean (Riede, 2006, 2009c, 2010b, 2011b, 2013b). While these phylogenetic aspects have not featured prominently throughout this book, the Laacher See scenario *in toto* adds a detailed, albeit far from exhaustive, case study to the roster of evolutionary archaeology. What is more, the immediate need to separate adaptive from mal-adaptive practices in the analytical mirror of extreme events adds a facet to the evolutionary archaeological approach that has not been considered before: risk reduction research. Here, Darwinian approaches are also being explored (McLaughlin, 2011, 2012; McLaughlin and Dietz, 2008), thus promising a potentially productive integration of diachronic approaches of vulnerability and resilience in deep time and contemporary concerns. But how can archaeology in general and the Laacher See case study in particular contribute to contemporary risk reduction research?

7.4 The contribution of an 'extreme event archaeology'

Archaeologists and the public alike have been fascinated by past 'catastrophes' since the discovery of Pompeii. Yet, this fascination is rarely coupled with adequate notions of how such extreme events and the transformation into disasters through their interaction with contemporaneous social structures may contribute to the patterns and processes of history unfolding. The Laacher See case study underlines that calamities such as volcanic eruptions can lead to cascading effects that reverberate through social and demographic networks at variable speeds. Placed in a broader comparative perspective, it seems that such events can have long-term social and political legacies, and their effects are often indirect, mediated by culturally specific components such as religion, and that these effects can occur, or indeed be amplified, in the far-field (Cashman and Giordano, 2008; Grattan et al., 2007; Grattan, 2006; Torrence and Grattan, 2002). Clearly, issues of data resolution often plague the study of past disasters, but these limitations are counterbalanced by privileged access to unique long-term information on societies and their material expressions of livelihood, as well as a similarly long-term perspective on the critical magnitude/frequency relationship of the natural hazards, by the opportunity to carefully select case studies, and by the number of data-points proffered (in principle) by the archaeological record.

It can be argued that information from past calamities may be used to inform planning for future extreme events. Indeed, the stakes are high, given the potentially destructive and disruptive impacts. Clarke (1999, 2004, 2006, 2007, 2008a, 2008b), for instance, has long argued that not only probable but also possible events should be the subject of serious debate and realistic planning efforts. Whilst such 'possibilism' carries with it the danger of hysteria, archaeological and historical data can be effectively used to "discipline possibilistic reasoning" (Clarke, 2007: 192) by offering historically informed, evidence-based information on both the geophysical as well as sociocultural parameters of past extreme events that, critically, retains a great deal of immediacy and intimacy. Such an approach could diminish the risk of being surprised by unforeseeable and catastrophic events that, following Taleb (2010), have popularly been termed 'black swans'. A suitably wide temporal angle could turn unforeseeable black swans into foreseeable, albeit still difficult to handle, 'gray swans' (Stein and Stein, 2014: 1279) or indeed merely 'gray cygnets' (Rissland, 2009: 6); chronological largess enables comparison, which in turn may facilitate learning from the past (cf. Riede et al, 2016).

The current discourse about climate change and the impacts of extreme events is strongly catastrophic and apocalyptic in its rhetoric (see Dawdy, 2009; Dörries, 2010; Hulme, 2008; Mauelshagen, 2009; Nielsen, Esben B. 2013), and it is strongly focused on global 'future narratives' rather than narratives that are centred on particular locales or regions and their histories. With a heavy technochratic and natural scientific focus the important milestone publications of, for instance, the Intergovernmental Panel on Climate Change (IPCC; see, for instance, Field et al., 2012; Smith, V. H. et al., 2009), remain distant and abstract for many. Ironically, as Van de Noort (2011) has noted, the IPCC draws heavily on palaeoclimatic data as a foundation for its prediction of future climate change, but does not draw to any meaningful degree on corresponding palaeosocietal – archaeological, historical – data when it comes to addressing future social change. Studies of past volcanism are plagued by a very similar dilemma: A suite of excellent databases of past volcanic activity as well as of other palaeo-hazards (e.g. www.ngdc.noaa.gov/hazard/tsu_db.shtml) exist, some of which are expressly constructed to aid in risk reduction research (Bryson et al., 2006; Crosweller et al., 2012; Siebert et al., 2010). Yet, none of these databases contain any or none other than trivial information on the societies actually affected

by these eruptions. Whilst fully appreciating their utility in studies of past geological processes (e.g. Deligne et al., 2010) and whilst also fully appreciating the large amounts of labour that have gone into assembling these databases in the first place, they do not contribute to the investigation of past human vulnerability, resilience or responses in a historically specific and historically informed manner. Similarly, current efforts to model the interaction between earth systems' processes and human behaviours (Palmer and Smith, 2014) could benefit from including past events (Riede, 2014c).

Hulme (2008: 5) has noted that:

"we are living in a climate of fear about our future climate. The language of the public discourse around global warming routinely uses a repertoire which includes words such as 'catastrophe', 'terror', 'danger', 'extinction' and 'collapse'. To help make sense of this phenomenon the story of the complex relationships between climates and cultures in different times and in different places is in urgent need of telling. If we can understand from the past something of this complex interweaving of our ideas of climate with their physical and cultural settings we may be better placed to prepare for different configurations of this relationship in the future".

The archaeological debate on collapse aside (see Middleton, 2012, 2013; Tainter, 2008), the fact that current climate change is perceived and talked about as catastrophic alone warrants a focus on catastrophic climatic change: in other words, extreme events in the past. Better understanding these past configurations will inform current debate. What archaeology can add is immediacy and intimacy to specific volcanic hazard forecast scenarios (e.g. Mastrolorenzo et al., 2006; Schmidt et al., 2011) by focusing on both the vulnerability and the resilience of past communities. This is not to say that archaeology can, except perhaps in very rare circumstances (e.g. Cooper and Sheets, 2012; Guttmann-Bond, 2010), provide concise blueprints for designing sustainable adaptations to volcanic hazards or other climate-induced challenges, or provide pointers to how businesses and institutions can manage crises (for an example of this, see Toft and Reynolds, 1994). Rather, archaeology can, in the form of 'climate change archaeology', contribute more broadly to a balanced understanding of the relationship between humans and the environment; archaeology can tell – on occasion using the narrative devices of catastrophe and apocalypse – stories of past successful and unsuccessful adaptive pathways; and archaeology can, through its established communication channels (i.e. museums, school curricula, etc.) contribute to environmental literacy and thus to an increased resilience of, in particular, local and regional communities (Dix and Röhrs, 2007; Van de Noort, 2013); archaeology can suggest historically informed, evidence-based and future-oriented *adaptive measures* or exaptations that mimic true adaptations precisely because they are designed with the past in mind. Given the ecological engineering or niche constructing power humans have in the present, such measures can have significant local, regional, or even global effects not only on non-human ecological relationships (Laland et al., 2014; Odling-Smee et al., 2013) but also on those aspects of human ecology and adaptation that relate directly to disaster vulnerability and resilience. In fact, drawing on the lessons of (pre)history, we are in the position to share the hard-won adaptations of one population in order to design exaptations, i.e. to nudge the evolution of socio-ecological systems (cf. Farrell and Thiel, 2013) and to thus design generic resilience in advance of specific hazards elsewhere (see Table 2.1). Archaeology, in focusing on the materiality of vulnerability and of resilience, can be one contributing discipline in the making of what Jasanoff (2007: 33) terms 'technologies of humility'.

Yet, some researchers concerned with such an archaeology of climate change and impact actively suggest discounting narratives of collapse and catastrophe in favour of narratives of resilience and coping (Hudson et al., 2012; Rowland, 2010). Whilst the empirical issues surrounding episodes of past societal collapse are hotly debated (Diamond, 2010b; McAnany and Yoffee, 2010; Middleton, 2012, 2013), the denial of catastrophic risks and the potential

impact of extreme events and their disastrous societal consequences may come at a high cost (e.g. Kieffer, 2013; Plag, 2014); complacency will only aggravate the next disaster (Sparks, 2007). Modern societies are, due to the inherent potential destructiveness of extreme events and the entanglement of modern societies in and dependence on expansive networks, patently not immune to such events (Donovan and Oppenheimer, 2013; Plag, 2014). In addition, to the degree that natural hazards do not belong to 'pre-modernity', the difference in contemporary and past responses may not be so great (e.g. Gerrard and Petley, 2013). In sum, the existentialist questions posed by the threat of natural hazards ought not to be avoided in either scientific or public discourse (Rees, 2013).

Complementing Van de Noort's (2013) 'climate change archaeology' with an 'extreme event archaeology' must humbly engage the delicate balance between hysterical catastrophism and myopic naiveté; it must remain explicit in viewing societies as internally heterogeneous so that simplistic blanket notions of collapse can be avoided. Some archaeological efforts in this direction are already underway. Japanese scholars and authorities, for instance, strive to exchange information on earthquake and tsunami risks (Okamura et al., 2013) and there is even a dedicated Disaster Reduction Museum at the Disaster Reduction and Human Renovation Institution in Kobe (http://www.dri.ne.jp/english/kanran/). Indeed, Japan is dotted with disaster museums often dedicated to specific and locally traumatic events. These museums attempt to raise awareness and to keep oral traditions of impact and response alive. The National Museum of American History curates a collection of artefacts from the 2005 hurricane Katrina (Shayt, 2006), while numerous recent temporary exhibitions raise similar issues (see Höfchen et al., 2014; Schenk et al., 2014). Likewise, the Edurisk website (http://www.edurisk.it/eng/) in Italy is also attempting to actively engage the public – in this case primarily children – in risk reduction efforts, although the role of archaeological information is limited in the latter case. Most importantly, however, all these efforts are *post hoc*, they fol-

Figure 7.2 *Current population densities in Europe with the Laacher See volcano marked in the region's centre. Source: ESRI.*

low events that already have caused great loss of life and property in these specific regions, their focus is primarily local and their time perspectives usually shallow. There is no reason why the information on past disasters and on past vulnerability that we can wrest from the archaeological record should not be used more proactively as part of an educational strategy intended to raise resilience and to allow communities to live sustainably with, for instance, volcanic risks (Kelman and Mather, 2008). Archaeology could here contribute substantially to what has been termed "humanistic volcanology" (Lockwood and Hazlett, 2010: 395) or "social volcanology" (Donovan, 2010: 117) precisely because the past feeds into processes of identify creation and furnishes a resource for action. In this way, the rich data provided by these elements of geo-cultural heritage – our "usable past" (Stump, 2013: 268) – could play a more proactive role in present and future risk reduction strategies and in the strengthening of social resilience that emerges out of a coupling between traditional and scientific knowledge and methods, just as disasters emerge at the violent interface between geological and societal forces.

So, what – if anything – can we learn from the Laacher See case study? At present, the occurrence of a high-magnitude volcanic eruption from the Laacher See edifice – right in the heart of Europe – is only entertained in film (Janson, 2009), in fiction (Schreiber, 2006), and in the tabloid press (see, for example, http://www.bild.de/news/2007/news/forscher-ausbruch-deutschland-1399914.bild.html and discussion in http://www.wired.com/wiredscience/2012/01/fearmongering-gets-started-in-2012-laacher-see-is-not-ready-to-blow/) – indeed it is writers of fiction that excel at drafting scenarios of future calamities (Atwood, 2011; Horn, 2012, 2014). Yet, the sociologist Clarke (2006) has suggested that it is the potential impact of such extreme events – no matter how improbable – that should be countenanced in order to evaluate the "surge capacity" (Clarke, 2008a: 683) of emergency systems and thereby to increase both event-

Figure 7.3 *The location of power plants in Europe and the currently known distribution of Laacher See fallout. Stippled lines mark the proximal, medial, distal and ultra-distal hazard zones. Redrawn from http://maps.unomaha.edu/peterson.*

specific but also general resilience in the present day (cf. Michel-Kerjan, 2012). He argues that one tool for pondering such 'worst cases' is counterfactual reasoning. However, the notoriously 'presentist' approach of disaster sociology (cf. Beck, 2015; and see Lovekamp and Trainor, 2013) makes for a compatibility problem in relation to the use of historical or archaeological data.

The detailed information available from past eruptions such as the 13,000 BP Laacher See event can provide important clues for 'retrofactually' considering the impact that renewed volcanic activity in the Eifel would have locally, regionally, as well as super-regionally. One important observation may be, for instance, that migration and displacement are the most common responses to volcanic events past and present. Migration in the wake of climate change (Hugo, 1996) – or events (Oliver-Smith, 2009) – is also a major challenge for future policy-making and infrastructure planning, but one that should be tackled pro-actively (Black et al., 2011).

If we triangulate between the Laacher See scenario as well as other well-researched case studies of volcanic eruptions and their impacts on human communities from the deep past to the present day (e.g. Driessen and MacDonald, 1997; Meller et al., 2013; Ort et al., 2008; Sheets, 2008, 2012; Torrence and Swadling, 2008; VanderHoek and Nelson, 2007), much more robust scenarios of not just the possible but the likely impact of a future eruption of the Laacher See volcano can be derived. The full suite of mechanisms now known to link LST deposition to cultural consequences via their attendant impacts on ecosystems would also be relevant in future events of this kind, not only for agriculture and public health, but for aviation, trade and communication (Alexander, 2013; Donovan and Oppenheimer, 2014; Donovan and Oppenheimer, 2011). Self (2006) calculates the probability of a $M = 6$ eruption such as the LSE to occur in the 21st century to be 100%, and he tersely describes some of the likely consequences of an eruption of this size or larger. Although by no means the most probable candidate, such a low frequency/high magnitude mid-continent eruption in Europe lasting several weeks or months would affect a very large number of people both in the near – as well as the far – field (Fig. 7.2). In addition, it would likely lead to a prolonged closure of European or even Eurasian airspace, a temporary collapse of air- and water-based supply chains providing many daily consumables, and key power supply nodes would be at risk (Fig. 7.3). The economic implications of these immediate effects and their longer-term clean-up and repair efforts are staggering (see Leder et al., 2017), and would likely put European economic as well as political systems under considerable strain. Migration, political, but also religious changes were demonstrably the results of such eruptions in the past and must be taken seriously as potential effects of future eruptions (Chester, 2005b). Fortunately, given the very low probability of renewed activity at the Laacher See in the near future, the scenario sketched out here is no more than a thought experiment – although a potentially significant footnote here is that, as already noted in Chapter 3, periods of warm temperatures are linked globally, as well as specifically in Europe, to increased rates of volcanism (Nowell et al., 2006; Watt et al., 2013). The implication of this relationship may very well be that anthro-pogenic warming will re-activate volcanism in hitherto dormant provinces in Europe.

At any rate, the far-field effects such as those described in the preceding chapters could also occur as the result of eruptions at the volcanically highly active European periphery (i.e. Iceland or the Mediterranean) or even further afield. In addition, there are many regions in the world that are active volcanically and where, in particular, the steadily more numerous urban poor are at risk (Chester et al., 2001; Small and Naumann, 2001). Here, archaeologically/historically informed resilience strategies cannot only be potentially put to the test, but they can also become part of mitigation strategies that already attempt to seriously incorporate indigenous views, geo-cultural heritage, and traditional ecological knowledge of the recent past (e.g. Cashman and Cronin, 2008; Cronin et al., 2004a; Cronin and Cashman, 2007; Cronin et al., 2004b; Dove, 2008; Lavigne et al., 2008; Németh and Cronin, 2009). If indeed a necessarily transdisciplinary and wisely deployed archaeology of global climate change and of extreme events has the "ability to reduce distance and therefore reduce uncertainty" (Hudson et al., 2012: 314), it could make a major contribution in this age of insecurity, fear and constant catastrophe.

References

Aaris-Sørensen, K., 1995. Palaeoecology of a Late Weichselian vertebrate fauna from Nørre Lyngby, Denmark. *Boreas* 24, 355-365.

Aaris-Sørensen, K., 1999. *Danmarks Forhistoriske Dyreverden*. Gyldendal, Copenhagen.

Aaris-Sørensen, K., 2009. Diversity and dynamics of the mammalian fauna in Denmark throughout the last glacial–interglacial cycle, 115-0 kyr BP. *Fossils and Strata* 57, 1-59.

Aaris-Sørensen, K., Liljegren, R., 2004. Late Pleistocene remains of giant deer (*Megaloceros giganteus* Blumenbach) in Scandinavia: chronology and environment. *Boreas* 33, 61-73.

Abbot, P.M., Davies, S.M., 2012. Volcanism and the Greenland ice-cores: the tephra record. *Earth-Science Reviews* 115, 173-191.

Adams, P.R., Adams, G.R., 1984. Mount Saint Helens's ashfall: Evidence for a disaster stress reaction. *American Pychologist* 39, 252-260.

Adger, W.N., 2006. Vulnerability. *Global Environmental Change* 16, 268-281.

Aeschbach-Hertig, W., Kipfer, R., Hofer, M., Imboden, D.M., Wieler, R., Signer, P., 1996. Quantification of gas fluxes from the subcontinental mantle: The example of Laacher See, a maar lake in Germany. *Geochimica Et Cosmochimica Acta* 60, 31-41.

Agrawal, A., 1995. Dismantling the Divide Between Indigenous and Scientific Knowledge. *Development and Change* 26, 413-439.

Ahl, C., Meyer, B., 1994. Zur bodenkundlich-sedimentologischen Horizontabfolge der Hauptabris im Buntsandsteingebiet von Reinhausen. In: Grote, K. (Ed.), *Die Abris im südlichen Leinebergland bei Göttingen. Archäologische Befunde zum Leben unter Felsschutzdächern in urgeschichtlicher Zeit*. Isensee Verlag, Oldenburg, pp. 37-52.

Ahrens, W., 1927. Das Alter des großen mittelrheinischen Bimssteinausbruchs und sein Verhältnis zu den jüngsten Rheinterrassen. *Geologische Rundschau* 18, 45-59.

Alaux, J.-F., 1972. L'industrie magdalénienne de l'abri de Blassac II, commune de Blassac (Haute-Loire). *Bulletin de la Société Préhistorique Française* 69, 499-507.

Alexander, D.E., 1995. A survey of the field of natural hazards and disaster studies. In: Carrara, A., Guzetti, F. (Eds.), *Geographical Information Systems in Assessing Natural Hazards*. Kluwer Academic, Amsterdam, pp. 1-19.

Alexander, D.E., 1997. The study of natural disasters, 1977-1997: some reflection on a changing field of knowledge. *Disasters* 21, 284-304.

Alexander, D.E., 2000. *Confronting Catastrophe*. Oxford University Press, Oxford.

Alexander, D.E., 2007. Misconception as a barrier to teaching about disasters. *Prehosp Disaster Med* 22, 95-103.

Alexander, D.E., 2013. Volcanic ash in the atmosphere and risks for civil aviation: A study in European crisis management. *Int J Disaster Risk Sci* 4, 9-19.

Alloway, B.V., Larsen, G., Lowe, D.J., Shane, P.A.R., Westgate, J.A., 2007. QUATERNARY STRATIGRAPHY | Tephrochronology. In: Scott, A.E. (Ed.), *Encyclopedia of Quaternary Science*. Elsevier, Oxford, pp. 2869-2898.

Álvarez-Fernández, E., 2001. L'axe Rhin-Rhône au Paléolithique supérieur récent: l'exemple des mollusques utilisés comme objets de parure. *L'Anthropologie* 105, 547-564.

Álvarez-Fernández, E., 2009. Magdalenian personal ornaments on the move: A review of the current evidence in Central Europe. *Zephyrus* 63, 45-59.

Álvarez-Fernández, E., 2011. Humans and marine resource interaction reappraised: Archaeofauna remains during the late Pleistocene and Holocene in Cantabrian Spain. *Journal of Anthropological Archaeology* 30, 327-343.

Ammerman, A.J., Feldman, M.W., 1974. On the "Making" of an Assemblage of Stone Tools. *American Antiquity* 39, 610-616.

Andersen, K.K., Azuma, N., Barnola, J.M., Bigler, M., Biscaye, P., Caillon, N., Chappellaz, J., Clausen, H.B., Dahl-Jensen, D., Fischer, H., Fluckiger, J., Fritzsche, D., Fujii, Y., Goto-Azuma, K., Gronvold, K., Gundestrup, N.S., Hansson, M., Huber, C., Hvidberg, C.S., Johnsen, S.J., Jonsell, U., Jouzel, J., Kipfstuhl, S., Landais, A., Leuenberger, M., Lorrain, R., Masson-Delmotte, V., Miller, H., Motoyama, H., Narita, H., Popp, T., Rasmussen, S.O., Raynaud, D., Rothlisberger, R., Ruth, U., Samyn, D., Schwander, J., Shoji, H., Siggard-Andersen, M.L., Steffensen, J.P., Stocker, T., Sveinbjornsdottir, A.E., Svensson, A., Takata, M., Tison, J.L., Thorsteinsson, T., Watanabe, O., Wilhelms, F., White, J.W., 2004. High-resolution record of Northern Hemisphere climate extending into the last interglacial period. *Nature* 431, 147-151.

Andersen, S.H., 1970. Senglaciale bopladser ved Bro. *Fynske Minder* 1970, 85-100.

Andersen, S.H., 1972. Bro. En senglacial boplads på Fyn. *Kuml* 1972, 6-60.

Andersen, S.H., 1977. En boplads fra ældre stenalder i Hjarup Mose. *Nordslesvigske Museer* 4, 18-27.

Andersen, S.H., 2016. Rensdyrjægere på farten. Kuml 2016, 9-53.

Andersen, S.H., Sterum, N., 1971. Gudenåkulturen. *Holstebro Museums årsskrift* 1970-1971, 14-32.

Anderson, R., Gathman, S., Hughes, J., Björnsson, S., Jónasson, S., Blanchard, D.C., Moore, C.B., Survilas, H.J., Vonnegut, B., 1965. Electricity in Volcanic Clouds: Investigations show that lightning can result from charge-separation processes in a volcanic crater. *Science* 148, 1179-1189.

Andersson, M., Karsten, P., Knarrström, B., Svensson, M., 2004. *Stone Age Scania. Significant places dug and read by contract archaeology*. Riksantikvarieämbetet, Lund.

Andres, W., Bos, J.A.A., Houben, P., Kalis, A.J., Nolte, S., Rittweger, H., Wunderlich, J., 2001. Environmental change and fuvial activity during the Younger Dryas in central Germany. *Quaternary International* 79, 89-100.

Andronikov, A., Lauretta, D.S., Subetto, D.A., Verbruggen, C., van der Putten, N., Andronikova, I., Sapelko, T.V., Drosenko, D., 2012. Tale of two lakes: HR-ICP-MS study of Late-Glacial lake sediments from the Snellegem Pond in Belgium and the Lake Medvedevskoye in NW Russia. In search for fingerprints of the Late Pleistocene extraterrestrial event. In: Zhirov, A., Kuznetsov, V., Subetto, D.A., Thiede, J. (Eds.), *"Geomorphology and Paleogeography of Polar Regions": Proceedings of the Joint Conference "Geomorphology and Quaternary Paleogeography of Polar Regions", Symposium "Leopoldina" and the INQUA Peribaltic working group Workshop. Saint-Petersburg, SPbSU, 9-17 September 2012*. Saint Petersburg University, Saint Petersburg, pp. 402-405.

Andronikov, A.V., Rudnickaitė, E., Lauretta, D.S., Andronikova, I.E., Kaminskas, D., Šinkūnas, P., Melešytė, M., 2015. Geochemical evidence of the presence of volcanic and meteoritic materials in Late Pleistocene lake sediments of Lithuania. *Quaternary International* 386, 18-29.

Andronikov, A.V., Subetto, D.A., Lauretta, D.S., Andronikova, I.E., Drosenko, D.A., Kuznetsov, D.D., Sapelko, T.V., Syrykh, L.S., 2014. In search for fingerprints of an extraterrestrial event: Trace element characteristics of sediments from the lake Medvedevskoye (Karelian Isthmus, Russia). *Doklady Earth Sciences* 457, 819-823.

Annen, C., Wagner, J.-J., 2003. The Impact of Volcanic Eruptions During the 1990s. *Natural Hazards Review* 4, 169-175.

Araya, O., Wittwer, F., Villa, A., Ducom, C., 1990. Bovine fluorosis following volcanic activity in the southern Andes. *The Veterinary Record* 126, 641-642.

Arnold, J.R., Libby, W.F., 1949. Age Determinations by Radiocarbon Content: Checks with Samples of Known Age. *Science* 110, 678-680.

Arnórsson, S., 2000. Exploitation of geothemral resources. In: Sigurdsson, H., Houghton, B.F., McNutt, S.R., Rymer, H., Stix, J. (Eds.), *Encyclopedia of Volcanoes*. Academic Press, San Diego, CA, pp. 1243-1258.

Atkinson, Q.D., Gray, R.D., 2005. Curious Parallels and Curious Connections – Phylogenetic Thinking in Biology and Historical Linguistics. *Systematic Biology* 54, 513-526.

Atwood, M., 2011. *In other worlds: science fiction and the human imagination*. Virago, London.

Auchmann, R., Brönnimann, S., Breda, L., Bühler, M., Spadin, R., Stickler, A., 2012. Extreme climate, not extreme weather: the summer of 1816 in Geneva, Switzerland. *Climate of the Past* 8, 325-335.

Audouze, F., Valentin, B., 2010. A Paleohistorical Approach to Upper Paleolithic Structural Changes. In: Bolender, D.J. (Ed.), *Eventful archaeologies: New approaches to social transformation in the archaeological record*. State University of New York, Albany, NY, pp. 29-47.

Bacon, C.R., Lanphere, M.A., 2006. Eruptive history and geochronology of Mount Mazama and the Crater Lake region, Oregon. *Geological Society of America Bulletin* 118, 1331-1359.

Bagniewski, Z., 1997. O schyłkowopaleolitycznych kulturach kompleksu z liściakami na Pomorzu. *Studia Archeologiczne* 29, 25-92.

Bagniewski, Z., 1999. Tanged-Points and the Problem of Palaeolithic Settlement in Pomerania. In: Kozlowski, S.K., Gurba, J., Zaliznyak, L.L. (Eds.), *Tanged Point Cultures in Europe. Read at the International Archaeological Symposium. Lublin, September, 13-16, 1993*. Maria Curie-Sklodowska University Press, Lublin, pp. 131-145.

Baillie, M.G.L., 1991. Suck-in and smear: two related chronological problems for the 90s. *Journal of Theoretical Achaeology* 2, 12-16.

Baker, C.M., 1978. The Size Effect: An Explanation of Variability in Surface Artifact Assemblage Content. *American Antiquity* 43, 288-293.

Balascio, N.L., Wickler, S., Narmo, L.E., Bradley, R.S., 2011. Distal cryptotephra found in a Viking boathouse: the potential for tephrochronology in reconstructing the Iron Age in Norway. *Journal of Archaeological Science* 38, 934-941.

Bandi, H.-G., 1968. Das Jungpaläolithikum. *Ur- und Frühgeschichtliche Archäologie der Schweiz* 1, 107-122.

Bankoff, G., 2004. Time is of the Essence: Disasters, Vulnerability and History. *International Journal of Mass Emergencies and Disasters* 22, 23-42.

Barber, E.J.W., Barber, P., 2006. *When they severed earth from sky: How the human mind shapes myth*. Princeton University Press, Princeton, NJ.

Barton, R.N.E., 1992. *Hengistbury Head, Dorset*. Volume 2: *The Late Upper Palaeolithic & Early Mesolithic Sites*. Oxford Committee for Archaeology, Oxford.

Barton, R.N.E., Berridge, P.J., Walker, M.J.C., Bevins, R.E., 1995. Persistent places in the Mesolithic Landscape: an example from the Black Mountain Uplands of South Wales. *Proceedings of the Prehistoric Society* 61, 81-116.

Barton, R.N.E., Roberts, A.J., 2001. A Lyngby point from Mildenhall, Suffolk and its implications for the British Late Upper Palaeolithic. In: Milliken, S., Cook, J. (Eds.), *A Very Remote Period Indeed. Papers on the Palaeolithic presented to Derek Roe*. Oxbow, Oxford, pp. 234-241.

Barton, R.N.E., Roberts, A.J., Roe, D. (Eds.), 1991. *The Late Glacial in north-west Europe: human adaptation and environmental change at the end of the Pleistocene Council for British Archaeology Research Report*. CBA, London.

Baxter, P.J., 2005. Human impacts of volcanoes. In: Martí, J., Ernst, G.G.J. (Eds.), *Volcanoes and the Environment*. Cambridge University Press, Cambridge, pp. 273-303.

Baxter, P.J., Ing, R., Falk, H., Pliakaytis, B., 1983. Mount St. Helens eruptions: the acute respiratory effects of volcanic ash in a North American community. *Archives of Environmental Health* 38, 138-143.

Beaudoin, A.B., Oetelaar, G.A., 2003. The changing ecophysical landscape of Southern Alberta during the late Pleistocene and early Holocene. *Plains Anthropologist* 48, 187-187.

Beaudoin, A.B., Oetelaar, G.A., 2006. The Day the Dry Snow fell: The Record of a 7627-year-old Disaster. In: Payne, M., Wetherell, D., Kavanaugh, C. (Eds.), *Alberta Formed Alberta Transformed*. Volume 1: *E-SCAPE Contribution 5*. University of Alberta Press/University of Calgary Press, Edmonton, AB, pp. 36-53.

Beck, J.R.A., Bolender, D.J., Brown, J.A., Earle, T.K., 2007. Eventful Archaeology: The Place of Space in Structural Transformation. *Current Anthropology* 48, 833-860.

Beck, U., 2003. *Risikogesellschaft: Auf dem Weg in eine andere Moderne*. Suhrkamp, Frankfurt a. M.

Beck, U., 2015. Emancipatory catastrophism: What does it mean to climate change and risk society? *Current Sociology* 63, 75-88.

Becker, C.J., 1950. The Pitted-Ware Culture in Denmark. *Aarbøger for nordisk Oldkyndighed og Historie* 1950, 153-274.

Becker, C.J., 1971. Late Palaeolithic finds from Denmark. *Proceedings of the Prehistoric Society* 37, 131-139.

Becker, D., Benecke, N., 2002. *Die neolithische Inselsiedlung am Löddigsee bei Parchim*. Buck, Lübstorf.

Becker, E., 1967. Zur stratigraphischen Gliederung der jungpleistozänen Sedimente im nördlichen Oberrheintalgraben. *Eiszeitalter & Gegenwart* 18, 5-50.

Beckhoff, K., 1966. Zur Morphogenese der steinzeitlichen Pfeilspitze. *Die Kunde N.F.* 17, 34-65.

Behlen, H., 1905. Eine neue Nachgrabung vor der Steedener Höhle Wildscheuer. *Annalen des Vereins für Nassauische Alterthumskunde und Geschichtsforschung* 35, 290-307.

Bell, M., 2012. Climate change, extreme weather events and issues of human perception. *Archaeological Dialogues* 19, 42-46.

Benediktsson, K., Lund, K.A., Huijbens, E., 2011. Inspired by Eruptions? Eyjafjallajökull and Icelandic Tourism. *Mobilities* 6, 77-84.

Bennike, O., Sarmaja-Korjonen, K., Seppänen, A., 2004. Reinvestigation of the classic late-glacial Bølling Sø sequence, Denmark: chronology, macrofossils, Cladocera and chydorid ephippia. *Journal of Quaternary Science* 19, 465-478.

Bentley, R.A., Hahn, M.W., Shennan, S.J., 2004. Random drift and culture change. *Proceedings of the Royal Society B: Biological Sciences* 271, 1443-1450.

Berkes, F., 2007. Understanding uncertainty and reducing vulnerability: lessons from resilience thinking. *Natural Hazards* 41, 283-295.

Berthelsen, W., 1944. *Stenalderbopladser i Sønderkjær og Vejledalen. Bidrag til Kendskabet til den mesolitiske Kulturperiode i Sydøstjylland*. Munksgaard, Copenhagen.

Berthold, P., 2001. *Bird Migration. A General Survey*. Oxford University Press, Oxford.

Bille, M., Sørensen, T.F., 2007. An Anthropology of Luminosity: The Agency of Light. *Journal of Material Culture* 12, 263-284.

Binford, L.R., 2001. *Constructing Frames of Reference: An Analytical Method for Archaeological Theory Building Using Hunter-Gatherer and Environmental Data Sets*. University of California Press, Berkeley, CA.

Bingham, P.M., Souza, J., Blitz, J.H., 2013. Introduction: Social Complexity and the Bow in the Prehistoric North American Record. *Evolutionary Anthropology: Issues, News, and Reviews* 22, 81-88.

Bird, D., Gísladóttir, G., 2012. Residents' attitudes and behaviour before and after the 2010 Eyjafjallajökull eruptions—a case study from southern Iceland. *Bulletin of Volcanology* 74, 1263-1279.

Bird, D., Gísladóttir, G., Dominey-Howes, D., 2011. Different communities, different perspectives: issues affecting residents' response to a volcanic eruption in southern Iceland. *Bulletin of Volcanology* 73, 1209-1227.

Birkmann, J., Buckle, P., Jaeger, J., Pelling, M., Setiadi, N., Garschagen, M., Fernando, N., Kropp, J., 2010. Extreme events and disasters: a window of opportunity for change? Analysis of organizational, institutional and political changes, formal and informal responses after mega-disasters. *Natural Hazards* 55, 637-655.

Birkmann, J., Cardona, O.D., Carreño, M.L., Barbat, A.H., Pelling, M., Schneiderbauer, S., Kienberger, S., Keiler, M., Alexander, D., Zeil, P., Welle, T., 2013. Framing vulnerability, risk and societal responses: the MOVE framework. *Natural Hazards* 67, 193-211.

Birks, H.J.B., Lotter, A.F., 1994. The impact of the Laacher See Volcano (11000 yr B.P.) on terrestrial vegetation and diatoms. *Journal of Paleolimnology* 11, 313-322.

Bishop, S.E., 1886a. The remarkable sunsets. *Nature* 29, 259-260.

Bishop, S.E., 1886b. The origin of the red glows. *American Meteorological Journal* 3, 127-136, 193-196.

Bjurström, A., Polk, M., 2011. Physical and economic bias in climate change research: a scientometric study of IPCC Third Assessment Report. *Climatic Change* 108, 1-22.

Black, R., Bennett, S.R.G., Thomas, S.M., Beddington, J.R., 2011. Climate change: Migration as adaptation. *Nature* 478, 447-449.

Blockley, S.P.E., Pyne-O'Donnell, S.D.F., Lowe, J.J., Matthews, I.P., Stone, A., Pollard, A.M., Turney, C.S.M., Molyneux, E.g. 2005. A new and less destructive laboratory procedure for the physical separation of distal glass tephra shards from sediments. *Quaternary Science Reviews* 24, 1952-1960.

Blong, R.J., 1982. *The Time of Darkness. Local legends and volcanic reality in Papua New Guinea*. University of Washington Press, Seattle, WA.

Blong, R.J., 1984. *Volcanic Hazards. A Sourcebook on the Effects of Eruptions*. Academic Press, Sydney.

Blumberg, A.E., 1976. *Logic: A First Course*. Alfred E. Knopf, New York, NY.

Bocquet-Appel, J.-P., Demars, P.-Y., Noiret, L., Dobrowsky, D., 2005. Estimates of Upper Palaeolithic meta-population size in Europe from archaeological data. *Journal of Archaeological Science* 32, 1656-1668.

Bodu, P., 1998. Magdalenians-Early Azilians in the centre of the Paris Basin: a filiation? The example of Le Closeau (Rueil-Malmaison, France). In: Milliken, S. (Ed.), *The Organization of Lithic Technology in Late Glacial and Early Postglacial of Europe*. Oxbow, Oxford, pp. 131-147.

Bodu, P., Valentin, B., 1997. Groupes à Federmesser ou Aziliens dans le sud et l'ouest du Bassin parisien. Propositions pour un nouveau modèle d'évolution. *Bulletin de la Société Préhistorique Française* 94, 349-359.

Bokelmann, K., 1978. Ein Federmesserfundplatz bei Schalkholz, Kreis Dithmarschen. *Offa* 35, 36-54.

Bokelmann, K., Heinrich, D., Menke, B., 1983. Fundplätze des Spätglazials am Hainholz-Esinger Moor, Kreis Pinneberg. *Offa* 40, 199-239.

Bolender, D.J. (Ed.), 2010. *Eventful archaeologies: New approaches to social transformation in the archaeological record*. State University of New York, Albany, NY.

Bolt, B.A., Horn, W.L., MacDonald, G.A., Scott, R.F., 1975. *Geological Hazards. Earthquakes – Tsunamis – Volcanoes – Avalanches – Landslides – Floods*. Springer Verlag, Berlin.

Bolus, M., 1992. *Die Siedlungsbefunde des späteiszeitlichen Fundplatzes Niederbieber (Stadt Neuwied): Ausgrabungen 1981-1988; mit Beiträgen von Gabriele Roth, Siegfried Stephan, Rolf C. Rottländ*. Rudolf Habelt GmbH, Bonn.

Bolus, M., 2012. Schleifsteine mit Rille (Pfeilschaftglätter). In: Floss, H. (Ed.), Steinartefakte vom Altpaläolithikum bis in die Neuzeit. Archaeologica Venatoria. Kerns-Verlag, Tübingen, pp. 525-534.

Bonadonna, C., 2006. Probabilistic modelling of tephra dispersion. In: Mader, H.M., Coles, S.G., Connor, C.B., Connor, L.J. (Eds.), *Statistics in Volcanology*. Special Publications of IAVCEI 1. Geological Society, London, pp. 243-259.

Bonadonna, C., Ernst, G.G.J., Sparks, R.S.J., 1998. Thickness variations and volume estimates of tephra fall deposits: the importance of particle Reynolds number. *Journal of Volcanology and Geothermal Research* 81, 173-187.

Boonstra, W., de Boer, F., 2014. The Historical Dynamics of Social–Ecological Traps. *AMBIO* 43, 260-274.

Bos, J.A.A., 2001. Lateglacial and Early Holocene vegetation history of the northern Wetterau and the Amöneburger Basin (Hessen), central-west Germany. *Review of Palaeobotany and Palynology* 115, 177-212.

Bos, J.A.A., Janssen, C.R., 1996. Local Impact of Palaeolithic Man on the Environment During the End of the Last Glacial in the Netherlands. *Journal of Archaeological Science* 23, 731-739.

Bos, J.A.A., Urz, R., 2003. Late Glacial and early Holocene environment in the middle Lahn river valley

(Hessen, central-west Germany) and the local impact of early Mesolithic people—pollen and macrofossil evidence. *Vegetation History and Archaeobotany* 12, 19-36.

Bosinski, G., 1979. *Die Ausgrabungen in Gönnersdorf 1968-1976 und die Siedlungsbefunde der Grabung 1968*. Franz Steiner, Wiesbaden.

Bosinski, G., 2007. *Gönnersdorf und Andernach-Martinsberg: Späteiszeitliche Siedlungsplätze am Mittelrhein*. Gesellschaft für Archäologie an Mittelrhein und Mosel e.V., Koblenz.

Bosinski, G., Hahn, J., 1973. Der Magdalenien Fundplanz Andernach (Martinsberg). *Rheinische Ausgrabungen* 11, 81-264.

Bourdelle, Y., 1979. L'abri Durif a Enval (Vic-le-Comté, Puy-de-Dome). I. *Étude préliminaire du Magdalénien final du Fond de l'Abri Gallia Préhistoire* 22, 87-111.

Bourdelle, Y., Merlet, J.-C., 1991. Le site d'Enval. Commune de Vic-le-Comte (Puy-de-Dôme). *Bulletin de la Société Préhistorique Française* 88, 109-113.

Bourdieu, P., 1977. *Outline of a theory of practice*. Cambridge University Press, Cambridge.

Bratlund, B., 1993. Ein Riesenhirschschädel mit Bearbeitungsspuren aus Lüdersdorf, Kreis Grevesmühlen. *Offa* 49/50, 7-14.

Bratlund, B., 1999. A revision of the rarer species from the Ahrensburgian assemblage of Stellmoor. In: Benecke, N. (Ed.), *The Holocene History of the European Vertebrate Fauna. Modern Aspects of Research*. Archäologie in Eurasien 6. Verlag Marie Leidorf, Rahden, pp. 39-42.

Brauer, A., Endres, C., Negendank, J.F.W., 1999. Lateglacial calendar year chronology based on annually laminated sediments from Lake Meerfelder Maar, Germany. *Quaternary International* 61, 17-25.

Braun, A., Pfeiffer, T., 2002. Cyanobacterial Blooms as the Cause of a Pleistocene Large Mammal Assemblage. *Paleobiology* 28, 139-154.

Brauns, R., 1886. Bimssteine auf primärer Lagerstätte von Görzhausen bei Marburg. *Zeitschrift der deutschen geologischen Gesellschaft* 38, 234-236.

Brauns, R., 1892. Hauyn in den Bimssteinsanden der Umgegend von Marburg. *Zeitschrift der deutschen geologischen Gesellschaft* 44, 149-150.

Breest, K., 2004. Alt-, mittel, und jungsteinzeitliche Funde aus der Umgebung von Tostedt, Ldkr. Harburg. Die Sammlung Albert Bartels. *Nachrichten aus Niedersachsens Urgeschichte* 73, 3-6.

Breest, K., Böhmer, M., Renner, F., 1999. Ein spätpaläolithischer Oberflächenfundplatz mit Rücken- und Bromme (Lyngby)-Spitzen bei Dohnsen, Ldkr. Celle. *Nachrichten aus Niedersachsens Urgeschichte* 68, 3-18.

Breest, K., Gerken, K., 2003. Sassenholz FStNr. 78, Gde. Heeslingen, Ldkr. Rotenburg (Wümme), Reg. Bez. Lü. *Fundchronik Niedersachsen* 2003, 10-11.

Breest, K., Gerken, K., 2008. Kulturelle Einflüsse und Beziehungen im Spätpaläolithikum Nieder-

sachsens – Ein Diskussionsbeitrag Sassenholz 78 und 82, Ldkr. Rotenburg (Wümme). *Die Kunde N.F.* 59, 1-38.

Breest, K., Graff, K.-H., 2007. Mittel- und spätpaläolithische Funde von Handeloh, Gde. Höckel, Ldkr. Harburg. *Nachrichten aus Niedersachsens Urgeschichte* 76, 3-16.

Bretzke, K., Marks, A.E., Conard, N.J., 2006. Projektiltechnologie und kulturelle Evolution in Ostafrika. *Mitteilungen der Gesellschaft für Urgeschichte* 15, 63-81.

Brinch Petersen, E., 1970. Le Brommeen et le cycle de Lyngby. *Quartär* 21, 93-95.

Brinch Petersen, E., 2009. The human settlement of southern Scandinavia 12500-8700 cal BC. In: Street, M., Barton, R.N.E., Terberger, T. (Eds.), *Humans, environment and chronology of the late glacial of the North European Plain. RGZM – Tagungen*, Band 6. Verlag des Römisch-Germanischen Zentralmuseums, Mainz, pp. 89-129.

Bronk Ramsey, C., 2009. Bayesian Analysis of Radiocarbon Dates. *Radiocarbon* 51, 337-360.

Bronk Ramsey, C., Albert, P.G., Blockley, S.P.E., Hardiman, M., Housley, R.A., Lane, C.S., Lee, S., Matthews, I.P., Smith, V.C., Lowe, J.J., 2015a. Improved age estimates for key Late Quaternary European tephra horizons in the RESET lattice. *Quaternary Science Reviews* 118, 18-32.

Bronk Ramsey, C., Higham, T.F.G., Brock, F., Baker, D., Ditchfield, P., Staff, R.A., 2015b. Radiocarbon Dates from the Oxford AMS System: Archaeometry Datelist 35. *Archaeometry* 57, 177-216.

Bronk Ramsey, C., Housley, R.A., Lane, C.S., Smith, V.C., Pollard, A.M., 2015c. The RESET tephra database and associated analytical tools. *Quaternary Science Reviews* 118, 33-47.

Brooks, N., Neil Adger, W., Mick Kelly, P., 2005. The determinants of vulnerability and adaptive capacity at the national level and the implications for adaptation. *Global Environmental Change* 15, 151-163.

Bryson, R.U., Bryson, R.A., Ruter, A., 2006. A calibrated radiocarbon database of late Quaternary volcanic eruptions. *eEarth Discussions* 1, 123-134.

Buck Pedersen, K., 2009. *Stederne og menneskerne. Istidsjægere omkring Knudshoved Odde*. Museerne.dk, Vordingborg.

Budd, L., Griggs, S., Howarth, D., Ison, S., 2011. A Fiasco of Volcanic Proportions? Eyjafjallajökull and the Closure of European Airspace. *Mobilities* 6, 31-40.

Burdukiewicz, J.M., 1999. Late Palaeolithic amber in Northern Europe. In: Kosmowska-Ceranowicz, B., Paner, H. (Eds.), *Investigations into Amber*. The Archaeological Museum in Gdansk, Gdansk, pp. 99-109.

Burdukiewicz, J.M., 2001. The last Ice Age and settlement break in the northern part of Central Europe. *Fontes Archaeologici Posnanienses* 39, 15-29.

Burdukiewicz, J.M., 2009. Further Research on Amber in Palaeolithic Archaeology. In: Burdukiewicz, J.M., Krysztof, C., Dyczek, P., Szymzcak, K. (Eds.), *Understanding the Past. Papers offered to Stefan K. Kozlowski*. University of Warsaw, Warsaw, pp. 69-74.

Burdukiewicz, J.M., Kobusiewicz, M. (Eds.), 1987. *Late Glacial in Central Europe. Culture and Environment*. Prace Komisji Archeologicznej, Kracow.

Burroughs, W.J., 2005. *Climate Change in Prehistory. The End of the Reign of Chaos*. Cambridge University Press, Cambridge.

Butzer, K.W., 1982. *Archaeology as Human Ecology. Method and Theory for a Contextual Approach*. Cambridge University Press, Cambridge.

Butzer, K.W., 1990. The Realm of Cultural-Human Ecology: Adaptation and Change in Historical Perspective. In: Turner, B.L.I., Clark, W.C., Kates, R.W., Richards, J.F., Mathews, J.T., Meyer, W.B. (Eds.), *The Earth as Transformed by Human Action: Global and Regional Changes in the Biosphere over the Past 300 Years*. Cambridge University Press, Cambridge, pp. 685-701.

Byron, G.G.N., 1839. *The Poetical Works of Lord Byron*. Volume IV. John Murray, London.

Böttger, T., Hiller, A., Junge, F.W., Litt, T., Mania, D., Scheele, N., 1998. Late Glacial stable isotope record, radiocarbon stratigraphy, pollen and mollusc analyses from the Geiseltal area, Central Germany. *Boreas* 27, 88-100.

Baales, M., 1996. *Umwelt und Jagdökonomie der Ahrensburger Rentierjäger im Mittelgebirge*. Verlag Rudolf Habelt GmbH, Bonn.

Baales, M., 2001. From Lithics to Spatial and Social Organization: Interpreting the Lithic Distribution and Raw Material Composition at the Final Palaeolithic Site of Kettig (Central Rhineland, Germany). *Journal of Archaeological Science* 28, 127-141.

Baales, M., 2002a. *Der spätpaläolithische Fundplatz Kettig: Untersuchungen zur Siedlungsarchäologie der Federmesser-Gruppen am Mittelrhein*. Verlag Rudolf Habelt GmbH, Bonn.

Baales, M., 2002b. Vulkanismus und Archäologie des Eiszeitalters am Mittelrhein. Die Forschungsergebnisse der letzten dreissig Jahre. *Jahrbuch des Römisch-Germanischen Zentralmuseums Mainz* 49, 43-80.

Baales, M., 2006. Final Palaeolithic environment and archaeology in the Central Rhineland (Rhineland-Palatinate, western Germany): conclusions of the last 15 years of research. *Anthropologie* 110, 418-444.

Baales, M., Bittmann, F., Kromer, B., 1999. Verkohlte Bäume im Trass der Laacher See-Tephra bei Kruft (Neuwieder Becken). Ein Beitrag zur Datierung des Laacher See-Ereignisses und zur Vegetation der Alleröd-Zeit am Mittelrhein. *Archäologisches Korrespondenzblatt* 28, 191-204.

Baales, M., Jöris, O., 2001. Zwischen Nord und Süd. Ein spätallrödzeitlicher Rückenspitzen-Fundplatz bei Bad Breisig, Kr. Ahrweiler (Mittelrhein, Rheinland-Pfalz). *Die Kunde N.F.* 52, 275-292.

Baales, M., Jöris, O., 2002. Between North and South – a site with backed points from the final Allerod: Bad Breisig, Kr. Ahrweiler (Central Rhineland, Germany). *L'Anthropologie* 106, 249-267.

Baales, M., Jöris, O., Street, M., Bittmann, F., Weninger, B., Wiethold, J., 2002. Impact of the Late Glacial Eruption of the Laacher See Volcano, Central Rhineland, Germany. *Quaternary Research* 58, 273-288.

Baales, M., Mewis, S.U., Street, M., 1998. Der Federmesser-Fundplatz Urbar bei Koblenz. Mit einem Beitrag von Horst Kierdorf. *Jahrbuch des Römisch-Germanischen Zentralmuseums Mainz* 43, 241-279.

Baales, M., Street, M., 1996. Hunter-Gatherer Behavior in a Changing Late Glacial Landscape: Allerød Archaeology in the Central Rhineland, Germany. *Journal of Anthropological Research* 52, 281-316.

Baales, M., Street, M., 1998. Late Palaeolithic backed-point assemblages in the northern Rheineland: current research and changing views. *Notae Praehistoricae* 18, 77-92.

Baales, M., Street, M., 1999. Late Glacial Federmesser-gruppen in the Central Rhineland. In: Thévenin, A., Bintz, P. (Eds.), *L'Europe des derniers chasseurs. Epipaléolithique et Mésolithique, Paris, Comité des Travaux historiques et scientifiques. UISPP – Commission XII, Grenoble,* Editions du CNRS, Paris, pp. 225-235.

Baales, M., von Berg, A., 1997. Tierfährten in der allerödzeitlichen Vulkanasche des Laacher See-Vulkans bei Mertloch, Kreis Mayen-Koblenz. *Archäologisches Korrespondenzblatt* 27, 1-12.

Campbell, J.B., 1977. *The Upper Palaeolithic of Britain: a Study of Man and Nature in the Late Ice Age*. Volume 2. Clarendon Press, Oxford.

Carlsson, T., Gruber, G., Molin, F., 2005. The Mesolithic in Östergötland – An Introduction. In: Gruber, G. (Ed.), *Identities in Transition. Mesolithic Strategies in the Swedish Province of Östergötland*. Riksantikvarieämbetet, Linköping, pp. 8-23.

Carr, C., 1995. Building a Unified Middle-Range Theory of Artifact Design. In: Carr, C., Neitzel, J. (Eds.), *Style, Society, and Person: Archaeological and Ethnological Perspectives*. Plenum, New York, NY, pp. 151-170.

Carson, R., 2000. *Mount St. Helens: the eruption and recovery of a volcano*. Sasquatch Books, Seattle, WA.

Casati, C., Sørensen, L., 2006. Bornholm i ældre stenalder. Status over kulturel udvikling og kontakter. *Kuml* 2006, 9-57.

Cashman, K.V., Cronin, S.J., 2008. Welcoming a monster to the world: Myths, oral tradition, and modern societal response to volcanic disasters.

Journal of Volcanology and Geothermal Research 176, 407-418.

Cashman, K.V., Giordano, G., 2008. Volcanoes and human history. *Journal of Volcanology and Geothermal Research* 176, 325-329.

Caspar, J.-P., De Bie, M., 1996. Preparing for the Hunt in the Late Palaeolithic Camp at Rekem, Belgium. *Journal of Field Archaeology* 23, 437-460.

Caspers, G., 1993. Fluviatile Geomorphodynamik und Vegetationsentwicklung im Tal der Weser seit dem Spätglazial. *Berichte der Naturhistorischen Gesellschaft Hannover* 135, 29-48.

Cattelain, P., 1997. Hunting during the Upper Paleolithic: Bow, Spearthrower, or Both? In: Knecht, H. (Ed.), *Projectile Technology*. Plenum Press, New York, NY, pp. 213-240.

Cattelain, P., 2004. Un propulseur de la Grotte du Placard (Vilhonneur, Charente, France). *Notae Praehistoricae* 24, 61-67.

Cattelain, P., 2005. Propulseurs magdaléniens: marqueurs culturels régionaux? In: Dujardin, V. (Ed.), *Industrie osseuse et parures du Solutréen au Magdalénien en Europe*. Mémoires de la Société Préhistorique Française 39. Société Préhistorique Française, Paris, pp. 301-317.

Caumann, L.S., 1998. *First-order Logic. An Introduction*. De Gruyter, Berlin.

Célérier, G., Chollet, A., Hantai, A., 1997. Nouvelles observations sur l'évolution de l'Azilien dans les gisements de Bois-Ragot (Vienne) et de Pont-d'Ambon (Dordogne). *Bulletin de la Société Préhistorique Française* 94, 331-336.

Champagne, F., Espitalié, R., 1970. L'abri du roc d'abeilles à Calviac (Dordogne). *Gallia Préhistoire* 13, 1-23.

Charman, D.J., West, S., Kelly, A., Grattan, J., 1995. Environmental Change and Tephra Deposition: the Strath of Kildonan, Northern Scotland. *Journal of Archaeological Science* 22, 799-809.

Charmley, J., 1999. *Splendid isolation? Britain, the balance of power and the origins of the First World War*. Hodder & Stoughton, London.

Cheshier, J., Kelly, R.L., 2006. Projectile Point Shape and Durability: The Effect of Thickness: Length. *American Antiquity* 71, 353-363.

Chester, D.K., 2005a. Theology and disaster studies: The need for dialogue. *Journal of Volcanology and Geothermal Research* 146, 319-328.

Chester, D.K., 2005b. Volcanoes, society, and culture. In: Martí, J., Ernst, G.G.J. (Eds.), *Volcanoes and the Environment*. Cambridge University Press, Cambridge, pp. 404-439.

Chester, D.K., Degg, M., Duncan, A.M., Guest, J.E., 2001. The increasing exposure of cities to the effects of volcanic eruptions: a global survey. *Environmental Hazards* 2, 89-103.

Chester, D.K., Duncan, A.M., 2007. Geomythology, Theodicy, and the Continuing Relevance of Religious Worldviews on Responses to Volcanic Eruptions. In: Grattan, J., Torrence, R. (Eds.), *Living Under The Shadow. Cultural Impacts of Volcanic Eruptions*. Left Coast Press, Walnut Creek, CA, pp. 203-224.

Chester, D.K., Duncan, A.M., Sangster, H., 2012. Human responses to eruptions of Etna (Sicily) during the late-Pre-Industrial Era and their implications for present-day disaster planning. *Journal of Volcanology and Geothermal Research* 225-226, 65-80.

Chmielewska, M., 1962. A Late Palaeolithic and Mesolithic site at Witów, district Łęczyca. *Archaeologia Polona* 4, 77-87.

Choi, S.W., Preusser, F., Radtke, U., 2007. Dating of lower terrace sediments from the Middle Rhine area, Germany. *Quaternary Geochronology* 2, 137-142.

Chollet, A., Fouéré, P., Hantai, A., Le Licon, G., 1999. L'evolution des choix techniques et economiques entre le Magdalenien superieur et l'Azilien. In: Bintz, P., Thévenin, A. (Eds.), *L'Europe des derniers chasseurs. Epipaléolithique et Mésolithique, Paris, Comité des Travaux historiques et scientifiques. UISPP – Commission XII, Grenoble*, Editions du CNRS, Paris, pp. 275-285.

Christensen, A.L., 1986. Projectile point size and projectile aerodynamics: An exploratory study. *Plains Anthropologist* 31, 109-128.

Christiansen, J., 2008. *Vegetationsgeschichtliche Untersuchungen in der westlichen Prignitz, dem östlichen Hannoverschen Wendland und der nördlichen Altmark*. Georg-August-Universität, Göttingen.

Churchill, S.E., 1993. Weapon Technology, Prey Size Selection, and Hunting Methods in Modern Hunter-Gatherers: Implications for Hunting in the Palaeolithic and Mesolithic. In: Peterkin, G.L., Bricker, H.M., Mellars, P. (Eds.), *Hunting and Animal Exploitation in the Later Palaeolithic and Mesolithic of Eurasia*. Archeological Papers of the American Anthropological Association 4. American Anthropological Association, Washington, DC, pp. 11-24.

Clark, J.G.D., 1936. *The Mesolithic Settlement of Northern Europe*. Greenwood, New York, NY.

Clark, J.G.D., 1950. The Earliest Settlement of the West Baltic Area in the Light of Recent Research. *Proceedings of the Prehistoric Society* 16, 87-100.

Clark, J.G.D. (Ed.), 1989. *Economic prehistory: papers on archaeology*. Cambridge University Press, Cambridge.

Clarke, L., 1999. *Mission Improbable. Using Fantasy Documents to Tame Disaster*. The University of Chicago Press, Chicago, IL.

Clarke, L., 2003. Coneptualizing responses to extreme events: The problem of panic and failing gracefully. In: Clarke, L. (Ed.), *Terrorism and disaster: New threats, new ideas*. Research in Social Problems and Public Policy 11. Elsevier, Amsterdam, pp. 123-141.

Clarke, L., 2004. Using Disaster to See Society. *Contemporary Sociology* 33, 137-139.

Clarke, L., 2006. *Worst Cases. Terror and Catastrophe in the Popular Imagination*. University of Chicago Press, Chicago, IL.

Clarke, L., 2007. Thinking possibilistically in a probabilistic world. *Significance* 4, 190-192.

Clarke, L., 2008a. Possibilistic Thinking: A New Conceptual Tool for Thinking about Extreme Events. *Social Research* 75, 669-690,1033.

Clarke, L., 2008b. Thinking about Worst-Case Thinking. *Sociological Inquiry* 78, 154-161.

Clausen, I., 2003. Das allerødzeitliche Rengeweihbeil aus Klappholz LA 63, Kreis Schleswig-Flensburg. Ein Relikt der Federmesser-, der Bromme- oder der Ahrensburger Kultur? *Offa* 59/60, 15-39.

Clausen, I., 2004. The reindeer antler axe of the Allerød period from Klappholz LA 63, Kreis Schleswig-Flensburg/Germany. Is it a relict of the Federmesser, Bromme or Ahrensburg culture? In: Terberger, T., Eriksen, B.V. (Eds.), *Hunters in a Changing World. Environment and Archaeology of the Pleistocene – Holocene Transition (c. 11000 – 9000 B.C. in Northern Central Europe)*. Verlag Marie Leidorf GmbH, Rahden, pp. 141-164.

Clausen, I., Hartz, S., 1988. Fundplätze des Spätglazials am Sorgetal bei Alt Duvenstedt, Kreis Rendsburg-Eckernförde. Offa 45, 17-41.

Cohen, K.M., 2003. *Differential subsidence within a coastal prism: Late-Glacial – Holocene tectonics in the Rhine-Meuse delta, The Netherlands*. Koninklijk Nederlands Aardrijkskundig Genootschap/Faculteit Ruimtelijke Wetenschappen, Universiteit Utrecht, Utrecht.

Cole-Dai, J., 2010. Volcanoes and climate. *Wiley Interdisciplinary Reviews: Climate Change* 1, 824-839.

Collard, M., Ruttle, A., Buchanan, B., O'Brien, M.J., 2013. Population Size and Cultural Evolution in Nonindustrial Food-Producing Societies. *PLoS ONE* 8, e72628.

Combier, J., Desbrosse, R., 1964. Magdalénien final à pointe de Teyjat dans le Jura méridional. *L'Anthropologie* 68, 190-194.

Conard, N.J., 1992. *Tönchesberg and its position in the paleolithic prehistory of Northern Europe*. Verlag Rudolf Habelt GmbH, Bonn.

Conneller, C., 2007. Inhabiting new landscapes: Settlement and mobility in Britain after the Last Glacial Maximum. *Oxford Journal of Archaeology* 26, 215-237.

Coope, G.R., Bocher, J., 2000. Coleoptera from the Late Weichselian deposits at Nørre Lyngby, Denmark and their bearing on palaeoecology, biogeography and palaeoclimate. *Boreas* 29, 26-34.

Coope, G.R., Lemdahl, G., 1995. Regional differences in the Lateglacial climate of northern Europe based on coleopteran analysis. *Journal of Quaternary Science* 10, 391-395.

Coope, G.R., Lemdahl, G., Lowe, J.J., Walkling, A., 1998. Temperature gradients in northern Europe during the last glacial–Holocene transition (14-9 14C kyr BP) interpreted from coleopteran assemblages. *Journal of Quaternary Science* 13, 419-433.

Cooper, J., 2012. Weathering climate change. The value of social memory and ecological knowledge. *Archaeological Dialogues* 19, 46-51.

Cooper, J., Sheets, P.D. (Eds.), 2012. *Surviving Sudden Environmental Change*. University of Colorado Press, Boulder, CO.

Cosgrove, R., 1995. *The Illusion of Riches. Scale, resolution and explanation in Tasmanian Pleistocene human behaviour*. Oxbow, Oxford.

Cotterell, B., Kamminga, J., 1990. *Mechanics of pre-industrial technology: an introduction to the mechanics of ancient and traditional material culture*. Cambridge University Press, Cambridge.

Crombé, P., Sergant, J., Robinson, E., De Reu, J., 2011. Hunter-gatherer responses to environmental change during the Pleistocene-Holocene transition in the southern North Sea basin: Final Palaeolithic-Final Mesolithic land use in northwest Belgium. *Journal of Anthropological Archaeology* 30, 454-471.

Crombé, P., Sergant, J., Verbrugge, A., De Graeve, A., Cherretté, B., Mikkelsen, J., Cnudde, V., De Kock, T., Huisman, H.D.J., van Os, B.J.H., Van Strydonck, M., Boudin, M., 2014. A sealed flint knapping site from the Younger Dryas in the Scheldt valley (Belgium): Bridging the gap in human occupation at the Pleistocene–Holocene transition in W Europe. *Journal of Archaeological Science* 50, 420-439.

Crombé, P.H., Robinson, E., Van Strydonck, M., Boudin, M., 2013. Radiocarbon dating of Mesolithic open-air sites in the coversand area of the North-west European Plain: Problems and prospects. *Archaeometry* 55, 545-562.

Crommelin, R.D., 1963. Een vulkanasch sediment in de ondergrond van de Betuwe. *Geologie En Mijnbouw* 42, 112-113.

Cronin, S.J., Cashman, K.V., 2007. Volcanic Oral Traditions in Hazard Assessment and Mitigation. In: Grattan, J., Torrence, R. (Eds.), *Living Under The Shadow. Cultural Impacts of Volcanic Eruptions*. Left Coast Press, Walnut Creek, CA, pp. 175-202.

Cronin, S.J., Petterson, M., Taylor, P., Biliki, R., 2004a. Maximising Multi-Stakeholder Participation in Government and Community Volcanic Hazard Management Programs; A Case Study from Savo, Solomon Islands. *Natural Hazards* 33, 105-136.

Cronin, S.J., Gaylord, D.R., Charley, D., Alloway, B.V., Wallez, S., Esau, J.W., 2004b. Participatory methods of incorporating scientific with traditional knowledge for volcanic hazard management on Ambae Island, Vanuatu. *Bulletin of Volcanology* 66, 652-668.

Cronin, S.J., Manoharan, V., Hedley, M.J., Loganathan, P., 2000. Fluoride: A review of its fate, bioavailability, and risks of fluorosis in grazed-pasture systems in New Zealand. *New Zealand Journal of Agricultural Research* 43, 295-321.

Cronin, S.J., Neall, V.E., Lecointre, J.A., Hedley, M.J., Loganathan, P., 2003. Environmental hazards of fluoride in volcanic ash: a case study from Ruapehu volcano, New Zealand. *Journal of Volcanology and Geothermal Research* 121, 271-291.

Crosweller, H.S., Arora, B., Brown, S.K., Cottrell, E., Deligne, N.I., Guerrero, N.O., Hobbs, L., Kiyosugi, K., Loughlin, S.C., Lowndes, J., Nayembil, M., Siebert, L., Sparks, R.S.J., Takarada, S., Venzke, E., 2012. Global database on large magnitude explosive volcanic eruptions (LaMEVE). *Journal of Applied Volcanology* 1, 4.

Currant, A., Jacobi, R., 2001. A formal mammalian biostratigraphy for the Late Pleistocene of Britain. *Quaternary Science Reviews* 20, 1707-1716.

Cutter, S.L. 1996. Vulnerability to environmental hazards. *Progress in Human Geography* 20, 529-539.

Cutter, S.L., Boruff, B.J., Shirley, W.L., 2003. Social Vulnerability to Environmental Hazards. *Social Science Quarterly* 84, 242-261.

Cziesla, E., 2001. Neue Altfunde aus Pritzerbe (Brandenburg). Zugleich ein Beitrag zum Fischfang und zum steinzeitlichen Angelhaken. *Ethnographisch-Archäologische Zeitschrift* 42, 473-504.

Cziesla, E., Pettitt, P., 2003. AMS-14C-Datierungen von Spätpaläolithischen und Mesolithischen Funden aus dem Bützsee (Brandenburg). *Archäologisches Korrespondenzblatt* 33, 21-38.

D'Alessandro, W., 2006. Human fluorosis related to volcanic activity: a review. In: Kungolos, A., Samaras, C.P., Brebbia, C.A., Popov, V.V. (Eds.), *Environmental Toxicology*. WIT Press, Southampton, pp. 21-30.

Dale, V.H., Delgado-Acevedo, J., MacMahon, J., 2005. Effects of modern volcanic eruptions on vegetation. In: Martí, J., Ernst, G.G.J. (Eds.), *Volcanoes and the Environment*. Cambridge University Press, Cambridge, pp. 227-249.

Damm, A., Thorndahl, J. (Eds.), 1987. *Danskeren og den ædle vilde: vore forestillinger om os selv og andre folk i fortid og nutid*. Hovedland/Moesgård, Risskov.

Daniel, R., 1970. L'abri de la Font-Brunel à Limeuil (Dordogne) Contribution à l'étude de son outillage lithique. Bulletin de la Société préhistorique française. *Comptes rendus des séances mensuelles* 67, 81-84.

Darasse, P., Guffroy, S., 1960. Le Magdalénien supérieur de l'abri de Fontalès près de Saint Antonin (Tarn-et-Garonne). *L'Anthropologie* 64, 1-35.

Davey P.J., Innes, J.J., 2002. Innovation, continuity and insular development in the Isle of Man. In: Waldren, W.H., Ensenyat, J.A. (Eds.), *World islands in prehistory. International insular investigations V Deia international conference in prehistory*. British

Archaeological Reports (International Series) 1095. Oxbow, Oxford, pp. 44-56.

David, S., 1984. Pointes de type nord-européen dans le Magdalénien final et l'Épipaléolithique de Franche-Comté. *Revue archéologique de l'est et du centre-est* 35, 144-149.

Davies, A., 2012. Palaeo-environments and human experience. *Archaeological Dialogues* 19, 51-54.

Davies, S.M., Abbott, P.M., Pearce, N.J.G., Wastegård, S., Blockley, S.P.E., 2012. Integrating the INTIMATE records using tephrochronology: rising to the challenge. *Quaternary Science Reviews* 36, 11-27.

Davies, S.M., Hoek, W.Z., Bohncke, S.J.P., Lowe, J.J., Pyne-O'Donnell, S., Turney, C.S.M., 2005. Detection of Lateglacial distal tephra layers in the Netherlands. *Boreas* 34, 123-135.

Davies, S.M., Larsen, G., Wastegård, S., Turney, C.S.M., Hall, V.A., Coyle, L., Thordarson, T., 2010. Widespread dispersal of Icelandic tephra: how does the Eyjafjöll eruption of 2010 compare to past Icelandic events? *Journal of Quaternary Science* 25, 605-611.

Davies, W., 2001. A Very Model of a Modern Human Industry: New Perspectives on the Origins and Spread of the Aurignacian in Europe. *Proceedings of the Prehistoric Society* 67, 195-217.

Dawdy, S.L., 2009. Millennial archaeology. Locating the discipline in the age of insecurity. *Archaeological Dialogues* 16, 131-142.

De Bélizal, É., Lavigne, F., Gaillard, J.C., Grancher, D., Pratomo, I., Komorowski, J.-C., 2012. The 2007 eruption of Kelut volcano (East Java, Indonesia): Phenomenology, crisis management and social response. *Geomorphology* 136, 165-175.

De Bie, M., 1999. Techniques de débitage du Paléolithique supérieur final au Mésolithique ancien en Flandres (Belgique): observations préliminaires = Knapping techniques from the Late Palaeolithic to the Early Mesolithic in Flanders (Belgium): preliminary observations. In: Bintz, P., Thévenin, A. (Eds.), *L'Europe des derniers chasseurs. Epipaléolithique et Mésolithique. UISPP – Commission XII, Grenoble*, Editions du CNRS, Paris, pp. 179-188.

De Bie, M., Caspar, J.-P., 2000. *Rekem. A Federmesser Camp on the Meuse River Bank*. Leuven University Press, Leuven.

De Bie, M., Vermeersch, P.M., 1998. Pleistocene-Holocene transition in the Benelux. *Quaternary International* 49/50, 29-43.

de Boer, J.Z., Sanders, D.T., 2002. *Volcanoes in Human History. The Far-Reaching Effects of Major Eruptions*. Princeton University Press, Princeton, NJ.

de Klerk, P., 2004. Confusing concepts in Lateglacial stratigraphy and geochronology: origin, consequences, conclusions (with special emphasis on the type locality Bøllingsø). *Review of Palaeobotany and Palynology* 129, 265-298.

de Klerk, P., 2006. Lateglacial and Early Holocene vegetation history near Hennigsdorf (C Brandenburg, NE Germany): a new interpretation of palynological data of Klaus Kloss. *Archiv für Naturschutz und Landschaftsforschung* 45, 37-52.

de Klerk, P., Helbig, H., Janke, W., 2008b. Vegetation and environment in and around the Reinberg basin (Vorpommern, NE Germany) during the Weichselian late Pleniglacial, Lateglacial, and Early Holocene. *Acta Palaeobotanica* 48, 301-324.

de Klerk, P., Janke, W., Kühn, P., Theuerkauf, M., 2008a. Environmental impact of the Laacher See eruption at a large distance from the volcano: Integrated palaeoecological studies from Vorpommern (NE Germany). *Palaeogeography, Palaeoclimatology, Palaeoecology* 270, 196-214.

De Molyn, J.C.M., 1954. The Bromme Culture. Notes on Denmarks most ancient culture. *Quartär* 6, 109-117.

de Sonneville-Bordes, D., 1959. Problèmes généraux du Paléolithique supérieur dans le sud-ouest de la France. *L'Anthropologie* 63, 1-36.

de Sonneville-Bordes, D., 1963. Upper Palaeolithic Cultures in Western Europe. *Science* 142, 347-355.

de Sonneville-Bordes, D., 1969. A propos des pointes pédonculées du Nord de l'Europe: pointe de Lingby et pointe de Teyjat. *Quartär* 20, 183-188.

de Sonneville-Bordes, D., 1988. Les pointes a afinites nordiques dans le Paleolithique final au sud de la Loire. In: Otte, M. (Ed.), *De la Loire à l'Oder. Les civilisations du Paléolithique final dans le nord-ouest européen*. British Archaeological Reports (International Series) 444. Oxbow, Oxford, pp. 621-643.

Dehn, J., McNutt, S.R., 2000. Volcanic materials in commerce and industry. In: Sigurdsson, H., Houghton, B.F., McNutt, S.R., Rymer, H., Stix, J. (Eds.), *Encyclopedia of Volcanoes*. Academic Press, San Diego, CA, pp. 1271-1282.

Deligne, N.I., Coles, S.G., Sparks, R.S.J., 2010. Recurrence rates of large explosive volcanic eruptions. *Journal of Geophysical Research* 115, B06203.

Derex, M., Beugin, M.-P., Godelle, B., Raymond, M., 2013. Experimental evidence for the influence of group size on cultural complexity. *Nature advance online publication*.

Desbrosse, R., 1980. Le Paléolithique du Jura méridional. *Bulletin de l'Association française pour l'étude du quaternaire* 17, 135-142.

Dev, S., Riede, F., 2012. Quantitative functional analysis of Late Glacial projectile points from northern Europe. *Lithics* 33, 40-55.

Dewez, M.C., 1975. Nouvelles recherches à la Grotte du Coléoptère à Bomal-sur-Ourthe (province du Luxembourg). Rapport provisoire de la première campagne de fouille. *Helinium* 15, 105-133.

Diamond, J.M., 1978. The Tasmanians: the longest isolation, the simplest technology. *Nature* 273, 185-186.

Diamond, J.M., 2010a. Intra-Island and Inter-Island Comparisons. In: Diamond, J.M., Robinson, J.A. (Eds.), *Natural Experiments of History*. Belknap Press, Cambridge, MA, pp. 120-141.

Diamond, J.M., 2010b. Two views of collapse. *Nature* 463, 880-881.

Diamond, J.M., Robinson, J.A. (Eds.), 2010. *Natural Experiments of History*. Belknap Press, Cambridge, MA.

Dietrich, J., 2012. Katastrophen im Altertum aus kulturanthropologischer und kulturphilosophischer Perspektive. In: Berlejung, A. (Ed.), *Disaster and Relief Management. Katastrophen und ihre Bewältigung*. Forschungen zum Alten Testament 81. Mohr Siebeck, Tübingen, pp. 85-116.

Dietz, C., Grahle, H.O., Müller, H., 1958. Ein spätglaziales Kalkmudde-Vorkommen im Seck-Bruch bei Hannover. *Geologisches Jahrbuch* 76, 67-102.

Dirksen, O., Danhara, T., Diekmann, B., 2009. Marker ash layers at Two-Yurts lake, Kamchatka: chronological significance and environmental impact. *Geophysical Research Abstracts* 11, 6495.

Dix, A., 2008. Historische Ansätze in der Hazard- und Risikoanalyse. In: Felgentreff, C., Glade, T. (Eds.), *Naturrisiken und Sozialkatastrophen*. Spektrum Akademischer Verlag, Berlin, pp. 201-211.

Dix, A., Röhrs, M., 2007. Vergangenheit versus Gegenwart? Anmerkungen zu Potentialen, Risiken und Nebenwirkungen einer Kombination historischer und aktueller Ansätze der Naturgefahrenforschung. *Historical Social Research* 32, 215-234.

Djindjian, F., 2011. The Role of the Archaeologist in Present-Day Society. *Diogenes* 58, 53-63.

Dobres, M.-A., Robb, J. (Eds.), 2000. *Agency in Archaeolgy*. Routledge, London.

Dodds, W.K., Whiles, M.R., 2010. *Freshwater Ecology*. Academic Press, London.

Donahue, R.E., Fischer, A., 2015. A Late Glacial family at Trollesgave, Denmark. *Journal of Archaeological Science* 54, 313-324.

Donovan, A., Oppenheimer, C., 2014. Extreme volcanism: disaster risk and societal implications. In: Ismail-Zadeh, A., Fucugauchi, J.U., Kijko, A., Takeuchi, K., Zaliapin, I. (Eds.), *Extreme natural hazards: Disaster risks and societal implications*. Cambridge University Press, Cambridge, pp. 29-46.

Donovan, A.R., Oppenheimer, C., 2011. The 2010 Eyjafjallajökull eruption and the reconstruction of geography. *The Geographical Journal* 177, 4-11.

Donovan, A.R., Oppenheimer, C., 2012. Governing the lithosphere: Insights from Eyjafjallajokull concerning the role of scientists in supporting decision-making on active volcanoes. *Journal of Geophysical Research: Solid Earth* 117, B03214.

Donovan, A.R., Oppenheimer, C., 2013. Managing the uncertain earth: geophysical hazards in the risk society. *The Geographical Journal* 180(1), 89-95.

Donovan, A.R., Oppenheimer, C., Bravo, M., 2011. Rationalising a volcanic crisis through literature: Montserratian verse and the descriptive reconstruction of an island. *Journal of Volcanology and Geothermal Research* 203, 87-101.

Donovan, K., 2010. Doing social volcanology: exploring volcanic culture in Indonesia. *Area* 42, 117-126.

Dornan, J.L., 2002. Agency and Archaeology: Past, Present, and Future Directions. *Journal of Archaeological Method and Theory* 9, 303-329.

Dorsten, I., Harries, D., 2007. Fund von Laacher-See-Bims im Herbstlabyrinth-Adventhöhlen-System (Hessen). *Jahrbuch des nassauischen Vereins für Naturkunde* 127, 131-136.

Dorsten, I., Hülsmann, T., Hüser, A., 2007. Das Herbstlabyrinth-Adventhöhle-System – Neue Forschungsergebnisse aus der größten hessischen Höhle. *Jahrbuch des nassauischen Vereins für Naturkunde* 127, 103-130.

Dove, M.R., 2008. Perception of volcanic eruption as agent of change on Merapi volcano, Central Java. *Journal of Volcanology and Geothermal Research* 172, 329-337.

Dove, M.R., 2010. The panoptic gaze in a non-western setting: Self-surveillance on Merapi volcano, Central Java. *Religion* 40, 121-127.

Driessen, J., MacDonald, C.F., 1997. *The Troubled Island: Minoan Crete before and after the Santorini eruption*. Université de Liège, Liège.

Drucker, D.G., Bridault, A., Iacumin, P., Bocherens, H., 2009. Bone stable isotopic signatures (^{15}N, ^{18}O) as tracers of temperature variation during the Lateglacial and early Holocene: case study on red deer *Cervus elaphus* from Rochedane (Jura, France). *Geological Journal* 44, 593-604.

Drucker, D.G., Kind, C.J., Stephan, E., 2011. Chronological and ecological information on Late-glacial and early Holocene reindeer from northwest Europe using radiocarbon (14C) and stable isotope (13C, 15N) analysis of bone collagen: Case study in southwestern Germany. *Quaternary International* 245, 218-224.

Druitt, T.H., Costa, F., Deloule, E., Dungan, M., Scaillet, B., 2012. Decadal to monthly timescales of magma transfer and reservoir growth at a caldera volcano. *Nature* 482, 77-80.

Dugmore, A., Newton, A., 2009. Tephrochronology. In: Gornitz, V. (Ed.), *Encyclopedia of Paleoclimatology and Ancient Environments*. Encyclopedia of Earth Sciences Series. Springer, Amsterdam, pp. 937-938.

Dugmore, A.J., Church, M.J., Mairs, K.-A., McGovern, T.H., Perdikaris, S., Vésteinsson, O., 2007. Abandoned Farms, Volcanic Impacts, and Woodland Management: Revisiting Þjórsárdalur, the "Pompeii Of Iceland". *Arctic Anthropology* 44, 1-11.

Dugmore, A.J., McGovern, T.H., Vésteinsson, O., Arneborg, J., Streeter, R., Keller, C., 2012. Cultural adaptation, compounding vulnerabilities and conjunctures in Norse Greenland. *Proceedings of the National Academy of Sciences* 109, 3658-3663.

Dumond, D.E., 2004. Volcanism and History on the Northern Alaska Peninsula. *Arctic Anthropology* 41, 112-125.

Dunnell, R.C., 1970. Seriation method and its evaluation. *American Antiquity* 35, 305-319.

Dunnell, R.C., Simek, J.F., 1995. Artifact Size and Plowzone Processes. *Journal of Field Archaeology* 22, 305-319.

Durand, M., Grattan, J., 2001. Effects of volcanic air pollution on health. *The Lancet* 357, 164.

Durant, A.J., Rose, W.I., Sarna-Wojcicki, A.M., Carey, S., Volentik, A.C.M., 2009. Hydrometeor-enhanced tephra sedimentation: Constraints from the 18 May 1980 eruption of Mount St. Helens. *Journal of Geophysical Research: Solid Earth* 114, B03204.

Dyer, C.L., 2002. Punctuated Entropy as Culture-Induced Change: The case of the *Exxon Valdez* Oil Spill. In: Hoffman, S.M., Oliver-Smith, A. (Eds.), *Catastrophe & culture: the anthropology of disaster*. School of American Research Press, Santa Fe, NM, pp. 159-185.

Dörries, M., 2010. Climate catastrophes and fear. Wiley Interdisciplinary Reviews: *Climate Change* 1, 885-890.

Edwards, J.S., 2005. Animals and volcanoes: survival and revival. In: Martí, J., Ernst, G.G.J. (Eds.), *Volcanoes and the Environment*. Cambridge University Press, Cambridge, pp. 250-272.

Eicher, U., 1987. Die spätglazialen sowie die frühpostglazialen Klimaverhaltnisse im Bereiche der Alpen: Sauerstoffisotopenkurven kalkhaltiger Sedimente. *Geographica Helvetica* 42, 99-104.

Ekholm, G., 1925. Die erste Besiedlung des Ostseegebietes. *Wiener Prähistorische Zeitschrift* 12, 1-16.

Ekholm, G., 1926. Lyngby-Kultur. In: Ebert, M. (Ed.), *Reallexikon der Vorgeschichte*. Band 7. Verlag Walter de Gruyter & Co., Berlin, pp. 324-326.

Eldredge, N., Gould, S.J., 1972. Punctuated Equilibria: an Alternative to Phyletic Gradualism. In: Schopf, T.M. (Ed.), *Models in Palaeobiology*. Freeman Cooper, San Francisco, CA, pp. 82-115.

Elphick, J. (Ed.), 2007. *The Atlas of Bird Migration*. The Natural History Museum, London.

Enters, D., Kirilova, E., Lotter, A., Lücke, A., Parplies, J., Jahns, S., Kuhn, G., Zolitschka, B., 2010. Climate change and human impact at Sacrower See (NE Germany) during the past 13,000 years: a geochemical record. *Journal of Paleolimnology* 43, 719-737.

Eriksen, B.V., 1996. Regional Variation in Late Pleistocene Subsistence Strategies. Southern Scandinavian Reindeer Hunters in a European Context. In: Larsson, L. (Ed.), *The Earliest Settlement of Scandinavia and its relationship with neighbouring areas*. Acta Archaeologica Lundensia Series IN 8°, 24. Almqvist & Wicksell, Stockholm, pp. 7-22.

Eriksen, B.V., 1999. Late Palaeolithic settlement in Denmark – how do we read the record? In: Kobusiewicz, M., Kozlowski, J.K. (Eds.), *Post-Pleniglacial Re-Colonisation of the Great European Lowland*. Polska Akademia Umiejetnosci, Kraków, pp. 157-174.

Eriksen, B.V., 2000. Patterns of Ethnogeographic Variability in Late Pleistocene Western Europe. In: Peterkin, G.L., Price, H.A. (Eds.), *Regional Approaches to Adaptation in Late Pleistocene Western Europe*. British Archaeological Reports (International Series) 896. Oxbow, Oxford, pp. 147-168.

Eriksen, B.V., 2002. Reconsidering the geochronological framework of Lateglacial hunter-gatherer colonization of southern Scandinavia. In: Eriksen, B.V., Bratlund, B. (Eds.), *Recent studies in the Final Palaeolithic of the European plain*. Jutland Archaeological Society, Højbjerg, pp. 25-42.

Eriksen, B.V. (Ed.), 2010. *Lithic technology in metal using societies*. Jutland Archaeological Society, Højbjerg.

Eriksen, P. (Ed.), 2012. *Erik Westerby: arkæolog og politifuldmægtig i Ringkøbing*. Ringkøbing-Skjern Museum, Skjern.

Erkens, G., Hoffmann, T., Gerlach, R., Klostermann, J., 2011. Complex fluvial response to Lateglacial and Holocene allogenic forcing in the Lower Rhine Valley (Germany). *Quaternary Science Reviews* 30, 611-627.

Fagnart, J.-P., Coudret, P., 1997. Les industries à Federmesser dans le bassin de la Somme: chronologie et identité des groupes culturels. *Bulletin de la Société Préhistorique Française* 94, 349-360.

Fagnart, J.-P., Munaut, A.V., Limondin-Lozouet, N., Antoine, P., 2000. Le Tardiglaciaire du bassin de la Somme: éléments de synthèse et nouvelles données. *Quaternaire* 11, 85-98.

Fahlke, J.M., 2009. *Der Austausch der terrestrischen Säugetierfauna an der Pleistozän/Holozän-Grenze in Mitteleuropa*. Unpublished Ph.D. thesis: Universität Bonn, Bonn.

Farrell, K.N., Thiel, A., 2013. Nudging Evolution? *Ecology and Society* 18.

Fejerskov, O., Manji, F., Baelum, V., Møller, I.J., 1988. *Dental fluorosis – a handbook for health workers*. Munksgaard, Copenhagen.

Felgentreff, C., Glade, T. (Eds.), 2008. *Naturrisiken und Sozialkatastrophen*. Spektrum Akademischer Verlag, Berlin.

Fenenga, F., 1953. The Weights of Chipped Stone Points: A Clue to Their Functions. Southwestern *Journal of Anthropology* 9, 309-323.

Feustel, R., Kerkmann, K., Schmid, E., Musil, R., Jacob, H., 1971. Der Bärenkeller bei Königsee-Garsitz, eine jungpaläolithische Kulthöhle. (I). *Alt-Thüringen* 11, 81-130.

Fiedel, S.J., Southon, J.R., Brown, T.A., Zielinski, G.A., Mayewski, P.A., Meeker, L.D., Whitlow, S., Twickler, M.S., Morrison, M., Meese, D.A., Gow, A.J., Alley, R.B., 1995. The GISP Ice Core Record of Volcanism Since 7000 B.C. *Science* 267, 256-258.

Fiedler, L., 1976. Ein endpaläolithischer Fundplatz bei Rothenkirchen, Kreis Fulda. *Archäologisches Korrespondenzblatt* 6, 267-269.

Fiedler, L., 1994. *Alt- und mittelsteinzeitliche Funde in Hessen*. Theiss, Stuttgart.

Field, C.B., Barros, V., Stocker, T.F., Qin, D., Dokken, D.J., Ebi, K.L., Mastrandrea, M.D., Mach, K.J., Plattner, G.-K., Allen, S.K., Tignor, M., Midgley, P.M. (Eds.), 2012. *Managing the Risks of Extreme Events and Disasters to Advance Climate Change Adaptation. Working Groups I and II of the Intergovernmental Panel on Climate Change, Special Report*. Cambridge University Press, Cambridge.

Finsinger, W., Belis, C., Blockley, S.P.E., Eicher, U., Leuenberger, M., Lotter, A.F., Ammann, B., 2008. Temporal patterns in lacustrine stable isotopes as evidence for climate change during the late glacial in the Southern European Alps. *Journal of Paleolimnology* 40, 885-895.

Firbas, F., 1949. *Spät- und nacheiszeitliche Waldgeschichte Mitteleuropas nördlich der Alpen. Erster Band: Allgemeine Waldgeschichte*. Verlag von Gustav Fischer, Jena.

Firbas, F., 1953. Das absolute Alter der jüngsten vulkanischen Eruptionen im Bereich des Laacher Sees. *Naturwissenschaften* 40, 54-55.

Fischer, A., 1978. På sporet af overgangen mellem palæolitikum og mesolitikum i Sydskandinavien. *Hikuin* 4, 27-50.

Fischer, A., 1985. Late Paleolithic Finds. In: Kristiansen, K. (Ed.), *Archaeological Formation Processes. The representativity of archaeological remains from Danish Prehistory*. The National Museum, Copenhagen, pp. 81-88.

Fischer, A., 1988. A Late Palaeolithic Flint Workshop at Egtved, East Jutland. *Journal of Danish Archaeology* 7, 7-23.

Fischer, A., 1989. Hunting with Flint-Tipped Arrows: Results and Experiences from Experiments. In: Bonsall, C. (Ed.), *The Mesolithic in Europe*. John Donald, Edinburgh, pp. 29-39.

Fischer, A., 1991. Pioneers in deglaciated landscapes: The expansion and adaptation of Late Palaeolithic societies in Southern Scandinavia. In: Barton, R.N.E., Roberts, A.J., Roe, D.A. (Eds.), *Late Glacial in north-west Europe: human adaptation and environmental change at the end of the Pleistocene*. CBA, Oxford, pp. 100-122.

Fischer, A., 1996. At the border of human habitat: the Late Palaeolithic and Early Mesolithic in Scandinavia. In: Larsson, L. (Ed.), *The Earliest Settlement of Scandinavia and Its Relationship with Neighbouring Areas*. Almquist & Wiksell, Stockholm, pp. 157-176.

Fischer, A., 2002. Arkæologen Erik Westerby: frontforsker på fritidsbasis. *Kuml* 2002, 35-64.

Fischer, A., 2012. En ø ved verdens ende. *VHM-nyt* 25, 6-9.

Fischer, A., 2013. The Fensmark settlement and the almost invisible Late Palaeolithic in Danish field archaeology. *Danish Journal of Archaeology* 1(2), 123-141.

Fischer, A., Clemmensen, L.B., Donahue, R.E., Heinemeier, J., Lykke-Andersen, H., Lysdahl, P., Mortensen, M.F., Olsen, J., Vang Petersen, P., 2013b. Late Palaeolithic Nørre Lyngby – a northern outpost close to the west coast of Europe. *Quartär* 60, 137-162.

Fischer, A., Hansen, P.V., Rasmussen, P., 1984. Macro and Micro Wear Traces on Lithic Projectile Points. Experimental Results and Prehistoric Examples. *Journal of Danish Archaeology* 3, 19-46.

Fischer, A., Mortensen, M.F., Henriksen, P.S., Mathiassen, D.R., Olsen, J., 2013a. Dating the Trollesgave site and the Bromme culture – chronological fix-points for the Lateglacial settlement of Southern Scandinavia. *Journal of Archaeological Science* 40, 4663-4674.

Fischer, A., Nielsen, F.O.S., 1986. Senistidens bopladser ved Bromme. En genbearbejdning af Westerby's og Mathiassen's fund. *Aarbøger for nordisk Oldkyndighed og Historie* 1986, 5-42.

Fisher, R.V., Schmincke, H.-U., 1984. *Pyroclastic Rocks.* Springer-Verlag, Berlin.

Fisher, R.V., Schmincke, H.-U., van den Bogaard, P., 1983. Origin and emplacement of a pyroclastic flow and surge unit at Laacher See, Germany. *Journal of Volcanology and Geothermal Research* 17, 375-392.

Fitzhugh, B., 2012. Hazards, Impacts, and Resilience among Hunter-Gatherers of the Kuril Islands. In: Cooper, J., Sheets, P.D. (Eds.), *Surviving Sudden Environmental Change.* University of Colorado Press, Boulder, CO, pp. 19-42.

Flohr, S., von Berg, A., Protsch von Zieten, R., 2004. Die verschollenen "pleistozänen" Menschenfunde von Weißenthurm, Kreis Mayen-Koblenz: Neue und alte Informationen. *Anthropologischer Anzeiger* 62, 1-10.

Floss, H., 1987. Silex-Rohstoffe als Belege für Fernverbindungen im Paläolithikum des nordwestlichen Mitteleuropa. *Archäologische Informationen* 10, 151-161.

Floss, H., 1994. Rohmaterialversorgung im Paläolithikum des Mittelrheingebietes. Rudolf Hablet GmbH, Bonn.

Floss, H., 2000. Le couloir Rhin-Saône-Rhône: axe de communication au Tardiglaciaire? In: Richard, A., Cupillard, C., Richard, H., Thevenin, A. (Eds.), *Les derniers chasseurs-cueilleurs d l'Europe occidentale: Actes du colloque international de Besançon 1998.* Presses Universitaires Franc-Comtoises, Besançon, pp. 313-321.

Floss, H., 2002. Climate and raw material behavior: A case study from late Pleistocene Hunter-gatherers in the Middle Rhine Area of Germany. In: Fisher, L.E., Eriksen, B.V. (Eds.), *Lithic raw material economies in late glacial and early postglacial Europe.* British Archaeological Reports (International Series) 1093. Oxbow, Oxford, pp. 79-88.

Flueck, W.T., Smith-Flueck, J.A.M., 2013. Severe dental fluorosis in juvenile deer linked to a recent volcanic eruption in Patagonia. *Journal of Wildlife Diseases* 49, 355-366.

Flaathen, T.K., Gislason, S.R., 2007. The effect of volcanic eruptions on the chemistry of surface waters: The 1991 and 2000 eruptions of Mt. Hekla, Iceland. *Journal of Volcanology and Geothermal Research* 164, 293-316.

Foley, R.A., 1981. Off-site archaeology: an alternative approach for the short-sited. In: Hodder, I., Isaac, G., Hammond, N. (Eds.), *Pattern of the past. Studies in honour of David Clarke.* Cambridge University Press, Cambridge, pp. 157-183.

Forster, P., 2004. Ice Ages and the mitochondrial DNA chronology of human dispersals: a review. *Philosophical Transactions of the Royal Society B: Biological Sciences* 359, 255-264.

Fort, J., Pujol, T., Cavalli-Sforza, L.L., 2004. Palaeolithic Populations and Waves of Advance. *Cambridge Archaeological Journal* 14, 53-61.

Francis, P., Oppenheimer, C., 2004. *Volcanoes.* Oxford University Press, Oxford.

Frechen, J., 1952. Die Herkunft der spätglazialen Bimsstuffe in mittel- und süddeutschen Mooren. *Geologisches Jahrbuch* 67, 209-230.

Frechen, J., 1953. *Der Rheinische Bimsstein.* Georg Fischer Verlag, Wittlich.

Frechen, M., 1995. Eruptionsgeschichte und Deckschichtenfolge der Wannenkopf-Vulkangruppe in der Osteifel. *Eiszeitalter & Gegenwart* 45, 109-129.

Freundt, A., Schmincke, H.-U., 1985. Lithic-enriched segregation bodies in pyroclastic flow deposits of Laacher See Volcano (East Eifel, Germany). *Journal of Volcanology and Geothermal Research* 25, 193-224.

Friedrich, M., Knipping, M., van der Kroft, P., Renno, A., Schmitt, S., Ullrich, O., Vollbrecht, J., 2001. Ein Wald vom Ende der Eiszeit – Aspekte zu Kultur- und Landschaftsentwicklung sowie zur Paläoökologie an einem verlandeten See im Tagebau Reichwalde (Niederschlesischer Oberlausitzkreis). *Arbeits- und Forschungsberichte der Sächsischen Bodendenkmalspflege* 43, 21-94.

Friedrich, M., Kromer, B., Spurk, H., Hofmann, J., Kaiser, K.F., 1999. Paleo-environment and radiocarbon calibration as derived from Lateglacial/Early Holocene tree-ring chronologies. *Quaternary International* 61, 27-39.

Friedrich, W.L., 2009. *Santorini: volcano, natural history, mythology.* Aarhus University Press, Aarhus.

Fries, J.E., 2005. Jagen und Sammeln in den Dünen. Alt- und mittelsteinzeitliche Fundplätze im Tagebau Cottbus-Nord. *Arbeitsberichte zur Bodendenkmalpflege in Brandenburg* 14, 157-166.

Friis-Hansen, J., 1990. Mesolithic cutting arrows: functional analysis of arrows used in the hunting of large game. *Antiquity* 64, 494-504.

Frogner Kockum, P.C., Herbert, R.B., Gislason, S.R., 2006. A diverse ecosystem response to volcanic aerosols. *Chemical Geology* 231, 57-66.

Fruth, H.-J., 1979. Ein spätpaläolithischer Fundplatz bei Mühlheim-Dietesheim, Kreis Offenbach. Archäologisches Korrespondenzblatt 9, 261-266.

Fruth, H.-J., 1994. Der spätpaläolithische Fundplatz Mühlheim-Dietesheim, Kreis Offenbach. *Fundberichte aus Hessen* 22/23, 1-67.

Fuchs, S., Birkmann, J., Glade, T., 2012. Vulnerability assessment in natural hazard and risk analysis: current approaches and future challenges. *Natural Hazards* 64, 1969-1975.

Fugl Petersen, B., 1973. Senpalæolitiske flækkespidser fra Knudshoved Odde, Sydsjælland. *Aarbøger for nordisk Oldkyndighed og Historie* 1973, 211-216.

Fugl Petersen, B., 1994. Rundebakke. En senpalæolitisk boplads på Knudshoved Odde, Sydsjælland. *Aarbøger for nordisk Oldkyndighed og Historie* 1992, 7-40.

Fugl Petersen, B., 2001. Senpalæolitiske opsamlingsfund fra Sydsjælland, Fejø og Nordsjælland – et bidrag til udforskningen af de senglaciale kulturer i Danmark. *Kulturhistoriske Studier* 2001, 7-64.

Fuglestvedt, I., 2012. The Pioneer Condition on the Scandinavian Peninsula: the Last Frontier of a 'Palaeolithic Way' in Europe. *Norwegian Archaeological Review* 45, 1-29.

Gal, F., Michel, B., Gilles, B., Frédéric, J., Karine, M., 2011. CO2 escapes in the Laacher See region, East Eifel, Germany: Application of natural analogue onshore and offshore geochemical monitoring. *International Journal of Greenhouse Gas Control* 5, 1099-1118.

Galinier, J., Becquelin, A.M., Bordin, G., Fontaine, L., Fourmaux, F., Ponce, J.R., Salzarulo, P., Simonnot, P., Therrien, M., Zilli, I., 2010. Anthropology of the Night: Cross-Disciplinary Investigations. *Current Anthropology* 51, 819-847.

Galiński, T., 2007. Rotnowo. *Stanowisko paleolityczne i mezolityczne w Dolnie Lubieszowej na Pomorzu Zachodnim*. Instytut Archeologii i Etnologii PAN, Warszawa.

Gamble, C.S., Davies, W., Pettitt, P., Richards, M., 2005. The Archaeological and Genetic Foundations of the European Population during the Late Glacial: Implications for 'Agricultural Thinking'. *Cambridge Archaeological Journal* 15, 193-223.

Gamble, C.S., Porr, M. (Eds.), 2005. *The hominid individual in context: archaeological investigations of lower and middle Palaeolithic landscapes, locales, and artefacts*. Routledge, London.

García-Acosta, V., 2002. Historical disaster research. In: Hoffman, S.M., Oliver-Smith, A. (Eds.), *Catastrophe & culture: the anthropology of disaster. School of American Research advanced seminar series*. School of American Research Press, Santa Fe, NM., pp. 49-66.

Garrod, D., 1955. Palaeolithic spear-throwers. *Proceedings of the Prehistoric Society* 21, 21-35.

Garrott, R.A., Eberhardt, L.L., Otton, J.K., White, P.J., Chaffee, M.A., 2002. A Geochemical Trophic Cascade in Yellowstone's Geothermal Environments. *Ecosystems* 5, 659-666.

Geist, V., 1999. *Deer of the World. Their Evolution, Behaviour, and Ecology*. Swan Hill Press, Shrewsbury.

Gelhausen, F., Kegler, J.F., Wenzel, S., 2004. Hütten oder Himmel? Latente Behausungsstrukturen im Spätpaläolithikum Mitteleuropas. *Jahrbuch des Römisch-Germanischen Zentralmuseum Mainz* 51, 1-22.

Georgsson, G., Petursson, G., 1972. Fluorosis of Sheep Caused by the Hekla Eruption in 1970. *Fluoride* 2, 58-66.

Gerken, K., 2001a. *Studien zur jung- und spätpaläolithischen sowie mesolithischen Besiedlung im Gebiet zwischen Wümme und Oste*. Isensee Verlag, Oldenburg.

Gerken, K., 2001b. Das Jung- und Spätpaläolithikum sowie Mesolithikum im Landkreis Rotenburg (Wümme). Aktueller Forschungsstand. *Die Kunde N.F.* 52, 255-274.

Gerken, K., 2001c. Westertimke 69 – eine Jagdstation der Federmesser-Gruppen. In: Gehlen, B., Heinen, M., Tillmann, A. (Eds.), *Zeit-Räume. Gedenkschrift für Wolfgang Taute*. Archäologische Berichte 14. Verlag Rudolf Habelt GmbH, Bonn, pp. 363-380.

Gerrard, C.M., Petley, D.N., 2013. A risk society? Environmental hazards, risk and resilience in the later Middle Ages in Europe. *Natural Hazards* 69, 1051-1079.

Giddens, A., 1984. *The Constitution of Society: Outline of a Theory of Structuration*. University of California Press, Berkeley, CA.

Ginibre, C., Davidson, J.P., Wörner, G., 2004a. Sr isotope zoning in feldspars at Laacher See Volcano, Germany. *Geochimica Et Cosmochimica Acta* 68, A654-A654.

Ginibre, C., Wörner, G., Kronz, A., 2004b. Structure and dynamics of the Laacher See magma chamber (Eifel, Germany) from major and trace element zoning in sanidine: A cathodoluminescence and electron microprobe study. *Journal of Petrology* 45, 2197-2223.

Ginter, B., 1974. *Spätpaläolithikum in Oberschlesien und im Flussgebiet der oberen Warta*. Nakladem Uniwersytetu Jagiellonskiego, Kraków.

Gislason, S.R., Hassenkam, T., Nedel, S., Bovet, N., Eiriksdottir, E.S., Alfredsson, H.A., Hem, C.P.,

Balogh, Z.I., Dideriksen, K., Oskarsson, N., Sigfusson, B., Larsen, G., Stipp, S.L.S., 2011. Characterization of Eyjafjallajökull volcanic ash particles and a protocol for rapid risk assessment. *Proceedings of the National Academy of Sciences* 108, 7307-7312.

Glørstad, H., 2013. Where are the Missing Boats? The Pioneer Settlement of Norway as Long-Term History. *Norwegian Archaeological Review* 46, 57-80.

Goepel, A., Lonschinski, M., Viereck, L., Büchel, G., Kukowski, N., 2014. Volcano-tectonic structures and CO2-degassing patterns in the Laacher See basin, Germany. *International Journal of Earth Sciences*, 1-13.

Goldhahn, J., 2002. Roaring Rocks: An Audio-Visual Perspective on Hunter-Gatherer Engravings in Northern Sweden and Scandinavia. *Norwegian Archaeological Review* 35, 29-61.

Gómez-Romero, M., Lindig-Cisneros, R., Galindo-Vallejo, S., 2006. Effect of tephra depth on vegetation development in areas affected by volcanism. *Plant Ecology* 183, 207-213.

Good, D.H., Reuveny, R., 2006. The fate of Easter Island: The limits of resource management institutions. *Ecological Economics* 58, 473-490.

Gosden, C., Lock, G., 1998. Prehistoric Histories. *World Archaeology* 30, 2-12.

Gould, D.H., 1998. Polioencephalomalacia. *Journal of Animal Science* 76, 309-314.

Gould, S.J., Eldredge, N., 1993. Punctuated equilibrium comes of age. *Nature* 366, 223.

Gould, S.J., Lewontin, R.C., 1979. The spandrels of San Marco and the Panglossian paradigm: a critique of the adaptationist programme. *Proceedings of the Royal Society B: Biological Sciences* 205, 581-598.

Graf, H.-F., Timmreck, C., 2001. A general climate model simulation of the aerosol radiative effects of the Laacher See eruption (10,900 B.C.). *Journal of Geophysical Research* 106, 14747-14756.

Gramsch, B., 1969. Ein Lagerplatz der Federmesser-Gruppe bei Golßen, Kr. Luckau. *Ausgrabungen & Funde* 14, 121-128.

Gramsch, B., 1987. The Late Palaeolithic in the Area Lying Between the River Oder and the Elbe/Havel. In: Burdukiewicz, J.M., Kobusiewicz, M. (Eds.), *Late Glacial in Central Europe. Culture and Environment*. Prace Komisji Archeologicznej, Wrocław, pp. 107-120.

Gramsch, B., Beran, J., Hanik, S., Sommer, R.S., 2013. A Palaeolithic fishhook made of ivory and the earliest fishhook tradition in Europe. *Journal of Archaeological Science* 40, 2458-2463.

Grattan, J.P., 2006. Aspects of Armageddon: An exploration of the role of volcanic eruptions in human history and civilization. *Quaternary International* 151, 10-18.

Grattan, J.P., 2010. Testing eventful archaeologies: Eventful archaeology and volcanic "disasters". In: Bolender, D.J. (Ed.), *Eventful archaeologies: New approaches to social transformation in the archaeological record*. State University of New York, Albany, NY, pp. 179-188.

Grattan, J.P., Brayshaw, M., Schüttenhelm, R.T.E., 2002. 'The end is nigh'? Social and environmental responses to volcanic gas pollution In: Torrence, R., Grattan, J.P. (Eds.), *Natural Disasters and Cultural Change*. Routledge, London, pp. 87-106.

Grattan, J.P., Charman, D.J., 1994. Non-climatic factors and the environmental impact of volcanic volatiles: implications of the Laki fissure eruption of AD 1783. *The Holocene* 4, 101-106.

Grattan, J.P., Durand, M., Taylor, S., 2003. Illness and Elevated Human Mortality in Europe Coincident with the Laki Fissure Eruption. In: Oppenheimer, C., Pyle, D.M., Barclay, J. (Eds.), *Volcanic Degassing*. Geological Society, London, pp. 410-414.

Grattan, J.P., Michnowicz, S., Rabartin, R., 2007. The Long Shadow: Understanding the Influence of the Laki Fissure Eruption on Human Mortality in Europe. In: Grattan, J.P., Torrence, R. (Eds.), *Living Under The Shadow. Cultural Impacts of Volcanic Eruptions*. Left Coast Press, Walnut Creek, CA., pp. 153-174.

Grattan, J.P., Torrence, R., 2007. Beyond Gloom and Doom: The Long-Term Consequences of Volcanic Disasters. In: Grattan, J.P., Torrence, R. (Eds.), *Living Under The Shadow. Cultural Impacts of Volcanic Eruptions*. Left Coast Press, Walnut Creek, CA., pp. 1-18.

Gravina, B., 2004. Agency, Technology and the 'Muddle in the Middle': The Case of the Middle Palaeolithic. In: Gardner, A. (Ed.), *Agency Uncovered: Archaeological perspectives on social agency, power, and being human*. UCL Press, London, pp. 65-77.

Grimm, S.B., 2004. Ein spätallerödzeitlicher Fundplatz bei Bad Breisig, Kreis Ahrweiler. *Berichte zur Archäologie an Mittelrhein und Mosel* 9, 11-32.

Grimm, S.B., Weber, M.-J., 2008. The chronological framework of the Hamburgian in the light of old and new ^{14}C dates. *Quartär* 55, 17-40.

Gronenborn, D., 2012. Yes and No. How applicable is a focus on palaeo-weather? *Archaeological Dialogues* 19, 54-56.

Grote, K., 1988. Die Buntsandsteinabris im südniedersächsischen Bergland bei Göttingen. Erfassung und Untersuchung ihrer ur- und frühgeschichtlichen Nutzung (1983 – 1987). *Die Kunde N.F.* 39, 1-43.

Grote, K., 1990. Das Buntsandsteinabri Bettenroder Berg IX im Reinhäuser Wald bei Göttingen – Paläolithikum und Mesolithikum. *Archäologisches Korrespondenzblatt* 20, 137-147.

Grote, K. (Ed.), 1994. *Die Abris im südlichen Leinebergland bei Göttingen. Archäologische Befunde zum Leben unter Felsschutzdächern in urgeschichtlicher Zeit*. Isensee Verlag, Oldenburg.

Grote, K., 1999a. Archäologische Landesaufnahme im Gebiet des Seeburger Sees, Luttersees und ehemaligen Westersees im Untereichsfeld, Ldkr. Göttingen. *Neue Ausgrabungen und Forschungen in Niedersachsen* 21, 13-136.

Grote, K., 1999b. Vom Leben unter Felsschutzdächern. Jäger und Sammler in Südniedersachsen am Ende der letzten Eiszeit. In: Boetzkes, M., Schweitzer, I., Vespermann, J. (Eds.), *EisZeit. Das große Abenteuer der Naturbeherrschung. Begleitbuch zur gleichnamigen Ausstellung*. Jan Thorbecke Verlag, Hildesheim.

Grote, K., Freese, H.-D., 1982. Die Felsschutzdächer (Abris) im südniedersächsischen Bergland – Ihre archäologischen Funde und Befunde. *Nachrichten aus Niedersachsens Urgeschichte* 51, 17-70.

Grove, M., 2009. Hunter-gatherer movement patterns: Causes and constraints. *Journal of Anthropological Archaeology* 28, 222-233.

Grünbaum, B., 1975. Venn Diagrams and Independent Families of Sets. *Mathematics Magazine* 48, 12-23.

Grünbaum, B., 1992a. Venn Diagrams I. *Geombinatorics* 1, 5-12.

Grünbaum, B., 1992b. Venn Diagrams II. *Geombinatorics* 2, 25-32.

Grünberg, J.M., 2006. New AMS Dates for Palaeolithic and Mesolithic Camp Sites and Single Finds in Saxony-Anhalt and Thuringia (Germany). *Proceedings of the Prehistoric Society* 72, 95-112.

Gräslund, B., 2010. Grahame Clark and Scandinavia. In: Marciniak, A., Coles, J. (Eds.), *Grahame Clark and his Legacy*. Cambridge Scholars Publishing, Newcastle, pp. 97-113.

Gräslund, B., Price, N., 2012. Twilight of the gods? The 'dust veil event' of AD 536 in critical perspective. *Antiquity* 86, 428-443.

Guiver, J., Jain, J., 2011. Grounded: Impacts of and Insights from the Volcanic Ash Cloud Disruption. *Mobilities* 6, 41 – 55.

Guttmann-Bond, E., 2010. Sustainability out of the past: how archaeology can save the planet. *World Archaeology* 42, 355-366.

Günther, K. (Ed.), 1988. *Alt- und mittelsteinzeitliche Fundplätze in Westfalen*. Westfälisches Museum für Archäologie, Münster.

Günther, K., 1973. Der Federmesser-Fundplatz von Westerkappeln, Kr. Tecklenburg. *Bodenaltertümer Westfalens* 13, 5-67

Haflidason, H., Eiriksson, J., Kreveld, S.V., 2000. The tephrochronology of Iceland and the North Atlantic region during the Middle and Late Quaternary: a review. *Journal of Quaternary Science* 15, 3-22.

Hajdas, I., Zolitschka, B., Ivyochs, S.D., Beer, J., Bonani, G., Leroy, S.A.G., Negendank, J.W., Ramrath, M., Suter, M., 1995. AMS Radiocarbon Dating of Annually Laminated Sediments from Lake Holzmaar, Germany. *Quaternary Science Reviews* 14, 137-143.

Hall, V.A., Pilcher, J.R., 2002. Late-Quaternary Icelandic tephras in Ireland and Great Britain: detection, characterization and usefulness. *Holocene* 12, 223-230.

Hallam, J.S., Edwards, B.J.N., Barnes, B., Stuart, A.J., 1973. The Remains of a Late Glacial Elk Associated with Barbed Points from High Furlong, near Blackpool, Lancashire. *Proceedings of the Prehistoric Society* 39, 100-128.

Hamilton, J., 2012. *Volcano: Nature and Culture*. Reaktion Books. Limited, London, pp. 208.

Hamilton, S., Whitehouse, R., Brown, K., Combes, P., Herring, E., Thomas, M.S., 2006. Phenomenology in Practice: Towards a p Methodology for a 'Subjective' Approach. *European Journal of Archaeology* 9, 31-71.

Hansell, A., Oppenheimer, C., 2004. Health Hazards from Volcanic Gases: A Systematic Literature Review. *Archives of Environmental Health* 59, 628-639.

Hardaker, T., Dunn, S., 2005. The Flip Test – a New Statistical Measure for Quantifying Symmetry in Stone Tools. *Antiquity* 79, project gallery.

Hardesty, D.L., 1972. The Human Ecological Niche. *American Anthropologist* 74, 458-466.

Hardesty, D.L., 1975. The niche concept: Suggestions for its use in human ecology. *Human Ecology* 3, 71-85.

Harms, E., Gardner, J.E., Schmincke, H.-U., 2004. Phase equilibria of the Lower Laacher See Tephra (East Eifel, Germany): constraints on pre-eruptive storage conditions of a phonolitic magma reservoir. *Journal of Volcanology and Geothermal Research* 134, 125-138.

Harms, E., Schmincke, H.-U., 2000. Volatile composition of the phonolitic Laacher See magma (12,900 yr BP): implications for syn-eruptive degassing of S, F, Cl and H_2O. *Contributions to Mineralogy and Petrology* 138, 84-98.

Hartz, S., 1987. Neue spätpaläolithische Fundplätze bei Ahrenshöft, Kreis Nordfriesland. *Offa* 44, 5-52.

Hastrup, K. (Ed.), 2009. *The Question of Resilience. Social Responses to Climate Change*. Historisk-filosofiske Meddelelser 66. Det Kongelige Danske Videnskabernes Selskab, Viborg.

Hazelwood, L., Steele, J., 2003. Colonizing new landscapes: archaeological detectability of the first phase. In: Rockman, M., Steele, J. (Eds.), *Colonization of Unfamiliar Landscapes: The archaeology of adaptation*. Routledge, London, pp. 203-221.

Heinemeier, J., Rud, N., 2001. AMS ^{14}C dateringer, Århus 1999. *Arkæologiske udgravninger i Danmark* 2000, 296-313.

Heinemeier, J., Rud, N., 2001. AMS ^{14}C dateringer, Århus 1999. Arkæologiske udgravninger i Danmark 2000**,** 296-313.

Heinen, M., Jöris, O., Riedmeier-Fischer, E., Thissen, J.P., 1996. Ein Federmesserfundplatz im Tal der Niers bei Goch, Kr. Kleve. Rekonstruktion eines kurzzeitigen Jagdaufenthaltes. *Archäologisches Korrespondenzblatt* 26, 111-120.

Helbing, D., 2013. Globally networked risks and how to respond. *Nature* 497, 51-59.

Helbing, D., Ammoser, H., Kühnert, C., 2006. Disasters as Extreme Events and the Importance of Network Interactions for Disaster Response Management. In: Albeverio, S., Jentsch, V., Kantz, H. (Eds.), *Extreme Events in Nature and Society*. The Frontiers Collection. Springer, Berlin, pp. 319-348.

Helbling, J., 2006. Coping with 'Natural' Disasters in Pre-industrial Societies: Some Comments. *The Medieval History Journal* 10, 429-446.

Henrich, J., 2004. Demography and Cultural Evolution: How Adaptive Cultural Processes Can Produce Maladaptive Losses – the Tasmanian Case. *American Antiquity* 69, 197-214.

Henry, J., 2013. Return or relocate? An inductive analysis of decision-making in a disaster. *Disasters* 37, 293-316.

Hewitt, G.M., 1999. Post-glacial re-colonization of European biota. *Biological Journal of the Linnean Society* 68, 87-112.

Hewitt, K. (Ed.), 1983. *Interpretations of Calamity*. Allen & Unwin Inc., Boston, MA.

Hewitt, K., 1995. Studying Disaster: A Review of the Main Conceptual Tools. *International Journal of Mass Emergencies and Disasters* 13, 231-240.

Hickman, C.N., 1937. The Dynamics of a Bow and Arrow. *Journal of Applied Physics* 8, 404-409.

Higgs, E. (Ed.), 1972. *Papers in Economic Prehistory*. Cambridge University Press, Cambridge.

Hijma, M.P., Cohen, K.M., Roebroeks, W., Westerhoff, W.E., Busschers, F.S., 2012. Pleistocene Rhine–Thames landscapes: geological background for hominin occupation of the southern North Sea region. *Journal of Quaternary Science* 27, 17-39.

Hirsch, K., Madsen, E.M., 2012. Istidsjægere i Sønderjylland. In: Heidemann Lutz, L., Sørensen, A.B. (Eds.), *Med graveske gennem Sønderjylland. Arkæologi på naturgas- of motovejstracé*. Årbog for Museum Sønderjylland 2012. Museum Sønderjylland, Haderslev, pp. 24-32.

Hodder, I., 1990. Style as Historical Quality. In: Conkey, M., Hastorf, C. (Eds.), *The Uses of Style in Archaeology*. Cambridge University Press, Cambridge, pp. 44-51.

Hodder, I. (Ed.), 2001. *Archaeological Theory Today*. Polity, Cambridge.

Hofbauer, H., 1985. *Grabungsbericht: Ein spätpaläolithischer Fundplatz bei Rothenkirchen, Kr. Fulda*. Hessisches Landesmuseum, Kassel.

Hofbauer, H., 1991. Felsschutzdächer im Umland des Amöneburger Beckens und in der nördlichen Wetterau. *Berichte der Kommission für archäologische Landesforschung in Hessen* 1, 14-17.

Hofbauer, H., 1992. Ein spätpaläolithischer Fundplatz bei Rothenkirchen, Kreis Fulda (Hessen). *Archäologisches Korrespondenzblatt* 22, 329-340.

Hofbauer, H., 1995. Abri-Kataster von Hessen: Ein Vorbericht. *Berichte der Kommission für archäologische Landesforschung in Hessen* 3, 99-105.

Hoffecker, J.F., 2005a. *A Prehistory of the North: Human Settlement of the Higher Latitudes*. Rutgers University Press, New Brunswick, NJ.

Hoffecker, J.F., 2005b. Innovation and technological knowledge in the Upper Paleolithic of Northern Eurasia. *Evolutionary Anthropology* 14, 186-198.

Hoffman, S.M., Oliver-Smith, A. (Eds.), 1999. *The Angry Earth. Disaster in Anthropological Perspective*. Routledge, London.

Hoffman, S.M., Oliver-Smith, A. (Eds.), 2002. *Catastrophe & culture: the anthropology of disaster. School of American Research advanced seminar series*. School of American Research Press, Santa Fe, NM.

Hofmann, F., 1963. Spätglaziale Bimsstaublagen des Laachersee-Vulkanismus in schweizerischen Mooren. *Eclogae geologicae Helveticae* 56, 147-164.

Holling, C.S., 1973. Resilience and Stability of Ecological Systems. *Annual Review of Ecology and Systematics* 4, 1-23.

Holm, J., 1972. Istidsjægere på Ærø. *Fynske Minder* 1972, 5-16.

Holm, J., 1991. Settlements of the Hamburgian and Federmesser Cultures at Slotseng, South Jutland. *Journal of Danish Archaeology* 10, 7-19.

Holm, J., 1992. *Senpalæolitisk materiale fra Jelssøerne i Jørn Fynbos oldsagssamling*. http://www.doggerland.dk.

Holm, J., 1996. The Earliest Settlement of Denmark. In: Larsson, L. (Ed.), *The Earliest Settlement of Scandinavia and its relationship with neighbouring areas*. Acta Archaeologica Lundensia Series IN 8°, 24. Almqvist & Wicksell, Stockholm, pp. 43-59.

Holm, J., Rieck, F., 1983. Jels 1 – the First Danish Site of the Hamburgian Culture. A Preliminary Report. *Journal of Danish Archaeology* 2, 7-11.

Holm, J., Rieck, F., 1987. Die Hamburger Kultur in Dänemark. *Archäologisches Korrespondenzblatt* 17, 151-168.

Holm, J., Rieck, F. (Eds.), 1992. *Istidsjægere ved Jelssøerne*. Skrifter fra Museumsrådet for Sønderjyllands Amt. Museumsrådet for Sønderjyllands Amt, Haderslev.

Holmberg, K., 2013. The Sound of Sulfur and Smell of Lightning: Sensing the Volcano. In: Day, J. (Ed.), *Making Senses of the Past: Toward a Sensory Archaeology*. Occasional Paper 40. Center for Archaeological Investigations, Carbondale, IL., pp. 49-68.

Hooper, P.R., 2000. Flood basalt provinces. In: Sigurdsson, H., Houghton, B.F., McNutt, S.R., Rymer, H., Stix, J. (Eds.), *Encyclopedia of Volcanoes*. Academic Press, San Diego, CA, pp. 345-360.

Horn, E., 2012. Das Wetter von Übermorgen. Kleine Imaginationsgeschichte der Klimakatastrophe. *Merkur* 12, 1091-1105.

Horn, E., 2014. *Zukunft als Katastrophe*. S. Fischer, Frankfurt a.M.

Horwell, C.J., 2007. Grain-size analysis of volcanic ash for the rapid assessment of respiratory health hazard. *Journal of Environmental Monitoring* 9, 1107-1115.

Horwell, C.J., Baxter, P.J., 2006. The respiratory health hazards of volcanic ash: a review for volcanic risk mitigation. *Bulletin of Volcanology* 69, 1-24.

Horwell, C.J., Fenoglio, I., Fubini, B., 2007. Iron-induced hydroxyl radical generation from basaltic volcanic ash. *Earth and Planetary Science Letters* 261, 662-669.

Horwell, C.J., Fenoglio, I., Ragnarsdottir, K.V., Sparks, R.S.J., Fubini, B., 2003b. Surface reactivity of volcanic ash from the eruption of Soufrière Hills volcano, Montserrat, West Indies with implications for health hazards. *Environmental Research* 93, 202-215.

Horwell, C.J., Sparks, R.S.J., Brewer, T.S., Llewellin, E.W., Williamson, B.J., 2003a. Characterization of respirable volcanic ash from the Soufrière Hills volcano, Montserrat, with implications for human health hazards. *Bulletin of Volcanology* 65, 346-362.

Hotes, S., Poschlod, P., Takahashi, H., 2006. Effects of volcanic activity on mire development: case studies from Hokkaido, northern Japan. *Holocene* 16, 561-573.

Hotes, S., Poschlod, P., Takahashi, H., Grootjans, A.P., Adema, E., 2004. Effects of tephra deposition on mire vegetation: a field experiment in Hokkaido, Japan. *Journal of Ecology* 92, 624-634.

Houben, P., 2003. Spatio-temporally variable response of fluvial systems to Late Pleistocene climate change: a case study from central Germany. *Quaternary Science Reviews* 22, 2125-2140.

Houghton, B.F., Swanson, D.A., Rausch, J., Carey, R.J., Fagents, S.A., Orr, T.R., 2013. Pushing the Volcanic Explosivity Index to its limit and beyond: Constraints from exceptionally weak explosive eruptions at Kīlauea in 2008. *Geology* 41(6), 627-631.

Housley, R.A., Gamble, C.S., Street, M., Pettitt, P.B., 1997. Radiocarbon evidence for the Late Glacial human recolonization of northern Europe. *Proceedings of the Prehistoric Society* 63, 25-54.

Housley, R.A., Lane, C.S., Cullen, V.L., Weber, M.J., Riede, F., Gamble, C.S., Brock, F., 2012. Icelandic volcanic ash from the Late-glacial open-air archaeological site of Ahrenshöft LA 58 D, North Germany. *Journal of Archaeological Science* 39, 708-716.

Housley, R.A., MacLeod, A., Armitage, S.J., Kabaciński, J., Gamble, C.S., 2014. The potential of cryptotephra and OSL dating for refining the chronology of open-air archaeological windblown sand sites: A case study from Mirkowice 33, northwest Poland. *Quaternary Geochronology* 20, 99-108.

Housley, R.A., MacLeod, A., Nalepka, D., Jurochnik, A., Masojć, M., Davies, L., Lincoln, P.C., Bronk Ramsey, C., Gamble, C.S., Lowe, J.J., 2013. Tephrostratigraphy of a Lateglacial lake sediment sequence at Węgliny, southwest Poland. *Quaternary Science Reviews* 77, 4-18.

Houtsma, P., Kramer, E., Newell, R.R., Smit, J.L., 1996. *The Late Palaeolithic Habitation of Haule V: From Excavation Report to the Reconstruction of Federmesser Settlement Patterns and Land-Use*. Van Gorcum, Assen.

Houtsma, P., Roodenberg, J.J., Schilstra, J., 1981. A Site of the Tjonger Tradition along the Schipsloot at Een (Gemeente of Norg, Province of Drenthe, the Netherlands). *Palaeohistoria* 23, 45-74.

Howes, D., 2006. Scent, Sound and Synaesthesia: Intersensoriality and Material Culture Theory. In: Tilley, C., Keane, W., Küchler, S., Rowlands, M., Spyer, P. (Eds.), *Handbook of Material Culture*. Sage, London, pp. 161-172.

Hudson, M.J., Aoyama, M., Hoover, K.C., Uchiyama, J., 2012. Prospects and challenges for an archaeology of global climate change. *Wiley Interdisciplinary Reviews: Climate Change* 3, 313-328.

Huff, W.D., Owen, L.A., 2013. Volcanic Landforms and Hazards. In: John, F.S. (Ed.), *Treatise on Geomorphology*. Academic Press, San Diego, pp. 148-192.

Hufschmidt, G., 2011. A comparative analysis of several vulnerability concepts. *Natural Hazards* 58, 621-643.

Hughes, S., 1998. Getting to the Point: Evolutionary Change in Prehistoric Weaponry. *Journal of Archaeological Method and Theory* 5, 345-408.

Hugo, G., 1996. Environmental Concerns and International Migration. *International Migration Review* 30, 105-131.

Hulme, M., 2008. The conquering of climate: discourses of fear and their dissolution. *Geographical Journal* 174, 5-16.

Huppert, H.E., Sparks, R.S.J., 2006. Extreme natural hazards: population growth, globalization and environmental change. *Philosophical Transactions of the Royal Society A: Mathematical, Physical and Engineering Sciences* 364, 1875-1888.

Hutchings, W.K., 2011. Measuring use-related fracture velocity in lithic armatures to identify spears, javelins, darts, and arrows. *Journal of Archaeological Science* 38, 1737-1746.

Höfchen, H., Limberg, K.M., Zuschlag, C. (Eds.), 2014. *Apocalypse Now! Visionen von Schrecken und Hoffnung in der Kunst vom Mittelalter bis heute*. Deutscher Kunstverlag, München/Berlin.

Högberg, A., Olausson, D., 2007. *Scandinavian flint: an archaeological perspective*. Aarhus University Press, Aarhus.

Høgh, L., 2008. Kulturheltens arv – Arkæologiens nationalvidenskabelige forpligtelse. *Arkæologisk Forum* 18, 2-7.

Høiris, O., 1999. Opfindelsen af stenalderen. Jæger-samler samfund i antropologien og arkæologien.

In: Høiris O., Madsen, H.J., Madsen, T., Vellev, J. (Eds.), *Menneskelivets mangfoldighed. Arkæologisk og antropologisk forskning på Moesgård.* Aarhus University Press, Aarhus, pp. 107-114.

Høiris, O., 2010. Danmarks oldtid – i historisk perspektiv. *Kuml* 2010, 213-255.

Ikinger, A., 1996. Bodentypes unter Laacher See-Tephra im Mittelrheinischen Becken und ihre Deutung. *Mainzer geowissenschaftliche Mitteilungen* 25, 223-284.

Ikinger, E.-M., 1998. *Der endeiszeitliche Rückenspitzen-Kreis Mitteleuropas.* LIT, Münster.

Ingold, T., 1986. *The appropriation of nature.* Manchester University Press, Manchester.

Ingold, T., 2000. *The Perception of the Environment: Essays on Livelihood, Dwelling and Skill.* Routledge, London.

Ingold, T. 2004. Culture on the Ground: The World Perceived Through the Feet. *Journal of Material Culture* 9, 315-340.

Ingold, T., 2005. The eye of the storm: visual perception and the weather. *Visual Studies* 20, 97-104.

Ingold, T., 2007. Earth, sky, wind, and weather. *Journal of the Royal Anthropological Institute* 13, S19-S38.

Ingold, T., 2010. Footprints through the weather-world: walking, breathing, knowing. *Journal of the Royal Anthropological Institute* 16, S121-S139.

Ingold, T., 2011. *Being alive: essays on movement, knowledge and description.* Routledge, London.

Iversen, J., 1942. En pollenanalytisk Tidsfæstelse af Ferskvandslagene ved Nørre Lyngby. *Meddelelser fra Dansk Geologisk Forening* 10, 130-151.

Iversen, J., 1946. Geologisk Datering af en senglacial Boplads ved Bromme. *Aarbøger for nordisk Oldkyndighed og Historie* 1946, 198-231.

Iversen, J., 1947. Plantevækst, Dyreliv og Klima i det senglaciale Danmark. *Geologiska Föreningen i Stockholm Förhandlingar* 69, 67-78.

Iversen, R., 2010. In a World of Worlds: The Pitted Ware Complex in a large scale perspective. *Acta Archaeologica* 81, 5-43.

Jacobi, R.M., 1980. The Upper Palaeolithic in Britain, with special reference to Wales. In: Taylor, J.A. (Ed.), *Culture and Environment in Prehistoric Wales.* British Archaeological Reports (British Series) 76. Oxbow, Oxford, pp. 15-99.

Jacoby, G.C., Workman, K.W., D'Arrigo, R.D., 1999. Laki eruption of 1783, tree rings, and disaster for northwest Alaska Inuit. *Quaternary Science Reviews* 18, 1365-1371.

Jahns, S., 2007. Palynological investigations into the Late Pleistocene and Holocene history of vegetation and settlement at the Löddigsee, Mecklenburg, Germany. *Vegetation History and Archaeobotany* 16, 157-169.

James, P., Chester, D.K., Duncan, A.M., 2000. Volcanic soils: their nature and archaeological significance. In: McGuire, W.J., Griffiths, D.R., Hancock, P.L.,

Stewart, I.S. (Eds.), *The Archaeology of Geological Catastrophes.* Geological Society, London, Special Publications 171, 317-338.

Janson, U., 2009. *Vulkan.* Warner Home Video.

Janssens, M.M., Kasse, C., Bohncke, S.J.P., Greaves, H., Cohen, K.M., Wallinga, J., Hoek, W.Z., 2012. Climate-driven fluvial development and valley abandonment at the last glacial-interglacial transition (Oude IJssel-Rhine, Germany). *Netherlands Journal of Geosciences-Geologie En Mijnbouw* 91, 37-62.

Jantsch, E., 1972. Towards Interdisciplinarity and Transdisciplinarity in Education and Innovation. In: Apostél, L., Berger, G., Briggs, A. (Eds.), *Interdisciplinarity. Problems of teaching and research in universities.* OECD Publications, Paris, pp. 97-121.

Jasanoff, S., 2007. Technologies of humility. *Nature* 450, 33.

Jessen, A.H., Nordmann, V.J.H., 1915. *Ferskvandslagene ved Nørre Lyngby.* C.A. Reitzel, Copenhagen.

Johansen, L., 2000. The Late Palaeolithic in Denmark. In: Bodu, P., Christensen, M., Valentin, B. (Eds.), *L'Europe centrale et septentrionale au Tardiglaciaire.* Mémoires du Musée de Préhistoire d'Ile-de-France 7, Nemours. APRAIF, Paris, pp. 19-54.

Johansson, A.D., 2003. *Stoksbjerg Vest. Et senpalæolitisk Fundkompleks ved Porsmose, Sydsjælland. Fra Bromme- til Ahrensburgkultur i Norden.* Det Kongelige Nordiske Oldskriftselskab, Copenhagen.

Johnsen, S.J., Dahl-Jensen, D., Gundestrup, N., Steffensen, J.P., Clausen, H.B., Miller, H., Masson-Delmotte, V., Sveinbjörnsdottir, A.E., White, J., 2001. Oxygen isotope and palaeotemperature records from six Greenland ice-core stations: Camp Century, Dye-3, GRIP, GISP2, Renland and NorthGRIP. *Journal of Quaternary Science* 16, 299-307.

Jones, M.T., Gislason, S.R., 2008. Rapid releases of metal salts and nutrients following the deposition of volcanic ash into aqueous environments. *Geochimica Et Cosmochimica Acta* 72, 3661-3680.

Jordan, P., 2003. *Material culture and sacred landscape: the anthropology of the Siberian Khanty.* AltaMira, Oxford.

Joyce, R.A., Lopiparo, J., 2005. Postscript: Doing Agency in Archaeology. *Journal of Archaeological Method and Theory* 12, 365-374.

Jungerius, P.D., Riezebos, P.A., Slotboom, R.T., 1968. The age of Eifel Maars as shown by the presence of Laacher See ash of Allerød age. *Geologie En Mijnbouw* 47, 199-205.

Junkmanns, J., 2001. *Pfeil und Bogen. Herstellung und Gebrauch in der Jungsteinzeit.* Museum Schwab, Biel.

Juvigné, E.H., 1977. La zone de dispersion des poussières émises par une des dernières éruptions du volcan du Laachersee (Eifel). *Zeitschrift für Geomorphologie* 21, 323-342.

Kabacinski, J., Sobkowiak-Tabaka, I., 2010. Between East and West – a new site of the Federmessergruppen in Poland. *Quartär* 57, 139-154.

Kaiser, K., 1996. Zur hydrologischen Entwicklung mecklenburgischer Seen im jüngeren Quartär. *Petermanns geographische Mitteilungen* 140, 323-342.

Kaiser, K., 1998. Die hydrologische Entwicklung der Müritz im jüngeren Quartär – Befunde und ihre Interpretation. *Zeitschrift für Geomorphologie N.F.* 112, 143-176.

Kaiser, K., Clausen, I., 2005. Palaeopedology and Stratigraphy of the Late Palaeolithic Alt Duvenstedt Site, Schleswig-Holstein (Northwest Germany). *Archäologisches Korrespondenzblatt* 35, 447-466.

Kaiser, K., de Klerk, P., Terberger, T., 1999. Die Riesenhirschfundstelle von Endingen: geowissenschaftliche und archäologische Untersuchungen an einem spätglazialen Fundplatz in Vorpommern. *Eiszeitalter & Gegenwart* 49, 102-123.

Kaiser, K., Hilgers, A., Schlaak, N., Jankowski, M., Kühn, P., Bussemer, S., Przegiętka, K., 2009. Palaeopedological marker horizons in northern central Europe: characteristics of Lateglacial Usselo and Finow soils. *Boreas* 38, 591-609.

Kaiser, K., Janke, W., 1998. Bodenkundlich-geomorphologische und paläobotanische Untersuchungen im Ryckbecken bei Greifswald. *Bodendenkmalpflege in Mecklenburg-Vorpommern* 45, 69-102.

Kasse, C., Hoek, W.Z., Bohncke, S.J.P., Konert, M., Weijers, J.W.H., Cassee, M.L., Van der Zee, R.M., 2005. Late Glacial fluvial response of the Niers-Rhine (western Germany) to climate and vegetation change. *Journal of Quaternary Science* 20, 377-394.

Kegler, J., 2002. Die federmesserzeitliche Fundschicht des paläolithischen Siedlungsplatzes Andernach-Martinsberg, Grabung 1994-1996. *Archäologisches Korrespondenzblatt* 32, 501-516.

Kelly, R.L., 1995. *The Foraging Spectrum: Diversity in Hunter-Gatherer Lifeways*. Smithsonian Institution Press, Washington, D.C.

Kelly, R.L., 2003. Colonization of new land by hunter-gatherers: expectations and implications based on ethnographic data. In: Rockman, M., Steele, J. (Eds.), *Colonization of Unfamiliar Landscapes: The archaeology of adaptation*. Routledge, London, pp. 44-58.

Kelly, R.L., Todd, L.C., 1988. Coming into the Country: Early Paleoindian Hunting and Mobility. *American Antiquity* 53, 231-244.

Kelman, I., Mather, T.A., 2008. Living with volcanoes: The sustainable livelihoods approach for volcano-related opportunities. *Journal of Volcanology and Geothermal Research* 172, 189-198.

Kestler, H.A., Müller, A., Gress, T.M., Buchholz, M., 2005. Generalized Venn diagrams: a new method of visualizing complex genetic set relations. *Bioinformatics* 21, 1592-1595.

Kestler, H.A., Müller, A., Kraus, J., Buchholz, M., Gress, T., Liu, H., Kane, D., Zeeberg, B., Weinstein, J., 2008. VennMaster: Area-proportional Euler diagrams for functional GO analysis of microarrays. *BMC Bioinformatics* 9, 67.

Kieffer, S.W., 2013. *The dynamics of disaster*. W. W. Norton & Co., New York, NY.

Kierdorf, H., Kierdorf, U., 1997. Disturbances of the secretory stage of amelogenesis in fluorosed deer teeth: a scanning electron-microscopic study. *Cell Tissue Research* 289, 125-135.

Kierdorf, H., Kierdorf, U., Sedlacek, F., Erdelen, M., 1996. Mandibular bone fluoride levels and occurrence of fluoride induced dental lesions in populations of wild red deer (Cervus elaphus) from Central Europe. *Environmental Pollution* 93, 75-81.

Kierdorf, U., Kierdorf, H., Fejerskov, O., 1993. Fluoride-induced developmental changes in enamel and dentine of European roe deer (Capreolus capreolus L.) as a result of environmental pollution. *Archives of Oral Biology* 38, 1071-1081.

Kirch, P.V., 2005. Archaeology and Global Change: The Holocene Record. *Annual Review of Environment and Resources* 30, 409-440.

Kittleman, L.R., 1973. Mineralogy, Correlation, and Grain-Size Distributions of Mazama Tephra and Other Postglacial Pyroclastic Layers, Pacific Northwest. *Geological Society of America Bulletin* 84, 2957-2980.

Kittleman, L.R., 1979. Geologic Methods in Studies of Quaternary Tephra. In: Sheets, P.D., Grayson, D.K. (Eds.), *Volcanic Activity and Human Ecology*. Academic Press, New York, NY, pp. 49-82.

Kjellgren, E., 2001. *Splendid isolation: Art of Easter Island*. Yale University Press, New Caven, CO.

Klee, R., Schmidt, R., Müller, J., 1993. Alleröd diatom assemblages in prealpine hardwater lakes of Bavaria and Austria as preserved by the Laacher See eruption event. *Limnologica* 23, 131-143.

Klindt-Jensen, O., 1975. *A History of Scandinavian Archaeology*. Thames & Hudson, London.

Kloss, K., Wechler, K.-P., 1987. Federmesserfundplatz und anthropogene Einflüsse in einem Pollendiagramm zum Spätglazial bei Henningsdorf, Kr. Oranienburg. *Ausgrabungen & Funde* 32, 54-62.

Knudsen, S.A., 1990. 361. Gamst Sønge. *Arkæologiske udgravninger i Danmark* 1989, 104.

Knuth, G., Thomae, M., 2003. Zur Tephra im Alleröd bei Schadeleben und Krumpa in Sachsen-Anhalt. *Hallesches Jahrbuch für Geowissenschaften* 25, 81-90.

Kobusiewicz, M., 2009a. The Lyngby point as a cultural marker. In: Street, M., Barton, R.N.E., Terberger, T. (Eds.), *Humans, environment and chronology of the late glacial of the North European Plain. RGZM – Tagungen*. Band 6. Verlag des Römisch-Germanischen Zentralmuseums, Mainz, pp. 169-178.

Kobusiewicz, M., 2009b. Whether the Bromme culture existed? *Folia Praehistorica Posnaniensia* 15, 75-91.

Koerper, H.C., Stickel, E.g. 1980. Cultural Drift: A Primary Process of Cultural Change. *Journal of Anthropological Research* 36, 463-469.

Kohl, P.L., Fawcett, C., 1995. *Nationalism, politics, and the practice of archaeology*. Cambridge University Press, Cambridge.

Kolstrup, E , 2002. Some classical methods used for reconstruction of Lateglacial environments in the European plain: potentials and limitations. In: Eriksen, B.V., Bratlund, B. (Eds.), *Recent studies in the final Palaeolithic of the European plain: proceedings of a U.I.S.P.P. symposium, Stockholm, 14.-17. October 1999*. Jutland Archaeological Society, Højbjerg, pp. 11-24.

Kooi, B.W., Bergman, C.A., 1997. An Approach to the Study of Ancient Archery Using Mathematical Modelling. *Antiquity* 71, 124-134.

Korfmann, M., 1972. *Schleuder und Bogen in Südwestasien: Von den frühesten Belegen bis zum Beginn der historischen Stadtstaaten*. Verlag Rudolf Habelt GmbH, Bonn.

Koutrafouri, V.G., Sanders, J. (Eds.), 2013. *Ritual Failure. Archaeological Perspectives*. Sidestone Press, Leiden.

Kovarovic, K., Aiello, L.C., Cardini, A., Lockwood, C.A., 2011. Discriminant function analyses in archaeology: are classification rates too good to be true? *Journal of Archaeological Science* 38, 3006-3018.

Kramer, F.E., 1995. 7. Attemose II. *Arkæologiske udgravninger i Danmark* 1995, 118.

Krause, W., Kollau, W., 1943. Die steinzeitlichen Wirbeltierfaunen von Stellmoor in Holstein. In: Rust, A. (Ed.), *Die Alt- und Mitelsteinzeitlichen Funde von Stellmoor*. Karl Wachholtz Verlag GmbH, Neumünster, pp. 40-59.

Kremer, B.P. (Ed.), 1995. *Laacher See. Landschaft, Natur, Kunst, Kultur*. Wienand Verlag, Köln.

Kreps, G.A., 1998. Disaster as systemic event and social catalyst. In: Quarantelli, E.L. (Ed.), *What is a disaster? Perspectives on the question*. Routledge, London, pp. 31-55.

Kristiansen, K., 2002. The Birth of Ecological Archaeology in Denmark. In: Fischer, A., Kristiansen, K. (Eds.), *The Neolithisation of Denmark. 150 years of debate*. J.R. Collins, Sheffield, pp. 9-32.

Krämer, D., 2009. Sie haben festgestellt, dass es keinen Sommer gegeben hat. Der Ausbruch des Tambora (Indonesien) am 10. April 1815 und seine Auswirkungen. In: Schenk, G.J. (Ed.), *Katastrophen. Vom Untergang Pompejis bis zum Klimawandel*. Jan Thorbecke Verlag, Ostfildern, pp. 132-146.

Kuhlicke, C., 2010. The dynamics of vulnerability: some preliminary thoughts about the occurrence of 'radical surprises' and a case study on the 2002 flood (Germany). *Natural Hazards* 55, 671-688.

Kuhn, S.L., 1994. A Formal Approach to the Design and Assembly of Mobile Toolkits. *American Antiquity* 59, 426-442.

Kusky, T.M., 2003. *Geological hazards: a sourcebook*. Greenwood Press, Westport, CN.

Kwadijk, J.C.J., 1991. Sensitivity of the river Rhine discharge to environmental change, a first tentative assessment. *Earth Surface Processes and Landforms* 16, 627-637.

Küssner, M., 2007. Mitteldeutsche Fundstellen der Zeit zwischen dem Weichsel-Pleniglazial und dem Ende des Allerød im Kartenbild. In: Speitel, E. (Ed.), *Terra praehistorica. Festschrift für Klaus-Dieter Jäger zum 70. Geburtstag. Neue Ausgrabungen und Funde in Thüringen, Sonderband 2007/Beiträge zur Ur- und Frühgeschichte Mitteleuropas*. Band 48. Beier & Beran, Langenweissbach, pp. 211-223.

Küssner, M., 2009. *Die späte Altsteinzeit im Einzugsgebiet der Saale. Untersuchungen an ausgewählten Fundstellen*. Beran & Beran, Langenweissbach.

Küssner, M., 2010. The Late Upper Palaeolithic in the catchment area of the River Saale – facts and considerations. *Quartär* 57, 125-137.

Lacasse, C., Garbe-Schonberg, C.D., 2001. Explosive silicic volcanism in Iceland and the Jan Mayen area during the last 6 Ma: sources and timing of major eruptions. *Journal of Volcanology and Geothermal Research* 107, 113-147.

Lacroix, D., 1993. Les minéraux denses transparents des dépôts de la grotte Walou à Trooz (Province de Liège, Belgique). In: Dewez, M.C. (Ed.), *Recherches à la grotte Walou à Trooz (province de Liège, Belgique). Premier rapport de fouille*. Société Wallonne de Palethnologie, Liège, pp. 25-31.

Laland, K.N., Boogert, N., Evans, C., 2014. Niche construction, innovation and complexity. *Environmental Innovation and Societal Transitions* 11, 71-86.

Laland, K.N., Brown, G.R., 2002. *Sense & Nonsense. Evolutionary Perspectives on Human Behaviour*. Oxford University Press, Oxford.

Laland, K.N., Brown, G.R., 2006. Niche Construction, Human Behavior, and the Adaptive-Lag Hypothesis. *Evolutionary Anthropology* 15, 95-104.

Laland, K.N., O'Brien, M.J., 2010. Niche Construction Theory and Archaeology. *Journal of Archaeological Method and Theory* 17, 303-322.

Laland, K.N., Odling-Smee, F.J., Feldman, M.W., 1999. Evolutionary consequences of niche construction and their implications for ecology. *Proceedings of the National Academy of Sciences of the United States of America* 96, 10242-10247.

Lamb, H.H., 1972. *Climate: present, past and future*. Methuen, London.

Lane, C.S., Brauer, A., Blockley, S.P.E., Dulski, P., 2013. Volcanic ash reveals time-transgressive abrupt climate change during the Younger Dryas. *Geology* 41(12), 1251-1254.

Lane, C.S., Cullen, V.L., White, D., Bramham-Law, C., Smith, V.C., 2014. Cryptotephra as a dating and correlation tool in archaeology. *Journal of Archaeological Science* 42, 42-50.

Lane, C.S., De Klerk, P., Cullen, V.L., 2012. A teph-rochronology for the Lateglacial palynological record of the Endinger Bruch (Vorpommern, north-east Germany). *Journal of Quaternary Science* 27, 141-149.

Lang, H.D., 1954. Ein Alleröd-Profil mit eingelagertem Laacher-See-Tuff bei Marburg/Lahn. *Neues Jahrbuch für Geologie und Paläontologie-Monatshefte* 8, 362-372.

Langmann, B., Folch, A., Hensch, M., Matthias, V., 2012. Volcanic ash over Europe during the eruption of Eyjafjallajökull on Iceland, April–May 2010. Atmospheric Environment 48, 1-8.

Lanting, J.N., Van der Plicht, J., 1996. De ^{14}C-chronologie van de Nederlandse pre- en protohistorie I: Laat-Paleolithikum. *Palaeohistoria* 37/38, 71-125.

Larsen, G., Eiríksson, J., 2008. Late Quaternary terrestrial tephrochronology of Iceland—frequency of explosive eruptions, type and volume of tephra deposits. *Journal of Quaternary Science* 23, 109-120.

Larsen, J.J., Noe-Nygaard, N., 2014. Lateglacial and early Holocene tephrostratigraphy and sedimentology of the Store Slotseng basin, SW Denmark: a multi-proxy study. *Boreas* 43, 349-361.

Larsson, L., 1991. The Late Palaeolithic in southern Sweden: Investigations in a marginal region. In: Barton, R.N.E., Roberts, A.J., Roe, D. (Eds.), *The Late Glacial in north-western Europe: human adaptation and environmental change at the end of the Pleistocene*. CBA, London, pp. 122-127.

Larsson, L., 1993. Neue Siedlungsfunde der Späteiszeit im südlichen Schweden. *Archäologisches Korrespondenzblatt* 23, 275-283.

Larsson, L. (Ed.), 1996. *The Earliest Settlement of Scandinavia and Its Relationship with Neighbouring Areas*. Acta Archaeologica Lundensia Series IN 8°, 24. Almqvist & Wiksell, Stockholm.

Larsson, L., Liljegren, R., Magnell, O., Ekström, J., 2002. Archaeo-faunal aspects of bog finds from Hässleberga, southern Scania, Sweden. In: Eriksen, B.V., Bratlund, B. (Eds.), *Recent studies in the Final Palaeolithic of the European plain*. Jutland Archaeological Society, Højbjerg, pp. 61-74.

Lartet, E., Christy, H., 1875. *Reliquae Aquitanicae: being contributions to the archaeology of Périgord and adjoining provinces of Southern France*. Norgate, London.

Lauer, T., Frechen, M., Klostermann, J., Krbetschek, M., Schollmayer, G., Tsukamoto, S., 2011. Luminescence dating of Last Glacial and Early Holocene fluvial deposits from the Lower Rhine – methodological aspects and chronological framework. *Zeitschrift der Deutschen Gesellschaft für Geowissenschaften* 162, 47-61.

Lavigne, F., De Coster, B., Juvin, N., Flohic, F., Gaillard, J.-C., Texier, P., Morin, J., Sartohadi, J., 2008. People's behaviour in the face of volcanic hazards: Perspectives from Javanese communities, Indonesia. *Journal of Volcanology and Geothermal Research* 172, 273-287.

Lawson, I.T., Swindles, G.T., Plunkett, G., Greenberg, D., 2012. The spatial distribution of Holocene cryptotephras in north-west Europe since 7 ka: implications for understanding ash fall events from Icelandic eruptions. *Quaternary Science Reviews* 41, 57-66.

Le Gall, O., 1992. Les Magdaléniens et l'ichtyofaune dulçaquicole. In: Rigaud, J.P., Laville, H., Vandermeersch, B. (Eds.), *Le peuplement Magdalénien. Paléogéographie physique et humaine*. Editions du CNRS, Paris, pp. 277-285.

Le Gall, O., 2003. Des Magdaléniens et...des Poissons. In: Costamagno, S., Laroulandie, V. (Eds.), *Zooarchaeological insights into Magdalenian Lifeways*. British Archaeological Reports (International Series) 1144. Archaeopress, Oxford, pp. 119-128.

Le Maitre, R.W. (Ed.), 2002. *Igneous rocks: a classification and glossary of terms. Recommendations of the International Union of Geological Sciences, Subcommission on the Systematics of Igneous Rocks*. Cambridge University Press, Cambridge.

Leder, J., Wenzel, F., Daniell, J.E., Gottschämmer, E., 2017. Loss of residential buildings in the event of a re-awakening of the Laacher See Volcano (Germany). *Journal of Volcanology and Geothermal Research* 337, 111-123.

Lehman, S.J., Keigwin, L.D., 1992. Sudden changes in North Atlantic circulation during the last deglaciation. *Nature* 356, 757-762.

Lemdahl, G., Buckland, P.I., Mortensen, M.F., 2014. Lateglacial insect assemblages from the Palaeolithic site Slotseng: New evidence concerning climate and environment in SW Denmark. *Quaternary International* 341, 172-183.

Leroy, S.A.G., 2006. From natural hazard to environmental catastrophe: Past and present. *Quaternary International* 158, 4-12.

Lewontin, R.C., 1978. Adaptation. *Scientific American* 239, 156-169.

Liabeuf, R., Bourdelle, Y., Fontana, L., Surmely, F., 1997. Nouveaux éléments apportés à l'étude du site magdalénien d'Enval (Vic-le-Comte, Puy-de-Dôme, France) et du peuplement de la Limagne d'Auvergne. *Bulletin de la Société Préhistorique Française* 94(2), 172-181.

Lie, R., 1990. Blomvågfunnet, de eldste spor etter mennesker i Norge? *Viking* 53, 7-20.

Lipps, S., Caspers, G., 1990. Spätglazial und Holozän auf der Stolzenauer Terrasse im Mittelwesertal. *Eiszeitalter & Gegenwart* 40, 111-119.

Litt, T., Schmincke, H.-U., Frechen, M., Schlüchter, C., 2008. Quaternary. In: McCann, T. (Ed.), *The Geology of Central Europe*. Volume 2: *Mesozoic and Cenozoic*. Geological Society of London, London, pp. 1287-1340.

Litt, T., Schmincke, H.-U., Kromer, B., 2003. Environmental response to climatic and volcanic events in central Europe during the Weichselian Lateglacial. *Quaternary Science Reviews* 22, 7-32.

Lockwood, J.P., Hazlett, R.W., 2010. *Volcanoes. Global Perspective*. Wiley-Blackwell, Chichester.

Loew, S., 2003. Rüsselsheim 122 – ein Jagdcamp aus dem Endglazial. *hessenArchäologie* 2003, 22-26.

Loew, S., 2005. Der Federmesser-Fundplatz Rüsselsheim 122 am unteren Main (Hessen). *Archäologisches Korrespondenzblatt* 35, 143-158.

Loew, S., 2006. Wohnen im Spätglazial – die Siedlungsstrukturen von Rüsselsheim 122. *Denkmalpflege & Kulturgeschichte* 2006, 18-21.

Loew, S., 2009. Korrespondenzanalyse und Behausungsstrukturen. Siedlungsplatzanalyse des Federmesserfundplatzes Rüsselsheim 122 (Kr. Groß-Gerau, Hessen). *Archäologisches Korrespondenzblatt* 39, 309-324.

Loewe, G., 1998. *Kreis Schleswig (seit 1974 Kreis Schleswig-Flensburg)*. Wachholtz Verlag, Neumünster.

Loftus, J., 1982. Ein verzierter Pfeilschaftglätter von Fläche 64/74-73/78 des spätpaläolithischen Fundplatzes Niederbieber/Neuwieder Becken. *Archäologisches Korrespondenzblatt* 12, 313-316.

Lorenz, D.F., 2013. The diversity of resilience: contributions from a social science perspective. *Natural Hazards* 67, 7-24.

Lorenzen, E.D., Nogues-Bravo, D., Orlando, L., Weinstock, J., Binladen, J., Marske, K.A., Ugan, A., Borregaard, M.K., Gilbert, M.T.P., Nielsen, R., Ho, S.Y.W., Goebel, T., Graf, K.E., Byers, D., Stenderup, J.T., Rasmussen, M., Campos, P.F., Leonard, J.A., Koepfli, K.-P., Froese, D., Zazula, G., Stafford, T.W., Aaris-Sorensen, K., Batra, P., Haywood, A.M., Singarayer, J.S., Valdes, P.J., Boeskorov, G., Burns, J.A., Davydov, S.P., Haile, J., Jenkins, D.L., Kosintsev, P., Kuznetsova, T., Lai, X., Martin, L.D., McDonald, H.G., Mol, D., Meldgaard, M., Munch, K., Stephan, E., Sablin, M., Sommer, R.S., Sipko, T., Scott, E., Suchard, M.A., Tikhonov, A., Willerslev, R., Wayne, R.K., Cooper, A., Hofreiter, M., Sher, A., Shapiro, B., Rahbek, C., Willerslev, E., 2011. Species-specific responses of Late Quaternary megafauna to climate and humans. *Nature advance online publication*.

Lovekamp, W.E., Trainor, J.E., 2013. 30 Years of Dissertation Trends in Disaster Studies. *HazNet* 5, 11-14.

Lowe, D.J., 2011. Tephrochronology and its application: A review. *Quaternary Geochronology* 6, 107-153.

Lowe, D.J., Alloway, B.V., 2015. Tephrochronology. In: Rink, W.J., Thompson, J.W. (Eds.), *Encyclopaedia of Scientific Dating Methods*. Springer, Dordrecht, pp. 733-799.

Lowe, D.J., Newnham, R.M., McCraw, J.D., 2002. Volcanism and early Maori society in new Zealand. In: Torrence, R., Grattan, J. (Eds.), *Natural Disasters and Cultural Change*. Routledge, London, pp. 126-161.

Lowe, D.J., Newnham, R.M., McFadgen, B.G., Higham, T.F.G., 2000. Tephras and New Zealand Archaeology. *Journal of Archaeological Science* 27, 859-870.

Lowe, J., Barton, N., Blockley, S., Ramsey, C.B., Cullen, V.L., Davies, W., Gamble, C., Grant, K., Hardiman, M., Housley, R., Lane, C.S., Lee, S., Lewis, M., MacLeod, A., Menzies, M., Müller, W., Pollard, M., Price, C., Roberts, A.P., Rohling, E.J., Satow, C., Smith, V.C., Stringer, C.B., Tomlinson, E.L., White, D., Albert, P., Arienzo, I., Barker, G., Borić, D., Carandente, A., Civetta, L., Ferrier, C., Guadelli, J.-L., Karkanas, P., Koumouzelis, M., Müller, U.C., Orsi, G., Pross, J., Rosi, M., Shalamanov-Korobar, L., Sirakov, N., Tzedakis, P.C., 2012. Volcanic ash layers illuminate the resilience of Neanderthals and early modern humans to natural hazards. *Proceedings of the National Academy of Sciences* 109, 13532-13537.

Lowe, J.J., Rasmussen, S.O., Björck, S., Hoek, W.Z., Steffensen, J.P., Walker, M.J.C., Yu, Z.C., 2008. Synchronisation of palaeoenvironmental events in the North Atlantic region during the Last Termination: a revised protocol recommended by the INTIMATE group. *Quaternary Science Reviews* 27, 6-17.

Luhr, J.F., Simkin, T., 1993. *Parícutin: the volcano born in a Mexican cornfield*. Geoscience Press, Phoenix, AZ.

Lund, K.A., Benediktsson, K., 2011. Inhabiting a risky earth: The Eyjafjallajökull eruption in 2010 and its impacts. *Anthropology Today* 27, 6-9.

Lyman, R.L., O'Brien, M.J., 2006. Seriation and Cladistics: The Difference between Anagenetic and Cladogenetic Evolution. In: Lipo, C.P., O'Brien, M.J., Collard, M., Shennan, S.J. (Eds.), *Mapping our Ancestors. Phylogenetic Approaches in Anthropology and Prehistory*. AldineTransaction, New Brunswick, NJ., pp. 65-88.

Mace, A., 1959. An Upper Palaeolithic Open-site at Hengistbury Head, Christchurch, Hants. *Proceedings of the Prehistoric Society* 25, 233-259.

Mace, B.L., Bell, P.A., Loomis, R.J., 1999. Aesthetic, Affective, and Cognitive Effects of Noise on Natural Landscape Assessment. *Society & Natural Resources* 12, 225-242.

Madsen, B., 1983. New Evidence of Late Palaeolithic Settlement in East Jutland. *Journal of Danish Archaeology* 2, 12-31.

Madsen, B., 1986. De første spor. *Arkæologske Fund fra Randers Amt* 1986, 62-65.

Madsen, B., 1992. Hamburgkulturens flintteknologi i Jels (The Hamburgian Flint Technology at Jels). In: Holm, J., Rieck, F. (Eds.), *Istidsjægere ved Jelssøerne*. Skrifter fra Museumsrådet for Sønderjyllands Amt, Haderslev, pp. 93-131.

Madsen, B., 1993. Flint – extraction, manufacture and distribution. In: Hvaas, S., Storgaard, B. (Eds.),

Digging into the Past. 25 Years of Archaeology in Denmark. Jutland Archaeological Society, Højbjerg, pp. 126-129.

Madsen, B., 1996. Late Palaeolithic cultures of south Scandinavia: tools, traditions and technology. In: Larsson, L. (Ed.), *The Earliest Settlement of Scandinavia and Its Relationship with Neighbouring Areas*. Acta Archaeologica Lundensia Series IN 8°, 24. Almqvist & Wiksell, Stockholm, pp. 61-73.

Madsen, T., 1988. Multivariate statistics and archaeology. In: Madsen, T. (Ed.), *Multivariate archaeology: numerical approaches in Scandinavian archaeology*. Jutland Archaeological Society, Højbjerg, pp. 7-27.

Mandryk, C.A.S., 1993. Hunter-Gatherer Social Costs and the Nonviability of Submarginal Environments. *Journal of Anthropological Research* 49, 39-71.

Mangerud, J., Andersen, S.T., Berglund, B.E., Donner, J., 1974. Quaternary stratigraphy of Norden, a proposal for terminology and classification. *Boreas* 4, 109-128.

Mania, D., 1967. Das Quartär der Ascherslebener Depression im Nordharzvorland. *Hercynia* 4, 51-82.

Mania, D., 2003. Ascheregen vor 13 000 Jahren im Elbe-Saalegebiet. *Praehistoria Thuringica* 9, 51-79.

Mania, D., Toepfer, V., 1971. Zur jungquartären Landschaftsgeschichte und mesolithischen Besiedlung des Geiseltals. *Jahresschrift Mitteldeutsche Vorgeschichte* 55, 11-34.

Marchant, R., Lane, P., 2014. Past perspectives for the future: foundations for sustainable development in East Africa. *Journal of Archaeological Science* 51, 12-21.

Martin, C.G., 1913. The Recent Eruption of Katmai Volcano in Alaska. An Account of One of the Most Tremendous Volcanic Explosions Known in History. *National Geographic* 24, 131-181.

Martini, J., 1971. Recherches de tetombées volcaniques quaternaires dans le S.E. de la France et la Suisse occidentale. *Archives des Sciences* 23, 641-674.

Maschner, H., Mason, O.K., 2013. The Bow and Arrow in Northern North America. *Evolutionary Anthropology: Issues, News, and Reviews* 22, 133-138.

Maschner, H.D.G., Jordan, J.W., 2008. Catastrophic Events and Punctuated Culture Change: The Southern Bering Sea and North Pacific in a Dynamic Global System. In: Papagianni, D., Layton, R.H., Maschner, H.D.G. (Eds.), *Time and Change. Archaeological and Anthropological Perspectives on the Long-Term in Hunter-Gatherer Societies*. Oxbow, Oxford, pp. 95-113.

Masojć, M., 2006. Selected technological aspects of Bromme-Lyngby culture flint-working as exemplified by the Pomeranian site Jaglisko 3 in the Dobiegniew Lake District. In: Wiśniewski, A., Płonka, T., Burdukiewicz, J.M. (Eds.), *The Stone: Technique*

and Technology. Institute of Archaeology Wrocław, Wrocław, pp. 167-170.

Masojć, M., Malkiewicz, M., Sadowski, K., Włodarski, W., 2007. Final Palaeolithic sites at Węgliny, distr. Gubin SW Poland. Preliminary results of archaeological and palaeoenvironmental studies. *Śląskie Sprawozdania Archeologiczne* 48, 61-74.

Mason, B.G., Pyle, D.M., Oppenheimer, C., 2004. The size and frequency of the largest explosive eruptions on Earth. *Bulletin of Volcanology* 66, 735-748.

Mastrolorenzo, G., Petrone, P., Pappalardo, L., Sheridan, M.F., 2006. The Avellino 3780-yr-B.P. catastrophe as a worst-case scenario for a future eruption at Vesuvius. *Proceedings of the National Academy of Sciences of the United States of America* 103, 4366-4370.

Mather, T.A., Pyle, D.M., Oppenheimer, C., 2003. Tropospheric Volcanic Aerosol. In: Robock, A., Oppenheimer, C. (Eds.), *Volcanism and the Earth's Atmosphere*. Geophysical Monograph 139. American Geophysical Union, Washington, D.C., pp. 189-212.

Mathiassen, T., 1946. En senglacial Boplads ved Bromme. *Aarbøger for nordisk Oldkyndighed og Historie* 1946, 121-197.

Mathiassen, T., 1959. *Nordvestsjællands Oldtidsbebyggelse*. National Museum, Copenhagen.

Matsumura, S., Forster, P., 2008. Generation time and effective population size in Polar Eskimos. *Proceedings of the Royal Society B: Biological Sciences* d275, 1501-1508.

Mauch, C., Pfister, C. (Eds.), 2009. *Natural Disasters, Cultural Responses: Case Studies toward a Global Environmental History*. Lexington Books, Lanham, MD.

Mauelshagen, F., 2009. Die Klimakatastrophe. Szenen und Szenarien. In: Schenk, G.J. (Ed.), *Katastrophen. Vom Untergang Pompejis bis zum Klimawandel*. Jan Thorbecke Verlag, Ostfildern, pp. 205-223.

McAnany, P.A., Yoffee, N., 2010. Questioning how different societies respond to crises. *Nature* 464, 977-977.

McCormick, M., 2008. Karl der Große und die Vulkane: Naturwissenschaft, Klimageschichte und Mittelalterforschung. *Ethnographisch-archäologische Zeitschrift* 49, 129-145.

McCormick, M., Dutton, P.E., Mayewski, P.A., 2007. Volcanoes and the Climate Forcing of Carolingian Europe, a.d. 750-950. *Speculum* 82, 865-895.

McGuire, W.J., Howarth, R.J., Firth, C.R., Solow, A.R., Pullen, A.D., Saunders, S.J., Stewart, I.S., Vita-Finzi, C., 1997. Correlation between rate of sea-level change and frequency of explosive volcanism in the Mediterranean. *Nature* 389, 473-476.

McKibben, B., 2010. *Eaarth: Making a Life on a Tough New Planet*. Times Books, New York, NY.

McLaughlin, P., 2011. Climate Change, Adaptation, and Vulnerability: Reconceptualizing Societal–Environment Interaction Within a Socially Constructed Adaptive Landscape. *Organization & Environment* 24, 269-291.

McLaughlin, P., 2012. The Second Darwinian Revolution: Steps Toward a New Evolutionary Environmental Sociology. *Nature + Culture* 7, 231-258.

McLaughlin, P., Dietz, T., 2008. Structure, agency and environment: Toward an integrated perspective on vulnerability. *Global Environmental Change* 18, 99-111.

McNabb, J., 2012. *Dissent with modification: human origins, palaeolithic archaeology and evolutionary anthropology in Britain 1859-1901*. Archaeopress, Oxford.

Meischner, D., Grüger, E., 2008. Entstehung des Erdfallsees Jues in Herzberg am Harz vor 12.916 Jahren. In: Röhling, H.-G., Zellmer, H. (Eds.), *GeoTop 2008 "Landschaften lesen lernen". 12. Internationale Jahrestagung der Fachsektion GeoTop der Deutschen Gesellschaft für Geowissenschaften, 30. April-4. Mai 2008 in Königslutter im Geopark Harz, Braunschweiger Land, Ostfalen*. Schriftenreihe der Deutsche Gesellschaft für Geowissenschaften 56. Deutsche Gesellschaft für Geowissenschaften, Hannover, pp. 19.

Meller, H., Bertemes, F., Bork, H.-R., Risch, R. (Eds.), 2013. *1600 – Kultureller Umbruch im Schatten des Thera-Ausbruchs? Tagungen des Landesmuseums für Vorgeschichte Halle*. Band 9: *Landesamt fur Denkmalpflege und Archäologie Sachsen-Anhalt*, Halle.

Merkt, J., Müller, H., 1999. Varve chronology and palynology of the Lateglacial in Northwest Germany from lacustrine sediments of Hamelsee in Lower Saxony. *Quaternary International* 61, 41-59.

Mesoudi, A., 2007. A Darwinian Theory of Cultural Evolution Can Promote an Evolutionary Synthesis for the Social Sciences. *Biological Theory* 2, 263-275.

Mesoudi, A., 2008. Foresight in cultural evolution. *Biology & Philosophy* 23, 243-255.

Mesoudi, A., O'Brien, M.J., 2009. Placing archaeology within a unified science of cultural evolution. In: Shennan, S.J. (Ed.), *Pattern and Process in Cultural Evolution*. University of California Press, Berkeley, CA., pp. 21-32.

Mesoudi, A., Veldhuis, D., Foley, R.A., 2010. Why aren't the social sciences Darwinian? *Journal of Evolutionary Psychology* 8, 93-104.

Mesoudi, A., Whiten, A., Laland, K.N., 2004. Is Human Cultural Evolution Darwinian? Evidence Reviewed from the Perspective of *The Origin of Species*. *Evolution* 58, 1-11.

Mesoudi, A., Whiten, A., Laland, K.N., 2006. Towards a unified science of cultural evolution. *Behavioural and Brain Sciences* 29, 329-383.

Metcalf, C.J.E., Pavard, S., 2007a. All paths to fitness lead through demography. *Trends in Ecology and Evolution* 22, 563-564.

Metcalf, C.J.E., Pavard, S., 2007b. Why evolutionary biologists should be demographers. *Trends in Ecology and Evolution* 22, 206-212.

Mey, W., 1962. Die Grabung 1961 auf dem endpaläolithischen Fundplatz Berlin-Tegel A (Vorbericht). *Berliner Jahrbuch für Vor- und Frühgeschichte* 2, 190-197.

Michel-Kerjan, E., 2012. How resiliant is your country? *Nature* 491, 497.

Middleton, G., 2012. Nothing Lasts Forever: Environmental Discourses on the Collapse of Past Societies. *Journal of Archaeological Research* 20, 257-307.

Middleton, G., 2013. That old devil called collapse. *E-International Relations* 1-7.

Mieth, A., Bork, H.-R., 2010. Humans, climate or introduced rats – which is to blame for the woodland destruction on prehistoric Rapa Nui (Easter Island)? *Journal of Archaeological Science* 37, 417-426.

Miller, T.P., Casadevall, T.J., 2000. Volcanic ash hazards to aviation. In: Sigurdsson, H. (Ed.), *Encyclopedia of Volcanoes*. Academic Press, San Diego, CA., pp. 915-930.

Minc, L.D., 1986. Scarcity and Survival: The Role of Oral Tradition in Mediating Subsistence Crises. *Journal of Anthropological Archaeology* 5, 39-113.

Mitchell, J.K., 2011. Looking backward to see forward: Historical changes of public knowledge about climate hazards in Ireland. *Irish Geography* 44, 7-26.

Mithen, S., 1990. *Thoughtful Foragers: A Study of Prehistoric Decision Making*. Cambridge University Press, Cambridge.

Morin, E., 2008. Evidence for declines in human population densities during the early Upper Paleolithic in western Europe. *Proceedings of the National Academy of Sciences* 105, 48-53.

Mortensen, M.F., 2007. *Biostratigraphy and chronology of the terrestrial late Weichselian in Denmark – New investigations of the vegetation development based on pollen and plant macrofossils in the Slotseng basin*. Unpublished Ph.D. thesis: University of Aarhus, Aarhus.

Mortensen, M.F., Birks, H.H., Christensen, C., Holm, J., Noe-Nygaard, N., Odgaard, B.V., Olsen, J., Rasmussen, K.L., 2011. Lateglacial vegetation development in Denmark – New evidence based on macrofossils and pollen from Slotseng, a small-scale site in southern Jutland. *Quaternary Science Reviews* 30, 2534-2550.

Mortensen, M.F., Henriksen, P.S., Bennike, O., 2014a. Living on the good soil: relationships between soils, vegetation and human settlement during the late Allerød period in Denmark. *Vegetation History and Archaeobotany* 23, 195-205.

Mortensen, M.F., Henriksen, P.S., Christensen, C., Petersen, P.V., Olsen, J., 2014b. Vegetation development in south-east Denmark during the Weichselian Late Glacial: palaeoenvironmental studies close to the Palaeolithic site of Hasselø. *Danish Journal of Archaeology* 3, 33-51.

Moseley, M.E., 1999. Convergent catastrophe: Past patterns and future implications of collateral natural disasters in the Andes. In: Oliver-Smith, A., Hoffman, S.M. (Eds.), *The Angry Earth. Disaster in Anthropological Perspective*. Routledge, London, pp. 59-71.

Mundel, G., 2002. Moorgeologisch-moorbodenkundliche Untersuchungen in Brandenburg. *Archives of Agronomy and Soil Science* 48, 7-18.

Müller, H., 1953. Zur spät- und nacheiszeitlichen Vegetationsgeschichte des mitteldeutschen Trockengebietes. *Nova Acta Leopoldina N.F.* 16, 1-67.

Németh, K., Cronin, S.J., 2009. Volcanic structures and oral traditions of volcanism of Western Samoa (SW Pacific) and their implications for hazard education. *Journal of Volcanology and Geothermal Research* 186, 223-237.

Neumann, J., 1990. The 1810s in the Baltic region, 1816 in particular: Air temperatures, grain supply and mortality. *Climatic Change* 17, 97-120.

Newell, R.R., Constandse-Westermann, T.S., 1996. The Use of Ethnographic Analyses for Researching Late Palaeolithic Settlement Systems, Settlement Patterns and Land Use in the Northwest European Plain. *World Archaeology* 27, 372-388.

Newell, R.R., Constandse-Westermann, T.S., 1999. *Late glacial-early postglacial hunting strategies and land-use practices in the Swabian Alb and surrounding regions (southwestern B.R.D.)*. Van Gorcum, Assen.

Newhall, C.G., Self, S., 1982. The Volcanic Explosivity Index (VEI): an estimate of explosive magnitude for historical volcanism. *Journal of Geophysical Research* 87, 1231-1238.

Newton, A.J., 1999. Report on the pumice. In: Crawford, B.E., Smith, B.B. (Eds.), *The Biggings, Papa Stour, Shetland: the history and archaeology of a royal Norwegian farm*. Society of Antiquaries of Scotland Monograph Series 13. Society of Antiquaries of Scotland, Edinburg, pp. 178.

Newton, A.J., 2001. The pumice. In: Mithen, S.J. (Ed.), *Hunter gather landscape archaeology: The Southern Hebrides Project 1988-98*. McDonald Institute Monographs, Cambridge, pp. 403-405.

Newton, A.J., 2003. Analysis of pumice from Baleshare. In: Barber, J. (Ed.), *Bronze Age farms and Iron Age farm mounds of the Outer Hebrides*. The Society of Antiquaries of Scotland with Historic Scotland and the Council for British Archaeology, Edinburgh, pp. 135-138.

Niekus, M.J.L.T., 1995. *The archaeological resolution of the Bromme in an anthropological context*. Unpublished MA dissertation: Groningen University, Groningen.

Nielsen, E.B., 2013. Klima, apokalypse og en topos om sted. *Rhetorica Scandinavica* 63, 39-53.

Nielsen, E.H., 2009. *Paläolithikum und Mesolithikum in der Zentralschweiz. Mensch und Umwelt zwischen 17'000 und 5500 v. Chr.* Kantonaler Lehrmittelverlag, Luzern.

Nielsen, E.H., 2013. Response of the Lateglacial fauna to climatic change. *Palaeogeography, Palaeoclimatology, Palaeoecology* 391, Part B, 99-110.

Nielsen, J.Ø., Sejersen, F., 2012. Earth System Science, the IPCC and the problem of downward causation in human geographies of Global Climate Change. *Geografisk Tidsskrift-Danish Journal of Geography* 112, 194-202.

Nilsson, T., 1989. Senglacial bosættelse i Vendsyssel. *Kuml* 1989, 47-75.

Noe-Nygaard, N., Knudsen, K.L., Houmark-Nielsen, M., 2006. Fra istid til og med jægerstenalder. In: Sand-Jensen, K., Larsen, G. (Eds.), *Naturen i Danmark. Geologien*. Gyldendal, Copenhagen, pp. 303-332.

November, V., 2008. Spatiality of risk. *Environment and Planning* A 40, 1523-1527.

Nowell, D.A.G., Jones, M.C., Pyle, D.M., 2006. Episodic Quaternary volcanism in France and Germany. *Journal of Quaternary Science* 21, 645-675.

O'Brien, M.J., Holland, T.D., 1990. Variation, Selection, and the Archaeological Record. In: Schiffer, M.B. (Ed.), *Archaeological Method and Theory*. University of Arizona Press, Tucson, AZ., pp. 31-79.

O'Brien, M.J., Holland, T.D., 1992. The Role of Adaptation in Archaeological Explanation. *American Antiquity* 57, 36-59.

O'Brien, M.J., Lyman, R.L., 1999. *Seriation, Stratigraphy, and Index Fossils. The Backbone of Archaeological Dating*. Kluwer Academic/Plenum, New York, NY.

O'Brien, M.J., Lyman, R.L., 2000. *Applying Evolutionary Archaeology. A Systematic Approach*. Kluwer Academic/Plenum, New York, NY.

O'Brien, M.J., Lyman, R.L., Collard, M., Holden, C.J., Gray, R.D., Shennan, S.J., 2008. Transmission, Phylogenetics, and the Evolution of Cultural Diversity. In: O'Brien, M.J. (Ed.), *Cultural Transmission and Archaeology: Issues and Case Studies*. Society for American Archaeology Press, Washington, DC, pp. 39-58.

O'Connor, A., 2007. *Finding time for the old Stone Age: a history of Palaeolithic archaeology and Quaternary geology in Britain, 1860-1960*. Oxford University Press, Oxford.

O'Hara, R.J., 1997. Population thinking and tree thinking in systematics. *Zoologica Scripta* 26, 323-329.

O'Keefe, P., Westgate, K., Wisner, B., 1976. Taking the naturalness out of natural disasters. *Nature* 260, 566-567.

O'Regan, M., 2011. On the Edge of Chaos: European Aviation and Disrupted Mobilities. *Mobilities* 6, 21-30.

Odell, G.H., Cowan, F., 1987. Estimating Tillage Effects on Artifact Distributions. *American Antiquity* 52, 456-484.

Odling-Smee, F.J., 2007. Niche Inheritance: A Possible Basis for Classifying Multiple Inheritance Systems in Evolution. *Biological Theory* 2, 276-289.

Odling-Smee, F.J., Laland, K.N., Feldman, M.W., 2003. *Niche Construction. The Neglected Process in Evolution*. Princeton University Press, Princeton, NJ.

Odling-Smee, J., Erwin, D.H., Palkovacs, E.P., Feldman, M.W., Laland, K.N., 2013. Niche Construction Theory: A Practical Guide for Ecologists. *The Quarterly Review of Biology* 88, 3-28.

Oetelaar, G.A., 2015. The days of the dry snow: vulnerabilities and transformations related to the Mazama ash fall on the northern Plains. In: Riede, F. (Ed.), *Past Vulnerability. Volcanic eruptions and human vulnerability in traditional societies past and present*. Aarhus University Press, Aarhus, pp. 205-228.

Oetelaar, G.A., Beaudoin, A.B., 2005. Darkened Skies and Sparkling Grasses: The Potential Impact of the Mazama Ash Fall on the Northwestern Plains. *Plains Anthropologist* 50, 285-305.

Oetelaar, G.A., Beaudoin, A.B., 2016. Evidence of cultural responses to the impact of the Mazama ash fall from deeply stratified archaeological sites in southern Alberta, Canada. *Quaternary International* 394, 17-36.

Offer, J., 2010. Social change and selectionist thought: on Spencer, Darwin and Runciman. *Sociological Review* 58, 305-326.

Okamura, K., Fujisawa, A., Kondo, Y., Fujimoto, Y., Uozu, T., Ogawa, Y., Kaner, S., Mizoguchi, K., 2013. The Great East Japan Earthquake and cultural heritage: towards an archaeology of disaster. *Antiquity* 87, 258-269.

Oliver-Smith, A., 1986. Disaster context and causation: an overview of changing perspectives in disaster research. In: Oliver-Smith, A. (Ed.), *Natural Disasters and Cultural Responses*. College of William and Mary, Williamsburg, VA.

Oliver-Smith, A., 1996. Anthropological Research on Hazards and Disasters. *Annual Review of Anthropology* 25, 303-328.

Oliver-Smith, A., 1998. Global changes and the definition of disaster. In: Quarantelli, E.L. (Ed.), *What is a disaster?* Routledge, London, pp. 178-194.

Oliver-Smith, A., 1999. "What is a Disaster?" Anthropological Perspectives on a Persistent Question. In: Oliver-Smith, A., Hoffman, S.M. (Eds.), *The Angry Earth. Disaster in Anthropological Perspective*. Routledge, London, pp. 18-34.

Oliver-Smith, A., 2004. Theorizing vulnerability in a globalized world: A political ecological perspective. In: Hilhorst, T., Frerks, G., Bankoff, G. (Eds.), *Mapping vulnerability: disasters, development, and people*. Earthscan Publications, London, pp. 10-24.

Oliver-Smith, A., 2009. Climate change and population displacement: disasters and diasporas in the twenty-first century. In: Crate, S.A., Nuttall, M. (Eds.), *Anthropology and climate change: from encounters to actions*. Left Coast Press, Walnut Creek, CA, pp. 116-136.

Oliver-Smith, A., Hoffman, S.M., 2002. Why Anthropologists Should Study Disaster. In: Hoffman, S.M., Oliver-Smith, A. (Eds.), *Catastrophe & culture: the anthropology of disaster*. School of American Research Press, Santa Fe, NM, pp. 3-22.

Oliver, W.C., Pharr, G.M., 2010. Nanoindentation in materials research: Past, present, and future. *MRS Bulletin* 35, 897-907.

Olshansky, R., Hopkins, L., Johnson, L., 2012. Disaster and Recovery: Processes Compressed in Time. *Natural Hazards Review* 13, 173-178.

Oman, L., Robock, A., Stenchikov, G., Schmidt, G.A., Ruedy, R., 2005. Climatic response to high-latitude volcanic eruptions. *Journal of Geophysical Research* 110, D13103.

Oppenheimer, C., 2003. Climatic, environmental and human consequences of the largest known historic eruption: Tambora volcano (Indonesia) 1815. *Progress in Physical Geography* 27, 230-259.

Oppenheimer, C., 2011. *Eruptions that shook the world*. Cambridge University Press, Cambridge.

Ort, M.H., Elson, M.D., Anderson, K.C., Duffield, W.A., Hooten, J.A., Champion, D.E., Waring, G., 2008. Effects of scoria-cone eruptions upon nearby human communities. *Geological Society of America Bulletin* 120, 476-486.

Óskarsson, N., 1980. The interaction between volcanic gases and tephra: Fluorine adhering to tephra of the 1970 Hekla eruption. *Journal of Volcanology and Geothermal Research* 8, 251-266.

Oswalt, W.H., 1972. *Habitat and technology: The evolution of hunting*. Holt, Rinehart and Winston, New York, NY.

Oswalt, W.H., 1976. *An Anthropological Analysis of Food-Getting Technology*. John Wiley & Sons, New York, NY.

Otte, M., Keeley, L.H., 1990. The Impact of Regionalism on Palaeolithic Studies. *Current Anthropology* 31, 577-582.

Paddayya, K., 1973. A Federmesser Site with Tanged Points at Norgervaart, Province of Drenthe (Netherlands). *Palaeohistoria* 15, 167-213.

Pagli, C., Sigmundsson, F., 2008. Will present day glacier retreat increase volcanic activity? Stress induced by recent glacier retreat and its effect on magmatism at the Vatnajökull ice cap, Iceland. *Geophysical Research Letters* 35, L09304.

Pakula, L., 1989. A note on Venn diagrams. *American Mathematical Monthly* 96, 38-39.

Palmer, P.I., Smith, M.J., 2014. Earth systems: Model human adaptation to climate change. *Nature* 512, 365-366.

Paniagua, A. de, 1926. *L'age du renne*. P. Catin, Paris.

Pargeter, J., 2011. Assessing the macrofracture method for identifying Stone Age hunting weaponry. *Journal of Archaeological Science* 38, 2882-2888.

Park, C., Schmincke, H.-U., 1997. Lake Formation and Catastrophic Dam Burst during the Late Pleistocene Laacher See Eruption (Germany). *Naturwissenschaften* 84, 521-525.

Park, C., Schmincke, H.-U., 2009. Apokalypse im Rheintal. *Spektrum der Wissenschaften* 2009, 78-87.

Pasda, C., 2001. Das Knochengerät vom spätpaläolithischen Fundplatz Kleinlieskow in der Niederlausitz. Ein Essay zum steinzeitlichen Angelhaken. In: Gehlen, B., Heinen, M., Tillmann, A. (Eds.), *Zeit-Räume. Gedenkschrift für Wolfgang Taute*. Archäologische Berichte 14. Verlag Rudolf Habelt GmbH, Bonn, pp. 397-408.

Pasda, C., 2002. Archäologie einer Düne im Baruther Urstromtal bei Groß Lieskow, Stadt Cottbus. *Veröffentlichungen des Brandenburger Museums für Ur- und Frühgeschichte* 33, 7-49.

Pasda, C., 2007. Living culturally in ice-age forests, dunes and swamps. Preliminary results of a study of backed retouched pieces of the Late Palaeolithic site Kleinlieskow 120 in Lower Lusatia (Brandenburg, FRG). In: Masojć, M., Plonka, T., Ginter, B., Kozlowski, J.K. (Eds.), *Contribution to the Central European Stone Age. Papers dedicated to the late Professor Zbigniew Bagniewski*. Instytut Archeologii, Wroclaw, pp. 43-42.

Pautasso, M., 2012. Observed impacts of climate change on terrestrial birds in Europe: an overview. *Italian Journal of Zoology* 79, 296-314.

Pazdur, A., Fogtman, M., Michcznski, A., Pawlyta, J., Zajac, M., 2004. ^{14}C Chronology of Mesolithic Sites from Poland and the Background of Environmental Changes. *Radiocarbon* 46, 809-826

Pedersen, R., 2010. *Eyjafjallajökull. Vulkanen der lammede Europa*. Gyldendal, Copenhagen.

Pentz, P., 2009. Arvestrid – Nationalarv og verdensarv. *Arkæologisk Forum* 20, 24-28.

Petersen, P.V., 2006. White Flint and Hilltops – Late Palaeolithic Finds in Southern Denmark. In: Møller Hansen, K., Buck Pedersen, K. (Eds.), *Across the Western Baltic Proceedings of the archaeological conference "The Prehistory and Early Medieval Period in the Western Baltic" in Vordingborg, South Zealand, Denmark, March 27th – 29th 2003*. Sydsjællands Museums Publikationer, Vordingborg, pp. 57-74.

Petersen, P.V., 2008. *Flint fra Danmarks Oldtid*. Museerne.dk, Vordingborg.

Petersen, P.V., 2009. Stortandede harpuner – og jagt på hjortevildt til vands. *Årbøger for nordisk Oldkyndighed og Historie* 2009, 43-54.

Petersen, P.V., Johansen, L., 1991. Sølbjerg I – An Ahrensburgian Site on a Reindeer Migration Route through Eastern Denmark. *Journal of Danish Archaeology* 10, 20-37.

Pétillon, J.-M., Bignon, O., Bodu, P., Cattelain, P., Debout, G., Langlais, M., Laroulandie, V., Plisson, H., Valentin, B., 2011. Hard core and cutting edge: experimental manufacture and use of Magdalenian composite projectile tips. *Journal of Archaeological Science* 38, 1266-1283.

Petrone, P., Giordano, M., Giustino, S., Guarino, F.M., 2011. Enduring Fluoride Health Hazard for the Vesuvius Area Population: The Case of AD 79 Herculaneum. *PLoS ONE* 6, e21085.

Pettitt, P., 2008. The British Upper Palaeolithic. In: Pollard, J. (Ed.), *Prehistoric Britain*. Blackwell, Oxford, pp. 18-57.

Pettitt, P., Gamble, C., Davies, W., Richards, M., 2003. Palaeolithic radiocarbon chronology: quantifying our confidence beyond two half-lives. *Journal of Archaeological Science* 30, 1685-1693.

Pettitt, P., White, M.J., 2012. *The British Palaeolithic. Human Societies at the Edge of the Pleistocene World*. Routledge, London.

Pfister, C., 2009. Learning from Nature-Induced Disasters: Theoretical Considerations and Case Studies from Western Europe. In: Mauch, C., Pfister, C. (Eds.), *Natural Disasters, Cultural Responses: Case Studies toward a Global Environmental History*. Lexington Books, Lanham, MD, pp. 17-40.

Pillatt, T., 2012a. Resilience theory and social memory. Avoiding abstraction. *Archaeological Dialogues* 19, 62-74.

Pillatt, T., 2012b. Experiencing Climate: Finding Weather in Eighteenth Century Cumbria. *Journal of Archaeological Method and Theory* 19, 564-581.

Ping, C.-L., 2000. Volcanic soils. In: Sigurdsson, H., Houghton, B.F., McNutt, S.R., Rymer, H., Stix, J. (Eds.), *Encyclopedia of Volcanoes*. Academic Press, San Diego, CA, pp. 1259-1270.

Pirson, S., Draily, C., Court-Picon, M., Damblon, F., Haesaerts, P., 2004. La nouvelle séquence stratigraphique de la grotte Walou (Belgique). *Notae Praehistoricae* 24, 31-45.

Pirson, S., Haesaerts, P., Court-Picon, M., Damblon, F., Toussaint, M., Debenham, N., Draily, C., 2006. Belgian cave entrance and rock-shelter sequences as palaeoenvironmental data recorders: The example of Walou Cave. *Geologica Belgica* 9, 275-286.

Pirson, S., Juvigné, É., 2011. Bilan sur l'etude des téphras à la grotte Walou. In: Pirson, S., Draily, C., Toussaint, M. (Eds.), *La grotte Walou à Trooz (Belgique). Fouilles de 1006 à 2004*. Volume 1: *Les sciences de la terre*. Institut du Patrimonie wallon, Namur, pp. 134-167.

Plag, H.-P., 2014. Foreword: extreme geohazards – a growing threat for a globally interconnected civilization. *Natural Hazards* 72, 1275-1277.

Platnick, N.I., Cameron, H.D., 1977. Cladistic Methods in Textual, Linguistic, and Phylogenetic Analysis. *Systematic Biology* 26, 380-385.

Plourde, A.M., 2008. The Origins of Prestige Goods as Honest Signals of Skill and Knowledge. *Human Nature* 19, 374-388.

Plumet, P., 2006. Le Grand Nord et la religion. *L'Anthropologie* 110, 383-400.

Plunket, P., Uruñuela, G., 2000. The Quick and the Dead: Decision-making in the Abandonment of Tetimpa. *Mayab* 13, 78-87.

Plunket, P., Uruñuela, G., 2003. From Episodic to Permanent Abandonment: Responses to Volcanic Hazards at Tetimpa, Puebla, Mexico. In: Inomata, T., Webb, R.W. (Eds.), *The Archaeology of Settlement Abandonment in Middle America*. University of Utah Press, Salt Lake City, UT, pp. 13-27.

Plunket, P., Uruñuela, G., 2008. Mountain of sustenance, mountain of destruction: The prehispanic experience with Popocatépetl Volcano. *Journal of Volcanology and Geothermal Research* 170, 111-120.

Pollard, A.M., Blockley, S.P.E., Lane, C.S., 2006. Some numerical considerations in the geochemical analysis of distal microtephra. *Applied Geochemistry* 21, 1692-1714.

Pomeroy, A.J., 2008. *Then it was Destroyed by the Volcano. The ancient world in film and on television*. Duckworth, London.

Powell, A., Shennan, S., Thomas, M.G., 2009. Late Pleistocene Demography and the Appearance of Modern Human Behavior. *Science* 324, 1298-1301.

Prentiss, W.C., Chatters, J.C., 2003. Cultural Diversification and Decimation in the Prehistoric Record. *Current Anthropology* 44, 33-58.

Pyle, D.M., 1989. The thickness, volume and grainsize of tephra fall deposits. *Bulletin of Volcanology* 51, 1-15.

Pyle, D.M., 2000. Sizes of volcanic eruptions. In: Sigurdsson, H., Houghton, B.F., McNutt, S.R., Rymer, H., Stix, J. (Eds.), *Encyclopedia of Volcanoes*. Academic Press, San Diego, CA, pp. 263-270.

Pyle, D.M., Mather, T.A., 2009. Halogens in igneous processes and their fluxes to the atmosphere and oceans from volcanic activity: A review. *Chemical Geology* 263, 110-121.

Pyne-O'Donnell, S.D.F., Blockley, S.P.E., Turney, C.S.M., Lowe, J.J., 2008. Distal volcanic ash layers in the Lateglacial Interstadial (GI-1): problems of stratigraphic discrimination. *Quaternary Science Reviews* 27, 72-84.

Pyne-O'Donnell, S.D.F., Hughes, P.D.M., Froese, D.G., Jensen, B.J.L., Kuehn, S.C., Mallon, G., Amesbury, M.J., Charman, D.J., Daley, T.J., Loader. N.J., Mauquoy, D., Street-Perrott, F.A., Woodman-Ralph, J., 2012. High-precision ultra-distal Holocene tephrochronology in North America. *Quaternary Science Reviews* 52, 6-11.

Påhlsson, I., Bergh Alm, K., 1985. Pollen-Analytical Studies of the Cores 14103-3 and 14102-1 from the Western Baltic. *Striae* 23, 74-82.

Paas, W., 1961. Rezente und fossile Böden auf niederrheinischen Terrassen und deren Deckschichten. *Eiszeitalter & Gegenwart* 12, 165-230.

Quarantelli, E.L. (Ed.), 1998. *What is a disaster? Perspectives on the question*. Routledge, London.

Quarantelli, E.L., 1991. *More and worse disasters in the future: The social factors involved, Disaster Research Center*. University of Delaware, Newark, DE.

Quarantelli, E.L., 1995. What is a disaster? *International Journal of Mass Emergencies and Disasters* 13, 221-229.

Rasmussen, S.O., Andersen, K.K., Svensson, A.M., Steffensen, J.P., Vinther, B.M., Clausen, H.B., Siggaard-Andersen, M.-L., Johnsen, S.J., Larsen, L.B., Dahl-Jensen, D., Bigler, M., Röthlisberger, R., Fischer, H., Goto-Azuma, K., Hansson, M.E., Ruth, U., 2006. A new Greenland ice core chronology for the last glacial termination. *Journal of Geophysical Research – Atmospheres* 111, D06102.

Ratter, B., 2013. Surprise and Uncertainty – Framing Regional Geohazards in the Theory of Complexity. *Humanities* 2, 1-19.

Rauken, T., Kelman, I., 2010. River flood vulnerability in Norway through the pressure and release model. *Journal of Flood Risk Management* 3, 314-322.

Raynal, J.-P., Dougas, J.-P., 1984. Volcanisme et occupation humaine préhistorique dans le Massif Central français: quelques observations. *Revue archéologique du Centre de la France* 23, 7-20.

Raynal, J.-P., Vernet, G., Fain, J., Miallier, D., Montret, M., Pilleyre, T., Sanzelle, S., Daugas, J.-P., 1994. Téphrostratigraphie et Préhistoire des 160 derniers millénaires en Limagne d'Auvergne (Massif Central, France). *Bulletin de la Société Préhistorique Française* 91, 149-157.

Read, D., 2006. Tasmanian Knowledge and Skill: Maladaptive Imitation or Adequate Technology? *American Antiquity* 71, 164-184.

Read, D., 2008. An Interaction Model for Resource Implement Complexity Based on Risk and Number of Annual Moves. *American Antiquity* 73, 599-625.

Redman, C.L., 2005. Resilience Theory in Archaeology. American Anthropologist 107, 70-77.

Reed, S.E., Boggs, J.L., Mann, J.P., 2012. SPreAD-GIS: a GIS tool for modeling anthropogenic noise propagation in natural ecosystems. *Environmental Modelling & Software* 37, 1-5.

Rees, M., 2013. Denial of Catastrophic Risks. *Science* 339, 1123.

Reimer, P.J., Bard, E., Bayliss, A., Beck, J.W., Blackwell, P.G., Bronk Ramsey, C., Grootes, P.M., Guilderson, T.P., Haflidason, H., Hajdas, I., Hatté, C., Heaton, T.J., Hoffmann, D.L., Hogg, A.G., Hughen, K.A., Kaiser, K.F., Kromer, B., Manning, S.W., Niu, M., Reimer, R.W., Richards, D.A., Scott, E.M., Southon, J.R., Staff, R.A., Turney, C.S.M., van der Plicht, J., 2013. IntCal13 and Marine13 Radiocarbon Age

Calibration Curves 0-50,000 Years cal BP. *Radiocarbon* 55, 1869-1887.

Rennell, R., 2012. Landscape, Experience and GIS: Exploring the Potential for Methodological Dialogue. *Journal of Archaeological Method and Theory* 19, 510-525.

Rensink, E., 2000. Regional-scale variation and the Magdalenian record of northwestern Europe. In: Peterkin, G.L., Price, H.A. (Eds.), *Regional Approaches to Adaptation in Late Pleistocene Western Europe*. British Archaeological Reports (International Series) 896. Oxbow, Oxford, pp. 133-146.

Renson, V., Juvigné, E.H., Draily, C., 2002. Intérêt de la téphrostratigraphie dans le site archéologique et paléontologique du Pléistocène supérieur et de l'Holocène de la grotte Walou (Trooz, Belgique). In: Raynal, J.-P., Alborelivadie, C., Piperno, M. (Eds.), *Hommes et volcans. De l'éruption à l'objet*. Les dossiers de l'Archéo-Logis, Clermond-Ferrand, pp. 23-30.

Richerson, P.J., Boyd, R., Bettinger, R.L., 2009. Cultural Innovations and Demographic Change. *Human Biology* 81, 211-235.

Richter, H., Kierdorf, U., Richards, A., Kierdorf, H., 2010. Dentin abnormalities in cheek teeth of wild red deer and roe deer from a fluoride-polluted area in Central Europe. *Annals of Anatomy – Anatomischer Anzeiger* 192, 86-95.

Richter, J., 1990. Diversität als Zeitmass im Spätmagdalénien. *Archäologisches Korrespondenzblatt* 20, 249-257.

Richter, P.B., 2001. Ein spätpaläolithischer Schlagplatz innerhalb eines mehrphasigen Siedlungsareals bei Bienenbüttel, Ldkr. Uelzen. *Nachrichten aus Niedersachsens Urgeschichte* 70, 3-36.

Richter, P.B., 2002. Erste Ergebnisse der Ausgrabungen eines spätpaläolithischen und endneolithischen Siedlungsareals bei Häcklingen, Ldkr. Lüneburg. *Nachrichten aus Niedersachsens Urgeschichte* 71, 3-27.

Ridley, D.A., Solomon, S., Barnes, J.E., Burlakov, V.D., Deshler, T., Dolgii, S.I., Herber, A.B., Nagai, T., Neely, R.R., Nevzorov, A.V., Ritter, C., Sakai, T., Santer, B.D., Sato, M., Schmidt, A., Uchino, O., Vernier, J.P., 2014. Total volcanic stratospheric aerosol optical depths and implications for global climate change. *Geophysical Research Letters* 41, 2014GL061541.

Riede, F., 2005a. Darwin vs. Bourdieu. Celebrity Deathmatch or Postprocessual Myth? Prolegomenon for the Reconciliation of Agentive-Interpretative and Ecological-Evolutionary Archaeology. In: Cobb, H., Price, S., Coward, F., Grimshaw, L. (Eds.), *Investigating Prehistoric Hunter-Gatherer Identities: Case Studies from Palaeolithic and Mesolithic Europe*. British Archaeological Reports (International Series) 1411. Oxbow, Oxford, pp. 45-64.

Riede, F., 2005b. To Boldly Go Where No (Hu-)Man Has Gone Before. Some Thoughts on The Pioneer Colonisations of Pristine Landscapes. *Archaeological Review from Cambridge* 20, 20-38.

Riede, F., 2006. Chaîne Opèratoire – Chaîne Evolutionaire. Putting Technological Sequences in Evolutionary Context. *Archaeological Review from Cambridge* 21, 50-75.

Riede, F., 2007a. Der Ausbruch des Laacher See-Vulkans vor 12.920 Jahren und urgeschichtlicher Kulturwandel am Ende des Alleröd. Eine neue Hypothese zum Ursprung der Bromme Kultur und des Perstunien. *Mitteilungen der Gesellschaft für Urgeschichte* 16, 25-54.

Riede, F., 2007b. 'Stretched thin, like butter on too much bread…': some thoughts about journeying in the unfamiliar landscapes of late Palaeolithic Southern Scandinavia. In: Johnson, R., Cummings, V. (Eds.), *Prehistoric Journeys*. Oxbow, Oxford, pp. 8-20.

Riede, F., 2008a. Maglemosian Memes: Technological Ontology, Craft Traditions and the Evolution of Northern European Barbed Points. In: O'Brien, M.J. (Ed.), *Cultural Transmission and Archaeology: Issues and Case Studies*. Society for American Archaeology Press, Washington, DC, pp. 178-189.

Riede, F., 2008b. The Laacher See-eruption (12,920 BP) and material culture change at the end of the Allerød in Northern Europe. *Journal of Archaeological Science* 35, 591-599.

Riede, F., 2009a. Climate and Demography in Early Prehistory: Using Calibrated [14]C Dates as Population Proxies. *Human Biology* 81, 309-337.

Riede, F., 2009b. Climate change, demography and social relations: an alternative view of the Late Palaeolithic pioneer colonization of Southern Scandinavia. In: McCartan, S., Woodman, P.C., Schulting, R.J., Warren, G. (Eds.), *Mesolithic Horizons. Papers presented at the Seventh International Conference on the Mesolithic in Europe, Belfast 2005*. Volume 1. Oxbow, Oxford, pp. 3-10.

Riede, F., 2009c. Tangled Trees. Modeling Material Culture Change as Host-Associate Co-Speciation. In: Shennan, S.J. (Ed.), *Pattern and Process in Cultural Evolution*. University of California Press, Berkeley, CA., pp. 85-98.

Riede, F., 2009d. The loss and re-introduction of bow-and-arrow technology: a case study from the Southern Scandinavian Late Palaeolithic. *Lithic Technology* 34, 27-45.

Riede, F., 2010a. Hamburgian weapon delivery technology: a quantitative comparative approach. *Before Farming* 2010, article 1.

Riede, F., 2010b. Niche construction theory and human prehistory. Using artefact phylogenies and comparative methods to study past human ecosystem engineering. In: Escacena Carrasco, J.L., García Rivero, D., García Fernández, F.J. (Eds.), *Clasificación y Arqueología: Enfoques y métodos taxonómi-*

cos a la luz de la evolución darwiniana. University of Seville Press, Seville, pp. 175-204.

Riede, F., 2011a. Katastrofer – arkæologiske og flerfaglige perspektiver. *Jordens Folk* 46, 12-21.

Riede, F., 2011b. Steps Towards Operationalising an Evolutionary Archaeological Definition of Culture. In: Roberts, B.W., Vander Linden, M. (Eds.), *Investigating Archaeological Cultures. Material Culture, Variability, and Transmission*. Springer, New York, NY, pp. 245-270.

Riede, F., 2012a. A possible Brommian shaft-smoother from the site of Møllehøje, north-western Denmark. *Mesolithic Miscellany* 22, 10-18.

Riede, F., 2012b. Tephrochronologische Nachuntersuchungen am endpaläolithischen Fundplatz Rothenkirchen, Kreis Fulda. Führte der Ausbruch des Laacher See-Vulkans (10966 v. Chr.) zu einer anhaltenden Siedlungslücke in Hessen? *Jahrbuch des nassauischen Vereins für Naturkunde* 133, 47-68.

Riede, F., 2012c. Theory for the A-theoretical: Niche Construction Theory and Its Implications for Environmental Archaeology. In: Berge, R., Jasinski, M.E., Sognnes, K. (Eds.), *N-TAG TEN. Proceedings of the 10th Nordic TAG conference at Stiklestad, Norway 2009*. British Archaeological Reports (International Series) 2399. Archaeopress, Oxford, pp. 87-98.

Riede, F., 2013a. Towards a science of past disasters. *Natural Hazards*, 1-28.

Riede, F., 2013b. 'Brommeproblemet' – senglacial kulturtaksonomi og dens forståelses- og forvaltningsmæssige implikationer. *Arkæologisk Forum* 29, 8-14.

Riede, F., 2014a. Brommeproblemet 2.1 – et gensvar til Kristoffer Buck Pedersens kommentar. *Arkæologisk Forum* 31, 39-45.

Riede, F., 2014b. Eruptions and ruptures – a social network perspective on vulnerability and impact of the Laacher See eruption (c. 13,000 BP) on Late Glacial hunter-gatherers in northern Europe. *Archaeological Review from Cambridge* 29, 67-102.

Riede, F., 2014c. Climatic models: use archaeology record. *Nature* 513, 315.

Riede, F., 2014d. Success and failure during the Late Glacial pioneer human re-colonisation of southern Scandinavia. In: Riede, F., Tallavaara, M. (Eds.), *Lateglacial and postglacial pioneers in northern Europe*. British Archaeological Reports (International Series) 2599. Archaeopress, Oxford, pp. 33-52.

Riede, F., 2014e. The resettlement of northern Europe. In: Cummings, V., Jordan, P., Zvelebil, M. (Eds.), *Oxford Handbook of the Archaeology and Anthropology of Hunter-Gatherers*. Oxford University Press, Oxford, pp. 556-581.

Riede, F., 2014f. Towards a science of past disasters. Natural Hazards 71, 335-362.

Riede, F., 2014g. Volcanic activity. In: Smith, C. (Ed.), *Encyclopedia of Global Archaeology*. Springer, New York, NY, pp. 7657-7666.

Riede, F., 2015. 'Dominant' and 'radical' perspectives on material culture change in the wake of the catastrophic Laacher See volcanic eruption (c. 13,000 cal BP) in Northern Europe. In: Riede, F. (Ed.), *Past Vulnerability. Volcanic eruptions and human vulnerability in traditional societies past and present*. Aarhus University Press, Aarhus, pp. 229-256.

Riede, F., 2016. Changes in mid- and far-field human landscape use following the Laacher See eruption (c. 13,000 BP). *Quaternary International* 394, 37-50.

Riede, F., 2017. The 'Bromme problem' – notes on understanding the Federmessergruppen and Bromme culture occupation in southern Scandinavia during the Allerød and early Younger Dryas chronozones. In: Sørensen, M., Buck Pedersen, K. (Eds.), *Problems in Palaeolithic and Mesolithic Research*. Arkæologiske Studier vol. 12. University of Copenhagen & Museum of Southeast Denmark, Copenhagen, pp. 61-85.

Riede, F., Apel, J., Darmark, K., 2012. Cultural evolution and archaeology. Historical and current trends. In: Berge, R., Jasinski, M.E., Sognnes, K. (Eds.), *N-TAG TEN. Proceedings of the 10th Nordic TAG conference at Stiklestad, Norway 2009*. British Archaeological Reports (International Series) 2399. Archaeopress, Oxford, pp. 99-107.

Riede, F., Bazely, O., 2009. Testing the 'Laacher See hypothesis': a health hazard perspective. *Journal of Archaeological Science* 36, 675-683.

Riede, F., Bazely, O., Newton, A.J., Lane, C.S., 2011c. A Laacher See-eruption supplement to Tephrabase: Investigating distal tephra fallout dynamics. *Quaternary International* 246, 134-144.

Riede, F., Edinborough, K., 2012. Bayesian radiocarbon models for the cultural transition during the Allerød in southern Scandinavia. *Journal of Archaeological Science* 39, 744-756.

Riede, F., Grimm, S.B., Weber, M.-J., Fahlke, J.M., 2010. Neue Daten für alte Grabungen. Ein Beitrag zur spätglazialen Archäologie und Faunengeschichte Norddeutschlands. *Archäologisches Korrespondenzblatt* 40, 297-316.

Riede, F., Kierdorf, U., in prep. Did the eruption of the Laacher See-volcano (12,920 years BP) cause fluoride poisoning amongst contemporaneous fauna and foragers? *Medical Hypotheses*.

Riede, F., Kristensen, I.K., 2010. Skaftglatter. *Skalk* 2010, 3-6.

Riede, F., Laursen, S.T., Hertz, E., 2011a. Federmesser-Gruppen i Danmark. Belyst med udgangspunkt i en amatørarkæologs flintsamling. *Kuml* 2011, 9-38.

Riede, F., Laursen, S.T., Hertz, E., 2011b. Ingvor Filtenborgs flintsamling. Et diskussionsbidrag om senglacialtidens jagtvåbenteknologi. *By, marsk og geest* 23, 6-20.

Riede, F., Sørensen, A.H., Dietrich, J., Skaaning Høegsberg, M., Nordvig, M.V., Nielsen, E.B., 2016. Learning from the past – teaching past climate change and catastrophes as windows onto vulnerability and resilience. In: Siperstein, S., Lemenager, S., Hall, S. (Eds.), *Teaching Climate Change in the Humanities*. Routledge, New York, pp. 126-135.

Riede, F., Tallavaara, M., 2014. The Lateglacial and postglacial pioneer colonisation of northern Europe – an introduction. In: Riede, F., Tallavaara, M. (Eds.), *Lateglacial and postglacial pioneers in northern Europe*. British Archaeological Reports (International Series) 2599. Archaeopress, Oxford, pp. 3-10.

Riede, F., Thastrup, M., 2013. Tephra, tephrochronology and archaeology – a (re-)view from Northern Europe. *Heritage Science* 1, 15.

Riede, F., Wheeler, J.M., 2009. Testing the 'Laacher See hypothesis': tephra as dental abrasive. *Journal of Archaeological Science* 36, 2384-2391.

Rimantiene, R.J., 1971. *Paleolit i mezolit Litvy*. Akademiia nauk Litovskoi, Vilnius.

Rindel, P.O., 1993. 367. Estrup Mose. *Arkæologiske udgravninger i Danmark* 1992, 100.

Rindel, P.O., 1994a. 443. Estrup I. *Arkæologiske udgravninger i Danmark* 1993, 123.

Rindel, P.O., 1994b. 444. Estrup Mose I. *Arkæologiske udgravninger i Danmark* 1993, 124.

Rissland, E.L., 2009. Black Swans, Gray Cygnets and Other Rare Birds. In: McGinty, L., Wilson, D.C. (Eds.), *Case-Based Reasoning Research and Development. Lecture Notes in Computer Science*. Springer, Berlin/Heidelberg, pp. 6-13.

Ritter, J.R.R., Jordan, M., Christensen, U.R., Achauer, U., 2001. A mantle plume below the Eifel volcanic fields, Germany. *Earth and Planetary Science Letters* 186, 7-14.

Rittweger, H., 1997. *Spätquartäre Sedimente im Amöneburger Becken. Archive der Umweltgeschichte einer mittelhessischen Landschaft*. Landesamt für Denkmalpflege Hessen, Wiesbaden.

Rittweger, H., 2000. The "Black Floodplain Soil" in the Amöneburger Becken, Germany: a lower Holocene marker horizon and indicator of an upper Atlantic to Subboreal dry period in Central Europe? *Catena* 41, 143-164.

Rivers, W.H.R., 1912. The Disappearance of Useful Arts. In: Castrén, O., Hirn, Y., Lagerborg, R., Wallensköld, A. (Eds.), *Festskrift tillegnad Edvard Westermarck i anledning av hans femtioårsdag den 20 november 1912*. J. Simelii arvingars boktryckeri, Helsingfors, pp. 109-130.

Roach, N.T., Venkadesan, M., Rainbow, M.J., Lieberman, D.E., 2013. Elastic energy storage in the shoulder and the evolution of high-speed throwing in Homo. *Nature* 498, 483-486.

Roberts, L., 2011. 9 Billion? *Science* 333, 540-543.

Robertson, E.C., Klassen, J.A., 2006. Holocene Landscape Change in the Cypress Hills of Southeastern Alberta: Implications for Late Prehistoric Archaeological Site Formation and Paleoenvironmental Reconstruction. *Plains Anthropologist* 51, 425-442.

Robock, A., 2000. Volcanic eruptions and climate. *Reviews of Geophysics* 38, 191-219.

Robock, A., Oppenheimer, C. (Eds.), 2003. *Volcanism and the Earth's Atmosphere*. Geophysical Monograph 139. American Geophysical Union, Washington, DC.

Rockman, M., 2003. Knowledge and learning in the archaeology of colonization. In: Rockman, M., Steele, J. (Eds.), *Colonization of Unfamiliar Landscapes: the archaeology of adaptation*. Routledge, London, pp. 3-24.

Rockman, M., 2009. Landscape Learning in Relation to Evolutionary Theory. In: Prentiss, A.M., Kuijt, I., Chatters, J.C. (Eds.), *Macroevolution in Human Prehistory*. Springer, New York, NY, pp. 51-71.

Rolett, B., Diamond, J., 2004. Environmental predictors of pre-European deforestation on Pacific islands. *Nature* 431, 443-446.

Rolli, M., Filippi, M.L., Hadorn, P., Moscariello, A., 1994. Variazioni climatiche post-glaciali nei sedimenti lacustri del Lago di Loclat (Neuchatel, Svizzera): evidenze sedimentologiche, palinologiche, mineralogiche, geochimiche ed isotopiche – Dati preliminari. *Il Quaternario* 7, 335-342.

Rose, W.I., Durant, A.J., 2009. Fine ash content of explosive eruptions. *Journal of Volcanology and Geothermal Research* 186, 32-39.

Rosenberg, M., 1994. Pattern, Process, and Hierarchy in the Evolution of Culture. *Journal of Anthropological Archaeology* 13, 307-340.

Rots, V., Plisson, H., 2014. Projectiles and the abuse of the use-wear method in a search for impact. *Journal of Archaeological Science* 48, 154-165.

Rottländer, R.C.A., 1973. Der Bernstein und seine Bedeutung in der Ur- und Frühgeschichte. *Acta praehistorica et archaeologica* 4, 11-32.

Rowland, M.J., 2010. Will the sky fall in? Global warming – an alternative view. *Antiquity* 84, 1163-1171.

Rowley-Conwy, P., 2006. The Concept of Prehistory and the Invention of the Terms 'Prehistoric' and 'Prehistorian': the Scandinavian Origin, 1833-1850. *European Journal of Archaeology* 9, 103-130.

Rowley, S., 1985. Population Movements in the Canadian Arctic. *Études/Inuit/Studies* 9, 3-21.

Rozoy, J.-G., 1989. The Revolution of the Bowmen in Europe. In: Bonsall, C. (Ed.), *The Mesolithic in Europe*. John Donald, Edinburgh, pp. 13-28.

Rozoy, J.-G., Escalon de Fonton, M., 1978. *Les derniers chasseurs: l'epipaléolithique en France et en Belgique essai de synthése*. Chez l'auteur, Charleville.

Rues, S., Lenz, J., Türp, J.C., Schweizerhof, K., Schindler, H.J., 2008. Forces and motor control mechanisms during biting in a realistically balanced experimental occlusion. *Archives of Oral Biology* 53, 1119-1128.

Runciman, W.G., 2005. Culture does evolve. *History and Theory* 44, 1-13.

Rust, A., 1943. *Die Alt- und Mittelsteinzeitlichen Funde von Stellmoor*. Karl Wachholtz Verlag GmbH, Neumünster.

Rust, A., 1951. Über die Kulturentwicklung des endglazialen Jungpaläolithikums in Nordwesteuropa. In: Kersten, K. (Ed.), *Festschrift für Gustav Schwantes zum 65. Geburtstag*. Karl Wachholtz Verlag GmbH, Neumünster, pp. 48-58.

Rust, A., 1958. *Die jungpaläolithischen Zeltanlagen von Ahrensburg*. Karl Wachholtz Verlag GmbH, Neumünster.

Röhr, C., 1987. Laacher-See-Tephra in Bad Soden am Taunus. *Geologisches Jahrbuch Hessen* 115, 239-244.

Sabloff, J.A., 2008. *Archaeology matters. Action archaeology in the modern world*. West Coast Press, Walnut Creek, CA.

Salomonsson, B., 1962. Sveriges äldste kontakt med Västeuropa. In: Hamberg, P.G. (Ed.), *Proxima Thule. Sverige och Europa under Forntid och Medeltid*. P.A Norstedt & Söners Förlag, Stockholm, pp. 1-25.

Salomonsson, B., 1964. Decouverte d'un habilitation du Tardi-Glaciere a Segebro, Scanie, Suede. *Acta Archaeologica* 35, 1-28.

Sanchez, P., 1974. The unequal group size problem in discriminant analysis. *Journal of the Academy of Marketing Science* 2, 629-633.

Sandberger, F., 1882a. Das Alter der Bimsstein-Gesteine des Westerwaldes und der Lahngegend. *Zeitschrift der deutschen geologischen Gesellschaft* 34, 806-811.

Sandberger, F., 1882b. Ueber Bimsstein-Gesteine des Westerwaldes. *Zeitschrift der deutschen geologischen Gesellschaft* 34, 146-150.

Sarna-Wojcicki, A.M., 2000. Tephrochronology. In: Noller, J.S., Sowers, J.M., Lettis, W.R. (Eds.), *Quaternary Geochronology: Methods and Applications*. AGU Reference Shelf 4. American Geophysical Union, Washington, DC, pp. 357-377.

Šatavičius, E., 2004. Bromės (liungbiu) kultūra Lietuvoje. *Lietuvos Archeologija* 25, 17-44.

Sauer, F., 2017. Raw material procurement economy and mobility in Late Palaeolithic Northern Bavaria. *Quartär* 63, 125-135.

Scanlon, J., 1988. Winners and losers: Some thoughts about the political economy of disaster. *International Journal of Mass Emergencies and Disasters* 6, 47-63.

Scarth, A., 1994. *Volcanoes: An Introduction*. CRC Press, Boca Raton, FL.

Scasso, R.A., Corbella, H., Tiberi, P., 1994. Sedimentological analysis of the tephra from the 12-15 August 1991 eruption of Hudson volcano. *Bulletin of Volcanology* 56, 121-132.

Schafer, R.M., 1973. *The music of the environment*. Universal Edition, Wien.

Scharf, B.W., Bittmann, F., Boettger, T., 2005. Freshwater ostracods (Crustacea) from the Lateglacial site at Miesenheim, Germany, and temperature reconstruction during the Meiendorf Interstadial. *Palaeogeography, Palaeoclimatology, Palaeoecology* 225, 203-215.

Schaub, M., Büntgen, U., Kaiser, K.F., Kromer, B., Talamo, S., Andersen, K.K., Rasmussen, S.O., 2008. Lateglacial environmental variability from Swiss tree rings. *Quaternary Science Reviews* 27, 29-41.

Schenk, G.J. (Ed.), 2009a. *Katastrophen. Vom Untergang Pompejis bis zum Klimawandel*. Jan Thorbecke Verlag, Ostfildern.

Schenk, G.J., 2009b. Meeresmacht und Menschenwerk. Die Marcellusflut an der Nordseeküste im Januar 1219. In: Schenk, G.J. (Ed.), *Katastrophen. Vom Untergang Pompejis bis zum Klimawandel*. Jan Thorbecke Verlag, Ostfildern, pp. 52-66.

Schenk, G.J., Juneja, M., Wieczorek, A., Lind, C. (Eds.), 2014. *Von Atlantis bis heute – Mensch. Natur. Katastrophe*. Regensburg, Schnell und Steiner.

Schild, R., 1975. Pozny paleolit. In: Hensel, W., Bukowski, Z. (Eds.), *Prahistoria ziem polskich*. Paleolit i mezolit Ossolineum, Wrocław, pp. 159-338.

Schild, R., 1996. Radiochronology of the Early Mesolithic in Poland. In: Larsson, L. (Ed.), *The Earliest Settlement of Scandinavia and its relationship with neighbouring areas*. Almqvist & Wiksell, Stockholm, pp. 285-296.

Schild, R., Tobolski, K., Kubiak-Martens, L., Pazdur, M.F., Pazdur, A., Vogel, J.C., Stafford, T.W., 1999. Stratigraphy, Palaeoecology and Radiochronology of the Site of Calowanie. In: Kobusiewicz, M., Kozlowski, J.K. (Eds.), *Post-Pleniglacial Re-Colonisation of the Great European Lowland*. Instytut Nauk Geologicznych UJ, Krakow, pp. 239-268.

Schirmer, U., 1998. Spätglaziale Vegetationsgeschichte an der Lahn. *GeoArchaeoRhein* 2, 163-175.

Schirmer, U., 1999. Pollenstratigraphische Gliederung des Spätglazials im Rheinland. *Eiszeitalter & Gegenwart* 49, 132-143.

Schirmer, W., 1995. Pellenz- und Meile-Eruption des Laacher See-Vulkanismus. *Erlanger Beiträge zur petrographischen Mineralogie* 5, 87-98.

Schmidt, A., Ostro, B., Carslaw, K.S., Wilson, M., Thordarson, T., Mann, G.W., Simmons, A.J., 2011. Excess mortality in Europe following a future Laki-style Icelandic eruption. *Proceedings of the National Academy of Sciences* 108, 15710-15715.

Schmidt, R.R., 1908. Die späteiszeitichen Kulturepochen in Deutschland und die neuen paläolithischen Funde. *Korrespondenz-Blatt der Deutschen Gesellschaft für Anthropologie, Ethnologie und Urgeschichte* 1908, 75-82.

Schmincke, H.-U., 1988. *Vulkane im Laacher See-Gebiet. Ihre Entstehung und heutige Bedeutung*. Bode, Haltern.

Schmincke, H.-U., 1999. The Quaternary Volcanic Fields of the East and West Eifel (Germany). In: Orovetskii, Y.P. (Ed.), *Mantle Plumes*. A.A. Balkema, Rotterdam, pp. 241-322.

Schmincke, H.-U., 2004. *Volcanism*. Springer, Berlin.

Schmincke, H.-U., 2006. Environmental impacts of the Lateglacial eruption of the Laacher See Volcano, 12.900 cal BP. In: von Koenigswald, W., Litt, T. (Eds.), *150 years of Neanderthal Discoveries*. Terra Nostra, Bonn, pp. 149-153.

Schmincke, H.-U., 2010. *Vulkanismus*. WBG (Wissenschaftliche Buchgesellschaft)/Primus Verlag, Darmstadt.

Schmincke, H.-U., Mertes, H., 1979. Pliocene and Quaternary Volcanic Phases in the Eifel Volcanic Fields. *Naturwissenschaften* 66, 614-615.

Schmincke, H.-U., Park, C., Harms, E., 1999. Evolution and environmental impacts of the eruption of Laacher See Volcano (Germany) 12,900 a BP. *Quaternary International* 61, 61-72.

Schneider, R., 1977. Pollenanalytische Untersuchungen zur Kenntnis der spät- und postglazialen Vegetationsgeschichte am Südrand der Alpen zwischen Turin und Varese (Italien). *Botanische Jahrbücher für Systematik* 100, 26-109.

Schoknecht, U., 1959. Der mittelsteinzeitliche Wohnplatz "Stinthorst" bei Waren. *Bodendenkmalpflege in Mecklenburg-Vorpommern* 5, 7-24.

Schreiber, U.C., 2006. *Die Flucht der Ameisen*. Piper, München/Zürich.

Schröter, P., 1998. Zum spätpaläolithischen Schädelfund aus der Rauschermühle bei Plaidt. *Beiträge zur Vor- und Frühgeschichte des Kreises Mayen-Koblen* 7, 5-14.

Schumacher, R., Schmincke, H.-U., 1991. Internal Structure and Occurrence of Accretionary Lapilli – a Case-Study at Laacher See Volcano. *Bulletin of Volcanology* 53, 612-634.

Schwabedissen, H., 1944. Eine neue magdalénienartige Kulturgruppe im nordwesteuropäischen Flachland und deren Bedeutung für die Entstehung des Nordischen Kreises. *Forschungen und Fortschritte* 20, 51-52.

Schwabedissen, H., 1949. Hamburg-Rissen, ein wichtiger Fundplatz der frühen Menschheitsgeschichte. *Hammaburg* 2, 81-90.

Schwabedissen, H., 1951. Über das Vorkommen des Magdalénien im nordwesteuropäischen Flachland. *Eiszeitalter & Gegenwart* 1, 152-165.

Schwabedissen, H., 1954. *Die Federmessergruppen des nordwesteuropäischen Flachlandes. Zur Ausbreitung des Spät-Magdalénien*. Karl Wachholtz Verlag GmbH, Neumünster.

Schwabedissen, H., 1958. Das Alter der Federmesser-Zivilisation auf Grund neuer naturwissenschaftlicher Untersuchungen. *Quartär* 8/9, 200-209.

Schwantes, G., 1923a. Die Zivilisation von paläolithischem Gepräge in Holstein. *Mitteilungen der Anthropologischen Gesellschaft* 57, 158-161.

Schwantes, G., 1923b. Das Beil als Scheide zwischen Paläolithikum und Neolithikum. *Archiv für Anthropologie N.F.* XX(1), 13-41.

Schwarz, W., 1995. *Die Urgeschichte in Ostfriesland*. Schuster, Leer.

Schwendler, R.H., 2012. Diversity in social organization across Magdalenian Western Europe ca. 17-12,000 BP. *Quaternary International* 272-273, 333-353.

Schönweiß, W., 1992. *Letzte Eiszeitjäger in der Oberpfalz: Zur Verbreitung der Atzenhofer Gruppe des Endpaläolithikums in Nordbayern*. Bodner, Pressath.

Self, S., 2006. The effects and consequences of very large explosive volcanic eruptions. *Philosophical Transactions of the Royal Society* A: *Mathematical, Physical and Engineering Sciences* 364, 2073-2097.

Serwatka, K., Riede, F., 2016. 2D geometric morphometric analysis casts doubt on the validity of large tanged points as cultural markers in the European Final Palaeolithic. *Journal of Archaeological Science: Reports* 9, 150-159.

Sewell, W.H., Jr., 1996a. Historical Events as Transformations of Structures: Inventing Revolution at the Bastille. *Theory and Society* 25, 841-881.

Sewell, W.H., Jr., 1996b. Three Temporalities: Toward an Eventful Sociology. In: McDonald, T.J. (Ed.), *The Historic Turn in the Human Sciences*. The University of Michigan Press, Ann Arbor, MI, pp. 245-280.

Sewell, W.H., Jr., 2005. *Logics of history: Social theory and social transformation*. University of Chicago Press, Chicago, IL.

Shanks, M., Tilley, C., 1993. *Re-Constructing archaeology: theory and practice*. Routledge, London.

Shayt, D.H., 2006. Artifacts of Disaster. Creating the Smithsonian's Katrina Collection. *Technology and Culture* 47, 357-368.

Shea, J.J., 2006. The origins of lithic projectile point technology: evidence from Africa, the Levant, and Europe. *Journal of Archaeological Science* 33, 823-846.

Sheets, P.D., 2001. The effects of explosive volcanism on simple to complex societies in ancient Middle America. In: Markgraf, V. (Ed.), *Interhemispheric Climate Linkages*. Academic Press, London, pp. 73-86.

Sheets, P.D., 2002. *Before the Volcano Erupted: The Ancient Cerén Village in Central America*. University of Texas Press, Austin, TX.

Sheets, P.D., 2008. Armageddon to the Garden of Eden: Explosive Volcanic Eruptions and Societal Resilience in Ancient Middle America. In: Sandweiss, D., Quilter, J. (Eds.), *El Niño, Catastrophism, and Culture Change in Ancient America*. Harvard University Press, Cambridge, MA, pp. 167-186.

Sheets, P.D., 2011. Pilgrimages and persistent social memory in spite of volcanic disasters in the Arenal area, Costa Rica. *Ancient Mesoamerica* 22, 425-435.

Sheets, P.D., 2012. Responses to Explosive Volcanic Eruptions by Small to Complex Societies in Ancient Mexico and Central America. In: Cooper, J., Sheets, P.D. (Eds.), *Surviving Sudden Environmental*

Change. University of Colorado Press, Boulder, CO, pp. 43-63.

Sheets, P.D., Grayson, D.K. (Eds.), 1979. *Volcanic Activity and Human Ecology.* Academic Press, London.

Shennan, S.J., 1989. Archaeology as archaeology or as anthropology? Clarke's *Analytical Archaeology* and the Binfords' *New perspectives in archaeology* 21 years on. *Antiquity* 63, 831-835.

Shennan, S.J., 2000. Population, Culture History, and the Dynamics of Culture Change. *Current Anthropology* 41, 811-835.

Shennan, S.J., 2001. Demography and Cultural Innovation: a Model and its Implications for the Emergence of Modern Human Culture. *Cambridge Archaeological Journal* 11, 5-16.

Shennan, S.J., 2002. *Genes, Memes and Human History: Darwinian Archaeology and Cultural Evolution.* Thames and Hudson, London.

Shennan, S.J., 2004a. An evolutionary perspective on agency in archaeology. In: Gardner, A. (Ed.), *Agency Uncovered: Archaeological perspectives on social agency, power and being human.* UCL Press, London, pp. 19-32.

Shennan, S.J., 2004b. Analytical Archaeology. In: Bintliff, J.L. (Ed.), *A Companion to Archaeology.* Blackwell, Oxford, pp. 3-20.

Shennan, S.J., 2004c. Culture, society and evolutionary theory. *Archaeological Dialogues* 11, 107-114.

Shennan, S.J., 2006. From Cultural History to Cultural Evolution: An Archaeological Perspective on Social Information Transmission. In: Wells, J.C.K., Strickland, S., Laland, K.N. (Eds.), *Social Information Transmission and Human Biology.* CRC Press, London, pp. 173-190.

Shennan, S.J., 2008. Evolution in Archaeology. *Annual Review of Anthropology* 37, 75-91.

Shennan, S.J., 2011a. Descent with modification and the archaeological record. *Philosophical Transactions of the Royal Society B: Biological Sciences* 366, 1070-1079.

Shennan, S.J., 2011b. Social Evolution Today. *Journal of World Prehistory* 24, 201-212.

Shimoyama, S., 2002. Basic characteristics of disasters. In: Torrence, R., Grattan, J. (Eds.), *Natural Disasters and Cultural Change.* Routledge, London, pp. 19-27.

Shott, M.J., 1997. Stones and Shaft Redux: The Metric Discrimination of Chipped-Stone Dart and Arrow Points. *American Antiquity* 62, 86-101.

Shryock, A., Smail, D.L., Earle, T.K., 2011. *Deep history: the architecture of past and present.* University of California Press, Berkeley, CA.

Siebert, L., Simkin, T., Kimberly, P., 2010. *Volcanoes of the world* Smithsonian Institution, Washington, DC.

Siemaszko, J., 1999a. Tanged Points in the Basins of Lega and Elk Rivers. In: Kozlowski, S.K., Gurba, J., Zaliznyak, L.L. (Eds.), *Tanged Point Cultures in Europe. Read at the International Archaeological Symposium. Lublin, September, 13-16, 1993.* Maria Curie-Sklodowska University Press, Lublin, pp. 186-193.

Siemaszko, J., 1999b. Stone Age Settlement in the Lega Valley Microregion of North-East Poland. *European Journal of Archaeology* 2, 293-312.

Sigl, M., McConnell, J.R., Layman, L., Maselli, O., McGwire, K., Pasteris, D., Dahl-Jensen, D., Steffensen, J.P., Vinther, B., Edwards, R., Mulvaney, R., Kipfstuhl, S., 2013. A new bipolar ice core record of volcanism from WAIS Divide and NEEM and implications for climate forcing of the last 2000 years. *Journal of Geophysical Research: Atmospheres* 118, 1151-1169.

Sigmundsson, F., Pinel, V., Lund, B., Albino, F., Pagli, C., Geirsson, H., Sturkell, E., 2010. Climate effects on volcanism: influence on magmatic systems of loading and unloading from ice mass variations, with examples from Iceland. *Philosophical Transactions of the Royal Society A: Mathematical, Physical and Engineering Sciences* 368, 2519-2534.

Sigurdsson, H., 1999. *Melting the Earth. The history of ideas on volcanic eruptions.* Oxford University Press, Oxford.

Sigurdsson, H., 2000a. Volcanic episodes and rates of volcanism. In: Sigurdsson, H., Houghton, B.F., McNutt, S.R., Rymer, H., Stix, J. (Eds.), *Encyclopedia of Volcanoes.* Academic Press, San Diego, CA, pp. 271-279.

Sigurdsson, H., 2000b. Volcanoes in art. In: Sigurdsson, H. (Ed.), *Encyclopedia of Volcanoes.* Academic Press, San Diego, CA, pp. 1315-1338.

Sigurdsson, H., Carey, S., 1989. Plinian and co-ignimbrite tephra fall from the 1815 eruption of Tambora volcano. *Bulletin of Volcanology* 51, 243-270.

Sigurdsson, H., Lopes-Gautier, R., 2000. Volcanoes in literature and film. In: Sigurdsson, H. (Ed.), *Encyclopedia of Volcanoes.* Academic Press, San Diego, CA, pp. 1339-1360.

Simkin, T., Siebert, L., Blong, R., 2001. Volcano Fatalities--Lessons from the Historical Record. *Science* 291, 255.

Simpson, G.G., 1980. *Splendid isolation. The curious history of South American mammals.* Yale University Press, New Haven, CO.

Sinitsyna, G., 2002. Lyngby Points in Eastern Europe. *Archeologia Baltica* 5, 83-93.

Sinopoli, C.M., 1991. Style in arrows: a study of an ethnographic collection from the western United States. In: Miracle, P.T., Fisher, L.E., Brown, J. (Eds.), *Foragers in Context: Long-Term, Regional and Historical Perspectives in Hunter-Gatherer Studies.* University of Michigan Press, Ann Arbor, MI, pp. 63-87.

Sisk, M.L., Shea, J.J., 2009. Experimental use and quantitative performance analysis of triangular flakes (Levallois points) used as arrowheads. *Journal of Archaeological Science* 36, 2039-2047.

Smail, D.L., 2008. *On deep history and the brain*. University of California Press, Berkeley, CA.

Small, C., Naumann, T., 2001. The global distribution of human population and recent volcanism. *Environmental Hazards* 3, 93-109.

Smit, B., Wandel, J., 2006. Adaptation, adaptive capacity and vulnerability. *Global Environmental Change* 16, 282-292.

Smith, B.D., 2009. Resource resilience, human niche construction, and the long-term sustainability of Pre-Columbian susistence economies in the Mississippi river valley corridor. *Journal of Ethnobiology* 29, 167-183.

Smith, J.B., Schneider, S.H., Oppenheimer, M., Yohe, G.W., Hare, W., Mastrandrea, M.D., Patwardhan, A., Burton, I., Corfee-Morlot, J., Magadza, C.H.D., Füssel, H.-M., Pittock, A.B., Rahman, A., Suarez, A., van Ypersele, J.-P., 2009. Assessing dangerous climate change through an update of the Intergovernmental Panel on Climate Change (IPCC) "reasons for concern". *Proceedings of the National Academy of Sciences* 106, 4133-4137.

Smith, V.H., 2009. Eutrophication. In: Likens, G.E. (Ed.), *Encyclopedia of Inland Waters*. Academic Press, Oxford, pp. 61-73.

Smith, V.H., Tilman, G.D., Nekola, J.C., 1999. Eutrophication: impacts of excess nutrient inputs on freshwater, marine, and terrestrial ecosystems. *Environmental Pollution* 100, 179-196.

Sobel, E., Bettles, G., 2000. Winter Hunger, Winter Myths: Subsistence Risk and Mythology among the Klamath and Modoc. *Journal of Anthropological Archaeology* 19, 276-316.

Soffer, O., Gamble, C.S. (Eds.), 1990. *The World at 18,000 BP. Volume 1: High Latitudes*. Unwin Hyman, London

Solnit, R., 2010. *A Paradise Built in Hell: The Extraordinary Communities That Arise in Disaster*. Penguin, London.

Sommer, R.S., Fritz, U.W.E., Seppä, H., EkströM, J., Persson, A., Liljegren, R., 2011. When the pond turtle followed the reindeer: effect of the last extreme global warming event on the timing of faunal change in Northern Europe. *Global Change Biology* 17, 2049-2053.

Sommer, R.S., Kalbe, J., Ekström, J., Benecke, N., Liljegren, R., 2014. Range dynamics of the reindeer in Europe during the last 25,000 years. *Journal of Biogeography* 41, 298-306.

Sommer, U., 2000. Archaeology and Regional Identity in Saxony. *Public Archaeology* 1, 125-142.

Sommer, U., 2008. A choice of ancestors – the mechanisms of ethnic ascription in the age of patriotic antiquarianism (1815-1850). In: Schlanger, N., Nordbladh, J. (Eds.), *Archives, Ancestors, Practices, Archaeology in the lights of its history*. Cambridge University Press, Cambridge, pp. 233-246.

Sommer, U., 2009. Methods used to investigate the use of the past in the formation of regional identities. In: Sørensen, M.L.S., Carman, J. (Eds.), *Making the Means transparent: research methodologies in heritage studies*. Cambridge University Press, Cambridge, pp. 103-120.

Sparks, S., 2007. Use the calm between the storms. *Nature* 450, 354-354.

Stapert, D., 1986. The Vermaning stones: some facts and arguments. *Palaeohistoria* 28, 1-25.

Stapert, D., 2000. The Late Palaeolithic in the northern Netherlands. In: Valentin, B., Bodu, P., Christensen, M. (Eds.), *L'Europe centrale et septentrionale au Tardiglaciaire. Actes de la Table-Ronde internationale de Nemours, 13-16 mai 1997*. Mémoires du Musée de Préhistoire d'Ile de France, Paris, pp. 175-195.

Stapert, D., 2005. Het Laat-Paleolithicum in Noord-Nederland. In: Deeben, J., Drenth, E., van Oorsouw, M.-F., Verhart, L. (Eds.), *De Steentijd van Nederland*. Archeologie 11/12. J. A. Boom & Zoon Uitgevers, Meppel, pp. 143-169.

Steffensen, J.P., Andersen, K.K., Bigler, M., Clausen, H.B., Dahl-Jensen, D., Fischer, H., Goto-Azuma, K., Hansson, M., Johnsen, S.J., Jouzel, J., Masson-Delmotte, V., Popp, T., Rasmussen, S.O., Rothlisberger, R., Ruth, U., Stauffer, B., Siggaard-Andersen, M.L., Sveinbjornsdottir, A.E., Svensson, A., White, J.W., 2008. High-resolution Greenland ice core data show abrupt climate change happens in few years. *Science* 321, 680-684.

Stein, J.L., Stein, S., 2014. Gray swans: comparison of natural and financial hazard assessment and mitigation. *Natural Hazards* 72, 1279-1297.

Stensager, A.O., 2004. Nyt lys på gammelt fund. *Vendsyssel Nu og Da* 2004, 38-43.

Stevens, R.E., O'Connell, T.C., Hedges, R.E.M., Street, M., 2009. Radiocarbon and stable isotope investigations at the Central Rhineland sites of Gönnersdorf and Andernach-Martinsberg, Germany. *Journal of Human Evolution* 57, 131-148.

Stewart, J.R., Lister, A.M., 2001. Cryptic northern refugia and the origins of the modern biota. *Trends in Ecology and Evolution* 16, 608-613.

Stodiek, U., 1993. *Zur Technologie der jungpaläolithischen Speerschleuder. Eine Studie auf der Basis archäologischer, ethnologischer und experimenteller Erkenntnisse*. Archaeologica Venatoria, Tübingen.

Stodiek, U., Paulsen, H., 1996. *Mit dem Pfeil, dem Bogen…Technik der steinzeitlichen Jagd*. Isensee, Oldenburg.

Stommel, H., Stommel, E., 1983. *Volcano Weather. The story of 1816, the year without a summer*. Seven Seas Press, New Port, RI.

Stothers, R.B., 1984. The Great Tambora Eruption in 1815 and Its Aftermath. *Science* 224, 1191-1198.

Strahl, J., 2005. Zur Pollenstratigraphie des Weichselspätglazials von Berlin-Brandenburg. *Brandenburger geowissenschaftliche Beiträge* 12, 87-112.

Straus, L.G., Eriksen, B.V., Erlandson, J.M., Yesner, D.R. (Eds.), 1996. *Humans at the End of the Ice Age. The Archaeology of the Pleistocene-Holocene Transition.* Plenum Press, New York, NY.

Straus, L.G., Leesch, D., Terberger, T., 2012. The Magdalenian settlement of Europe: An introduction. *Quaternary International* 272-273, 1-5.

Street, M., 1986. Ein Wald der Allerödzeit bei Miesenheim, Stadt Andernach (Neuwieder Becken). *Archäologisches Korrespondenzblatt* 16, 13-22.

Street, M., 1996. The Late Glacial Faunal Assemblage from Endingen, Lkr. Nordvorpommern. *Archäologisches Korrespondenzblatt* 26, 33-42.

Street, M., Baales, M., 1997. Les groupes à Federmesser de l'Allerød en Rhénanie centrale (Allemagne). *Bulletin de la Société Préhistorique Française* 94, 373-386.

Street, M., Baales, M., 1999. Pleistocene/Holocene changes in the Rhineland fauna in a northwest European context. In: Benecke, N. (Ed.), *The Holocene History of the European Vertebrate Fauna. Modern Aspects of Research. Archäologie in Eurasien.* Band 6. Verlag Marie Leidorf, Rahden, pp. 9-38.

Street, M., Baales, M., Cziesla, E., Hartz, S., Heinen, M., Jöris, O., Koch, I., Pasda, C., Terberger, T., Vollbrecht, J., 2002. Final Palaeolithic and Mesolithic Research in Reunified Germany. *Journal of World Prehistory* 15, 365-453.

Street, M., Jöris, O., Turner, E., 2012. Magdalenian settlement in the German Rhineland – An update. *Quaternary International* 272-273, 231-250.

Street, M., Terberger, T., Orschiedt, J., 2006. A critical review of the German Paleolithic hominin record. *Journal of Human Evolution* 51, 551-579.

Strickland, S., 2006. Epilogue: Memory, Tradition, and Teleology. In: Wells, J.C.K., Strickland, S., Laland, K.N. (Eds.), *Social Information Transmission and Human Biology.* Society for the Study of Human Biology Series. CRC Press, London, pp. 269-281.

Stump, D., 2013. On Applied Archaeology, Indigenous Knowledge, and the Usable Past. *Current Anthropology* 54, 258-298.

Sulgostowska, Z., 1989. O Podstawach Wydzielenia Kultury Perstunskiej (Na Marginesie Dwoch Prac Karola Szymczaka). *Archeologia Polski* 34, 429-436.

Sundstrom, E., Bell, P.A., Busby, P.L., Asmus, C., 1996. Environmental Psychology 1989-1994. *Annual Review of Psychology* 47, 485-512.

Susman, P., O'Keefe, P., Wisner, B., 1983. Global disasters, a radical interpretation. In: Hewitt, K. (Ed.), *Interpretations of Calamity.* Allen & Unwin, London, pp. 263-283.

Swindles, G.T., De Vleeschouwer, F., Plunkett, G., 2010. Dating peat profiles using tephra: stratigraphy, geochemistry and chronology. *Mires & Peat* 7, 1-9.

Swindles, G.T., Lawson, I.T., Savov, I.P., Connor, C.B., Plunkett, G., 2011. A 7000 yr perspective on volca-nic ash clouds affecting northern Europe. *Geology* 39(9), 887-890.

Szmidt, C., Pétillon, J.-M., Cattelain, P., Normand, C., Schwab, C., 2009. Premières dates radiocarbone pour le Magdalénien d'Isturitz (Pyrénées-Atlantiques). *Bulletin de la Société préhistorique française* 106, 583-601.

Sztompka, P., 2000. Cultural Trauma: The Other Face of Social Change. *European Journal of Social Theory* 3, 449-466.

Szymczak, K., 1987. Perstunian Culture – The Eastern Equivalent of the Lyngby Culture in the Neman Basin. In: Burdukiewicz, J.M., Kobusiewicz, M. (Eds.), *Late Glacial in central Europe: culture and environment.* Polskiej Akademii Nauk, Wrocław, pp. 267-276.

Szymczak, K., 1999. Late Palaeolithic Cultural Units with Tanged Points in North Eastern Poland. In: Kozlowski, S.K., Gurba, J., Zaliznyak, L.L. (Eds.), *Tanged Point Cultures in Europe. Read at the International Archaeological Symposium. Lublin, September, 13-16, 1993.* Maria Curie-Sklodowska University Press, Lublin, pp. 93-101.

Sørensen, L., 2010. The Laacher See volcanic eruption. Challenging the idea of cultural disruption. *Acta Archaeologica* 81, 270-281.

Tainter, J.A., 2006. Archaeology of Overshoot and Collapse. *Annual Review of Anthropology* 35, 59-74.

Tainter, J.A., 2008. Collapse, Sustainability, and the Environment: How Authors Choose to Fail or Succeed. *Reviews in Anthropology* 37, 342-371.

Taleb, N., 2010. *The black swan: the impact of the highly improbable.* Penguin, London.

Tallavaara, M., Pesonen, P., Oinonen, M., 2010. Prehistoric population history in eastern Fennoscandia. *Journal of Archaeological Science* 37, 251-260.

Tallavaara, M., Seppä, H., 2012. Did the mid-Holocene environmental changes cause the boom and bust of hunter-gatherer population size in eastern Fennoscandia? *The Holocene* 22, 215-225.

Tanguy, J.C., Ribière, C., Scarth, A., Tjetjep, W.S., 1998. Victims from volcanic eruptions: a revised database. *Bulletin of Volcanology* 60, 137-144.

Taute, W., 1963. Funde der spätpaläolithischen "Federmesser-Gruppen" aus dem Raum zwischen mittlerer Elbe und Weichsel. *Berliner Jahrbuch für Vor- und Frühgeschichte* 3, 62-111.

Taute, W., 1968. *Die Stielspitzen-Gruppen im nördlichen Mitteleuropa. Ein Beitrag zur Kenntnis der späten Altsteinzeit.* Böhlau Verlag, Köln.

Taute, W., 1972. Die spätpaläolithisch-frühmesolithische Schichtenfolge im Zigeunerfels bei Sigmaringen (Vorbericht). *Archäologische Informationen* 1, 29-40.

Tehrani, J.J., Riede, F., 2008. Towards an archaeology of pedagogy: learning, teaching and the generation of material culture traditions. *World Archaeology* 40, 316-331.

Teit, J.A., 1930. The Salishan Tribes of the Western Plateau. *Annual Report of the Bureau of American Ethnology* 45, 23-396.

Terberger, K., 1993. *Das Lahntal-Paläolithikum. Landesamt für Denkmalpflege*, Wiesbaden.

Terberger, T., 1996. The early settlement of North-East Germany (Mecklenburg-Vorpommern). In: Larsson, L. (Ed.), *The Earliest Settlement of Scandinavia and its relationship with neighbouring areas*. Acta Archaeologica Lundensia Series IN 8°, 24. Almqvist & Wiksell, Stockholm, pp. 111-122.

Terberger, T., Kloss, K., Kreisel, H., 1996. Die "Riesenhirschfundstelle" von Endingen, Ldkr. Nordvorpommern. Spätglaziale Besiedlungsspuren in Nordostdeutschland. *Archäologisches Korrespondenzblatt* 26, 13-32.

Terberger, T., Street, M., 2002. Hiatus or continuity? New results for the question of pleniglacial settlement in Central Europe. *Antiquity* 76, 691-698.

Textor, C., Sachs, P.M., Graf, H.-F., Hansteen, T.H., 2003. The 12 900 years BP Laacher See eruption: estimation of volatile yields and simulation of their fate in the plume. *Geological Society, London, Special Publications* 213, 307-328.

Theuerkauf, M., 2002. Die Laacher See-Tephra in Nordostdeutschland: Paläoökologische Untersuchungen mit hoher zeitlicher und räumlicher Auflösung. *Greifswalder Geographische Arbeiten* 26, 171-174.

Theuerkauf, M., 2003. Die Vegetation NO-Deutschlands vor und nach dem Ausbruch des Laacher See-Vulkans (12880 cal. BP). *Greifswalder Geographische Arbeiten* 29, 143-189.

Thévenin, A., 1997. L'"Azilien" et les cultures à pointes à dos courbe: esquisse géographique et chronologique. *Bulletin de la Société Préhistorique Française* 94, 393-411.

Thissen, J.P., 1995. *Jäger und Sammler. Paläolithikum und Mesolithikum im Gebiet des Linken Niederrhein*. Band 2: *Jungpaläolithikum und Mesolithikum*. Unpublished Ph.D. thesis: Universität zu Köln, Cologne.

Thomas, D.H., 1978. Arrowheads and Atlatl Darts: How the Stones Got the Shaft. *American Antiquity* 43, 461-472.

Thomas, R.J., Krehbiel, P.R., Rison, W., Edens, H.E., Aulich, G.D., Winn, W.P., McNutt, S.R., Tytgat, G., Clark, E., 2007. Electrical Activity During the 2006 Mount St. Augustine Volcanic Eruptions. *Science* 315, 1097.

Thorarinsson, S., 1944. Tefrokronologiska studier på Island. *Geografiska Annaler* 26, 1-217.

Thorarinsson, S., 1958. The Öræfajökull Eruption of 1362. *Acta Naturalia Islandica* 2, 1-99.

Thorarinsson, S., 1979. On the Damage Caused by Volcanic Eruptions with Special Reference to Tephra and Gases. In: Sheets, P.D., Grayson, D.K. (Eds.), *Volcanic Activity and Human Ecology*. Academic Press, New York, NY, pp. 125-160.

Thorarinsson, S., 1981. Greetings from Iceland. ashfalls and volcanic aerosols in Scandinavia. *Geografiska Annaler* 63, 109-118.

Thordarson, T., Larsen, G., 2007. Volcanism in Iceland in historical time: Volcano types, eruption styles and eruptive history. *Journal of Geodynamics* 43, 118-152.

Thylstrup, A., 1978. Distribution of dental fluorosis in the primary dentition. *Community Dentistry And Oral Epidemiology* 6, 329-337.

Thylstrup, A., Fejerskov, O., 1978. Clinical appearance of dental fluorosis in permanent teeth in relation to histologic changes. *Community Dentistry And Oral Epidemiology* 6, 315-328.

Timmreck, C., Graf, H.-F., Lorenz, S.J., Niemeier, U., Zanchettin, D., Matei, D., Jungclaus, J.H., Crowley, T.J., 2010. Aerosol size confines climate response to volcanic super-eruptions. *Geophysical Research Letters* 37, L24705.

Toepfer, V., 1965. Paläolithische Fundstätten am ehemaligen Aschersleber-Gaterslebener See. *Ausgrabungen & Funde* 10, 3-10.

Toft, B., Reynolds, S., 1994. *Learning from Disasters. A Management Approach*. Butterworth-Heinemann, Oxford.

Tolksdorf, J.F., Turner, F., Kaiser, K., Eckmeier, E., Stahlschmidt, M., Housley, R.A., Breest, K., Veil, S., 2013. Multiproxy Analyses of Stratigraphy and Palaeoenvironment of the Late Palaeolithic Grabow Floodplain Site, Northern Germany. *Geoarchaeology* 28, 50-65.

Tomášková, S., 2003. Nationalism, Local Histories and the Making of Data in Archaeology. *The Journal of the Royal Anthropological Institute* 9, 485-507.

Tomka, S.A., 2013. The Adoption of the Bow and Arrow: A Model Based Experimental Performance Characteristics. *American Antiquity* 78, 553-569.

Torrence, R., 2016. Social resilience and long-term adaptation to volcanic disasters: The archaeology of continuity and innovation in the Willaumez Peninsula, Papua New Guinea. *Quaternary International* 394, 6-16.

Torrence, R., Grattan, J. (Eds.), 2002. *Natural Disasters and Cultural Change*. Routledge, London.

Torrence, R., Swadling, P., 2008. Social networks and the spread of Lapita. *Antiquity* 82, 600-616.

Toussaint, M., Becker, A., 1992. Le paléolithique supérieur récent du Trou Jadot à Comblain-au-Pont (Province de Liège, Belgique) et son paléoenvironnement. *Bulletin de la Société Préhistorique Française* 89, 12-18.

Trigger, B.G., 1989. *A History of Archaeological Thought*. Cambridge University Press, Cambridge.

Tromnau, G., 1975. *Neue Ausgrabungen im Ahrensburger Tunneltal. Ein Beitrag zur Erforschung des Jung-*

paläolithikums im Nordwesteuropäischen Flachland. Karl Wachholtz Verlag GmbH, Neumünster.

Tromnau, G., 1977. Jungpaläolithische Funde der Wehlener Grupper aus Hamburg-Poppenbüttel. *Hammaburg N.F.* 3/4, 141-145.

Trowbridge, T., 1976. Alaska's Volcanoes. Northern Link in the Ring of Fire. *Alaska Geographic* 4, 70-73.

Trölsch, O., 1976. Altsteinzeitliche Siedlungsplätze in der Umgebung von Mölln, Kreis Herzogtum Lauenburg. *Offa* 33, 5-42.

Turner, B.L., Kasperson, R.E., Matson, P.A., McCarthy, J.J., Corell, R.W., Christensen, L., Eckley, N., Kasperson, J.X., Luers, A., Martello, M.L., Polsky, C., Pulsipher, A., Schiller, A., 2003. A framework for vulnerability analysis in sustainability science. *Proceedings of the National Academy of Sciences* 100, 8074-8079.

Turner, F., Tolksdorf, J.F., Viehberg, F., Schwalb, A., Kaiser, K., Bittmann, F., von Bramann, U., Pott, R., Staesche, U., Breest, K., Veil, S., 2013. Lateglacial/early Holocene fluvial reactions of the Jeetzel river (Elbe valley, northern Germany) to abrupt climatic and environmental changes. *Quaternary Science Reviews* 60, 91-109.

Turney, C.S.M., Lowe, J.J., 2001. Tephrochronology. In: Last, W.M., Smol, P.J. (Eds.), *Tracking Environmental Change Using Lake Sediments. Volume 1: Basin Analysis, Coring, and Chronological Techniques.* Kluwer Academic, Dordrecht.

Turney, C.S.M., van den Burg, K., Wastegård, S., Davies, S.M., Whitehouse, N.J., Pilcher, J.R., Callaghan, C., 2006. North European last glacial–interglacial transition (LGIT; 15-9 ka) tephrochronology: extended limits and new events. *Journal of Quaternary Science* 21, 335-345.

Tøttrup, A.P., Thorup, K., Rainio, K., Yosef, R., Lehikoinen, E., Rahbek, C., 2008. Avian migrants adjust migration in response to environmental conditions en route. *Biology Letters* 4, 685-688.

Ugan, A., Bright, J., Rogers, A., 2003. When is technology worth the trouble? *Journal of Archaeological Science* 30, 1315-1329.

Ugolini, F.C., Zasoski, R.J., 1979. Soils Derived from Tephra. In: Sheets, P.D., Grayson, D.K. (Eds.), *Volcanic Activity and Human Ecology.* Academic Press, New York, NY, pp. 83-124.

Urry, J., 2007. *Mobilities.* Polity Press, Cambridge.

Urry, J., 2009. Aeromobilities and the global. In: Cwerner, S., Kesselring, S., Urry, J. (Eds.), *Aeromobilities.* Routledge, New York, NY, pp. 25-37.

Usinger, H., 1977. Bölling-Interstadial und Laacher Bimstuff in einem neuen Spätglazial-Profil aus dem Vallensgård Mose/Bornholm. Mit pollengrößenstatistischer Trennung der Birken. *Dansk Geologiske Undersøgelse* 1977, 5-29.

Vaesen, K., 2012. Cumulative Cultural Evolution and Demography. *PLoS ONE* 7, e40989.

Vale, G.L., Flynn, E.g. Kendal, R.L., 2012. Cumulative culture and future thinking: Is mental time travel a prerequisite to cumulative cultural evolution? *Learning and Motivation* 43, 220-230.

Valentin, B., 2008. Magdalenian and Azilian Lithic Productions in the Paris Basin: Disappearance of a Programmed Economy. *The Arkotek Journal* 2, 1-54.

Valentin, B., Fosse, G., Billard, C., 2004. Aspects et rythmes de l'azilianisation dans le Bassin parisien. *Gallia Préhistoire* 46, 171-209.

van Aalst, M.K., Cannon, T., Burton, I., 2008. Community level adaptation to climate change: The potential role of participatory community risk assessment. *Global Environmental Change* 18, 165-179.

Van de Noort, R., 2011. Conceptualising climate change archaeology. *Antiquity* 85, 1039-1048.

Van de Noort, R., 2013. *Climate Change Archaeology: Building Resilience from Research in the World's Coastal Wetlands.* Oxford University Press, Oxford.

van den Bogaard, C., Dörfler, W., Sandgren, P., Schmincke, H.-U., 1994. Correlating the holocene records: Icelandic tephra found in Schleswig-Holstein (Northern Germany). *Naturwissenschaften* 81, 554-556.

van den Bogaard, C., Schmincke, H.-U., 2002. Linking the North Atlantic to central Europe: a high-resolution Holocene tephrochronological record from northern Germany. *Journal of Quaternary Science* 17, 3-20.

van den Bogaard, P., 1983. *Die Eruption des Laacher See Vulkans.* Ruhr-Universität, Bochum.

van den Bogaard, P., 1995. $^{40}Ar/^{39}Ar$ ages of sanidine phenocrysts from Laacher See Tephra (12,900 yr BP): Chronostratigraphic and petrological significance. *Earth and Planetary Science Letters* 133, 163-174.

van den Bogaard, P., Hall, C.M., Schmincke, H.-U., York, D., 1987. $^{40}Ar/^{39}Ar$ laser dating of single grains: Ages of Quaternary tephra from the East Eifel volcanic field, FRG. *Geophysical Research Letters* 14, 1211-1214.

van den Bogaard, P., Hall, C.M., Schmincke, H.-U., York, D., 1989. Precise single-grain $^{40}Ar/^{39}Ar$ dating of a cold to warm transition in Central Europe. *Geophysical Research Letters* 14, 1211-1214.

van den Bogaard, P., Schmincke, H.-U., 1984. The Eruptive Center of the Late Quaternary Laacher See Tephra. *Geologische Rundschau* 73, 933-980.

van den Bogaard, P., Schmincke, H.-U., 1985. Laacher See Tephra: A widespread isochronous late Quaternary tephra layer in Central and Northern Europe. *Geological Society of America Bulletin* 96, 1554-1571.

van den Bogaard, P., Schmincke, H.-U., 1988. Aschelagen als quatäre Zeitmarken in Mitteleuropa. *Die Geowissenschaften* 6, 75-84.

van den Bogaard, P., Schmincke, H.-U., Freundt, A., Park, C., 1990. Evolution of Complex Plinian Eruptions: the Late Quaternary Laacher See Case

History. In: Hardy, D.A., Keller, J., Galanopoulos, V.P., Flemming, N.C., Druitt, T.H. (Eds.), *Thera and the Aegean World III. Volume 2: Earth Sciences*. The Thera Foundation, London, pp. 463-483.

van der Leeuw, S., Redman, C.L., 2002. Placing Archaeology at the centre of Socio-Natural Studies. *American Antiquity* 67, 597-605.

van Mourik, J.M., Slotboom, R.T., van der Plicht, J., Streurman, H.J., Kuijper, W.J., Hoek, W.Z., de Graaff, L.W.S., 2013. Geochronology of Betula extensions in pollen diagrams of Alpine Late-glacial lake deposits: A case study of the Late-glacial deposits of the Gasserplatz soil archives (Vorarlberg, Austria). *Quaternary International* 306, 3-13.

van Raden, U.J., Colombaroli, D., Gilli, A., Schwander, J., Bernasconi, S.M., van Leeuwen, J., Leuenberger, M., Eicher, U., 2013. High-resolution late-glacial chronology for the Gerzensee lake record (Switzerland): δ¹⁸O correlation between a Gerzensee-stack and NGRIP. *Palaeogeography, Palaeoclimatology, Palaeoecology* 391, Part B, 13-24.

VanderHoek, R., 2009. *The role of ecological barriers in the development of cultural boundaries during the Later Holocene of the Central Alaska Peninsula*. Unpublished Ph.D. thesis: University of Illionois, Urbana-Campaign.

VanderHoek, R., Nelson, R.E., 2007. Ecological Roadblocks on a Constrained Landscape: The Cultural Effects of Catastrophic Holocene Volcanism on the Alaska Peninsula, Southwest Alaska. In: Grattan, J., Torrence, R. (Eds.), *Living Under The Shadow. Cultural Impacts of Volcanic Eruptions*. Left Coast Press, Walnut Creek, CA, pp. 133-152.

Vanhaeren, M., d'Errico, F., 2005. Grave goods from the Saint-Germain-la-Rivière burial: Evidence for social inequality in the Upper Palaeolithic. *Journal of Anthropological Archaeology* 24, 117-134.

Veil, S., 1982. Der späteiszeitliche Fundplatz Andernach-Martinsberg. *Germania* 60, 391-424.

Veil, S., Breest, K., 2006. Origins of Mesolithic Art? A Recently Discovered Pendant and Other Objects of Amber from the Federmesser Site Weitsche, County of Lüchow-Dannenberg (Lower Saxony, Germany). In: Kind, C.-J. (Ed.), *After the Ice Age. Settlements, subsistence and social development in the Mesolithic of Central Europe*. Konrad Theiss Verlag, Stuttgart, pp. 285-296.

Veil, S., Breest, K., Grootes, P.M., Nadeau, M.-J., Hüls, M., 2012. A 14 000-year-old amber elk and the origins of northern European art. *Antiquity* 86, 660-673.

Veil, S., Geyh, M., Merkt, J., Müller, U., Staesche, U., 1991. Eine Widerhakenspite aus Lemförde am Dümmer, Landkreis Diepholz. *Neue Ausgrabungen und Forschungen in Niedersachsen* 19, 1-19.

Vencl, S., 1970. Die böhmischen Fazies der Federmesser-Gruppen. In: Gripp, G., Schütrumpf, R., Schwabedissen, H. (Eds.), *Mensch und Umwelt. Teil*

I: *Archäologische Beiträge. Fundamenta*. Böhlau Verlag, Köln, pp. 375-381.

Vencl, S., 1987. The Late Palaeolithic in Bohemia. In: Burdukiewicz, J.M., Kobusiewicz, M. (Eds.), *Late Glacial in Central Europe. Culture and Environment*. Prace Komisji Archeologicznej, Wrocław, pp. 121-130.

Venn, J., 1880. On the diagrammatic and mechanical representation of propositions and reasonings. *The London, Edinburgh, and Dublin Philosophical Magazine and Journal of Science* 9, 1-18.

Verbraeck, A., 1990. De Rijn aan het Einde van de Laaste Isjtijd: De Vorming van de jongste Afzettingen van de Formatie van Kreftenheye. *Geografisch Tijdsschtift* 23, 328-339.

Verheyleweghen, J., 1956. Le Paléolithique final de culture périgordienne du gisement préhistorique de Lommel (Province de Limbourg, Belgique). *Bulletin de la Société Royale Belge d'Anthropologie et de Préhistoire* 67, 1-79.

Vermeersch, P.M., 1977. Die stratigraphischen Probleme der postglazialen Kulturen in Dünengebieten. *Quartär* 27/28, 103-109.

Vermeersch, P.M., 2011. The human occupation of the Benelux during the Younger Dryas. *Quaternary International* 242, 267-276.

Vermeersch, P.M., 2013. *An Ahrensburgian site at Zonhoven-Molenheide (Belgium)*. Archaeopress, Oxford.

Vernet, G., Raynal, J.-P., 1995. *La Téphra des Roches, marqueur du volcanisme contemporain de la fin du Magdalénien dans le Massif central français*. Comptes-Rendus de l'Académie des Sciences, Série II 321, 713-720.

Vernet, G., Raynal, J.-P., 2000. Un cadre téphrostratigraphique réactualisé pour la préhistoire tardiglaciaire et holocène de Limagne (Massif central, France). *Comptes Rendus de l'Académie des Sciences – Series IIA – Earth and Planetary Science* 330, 399-405.

Vitaliano, D.B., 1968. Geomythology: the impact of geological events on history and legend with special reference to Atlantis. *Journal of the Folklore Institute* 5, 5-30.

Vitaliano, D.B., 2007. Geomythology: geological origins of myths and legends. *Geological Society, London, Special Publications* 273, 1-7.

Vollbrecht, J., 2005. *Spätpaläolithische Besiedlungsspuren aus Reichwalde, Reichwalde* 1. Landesamtes für Archäologie Sachsen, Dresden.

von Berg, A., 1994a. Allerödzeitliche Feuerstellen unter dem Bims im Neuwieder Becken (Rheinland-Pfalz). *Archäologisches Korrespondenzblatt* 24, 355-365.

von Berg, A., 1994b. Lebensspuren in der quartären Vulkanasche der Osteifel bei Mertloch. *Archäologie in Deutschland* 1994, 50-51.

von Dechen, H., 1881. Über Bimsstein im Westerwald. *Zeitschrift der deutschen geologischen Gesellschatt* 33, 442-453.

Waguespack, N.M., Surovell, T.A., Denoyer, A., Dallow, A., Savage, A., Hyneman, J., Tapster, D., 2009. Making a point: wood- versus stone-tipped projectiles. *Antiquity* 83, 786-800.

Waldmann, W., Jöris, O., Baales, M., 2001. Nach der Flut – Ein spätallerødzeitlicher Rückenspitzen-Fundplatz bei Bad Breisig. Mit einem Beitrag von Julian Wiethold. *Archäologisches Korrespondenzblatt* 31, 173-184.

Wastegård, S., 1998. Distribution of Lateglacial Tephra in Scandinavia. *Fróðskaparrit* 46, 297-303.

Wastegård, S., 2005. Late Quaternary tephrochronology of Sweden: a review. *Quaternary International* 130, 49-62.

Watt, S.F.L., Pyle, D.M., Mather, T.A., 2013. The volcanic response to deglaciation: Evidence from glaciated arcs and a reassessment of global eruption records. *Earth-Science Reviews* 122, 77-102.

Weber, M.-J., Grimm, S.B., 2009. Dating the Hamburgian in the Context of Lateglacial Chronology. In: Crombé, P., Van Strydonck, M., Sergant, J., Bats, M., Boudin, M. (Eds.), *Chronology and Evolution within the Mesolithic of North-West Europe: Proceedings of an International Meeting, Brussels, May 30th-June 1st 2007*. Cambridge Scholars Publishing, Newcastle, pp. 3-21.

Weber, M.-J., Grimm, S.B., Baales, M., 2011. Between warm and cold: Impact of the Younger Dryas on human behavior in Central Europe. *Quaternary International* 242, 277-301.

Wechler, K.-P., 1988. Zwei spätpaläolithische Feuersteinschlagplätze aus dem Altmoränengebiet der südwestlichen Niederlausitz. *Veröffentlichungen des Museums für Ur- und Frühgeschichte Potsdam* 22, 7-15.

Weinstein, P., 2005. Palaeopathology by proxy: the case of Egil's bones. *Journal of Archaeological Science* 32, 1077-1082.

Welinder, S., 1978. The concept of 'ecology' in Mesolithic research. In: Mellars, P.A. (Ed.), *The Early Postglacial Settlement of Northern Europe*. Duckworth, London, pp. 11-25.

Welinder, S., 1983. *The ecology of long-term change*. Gleerup, Lund.

Westerby, E., 1985. Da Danmarks ældste Stenalderboplads blev fundet. *Kuml* 1985, 164-186.

Weyl, R., 1961. Geländebefund und Petrographie der Bimsschicht. *Notizblatt des hessischen Landesamts für Bodenforschung* 89, 333-335.

Whallon, R., 2006. Social networks and information: Non-"utilitarian" mobility among hunter-gatherers. *Journal of Anthropological Archaeology* 25, 259-270.

White, G.F., 1974. Natural hazards research: concepts, methods and policy implications. In: White, G.F. (Ed.), *Natural Hazards: Local, National, Global*. Oxford University Press, Oxford, pp. 3-16.

Wiessner, P.W., 1983. Style and Social Information in Kalahari San Projectile Points. *American Antiquity* 48, 253-276.

Wilkinson, T.J., 2012. Weather and climate proxy records. *Archaeological Dialogues* 19, 57-62.

Willerslev, R., 2009. Hunting the elk by imitating the reindeer: A critical approach to ecological anthropology and the problems of adaptation and resilience among hunter-gatherers. In: Hastrup, K. (Ed.), *The Question of Resilience. Social Responses to Climate Change*. Historisk-filosofiske Meddelelser 66. Det Kongelige Danske Videnskabernes Selskab, Viborg, pp. 271-292.

Williams, R., 2008. Night Spaces: Darkness, Deterritorialization, and Social Control. *Space and Culture* 11, 514-532.

Wilson, T.M., Cole, J.W., Stewart, C., Cronin, S.J., Johnston, D.M., 2011. Ash storms: impacts of wind-remobilised volcanic ash on rural communities and agriculture following the 1991 Hudson eruption, southern Patagonia, Chile. *Bulletin of Volcanology* 73, 223-239.

Winchester, S., 2003. *Krakatoa: The day the world exploded, August 27, 1883*. Harper-Collins, New York, NY.

Wisner, B., 2010. Climate change and cultural diversity. *International Social Science Journal* 61, 131-140.

Wisner, B., Blaikie, P., Cannon, T., Davis, I., 2004. *At Risk. Natural hazards, people's vulnerability and disasters*. Routledge, London.

Witham, C.S., 2005. Volcanic disasters and incidents: A new database. *Journal of Volcanology and Geothermal Research* 148, 191-233.

Witze, A., Kanipe, J., 2014. *Island on Fire*. Profile Books, London.

Wolf, S., Hinkel, J., Hallier, M., Bisaro, A., Lincke, D., Ionescu, C., Klein, R.J.T., 2013. Clarifying vulnerability definitions and assessments using formalisation. *Int. J. Clim. Chang. Strateg. Manag.* 5, 54-70.

Woods, A.W., 1995. The dynamics of explosive volcanic eruptions. *Review of Geophysics* 33, 495-530.

Wulf, S., Ott, F., Słowiński, M., Noryśkiewicz, A.M., Dräger, N., Martin-Puertas, C., Czymzik, M., Neugebauer, I., Dulski, P., Bourne, A.J., Błaszkiewicz, M., Brauer, A., 2013. Tracing the Laacher See Tephra in the varved sediment record of the Trzechowskie palaeolake in central Northern Poland. *Quaternary Science Reviews* 76, 129-139.

Wörner, G., Schmincke, H.-U., 1984. Mineralogical and Chemical Zonation of the Laacher See Tephra Sequence (East Eifel, W. Germany). *Journal of Petrology* 25, 805-835.

Wörner, G., Viereck, L., Plaumann, S., Pucher, R., Schmincke, H.-U., 1988. The Quaternary Wehr Volcano: A multiphase evolved eruption center in the East Eifel Volcanic Field (FRG). *Neues Jahrbuch für Mineralogie-Abhandlungen* 159, 73-99.

Wörner, G., Wright, T.L., 1984. Evidence for magma mixing within the Laacher See magma chamber (East Eifel, Germany). *Journal of Volcanology and Geothermal Research* 22, 301-327.

Zahavi, A., Zahavi, A., 1997. *The Handicap Principle: A Missing Piece of Darwin's Puzzle*. Oxford University Press, Oxford.

Zaliznyak, L.L., 1999. Tanged Point Cultures in the Western Part of Eastern Europe. In: Kozlowski, S.K., Gurba, J., Zaliznyak, L.L. (Eds.), *Tanged Point Cultures in Europe. Read at the International Archaeological Symposium. Lublin, September, 13-16, 1993*. Maria Curie-Sklodowska University Press, Lublin, pp. 202-218.

Zdanowicz, C.M., Zielinski, G.A., Germani, M.S., 1999. Mount Mazama eruption: Calendrical age verified and atmospheric impact assessed. *Geology* 27, 621-624.

Zemek, F., Herman, M., Kierdorf, H., Kierdorf, U., Sedlacek, F., 2006. Spatial distribution of dental fluorosis in roe deer (Capreolus capreolus) from North Bohemia (Czech Republic) and its relationships with environmental factors. *Science of The Total Environment* 370, 491-505.

Zerefos CS, Tetsis P, Kazantzidis A, Amiridis V, Zerefos SC, Luterbacher J, Eleftheratos K, Gerasopoulos E, Kazadzis S, Papayannis A. 2014. Further evidence of important environmental information content in red-to-green ratios as depicted in paintings by great masters. *Atmospheric Chemistry and Physics* 14(6):2987-3015.

Zhu, H., Bozdag, E., Peter, D., Tromp, J., 2012. Structure of the European upper mantle revealed by adjoint tomography. *Nature Geoscience* 5, 493-498.

Zich, B., 1999. Das Hügelgräberfeld von Flintbek nach zwanzig Ausgrabungsjahren. *Jahrbücher für das ehemalige Amt Bordesholm* 1, 1-52.

Zielinski, G.A., Mayewski, P.A., Meeker, L.D., Whitlow, S., Twickler, M.S., 1996. A 110,000-yr record of explosive volcanism from the GISP2 (Greenland) ice core. *Quaternary Research* 45, 109-118.

Zielinski, G.A., Mayewski, P.A., Meeker, L.D., Whitlow, S., Twickler, M.S., Morrison, M., Meese, D.A., Gow, A.J., Alley, R.B., 1994. Record of Volcanism Since 7000 B.C. from the GISP2 Greenland Ice Core and Implications for the Volcano-Climate System. *Science* 264, 948-952.

Zolitschka, B., Negendank, J.F.W., Lottermoser, B.G., 1995. Sedimentological Proof and Dating of the Early Holocene Volcanic-Eruption of Ulmener Maar (Vulkaneifel, Germany). *Geologische Rundschau* 84, 213-219.

Zoller, D., 1981. Neue jungpaläolithische und mesolithische Fundstellen im nordoldenburgischen Geestgebiet. *Archäologische Mitteilungen aus Nordwestdeutschland* 4, 1-12.

Zylmann, P., 1933. *Ostfriesische Urgeschichte*. August Lax, Hildesheim.

#	Site name	Lat	Lon	Lab. code	BP	±	δ13C	Method	Dated material
26	Borneck§	53,66	10,24	KIA-33949	11940	50	-17,5	AMS	*Rangifer tarandus* (Humerus)
27	Grabow	53,28	11,59	KIA-26439	11980	120	-25,0	AMS	bone, species unidentified
28	Weitsche	53,03	11,13	KIA-26439	11980	120	-	AMS	burnt bone, *Castor fiber*
29	Klein Nordende CR	53,71	9,64	KI-2152	11990	100	-	conv	twig, *Hippophaë*
30	Klein Nordende CR	53,71	9,64	KI-2124	12035	110	-	conv	twig, *Hippophaë*
31	Grabow	53,28	11,59	KIA-41861	12070	98	-23,88	AMS	bone, species unidentified
32	Grabow	53,28	11,59	KIA-41862	12125	50	-27,7	AMS	charcoal, *Betula*

Sites marked with § have yielded large tanged points (i.e. 'Bromme' points) in association with arch-backed points. Associations given in brackets indicate that no diagnostic lithic material was found associated with the sample, or that the sample itself is not culturally diagnostic (i.e. Lyngby-axes). Evaluation criteria are from Pettitt et al. (2003) and are modified by Riede and Edinborough (2012) to best suit the analysis of specifically Late Glacial radiocarbon dates. FMG= Federmessergruppen; BR= Bromme culture. All auditing criteria are listed in Appendix II.

Association	Reference(s)	Country	I					II				
			a	b	c	d	e	a	b	c	d	Σ
FMG	Riede et al. (2010)	GER	4	1	5	4	5	3	2	2	2	28
FMG	Tolksdorf et al. (2013); Turner et al. (2013)	GER	4	4	5	3	3	4	3	4	4	34
FMG	Veil et al. (2012)	GER	1	2	5	2	5	3	3	2	2	25
(FMG)	Bokelmann et al. (1983)	GER	3	3	5	3	3	3	1	2	2	25
(FMG)	Bokelmann et al. (1983)	GER	3	3	5	3	3	3	1	2	2	25
FMG	Tolksdorf et al. (2013); Turner et al. (2013)	GER	4	4	5	3	3	4	3	4	4	34
FMG	Tolksdorf et al. (2013); Turner et al. (2013)	GER	5	4	5	3	3	4	3	4	4	35

Appendix II

Radiocarbon date auditing criteria

Auditing category		Score given 1	2
I	Chronometry		
Ia	Contamination by older/younger carbon and measurement of irrelevant carbon fractions	Carbon derives from a questionable chemical fraction, e.g. burnt bone, humic acid, oxalate crust, apatite, or the C/N ratio indicates potential contamination.	Amount of carbon measured too small to allow C/N evaluation.
Ib	¹⁴C dating of different chemical fractions	Measurements were on samples of the same material, and fall outside of a chronological sequence taking into account layers above and/or below.	Measurements were on samples of the same material but no available crosscheck with other dated horizons is available.
Ic	Accuracy	Sample dates to >30,000 BP and is the solitary date for a given horizon or falls outside of a sequence of dates from horizons above and/or below that from which it came.	>2 samples from a given horizon date to >30,000 BP and are generally in agreement with a chronological sequence with no more than 1/6 dates as outliers.
Id	Sample materials and ¹⁴C measurement	Sample is of riverine or marine derivation, and has not been corrected for a reservoir effect or sample is of wood charcoal and clearly not of a twig or small branch, which has not been identified to genus and for which therefore an 'old age' overestimation cannot be ruled out. Also, two chemical fractions of the same sample have been measured and differ at 2σ.	Carbon measured derived from a problematic chemical fraction, e.g. apatite, humic acids, carbonates, or carbon measured is exceptionally low, i.e. <0.5 mg or C/N ratio is outside of acceptable range for sample material.
Ie	Sample measurement and reporting	Sample was created from a bulked sample and/or measured conventionally before 1970.	Sample was pre-treated and/or measured at a laboratory that does not participate in International Radiocarbon Laboratory inter-comparisons.
II	Interpretation		
IIa	Certainty of association of dated sample with human activity	Low possibility (very poor archaeology, item recovered from mainly palaeontological (e.g. denning)	Reasonable possibility (archaeology scattered and/or fragmentary, low numbers).
IIb	Relevance of dated sample to specific archaeological entity of concern	Sample material (or genus if charcoal) is unknown.	No existing/published traces of hominin manufacture or modification of sample object exist.
IIc	Quantity and nature of dates for archaeological horizon	The date is the sole measurement for a given horizon, or is one of several that differ statistically at 2σ.	The date is one of only 2 dates for a given horizon, which are statistically the same age at 2σ.
IId	Sample materials and stratigraphic issues	Sample is a small fragment, which may be stratigraphically mobile, e.g. loose fleck of charcoal or individual bone fragment, with no refitting or spatial indication of its stratigraphic integrity.	Sample is <10 cm in maximum dimension with no clear indication of its stratigraphic integrity.

3	4	5
Carbon derives from a chemically complicated sample material from which numerous carbon sources cannot be ruled out by standard pre-treatment methods, e.g. rock art pigments, but that otherwise appears unproblematic, or from a sample with an unknown conservation history.	Carbon derives from collagen from bone, antler or ivory for which pre-treatment data are unproblematic.	Carbon derives from specific amino acid known to grow only in bone, or from the wood charcoal fraction of a charcoal sample identified to genus and for which the 'old age' effect can be eliminated.
Measurements were on samples of the same material and these are in agreement with samples of other materials from above or below the relevant horizon, i.e. fall into a clear sequence.	Measurements were upon at least a pair of charcoal (1 measurement) and one bone/antler/ivory pair, which were statistically the same age at 2σ.	Measurements were upon several discrete materials, at least one of which was charcoal and one of which was bone/antler/ivory, all clearly in association and statistically the same age at 2σ.
>2 samples from a given horizon date to >30,000 BP but fall into a clear chronological sequence with few or no outliers.	Samples date to <30,000 BP, fall into a clear chronological sequence with few or no outliers, and/or may be calibrated using IntCal09.	Samples date to <20,000 BP, fall into a clear chronological sequence and/or may be calibrated using IntCal09.
Collagen/cellulose yield and/or carbon yield relatively low (e.g. >0.5 mg carbon measured), but otherwise unproblematic.	Respectable yields from collagen/cellulose fractions and no indicators of pre-treatment problems.	As 3, and sample is statistically the same age as samples of *other materials* from same stratigraphic horizon.
Sample measurement is published without pre-treatment and measurement methods, or no laboratory comment that results satisfied the laboratory's assessment criteria.	Sample is published with such data, although some criteria fall outside of acceptable limits.	Sample is published with full pre-treatment, measurement and stable isotope data, all of which satisfy accepted criteria.
Probability (no demonstrable relationship but number of items and spatial patterning suggest association).	High probability (direct functional/contextual relationship).	Full certainty (anthropogenic object of concern dated).
Sample has high association with diagnostic archaeology, through incorporation in same horizon/level, but is in itself undiagnostic.	High probability of association, through incorporation into clear feature, e.g. hearth, pit, channel, very discrete occupation horizon, albeit undiagnostic itself.	Sample dated is either culturally diagnostic itself (or a hominin fossil), or bears both a high probability of association in addition to clear traces of hominin manufacture/modification.
The date is one of a group of >2 dates for a given horizon which are statistically the same age at 2σ.	The date is one of >3 dates for a given horizon, which are statistically the same age at 2σ.	The date is one of >5 dates for a given horizon which are statistically the same age at 2σ.
Sample is <10 cm in maximum dimension with a high probability of stratigraphic integrity.	Sample is >10 cm in maximum dimensions and clearly stratified within an identifiable feature.	Sample is >10 cm in maximum dimensions and meaningfully associated with comparable items, e.g. articulated skeleton, discrete organic spread.

Index

Upper Palaeolithic 99
Uruñuela, G. 114
Usselo horizon 81

V

Vallensgård Mose 71
Valogurian 81
Varve counting 66
VEI 51, 52
Venn diagrams 144
Volcanic eruptions 15, 21, 22
Volcanic Explosivity Index of Newhall and Self 51
Volcanism 49, 54, 77, 113, 154, 158
    explosive volcanism 79
Volcanological investigations 21
Volcanology 39
Vulnerability 20, 21, 22, 33, 35, 36, 37, 38, 39, 40,
    41, 42, 48, 78, 107, 109, 110, 111, 126, 132, 146,
    148, 149, 150, 152, 153, 154, 155, 156

W

Weaponry 141
Wehlener group 105
Wehlener scrapers 105
Wehlen scrapers 140
Wehr caldera 66
Weinberg Schadeleben 115
Weitsche 19, 104, 107
Welinder, S. 25
Westerby, E. 24, 135
White, G. 42
Wisner, B. 109, 110, 111
Workshop site 105

X

Xenolithic mantle 68

Y

Younger Dryas 69, 81, 104, 114, 117, 123, 133, 135,
    136, 137, 138, 146

Z

Zahavi, A. 104
Zooplankton 125